John Quincy Bittinger

History of Haverhill, N. H.

John Quincy Bittinger

History of Haverhill, N. H.

ISBN/EAN: 9783337327149

Printed in Europe, USA, Canada, Australia, Japan

Cover: Foto ©ninafisch / pixelio.de

More available books at **www.hansebooks.com**

HISTORY

OF

HAVERHILL, N. H.

BY

REV. J. Q. BITTINGER.

PREFACE.

This History had its origin in a conversation with the late N. B. Felton, Esq., who was much interested in having the history of the Town written, and suggested that I undertake the work. At first declined, but at last a multitude of facts and miscellaneous material having incidentally accumulated, I concluded about five years ago to undertake the work in earnest. The labor and expense have both been large, yet I do not regret having preserved in permanent form the history of the Town which in interest in many respects is the most historic of any town north and west of Concord.

I have availed myself of all sources of knowledge which were within reach. The Town and Proprietors' Records, Town Papers and State Papers, Records of Vermont Governor and Council, State Histories, private records, files of papers, and whatever could throw light upon the history of the Town; and I trust the record as now produced will be found trustworthy, though minor errors of date and in names have unavoidably escaped notice in some cases. I have not encumbered the pages with citation of authorities.

Several of the chapters are entirely biographical, which have been made quite full on the theory that a few leading and enterprising minds of every community make its history very largely. Much genealogy appears in these pages, but it is merely incidental to the general history, and in no case has completeness been aimed at in this respect. The History is not a genealogical work.

I have been greatly aided in many matters by others. To the late Hon. Samuel Swasey of Belvidere, Ill., and Hon. Nathaniel Wilson of Orono, Me., for a mass of information which was kindly communicated. To the late Hosea E. Baker and Miss Eliza Cross for much early traditional matter. To Hon. A. B. Thompson, Secretary of State, Isaac W. Hammond, M. D. librarian of New Hampshire Historical Society; Hon. A. S. Batchellor of Littleton; Gen. A. Harleigh Hill, author of Early Settlers of Groton, Vt.; Hon. Hiram Huse, state librarian, Vt.; J. J. Hazen, M. D., York, Me.; Henry K. Elkins of Chicago; Prof. Lewis Pollens, librarian of Dartmouth College; Rev. Henry A. Hazen of Boston, and others, for favors. Also to Ex-Gov. Charles H. Bell of Exeter for important papers on the early lawyers of Haverhill; to Phineas Spalding, M. D., for a like service in regard to some of the doctors, and to Charles B. Griswold, clerk of the court, for court matters.

I also am greatly indebted to Lieut. James A. Page for so complete a list of the names of soldiers who served in the War of the Rebellion, and for the information which is attached to many names; to the Town authorities for access to Town Records and papers, and especially to Town clerk, E. R. Weeks for his uniform willingness to aid the work; and last but not least to my neighbor, Mr. John Platt, for carrying me to various localities to inspect historic points.

The work is necessarily imperfect in some respects, the records outside the Town and Proprietors' Records are meager, and the time, 120 years, intervening between the foundation of the Town and the date of gathering material so great, that much that would have enhanced the value of the work, had passed beyond recovery. The work was undertaken none too soon, as all the older persons living and familiar with the earlier traditions of the Town, when I began the work, have answered the roll-call to a new Empire.

J. Q. B.

HAVERHILL, N. H., 1888.

CONTENTS.

CHAPTER I. 17–19
INTRODUCTION.

Author's aim—Early material imperfect—Official acts supplemented by tradition, conversations, and family records—Energy, courage, and perseverance of the founders—Changes in life and habits.

CHAPTER II. 20–28
GEOGRAPHY OF THE TOWN.

Name—Extent and value of farm products—Boundaries—Scenery—Area—Population—Villages—Mountains—Rivers and Streams—Ponds—Islands—Geology, Soil, and Minerals—Water-power—Roads.

CHAPTER III. 29–34
DISCOVERY AND EXPLORATION OF THE COHOS COUNTRY.

Early reports about it from hunters, trappers, and returned soldiers—Plan to explore and take possession of the Country—A doubt—Project failed—An event that led to a careful survey—A new route—The expedition of 1753—Capt. Power's scouting party, 1754—Missions of the Powers and Lovewell parties.

CHAPTER IV. 35–41
THE CHARTER PERIOD.

Influx of population—The Charter—Names of Grantees—Four divisions—House lots—Privileged "pitchers"—Governor Wentworth's "right"—Drawing—Numbering—Names of meadows Grantees common to Newbury and Haverhill—Gen. Jacob Bailey—Col. Jacob Kent—Gen. Moses Hazen.

CHAPTER V. 42-56

EARLY SETTLEMENT BEFORE THE CHARTER.

Two remarkable men—Michael Johnston and John Pattie the first settlers, 1761—Wintered at Ox Bow—Indians then in possession—Johnston and Pattie return to No. 4—A tragic end—Capt. Hazen comes to Cohos in 1762 with men and material for saw-mill and grist-mill—Leading position—Death—Moses Hazen and John Hazen confounded—William Hazen—Joshua Howard—Jessie Harriman—Simeon Stevens—Thomas Johnson—Col. Timothy Bedel and family—Capt. John Page and family—First Marriage—First Family—First Birth—First Death—Morse Meadow.

CHAPTER VI. 57-108

EARLY SETTLERS AFTER THE CHARTER.

Charter and energy of the men—Their training and education—Rapid settlement—Jesse Johnson—John White—James Bailey—Elisha Lock—Jonathan Sanders—James Woodward—Uriah Stone—Jonathan Elkins—John Taplin—Ezekiel Ladd—Moses Little—Haywards—Timothy Barron—James Abbott—William Eastman—John Hurd—Maxi Hazeltine—Joseph Hutchins—Simeon Goodwin—Jonathan Hale—Thomas Simpson—Ephraim Wesson—Charles Johnston—Asa Porter—William Porter—Andrew S. Crocker—Nathaniel Merrill—William Merrill—Joseph Pearson—Samuel Brooks—The Morses—Joseph Bliss—Joshua Young—Amos Kimball—William Cross—John Osgood—The Carrs—The Swans—Obadiah Swasey—Moor Russell—The Gookins—Asa Boynton—John Montgomery—Ross Coon—Glazier Wheeler—Parker Stevens—William Tarleton.

CHAPTER VII. 109-149

SETTLERS FROM 1800.

Division-line between early and late Settlers—River and back Settlements—Briar Hill—Along Oliverian—East Haverhill—Woodsville—Biographical Sketches—Noyses—Websters—Barstows—A character—Wilsons—Towles—Ephraim Kingsbury—Merrills—Timothy A. Edson—Bells—Noah Davis—Morses—Chester Farman—Perley Ayer—The Jeffers—Timothy Wilmot—Michael Carleton—Woodwards—Hosea S. Baker—StClairs—The Pikes—

Russell Kimball—James P. Brewer—Southards—Charles C. Kimball—Jos. B. Niles—Mansons—John McClary—Rixes—John L. Bunce—Stowes—Reding Brothers—Jonathan Nichols—William C. Marston—Haywards—Warrens—Jonathan B. Rowell—Elliotts Timothy K. Blaisdell—Cuttings—Clarks—Salmon Fish—Smiths—Alonzo W. Putnam—Cummings Brothers—Caleb Hunt—Jackson Brothers—Timothy R. Bacon—Daniel Batchelder—John Vose Bean—Bailey Brothers—Charles A. Gale—Darius K. Davis—Levi B. Ham—Currier Brothers—Augustus Whitney—The Stevenses—The Weekses—J. G. Blood—William H. Nelson—Joseph Powers—Meaders—Charles B. Griswold—Andrew J. Edgerly—Caleb Wells—Charles H. Day—R. D. Tucker—Woodsville settlers.

CHAPTER VIII.   150–8

TOWN AND PROPRIETORS' RECORDS FROM 1763 TO 1800.

First Town and Proprietors' Meeting—First Town Officers—Committee of Survey—Laying out of Lots—Drawing Lots—First Annual Town meeting—First full List of Town Officers—Town Expenses—Pound Wages for Town Work—Record Book—Danger of Wild Animals—Small Town Expenses—First Treasurer—Deer Reaves—Grant of Mill Privilege—Taxes Abated—Care of Imbecile—Census—Burial Places—Law suit—Town meeting Places—Waif—First Town-order for Aid—Legal Tenders—First Vote for Congressman and Presidential Electors—First Representative—First Vote for Governor and State Senator—Troublesome Persons—Special Choice of Selectmen—Question of Conscience—Traveling on the Sabbath—Small Pox—Old Debt—Care of Poor.

CHAPTER IX.   159–164

TOWN RECORDS FROM 1800 TO 1887.

Town in Relation to Condition of Country—War of 1812—Bounties for Soldiers—Small-pox—School Trouble—Town Farm—Town House—Fire Proof Vault—War of the Rebellion—Money Voted for Soldiers' Families—Bounties—Sum Total of Money Voted during the War for War Purposes—Funded Debt—Duty of Town to Needy Soldiers—Monument—Party Struggles—Character of Early Officers—A Memorable Contest—Improved Order.

CHAPTER X.   165-166

HAVERHILL IN THE REVOLUTION.

Prominence in the Revolution—Geographical Position—Able Leaders—Compact—Cohos well known to Enemy—Col. Johnston's Letter—Forts in the Upper Cohos—Rangers at Haverhill—Haverhill the Rendezvous for Troops and Scouting Parties—Character of the Ranger—Haverhill in constant Communication with Exeter and the Northern Army—Col. Wyman's Regiment—Four Stockades—Alarm from Indians in 1776—Retreat of our Army from St. Johns—Great consternation at Cohos—A Second Alarm in 1777—Again after the Fall of Ticonderoga—Military Road from Cohos to St. Johns—"Block Houses"—The Alarm of 1780—Town Authorities wide-awake—Frequent votes of Powder, Lead and Fire-arms—Efficient Committee of Safety Men—Conferences with other Towns—Vigilant eyes on Home-enemies—The Conspiracy of Col. Porter and others—Strong feeling—Persons who were obnoxious to the British—Rev. Peter Powers—Col. Johnson captured—Gen. Bailey's Escape—Dea. Elkins' Alarm—Quotas of Beef and Flour—Transportation of Grain from Cohos prohibited—Money-Patriots—Disastrous effects of the War—Rapid increase of Town Expenses—Sale of Rights—Decrease of Population during the War.

CHAPTER XI.   176-84

ENTERPRISES AND BUSINESS.

First Saw-mill and Grist-mill—General Progress—Liberal Offer for Blacksmith—First Saw-mill and Grist-mill at Hosmer Brook—Second Saw-mill—Other Mills—Fulling Mill—Side Light—Flax Mill—Water Power—Rafting Lumber—First Tannery—Cloth and Carding Mill—Potash Factory—Paper Mill—Other Mills and Shops—Pulp Mill—Swasey Mills—Other Factories and Shops—Woodsville Lumber Co.—Marble Works—Other Enterprises—A. F. Pike Manufacturing Co.—Stores and other business at Corner, North Haverhill, East Haverhill, Pike Station, Woodsville.

CHAPTER XII.   185-93

ROADS AND BRIDGES.

Roads and Civilization—First Roads little more than Bridle-paths—First Ox-team from Haverhill to Plymouth—Course of the Road

— Road from Portsmouth to Cohos—First mention of Town Roads—Road from the "Plain" to Coventry line, the Earliest Town Road—Ingress to Cohos—A Suggestive Vote—The Road from Piermont to Bath—Along the side-hill—The Oliverian Road—Highway Taxes and Labor—Public Ferry—County Road—Roads built before 1800—Roads extended and built as Population settled in Eastern part of Town—Character of Roads—Cohos Turnpike Corporators—Improvement in Roads—Room for further improvement—Permanent material—Grades—Road Engineers—Railroad—Canal—Bridges.

CHAPTER XIII. 194–205

MAILS, STAGES, TAVERNS.

Early Communication—First Mail—John Balch—State Routes—Postage—Haverhill Office—National Mails—Dutch Mail Wagon—Col. Silas May—Post Horn—Express—Bi-weekly Mail—First stage line—William Smart—Second stage line—Robert Morse—First Trip—Col. Silas May driver—Entrance into Haverhill—Almost an Accident—Tri-weekly Mails—Daily—Extras—The Drivers—Hanover Route—Six-horse Coaches—Haverhill a great stage center—Travel—Stage Lines—Famous Drivers—Their Character—Responsible Positions—Some Successful Men—Drinking Habits—Taverns: Bliss', Coon's, Towle's, Exchange, Sinclair's, Second Coon tavern, earliest tavern, Richardson's, Ladd's, Howard's, Morse's, Cobleigh's, Swan's, Morse Hill tavern—A great thoroughfare—Teams and Teamsters—Provisions—Lodgings—Large Teams—Crouch Tavern—A famous hostelry—The old-time tavern—Haverhill's stage-tavern—News Center—Bar room—Fire-place—Flip—Mental training—The Landlord.

CHAPTER XIV. 206–216

EDUCATION—ACADEMY.

Early Education—School lots laid out—School money—Earliest School Districts and School Houses—Second Class of School Houses—Re-districting—District Schools increase with population—Town system—First Board of Education—Town liberal in maintaining Schools—School Centres—The Corner and Woodsville Schools—Dartmouth College Grant—Incidents—Haverhill Academy.

CHAPTER XV.   217–236

RELIGION AND CHURCHES.

Religion and the founders—Early vote to call Rev. Peter Powers—Salary—Temporary preaching—First meetings at Newbury, Vt.—Parsonage Lot—Extent of Parish—Minister paid by Town—Protest—Certain Persons excused—Meeting House—Meetings in Houses and Barns—Union Meeting House in Newbury—Coming of Mr. Powers—People worshipped part of time in Newbury—Crossing river—Mr. Powers' Parish—Town divided into two Parishes—Propagating the Gospel—Church organizations—First Congregational Church—Pastors: Ethan Smith, John Smith, Grant Powers, Henry Wood, Joseph Gibbs, Archibald Fleming, Samuel Delano, Moses C. Searle, Edward H. Greeley, John D. Emerson, John Q. Bittinger, Eugene W. Stoddard—Methodist Episcopal Church: North Haverhill, Corner, East Haverhill—Baptist Church, North Haverhill—Free Will Baptist Church—Union Church—Advent Church—Protestant Episcopal Church, Woodsville—Methodist Episcopal Church, Woodsville.

CHAPTER XVI.   237–253

HAVERHILL IN WAR.

Her honorable position and officers of highest rank—List of Haverhill Soldiers in the several Wars—War of the Revolution—War of 1812—Mexican War—War of the Rebellion—Second Regiment—Fourth Regiment—Sixth Regiment—Ninth Regiment—Eleventh Regiment—Fifteenth Regiment—Eighteenth Regiment—First Regiment Heavy Artillery—First Cavalry.

CHAPTER XVII.   254–286

THE LAWYERS OF HAVERHILL.

Moses Dow—Alden Sprague—John Porter—Moses Dow, Jr.—George Woodward—Joseph Emerson Dow—John Nelson—Henry Hutchinson—David Sloan—Joseph Bell—Samuel Courtland—Edmund Carleton—Hale A. Johnston—Edward R. Olcott—Daniel Blaisdell—Jonathan Bliss—William H. Duncan—Samuel C. Webster—Nathan B. Felton—David Dickey—David H. Collins—Jonas Darius Sleeper—John S. Bryant—David Page—Charles E. Thompson—George W. Chapman—Charles R. Morrison—Nathaniel W. Westgate—George F. Putnam—Luther C. Morse—Samuel T. Page—Samuel B. Page—William F. Westgate.

CHAPTER XVIII. 287-309
DOCTORS.

Samuel White—John Porter—Samuel Hale—Martin Phelps—Isaac Moore—Amasa Scott—Edmund Carleton—Ezra Bartlett—Ezra Bartlett, Jr.—John Angier—Joel Angier—Anson Bracket—Simon B. Heath—Hiram Morgan—Henry Hayes—Edward Mattocks—Phineas Spalding—Henry B. Leonard—Homer H. Tenny—Samuel P. Carbee—Haven Palmer—Moses D. Carbee—Clarence H. Clark—Edward J. Brown—Henry P. Watson—Charles R. Gibson—Oliver D. Eastman—Charles Newcomb—Myron S. Wetherbee—James B. Clark, Dentist—Moses N. Howland, Dentist.

CHAPTER XIX. 310-353
HAVERHILL ABROAD.

Haverhill's honorable career Abroad—Charles J. Adams—J. Dorsey and George Angier—Louisa Page Babcock—Bacon Brothers—Barstow Brothers: Alfred, Anson, Gardner—George Barstow—Charles W.—John Barstow—Mary Barstow—Hazen Bedel—John Bedel—James W. Bell—John Bell—James P. Brewer—Samuel Brooks—Edwin Brooks—Edward C. and George Burbeck—James A. Cutting—Frederick Crocker—Noah Davis—Moses Elkins—D. L. Farnsworth—Charles N. Flanders—Lucien H. Frary—Warren Gookin—Michael Gray—Hunts: Caleb S., Horace, Prescott, Helen—Johnstons: Charles, Hannah—John Kimball—William H. Leith—Merrill Brothers; John L., Benjamin, Charles H.—William Merrill—Arthur Mitchell—Morse Brothers: Peabody A., George W., Isaac S.—Robert Morse—Joseph B. Morse—Thomas L. Nelson—Niles Brothers: Alonzo F., Horace L.—George B., Nellie and Clara Nichols—Person Noyes—John A. Page—Moses S. Page—James H. Pearson—Samuel P. Pike—Elizabeth Abbott, Mary Webster, Henrietta Mumford and George Carrington Powers—John Reding—Rodgers Brothers: Levi and M. Carleton—Jonathan H. and Chester Rowell—Horace O. Soper—Lyman D. Stevens—Smiths: Lyndon Arnold, Stephen, Sanford, Carlos—Frank A. Smith—William P. Stowe—The Tarletons—Towles: Frederick and James—Nathaniel Wilson—Edward B. Wilson—William F. Whitcher—Harvey B. Wilmont—John L. Woods—Franklin P. Wood.

CHAPTER XX. 354–362

DOMESTIC AND SOCIAL LIFE.

Time — Changes — Life Simple — Two Classes come to Haverhill, the Well-to-do and Enterprising, and the Dependent — The first House — Frame Houses, two sizes — The great Fire-place and Chimney — The Children and "Popped Corn" — "Lug Pole" — "Trammels" — Crane — Frying-pan — Dutch Oven — Spit — "The Goose Hangs High" — Furniture — Pots and Kettles — The Dresser — Pewter Dishes — Wooden Dishes — Two-tined Forks — Hemlock Brooms — Sanded Floors — Carpets Rare — Domestic Duties — Wants Few — Life Happy and Virtuous — Diet — Tea and Coffee — Drinks — Flip and Punch — Wine — Drinking Social — Sugar Making — Paring-bee — Games — Huskings — Muster-day — Social Character of Church-going — Society People — Official Position and Moral Worth — The Commencement of New Order — Rebellion against forced payment of Ministers' Taxes — Church-Going less Universal — The Stage-coach — Blinds, Pictures and Ornaments — Wooden Plates, sanded Floors, and Hemlock Brooms Yield — First Four-wheeled Carriage — First Piano — Chaises — Wagons — Clocks.

CHAPTER XXI.

MISCELLANEOUS. 362–417.

INDIAN NAMES,	362
INDIANS,	364
FAIRS AND MARKETS,	366
WILD ANIMALS, GAME AND FISH,	367
AN EGYPTIAN PLAGUE,	368
THE PIGEONS,	369
THE GREAT FLOOD,	369
HOUSES OF REFUGE,	370
A NOTED CHARACTER,	371
HORSE MEADOW,	373
THE POOR,	374
HOG REEVE,	374
TYTHING MAN,	374
COURTS AND COURT HOUSES,	375
TWO HISTORIC FARMS,	379
THE GREAT PINES,	381
DRINKING HABITS,	382
PIERMONT BOUNDARY DISPUTE,	383
THE VERMONT UNION,	387

LIBRARIES,	390
NEWSPAPERS,	391
TWO GREAT PLAGUES,	393
BANKS,	394
HANGINGS,	395
CYCLONE,	397
POWDER HOUSE,	398
STEAMBOATS,	398
MAKING CIDER,	399
TEAMING,	400
TRAINING DAY,	400
THE GREAT ACCIDENT,	403
THE GREAT FIRE,	404
FIRST JERSEY STOCK,	405
A ROMANCE,	406
THE CUCUMBER STORY,	407
LOCAL NAMES,	409
MASONRY,	413
PINE GROVE FARM,	415
ODD FELLOWS,	416
PATRIARCHS MILITANT,	417
GOOD TEMPLARS,	417

CHAPTER XXII.

APPENDIX,	419–431
CORRECTIONS,	433
INDEX,	435

DEDICATED

TO

THE MEMORY

OF

HAVERHILL'S MOST DISTINGUISHED CITIZEN,

BRAVE IN WAR, WISE IN COUNCIL, PUBLIC SPIRITED AND
EXEMPLARY IN LIFE,

COL. CHARLES JOHNSTON.

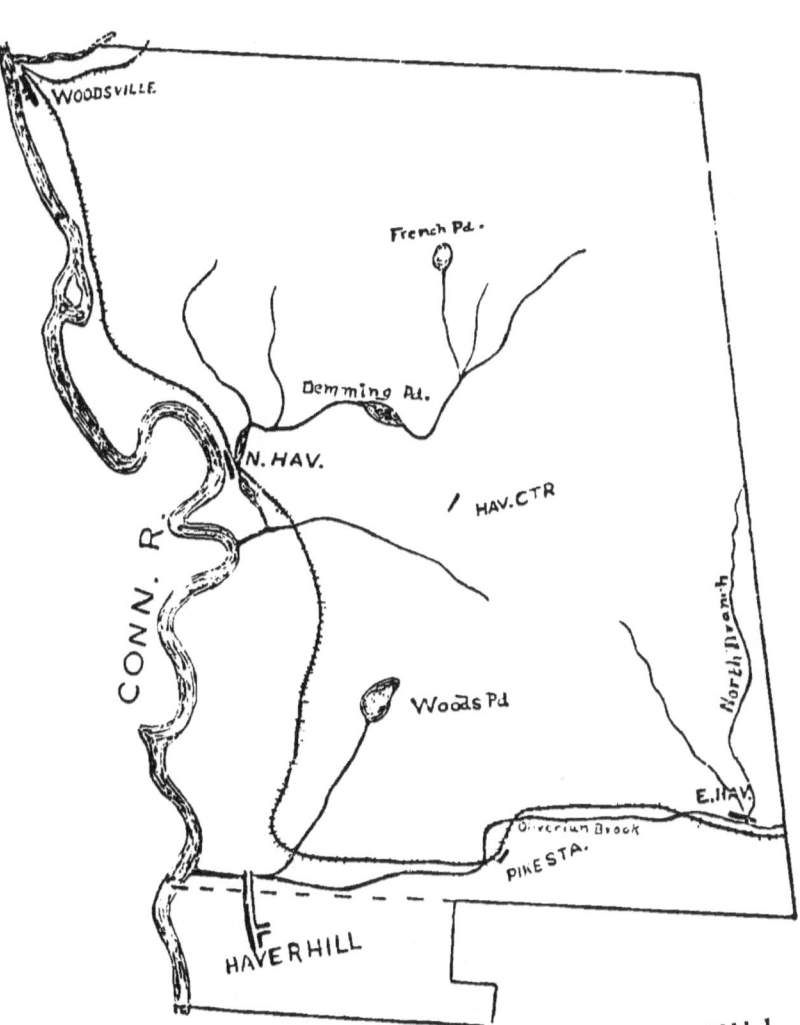

OUTLINE MAP—TOWN OF HAVERHILL

HISTORY OF HAVERHILL.

CHAPTER I.

INTRODUCTION.

Author's aim — Early material imperfect — Official acts supplemented by tradition, conversations, and family records — Energy, courage, and perseverance of the founders — Changes in life and habits.

It is my intention in the following pages to write the history of Haverhill from its first discovery by the white man down to the present time. The earlier years of this history, from the first occupancy of the Cohos Country, when Johnston and Pattie spent the winter of 1761-2 at the Ox Bow,* must necessarily be somewhat incomplete, as both the records of the Proprietors, as well as the records of the Town, are in some places imperfect; and even when they are complete and uninterrupted they record only the public acts of the Proprietors and of the Town, and give little information, except incidentally, of the character of the people and the spirit of the times.

However, with this material at hand, and with such other aids as I have been able to command, of family records, with the memory of the oldest inhabitants reaching back to the close of the last century, and handing down from that period the fresh conversations and traditions of an earlier generation, many of whom lived and died in the first quarter of the present century, I hope to be able to present the history of the Town as full and complete as possible. We shall see how a brave and resolute people, coming into these Indian wilds, laid the foundations of prosperity, of happiness, and of social order; how before their sturdy enterprise and indomitable energy the massive and dense forests disappeared from the broad river intervals, and the rich soil became

---

* In these pages "Ox Bow" stands for "Little Ox Bow."

a garden of fruitfulness, so that in times of scarcity or famine in the regions around Haverhill was a granary of abundance, an Egyptian storehouse, for the hungry and destitute: how through many perils and hardships mills were erected, water-powers trained into the service of man, and machinery in the absence of roads was dragged by human exertion over long reaches of bridle-path: how in the earlier years of the new settlement they lived in rude huts and log cabins with few conveniences and comforts, and suffered many self-denials and dangers: how the school and the church, those twin supports of all that is best and most hopeful in a community, were early established and maintained with praiseworthy self-sacrifice and devotion: how from scanty beginnings they rose to prosperity and riches, from dwelling in damp and uncomfortable homes to living in well-built houses, and surrounded with the comforts and conveniences of a better civilization: how the bridle-path and blazed way yielded to well-constructed and safe highways, and the tedious journeyings on horseback were exchanged for the comfortable and social conveyances of later times: how sanded floors, and rough benches, and bare walls, and simple table-ware gave way to mats, and carpets, and pictures, and pianos, to china and silver-service: how the huge fire-place with pot-hooks and trammels, the spinning-wheel and home-made fabrics, were displaced by modern inventions and conveniences.

We shall also see how in the long struggle between the mother country and her colonies our forefathers were fired with earnest zeal and lofty patriotism for the rights of man, and furnished both men and money beyond their means to advance the cause of religious and political liberty: how in the new demand which was laid upon their earlier descendants many of them have a proud place in the history of our common country; and later still how in the great War of the Rebellion when the Union was assailed from within and threatened with disruption, her citizens responded with patriotic promptness and to the full of their ability to the call of duty; how from their loins a goodly company of noble men and women have gone forth into other fields of labor and endeavor, and have won honor and eminence in professional life and in business enterprises, as teachers, lawyers, doctors, ministers, leaders of society and of progress as well as that larger number who, standing by the old fire-sides, have achieved an honorable name and a well-earned title to usefulness and esteem here.

We shall also note that the transition from the simplicity of life and habits of our forefathers to those of a later period, has its parallel in the contrast between the very general and heroic and stronger virtues, and the more effeminate and irresolute traits of their descendants. These and more than these we shall see in the unfolding of the Town's history as recorded in the following pages.

CHAPTER II.

GEOGRAPHY OF THE TOWN.

Name — Extent and value of farm products — Boundaries — Scenery — Area — Population — Villages — Mountains — Rivers and Streams — Ponds — Islands — Geology, Soil, and Minerals — Water-power — Roads.

The Town of Haverhill took its name from Haverhill, Mass., from the fact that the first white persons who permanently occupied its territory came from that town. It is one of the richest and most important agricultural sections of the state, cutting about one thousand tons more hay per annum than is cut in any other town, and whose farm products are only exceeded in value by that of one other town in the state.

From its southern limit on the town of Piermont to its northern limit on the Ammonoosuc is a distance of about ten miles; and from the Vermont bank of the Connecticut river, which winds in sweeping and tortuous curves through its western borders, to its eastern boundary on the town of Benton, it averages a breadth of about six miles.

The geographical features of the Town are of varied and picturesque beauty, embracing within its limits the broad and fertile intervals of the Connecticut — the heart of the famous Cohos Country in Indian history — with the uplands stretching away to the east till they swell into the foot-hills and outer bastions of grand Moosilauke, more familiarly known as "Moose Hillock," whose broad shoulders and massive granite walls can be seen from all parts of the Town.

The beauty and even grandeur of the scenery from many localities in the Town is unsurpassed. One of the sons of Haverhill, who has done honor to the Town in his professional career, now residing at the Golden Gate of the Pacific Coast, writing of the magnificent scenery of that region, says, "You have heard much of the Yosemite Valley and its magnificence, but standing on some elevated point in the

Town of Haverhill, and looking east toward Moosilauke you can on any clear day see a view which in beauty and grandeur far surpasses that of the Yosemite." Longfellow once on a visit to Haverhill, and walking down with a friend from the village to Powder House Hill, after taking in the view from that point up and down the river, with the broad intervals " dressed in living green," and the river quietly and peacefully winding in beautiful sweeps and reaches through the twenty mile valley in sight, said to his friend, a son of Haverhill, " I have seen the beauties of foreign lands, but the beauties from this spot surpass anything I have ever seen." Others have spoken in similar language, and many are the expressions of her loyal sons and daughters in writing to me, of their fresh and loving remembrance of the beautiful scenery of their childhood-home.

These praises of the beauty and picturesqueness of the scenery and physical features of Haverhill are not exaggerations, and their exactness can be verified from numerous points of observation. They are upon the lips of all who come here. The many roads through the Town furnish as charming and inviting drives as can be found any where in the state. Nothing can excel the bewitching and varying landscape which meets the eye as you follow the road eastward along the Oliverian. On either side the little valley is hemmed in by hills and mountains. Then spreading out into ample dimensions like a vast amphitheatre, with massive Moosilauke standing guard in the distance, Bald Face at the head of the broad Benton meadows, and the hills and mountains like guardian sentinels encircling the snug little village of East Haverhill, with cultivated fields running back from the brook to the foot-hills, and farm houses and shady ways breaking the view into beauty and variety.

On the wide expanse on which is built the village of North Haverhill the eye rests on an unsurpassed scene of picturesqueness and even grandeur, with Black Hill and

Hog Back, and again the broad front of Moosilauke to crown the view. The landscape any where from the Piermont line along the road through Haverhill village and Ladd Street is a succession of surprises and charms that have called forth from all whose eyes have ever lingered upon the view the most enthusiastic expressions of delight. Here the meadows are broad and well cultivated, and the valley in spring and summer resembles an immense floor of hightest emerald, through which the river in great curves winds its gleaming course. On the Vermont side is a line of high hills walling in the valley from the west, whilst Mt. Gardner with its solid front looks down from the north. Newbury, Wells River, Bradford, South Newbury, are within sweep of the eye, and grand Moosilauke stands perpetual watch over this charming landscape.

The area of the Town is about 35,000 acres, nearly two-thirds of which is favorable to cultivation, and has for the most part been brought under fruitful and profitable tillage. The remainder is pasturage and woodland. The former furnishes in great abundance most excellent and nutritious grass both for dairy and stock, whilst the latter is well covered with timber and wood, consisting chiefly of birch, beech, maple, and hemlock. The present standing of wood and timber, much of which is second growth, is estimated by persons of safe judgment to be greater in quantity than the wood and timber which was on the same area twenty years ago. The increase of growth, it is thought, has been more rapid than the loss by consumption and waste.

The population when the census of 1880 was taken was 2452. The number of families at that time was about 525, averaging nearly five persons to a family. The number of polls of those present in the Town is not far from 600. The population has varied very little during the last two decades, and is now about stationary. It is chiefly native except a small French element which the railroad has brought in at Woodsville, but this is not large enough to offset the general American character of the population and influence of the Town.

There are four villages in the Town, the most historic and prominent of these is Haverhill Corner which was early settled, within a year after of the first settlement at the Ox Bow in 1762. It is the west county seat of Grafton County, and contains the court house, jail, county building for county officers, the Academy, two churches, and the Exchange Hotel. In addition to these there are also business places: two good stores, a jeweller, druggist, fancy goods and millinery shops, lawyers' offices, and the Cohos Printing Press. Here is also printed and published the "Grafton County Register." The village numbers in all, including Ladd street, over one hundred private residences, many of which are large, substantial, square houses of the olden times, and give an air of respectability and prosperity to the place. In the center of the village is the large and beautiful Park around which is a fine growth of elms and maples, and fronting on the Park are many of the best residences of the village; the Exchange Hotel is on the west side of the Park, and the Congregational church and Academy are at the north-east corner. The village except in court time is ideal in its quiet and rest. In summer time, however, it is quite a resort for tourists and visitors, especially with those who seek a restful and invigorating atmosphere and pleasant social surroundings. With enterprise and well directed capital the place could be made one of the most popular and inviting in all New England. There is every element of a successful summer resort,—excellent society, scenery unrivalled, air pure and bracing, drives of great variety and comfort, two lakes within easy reach by carriage, boating and fishing, and frequent trains sweep near by on either side. Few houses have been built in the last forty years, and only one of marked modern style, that of Mrs. R. D. Tucker, which is a handsome Queen Ann structure. The village proper contains one Main street running north and south, and Court street on which are situated the court house and county building.

North Haverhill is a beautiful little village of some forty houses on the west end of a wide plain drained by Poole Brook. It contains a number of substantial private houses, several stores, a good sized hotel, shops, the Methodist church, and the new Town house and records building. The Boston and Lowell railroad runs close by the village, and the hotel has been generally well filled with visitors in summer months.

At the extreme north end of the Town, at the Junction of the Ammonoosuc with the Connecticut, is the village of Woodsville, named from John L. Woods who at one time was the owner of the land on which the village stands. For many years it was the terminus of the Boston, Concord and Montreal railroad, but is now an important railroad junction. The village is a bright, active, growing place, and does a large amount of business with the prospect of becoming a prominent center in this section. The White Mountain, Montpelier and Wells River, and the Passumpsic railroads connect at this point with the Boston and Lowell railroad. Woodsville is of quite recent growth, and in the past few years has doubled in size and population. Twenty-five years ago there was little more than the round-house and railroad station. Now there are a number of substantial residences and many pretty cottage houses, two churches, an excellent graded school building, two large hotels, stores, shops, a superior water supply, and the headquarters of the White Mountains division of the Boston and Lowell railroad.

These three villages are all on the western side of the Town,—Woodsville and North Haverhill near the banks of the Connecticut, whilst Haverhill Corner is situated on a high bluff about two hundred feet above the river bed and nearly a mile back, overlooking the river and having a commanding view of the valley north and south.

The other village is East Haverhill in the south-east part of the Town on the Oliverian about a mile from the Benton line. It is situated in the midst of the beautiful and wide expanse of meadow which is formed by the Oliverian and the North Branch. It contains pleasant and bright houses, two stores, shops, the Methodist church, and a station on the Boston and Lowell railroad.

A little hamlet has grown up at Pike Station in connection with the whet-stone works of the A. F. Pike Manufacturing Company, where there is also a store. The road from this point to East Haverhill is quite thickly settled, almost forming a continuous village between the two points. The remaining area of the Town under tillage is much of it somewhat sparsely settled.

There are no high mountains within the limits of the Town. The highest points of land are in the southern section,—Catamount Hill and Iron Ore Hill, the latter lying partly in Piermont. A range of well defined hills of considerable height, divided by Poole Brook, traverse the centre of the Town from south to north, of which Briar Hill forms the highest elevation. There is also an irregular range or cluster of hills in the north-western part of the Town, commencing east of Horse Meadow and running north to the Bath line. The surface of the Town may be described in general as irregular and broken, excepted along the river and in the plains already described, that at North Haverhill and the other at East Haverhill.

The Vermont bank of the Connecticut River marks the western boundary of Haverhill. The river flows in a very winding direction through the Town, traversing a distance of about eighteen miles in its course, and forming in the northern part the famous Ox Bow. The intervals or " meadows," as they are usually called, are of great breadth and of rare fertility, and are unsurpassed by any lands in the entire course of the river. Here are some of the largest and finest and most productive farms in the state, which are annually enriched by the Spring overflow of the Connecticut, sometimes filling the valley from side to side, and presenting the appearance of a large lake.

The Ammonoosuc, which comes down from the White Mountain range, is a large branch of the Connecticut and forms the boundary line at the extreme north-west end of the town. It furnishes excellent water-power. The Oliverian is the next most important stream in size and water-power. It rises in the western slope of Moosilauke, enters the Town near the south-east corner, and pursuing a westward direction empties into the Connecticut a little north of Haverhill Corner, after a rapid descent by a series of steep falls just above its mouth. This is a swift mountain stream, and gathers the water fall in a few hours after rains. It becomes angry and of full volume in the Spring and in rainy seasons, whilst in Summer months when the season is dry it shrinks to the dimensions of a moderate sized brook. Its principal tributary is North Branch which comes in from Benton, flows near the east line of the Town, and meets the main stream at East Haverhill.

Poole Brook with numerous small feeders has its spring in the north-east part of the Town, and running in a circuitous course through the center, forming Deming Pond in its way, reaches the Connecticut at the old Town farm. Its northern branch rises in French Pond. This brook traverses the wide and fertile plain at North Haverhill. The name of this brook was given to it from the fact that a man of that name lived in the earliest settlement of Haverhill on the north side of the brook not far from its mouth. Poole lost his life in the Connecticut at the "Narrows" as did his only child, Polly, who was drowned at the Ox Bow.

Within the limits of Haverhill there are no ponds of any

considerable size, which are so prominent a feature of other sections of the state. Woods' Pond in the southern part of the Town, Long Pond in the central, and French Pond in the northern are the only bodies of still water, and these are quite limited in extent.

The only island of any notable area is in the Connecticut River north of Ox Bow, known as "Howard Island," and was so named in honor of one of the earliest and most prominent settlers of the Town, Col. Joshua Howard, who lived to the age of ninety-nine years.

The general geologic rock area of the Town, according to Prof. Hitchcock, is known as "Bethlehem gneiss," and in this area is found the following varieties of stone: protogene, common gneiss, granite beds, hornblende chist, soapstone, and limestone. Along the Connecticut River the soil is alluvial, in the plain at North Haverhill a clayey loam, and at East Haverhill there is also alluvial soil. The remainder of the Town is of the ordinary soil of New Hampshire uplands.

Ores and minerals are found in the Town, iron in the region of Iron Ore Hill, which was formerly dug to some extent and drawn to a smelting furnace in Vermont. Native arsenic, a rare mineral in the United States, and almost wholly confined to New Hampshire, is found on Francis Kimball's farm. Soapstone was early discovered at the North End, and a few years ago efforts were made in quarrying and bringing it into market, but the attempt proved a financial failure. The vein is from twelve to fifteen feet wide, and the stone is said to be capable of a finer edge than any other similar stone in the country. Whetstone on Cutting Hill near the Piermont line, exists in immense beds which have been worked for over a half century and manufactured into all kinds of tool-sharpeners. There are granite quarries in the northern and southern parts of the Town. The stone of the latter is said to be of the very finest quality. Limestone is found along the valley of the North

Branch of the Oliverian, which has been quarried and burned in years past in large quantities. It is blue and gray, the former fine, the latter coarse. It is said lime can be made here much cheaper than at Thomaston, Maine.

The water-power of the Town,—that at Woodsville is ample enough to drive large machinery, whilst that of the Oliverian, which near its mouth makes a descent to the Connecticut river of about eighty feet in the short space of forty or fifty rods, furnishes sufficient head in seasons of ordinary water, but the power is very uncertain in the summer months, and is greatly crippled at that season of the year. Water storage in large quantities, it is said, could easily be secured by a comparatively small outlay on the North Branch back of Sugar Loaf. Water-power is also found at other points farther up the Oliverian and on the North Branch, whilst Poole Brook at North Haverhill a part of the year is very available for such purposes.

The Town is well provided with roads. Those running the length of the Town are the River road from Haverhill Corner through North Haverhill to Woodsville, the County road from Ladd street to Swiftwater, and a road from East Haverhill running in an irregular course near the Benton line commonly called the "Lime Kiln" road. Cross-roads connect these at convenient points, the most important of which are the road from Haverhill Corner, the Brook road, along the Oliverian, the Brushwood road, the road to the Centre from North Haverhill, and another to Briar Hill and Swiftwater, and one from the river to the Bath line, called the "Butler road."

CHAPTER III.

DISCOVERY AND EXPLORATION OF THE COHOS COUNTRY.

Early reports about it from hunters, trappers, and returned soldiers — Plan to explore and take possession of the Country — A doubt — Project failed — An event that led to a careful survey — A new route — The expedition of 1753 — Capt. Powers' scouting party, 1754 — Missions of the Powers and Lovewell parties.

Some years before the foot of any white Englishman or American had trod that part of the Connecticut Valley as a permanent abode, which afterwards became famous as the Cohos Country, reports of its great fertility and value had reached the settlements as far down on the Connecticut river as Massachusetts, and these reports were known also to the Provincial authorities of New Hampshire. They were brought by hunters and trappers who were accustomed to go up to the head-waters of the Pemigewasset and its tributaries and beyond, and also it is said by returned soldiers and captives who at the close of the French and Indian war came back from Canada by way of Lake Memphremagog and the Passumpsic and Connecticut rivers. Gen. Jacob Bailey, it is stated in the Life of Gen. Stark, passed from Canada to his home in Newbury, Mass., and was charmed with the Cohos meadows.

As early as 1752 the General Court of New Hampshire took measures to explore and take possession of the country. The farthest northern settlement as late as 1760 in the Connecticut Valley was at "No. 4," now Charleston, and there were only a few settlements south of that point within the limits of the Province of New Hampshire. The original plan of 1752 was to take possession of the Cohos Country, and hold it as a military post against the French and Indians. The government was to grant two townships to five hundred picked men who were to occupy the territory,—one on the Vermont side of the Connecticut river, and the other on the New

Hampshire side. In each of these townships a fort or stockade was to be built and garrisoned. The enclosures were to contain fifteen acres each, large enough to give shelter to the inhabitants and their cattle in case of an attack from the French and Indians. These enclosures were to be provided with public buildings and granaries. Courts were to be established for the settlement of all civil matters, and a strict military discipline was to be maintained. The settlement in Cohos was also to be connected with No. 4 by a military road cut through the forest.

Such was the general plan of occupancy as outlined in a letter of Col. Atkinson in the secretary's office of New Hampshire. And in order to carry out the scheme a committee was appointed to examine the lands and to locate the townships. The way of access at that time to the Cohos Country, was by way of No. 4, and the committee, it is said, after they had performed their duty, made a favorable report to the Provincial authorities, and four hundred men were actually enlisted to take possession of the Cohos Country.*

This project, however, was not carried out, as the aborigines who were in possession of the country not only as a hunting-ground, but had also cultivated some parts of it on both sides of the river, made earnest remonstrance and threats against the invasion of their territory by the whites.

Meantime, an event took place which led to an extensive and careful exploration of the Cohos Country. A party of four men whilst hunting on Baker's river in the spring of

---

* It has been held that the "committee" which was appointed in 1752 to examine and lay out the two townships, did not go to the Cohos Country, and that Capt. Powers and his party were the first explorers of this region. This view is founded on these facts, first, that no account of the committee's work is recorded, and second, that in 1754 the General Court in determining to send the Powers' party to the Cohos Country, call it an "hitherto unknown region."

1752 was surprised by Indians. Two of them were taken prisoners and carried away into Canada, one made his escape by flight, and the other was killed in the affray. One of the persons named was John Stark, who afterwards became the brave and distinguished Gen. Stark of the Revolutionary War, and the hero of the battle of Bennington. The Indians in taking their prisoners from Baker's river into Canada passed directly through the Cohos Country. Stark and his companion were soon released from captivity, and returned in the summer of the same year in which they were carried away. They gave an account of the Cohos Country, and their description of it was so favorable and enticing that the authorities were animated with new zeal and determination to send an expedition to the Connecticut river at Cohos.

The Indian trail from Baker's river to the Connecticut valley, over which Stark and his fellow-prisoners were taken, and which was followed in their return from Canada, suggested to the authorities of New Hampshire that the most direct and feasible way to reach the Cohos Country was to go up the Pemigewasset and Baker's rivers, and thence into the Connecticut valley by the Indian trail. And this route was the one chosen by the party sent out for the purpose of marking a road into Cohos, at the head of which was Col. Lovewell with John Stark, the returned prisoner, as their guide.

The party started from Concord, then called Rumford, March 10, 1753, and followed up the Merrimack, Pemigewasset, and Baker's rivers, using canoes whenever the water would permit. The party left Baker's river at the junction of Pond Brook, the north-west branch of the main stream, and reached the Connecticut river at Piermont through the north-east part of what is now the town of Orford. The round journey, a distance of about one hundred sixty miles, was made in twenty days. Col. Lovewell and his party remained on the Connecticut river only one night, and the next day they began their return to Concord.

In the following year, 1754, an expedition or scouting party was organized under the command of Capt. Peter Powers of Hollis. A detailed account of their journey is given in a diary or journal which was kept at the time, by Capt. Powers, and which was afterwards in possession of his youngest son, Samson Powers.

The expedition left Concord, June 15, 1754, and reached Contoocook the same day. The following day being Sunday, the Journal notes the fact that the party "tarried and went to meeting." A week later Capt. Powers and his associates had got as far as the mouth of Pond Brook on Baker's river, but perhaps on account of having penetrated beyond the limits of civilization and meeting houses, no mention is made of tarrying the second Sabbath for devotional purposes, and they marched on along Pond Brook. After advancing a short distance the party was compelled, "by reason of the dark weather," to follow the path which had been marked by Col. Lovewell and his men in March, 1753. The Connecticut river was reached on the 25th of June, the eleventh day after the expedition left Concord, at a point known as "Moose Meadow," afterwards owned by Maj. Nathaniel Merrill, and now in possession of Benjamin Hibbard, a descendant of his. Then skirting along the wide intervals of the Connecticut river the party encamped on the banks of a "large stream which came out of the east," and which is described as furnishing "the best falls and conveniences of all sorts of mills." The march of this day must have been about twenty miles, and the encampment on the night of June 25th was, in all probability, on the south side of Oliverean on the high plat of ground a little west of the Montgomery house, now owned by Capt. J. Leroy Bell. The river being much swollen by the frequent rains which are noted in the Journal, the explorers after a long and toilsome journey would hardly venture to cross.

In the Journal of the next day Capt. Powers noticed the fact of "clear intervals" on the Connecticut River. These intervals now known as Great Ox Bow in Newbury, Vermont, and Little Ox Bow in Haverhill, had been cultivated at times by the Indians. The hills of corn though swarded over and covered with a luxuriant growth of grass were visible at latter date, 1761, when Johnston and Pattie, the first white settlers, came to the Cohos Country. On reaching the Ammonoosuc the river was so deep and wide that the party were compelled to tarry and build a canoe before they were able to cross the stream. Capt. Powers and his men, after leaving the territory of the lower Cohos, within the limits of what is now Haverhill, continued their explorations as far as Lancaster. In their journey northward they passed along the high ground between the Connecticut and Ammonoosuc rivers. On the second day of July, finding their stores much reduced, with little hope of going forward with success, Capt. Powers resolved to return, and at once began preparations for the homeward journey. No Indians had been met by the exploring party in their long march, but on the day of their return whilst the men were mending their shoes, Capt. Powers with two others made a short excursion to the north of the encampment, in the course of which they came to a place where Indians had been making canoes, and which apparently they had abandoned only a short time before.

The last date in the Journal is July 6th, the expedition having reached on that day on the homeward journey as far as Haverhill, and on the night of that day the party encamped, according to the entry in the Journal, on the high ground near the Oliverian, which is described as "the best of upland," and covered by "some quantity of large white pine." This encampment was in all likelihood on the ground now covered by Haverhill Village.

The Powers' expedition as already stated was a scouting-party whose chief aim was a search for Indians. The exploration of the country was only incidental to its main purpose, and this was the first exploration of the Cohos Country unless the "committee" of 1752 actually went to Cohos. Col. Lovewell's party was sent to the Connecticut River and reached it at Piermont where it remained only one night, and then returned to Concord, and the object of this expedition was to mark a road to Cohos over the Indian trail between the Connecticut and Baker's rivers.

CHAPTER IV.

THE CHARTER PERIOD.

Influx of population—The Charter—Names of Grantees—Four divisions—House lots — Privileged "pitchers"— Governor Wentworth's "right"— Drawing — Numbering—Names of meadows—Grantees common to Newbury and Haverhill —Gen. Jacob Bailey—Col. Jacob Kent—Gen. Moses Hazen.

Although the Cohos Country was now fully explored by Capt. Powers and his party who gave a glowing account of its wonderful fertility and great resources, there was no immediate influx of emigration into the country till some years later. But after the conquest of Canada by the English in 1760, and when the frontiers were no longer exposed to the dangers and incursions of the French and their Indian allies, the spirit of emigration in the older settlements of New Hampshire and Massachusetts began again to revive, and large numbers of hardy and enterprising emigrants poured into the inviting openings of the Connecticut valley. In 1761 the Provincial authorities of New Hampshire made numerous grants of townships on both sides of the Connecticut River. The territory on the west side of the river as far as the New York line was at this time claimed as part of New Hampshire.

The charter of the Township of Haverhill bears date the 18th of May, 1763, and was granted to seventy-five persons. In addition to the seventy-five shares represented by these persons, His Excellency, Governor Benning Wentworth, Esq., was to have five hundred acres which were to be counted as two shares. Also, there was a share each for the Society for the Propagation of the Gospel in Foreign Parts, for a glebe for the Church of England, for the first settled minister of the gospel, and for the benefit of a common school. The charter with the names of grantees is given in the following pages, the document being printed exactly as it was originally written, — capitals, spelling, abreviations, and punctuations are left unchanged. This is the only document which is so printed in this history; all other papers of the olden time, as far as used, are made to conform to modern usage. This is printed as an example of the changes which have taken place in such matters since the days of the charter.

CHARTER.

PROVINCE OF
NEW HAMPSHIRE

{ Seal }. George The Third By the Grace of God of Grate Britean France and Ireland King Defender of The Faith &c &c

To all Parsons to whom These Presents shall [come] Greeting—

Know yee that we of our special Grace Certain Knowlige and mere motion for the Due Encouragement of Setting a New Plantation within our said Province by and with the advice of our Trusty and well Beloved Benning Wentworth Esq Our Governor and Commander in Chief of Our said Province of Newhampshire in New England and Our Council of the said Province, Have Upon The Conditions and Reservations herein after made Given and Granted and by These Presents for us Our Heirs and Successors Do Give and Grant in Equal Shares unto Our Loving Subjects Inhabitants of Our said Province of Newhampshire and Our Other Governments and thier Heirs and assigns for Ever whose Names Are Entered on this Grant to be Divided to and Amongst them into Eighty one Equal Shares all that Tract or Parcel of Land Situate Lying and being within Our said Province of Newhampshire Containing by Admeasurement
Acres which Tract is to Contain more Than Six Miles Square Out of which an allowance is to be made for high Ways and unimprovable Lands by Rocks Ponds Mountains and Rivers One Thousand and Forty Acres free according To a Plan and Survey thereof made by Our said Governors Order and Returned into the Secretary's Office and here unto anexed Budtted and Bounded as follows viz. Begining at a Tree marked Standing on the Bank of the Estern side of Connecticut river and on the southerly or south westedly side of the mouth of the Amonuck River Opposite to the South westedly Corner of Bath* from thence Down Connecticut river as that runs Till it comes to a marked Tree Standing on the Bank of the River and is about Sevn (7) Miles On a straight Line from the mouth of Amonusk River aforesaid from thence south Fiftey Three Degrees Eeast five Miles and Three Quarters to a Stake and Stones Thence North Twenty Five

---

* Bath was incorporated in 1761, though not settled till a few years later.

Degrees East about Eight Miles Until it Coms upon a line with the Lro [lower] Side Line of Bath Thence North Fifty Five Degress West as Bath Runs to the Tree by the River The Bounds Began at— and that the Same be and hereby is Incorporated into a Toundship by the Name of Haverhill and the Inhabitants that Do or Shall hereafter inhabit the said Toundship are hereby Declared to be Enfranchized with and Intitled to all and Every the Priviledges and Immunities that Other Tounds within Our Province by Law Enuse and injoy and further that the said Tound as soon as thire Shall be Fifty Families Resident and settled Thereon shall have the Liberty of Holding Two Feares one of Which shall be held on the   and the Other on the   annually which Fairs are not too Continue Longer then the Respective   Following the said   and that as soon as the said Tound shall Consist of Fifty families a Market may be Opened and Kept one or More Days in Each Week as may be Thought most advantageous to the Inhabitants also that the first Meeting For the Choice of Tound Officers agreable to the Laws of Our said Province Shall be held on ye Second Tuesday in June Next.

Which sd meeting Shall be Notifyed by Capt John Hazzen who is hereby also appointed the Moderator of the said First Meeting which he is To Notify and Govern agreeable to the Laws and Customs of Our said Province and that the Annual meetings forever hereafter for the Choice of such officers for the said Tound Shall be on the Second Tuesday of March annually—

To Have and To hold the said Tract of Land as above expressed together with all Privileges and appurtennance to them and Thire Respective heirs and assigns forever upon the following Considerations viz—

1. That Every Grantee his heres or assigns shall Plant and Cultivate Five acres of Land within the Term of Five Years for Every Fiftey acres Contained in his or Thire Shares or Propotion of Land in said Toundship and Continue to Improve and Settle the Same by additional Cultivations on Penalty of Forfeiture of his Grant or Share in the said Toundship and of its Reverting to us Our Heres and Successors to be by us and them Regranted to Such of Our Subjects as shall Effectually Settle and Cultivate the same—

2ly. That all White and Other Pine Trees within the Said Toundship Fit for Masting Our Royal Navy be carefully Preserved for that Use and not to be Cut or felled with Out our special Licence for so Doing First had and Obtained upon the Penalty of the Forfeiture of the Right of sutch Grantee his Hiers and assigns to us Our hiers and Successors as well as Being Subject to the Penalty of an act or acts of Parliament that Now are or here after Shall be Enacted—

3ly That before any Division of the Land be made, To and among the Grantees, a Tract of Land as near the Centre of the s [said] Toundship as the land will admit of: Shall be Reserved and marked Out For Tound Lotts one of which shall be allotted to Each Grantee of the Contents of One Acre—

4ly. Yielding and Paying therefor to us Our heirs and Successors for the Space of Ten Years to be Computed from the date hereof the rent of one Ear of Indian Corn only on the Twentey Fifth Day December annually if Lawfully Demanded the First Payment To be made on the Twentey Fifth Day of December: 1763.

5ly. Every Proprietor Settler or Inhabitant Shall Yield and pay unto us Our Heirs and Successors—yearly and Every Year forever from and After the Expiration of Ten years from the above sad Twentey Fifth Day of December Namely on the Twentey Fifth Day of December which will be the Year of Our Lord 1773 One Shillings Proclamation Money for Every Hundred [acres he so owns Settles or Possesses and So in Proportion For a Grater or Lesser Tract of the said Land: which money shall be Paid The Respective Parsons abovsaid thire Hiers or assigns in Our Council Chamber in Portsmouth or to sutch Officer or Officers as shall be appinted To Receive the same and This To be in Lieu of all Other Rents and Serviceses Whatsoever—

In Testimony whereof we have Caused the Seal of Our said Province to be hereunto affixed Witness Benning Wentworth Eqr Our Governor and Commander in Cheaf of Our said Province the 18th Day of May in the Year of Our Lord Christ One Thousand Seven Hundred and Sixty Three and in the Third Year of Our Reign—by his Excelleneys Command With the advice of Council—

B WENTWORTH

T ATKINSON JUNR. Secry—

Province of Newhampshire May ye 18 1763 Recorded in the Book of Charters Page 397 & 398

T ATKINSON JUNR. Secry—

THE NAMES OF THE GRANTEES OF HAVERHILL.

John Hazzen
Jacob Bayley Esq
Ephraim Bayley
James Philbrook
Gideon Gould
John Clark
John Swett
Thomas Emery
Benoney Colbourn
Reuben Mills
John Hazzen Junr
Jaasiel Harriman
Jacob Kent
Eleazer Hall
Samuel Hubbart
John Haile Esq
Maxey Hazelton
Thomas Johnson
John Mills
John Trusial
Abraham Dow
Uriah Morse

THE CHARTER PERIOD.

Edmond Cobley
David Hall
Lemuel Tucker
Edmond Moores Esq
John White
Benjamin Moores
William Hazzen
Moses Hazzen
Robert Peaslee
Timothy Bedel
John Spafford
Enoch Heath
William Page
Joseph Kelley
Aaron Hosmer
John Harriman
John Lampson
Stephen Knight
John Hall
David Hulbart
Simon Stevens
John Moores
William Toborn
David Page
James White
Benj Merrill
Nathaniel Merrill
John Church
Enoch Hall
Jacob Hall
Benoney Wright
John Page
Josiah Little
John Taplin Esq
Jona Foster
Joseph Blanchard Esq
Richard Pettey
Moses Foster
The Honorable
James Nevin Esq
John Nelson Esq
Theodore Atkinson Junr
Nathaniel Barrel
Col William Symes
William Porter
John Hastings
Capt George Marsh
Maj Richard Emery
Capt Nehemiah Lovell
Hon Henry Shorbern Esq
Maj John Wentworth
Saml Wentworth Esq of Boston
Bypeld Loyd Boston
And his Excellency Governor Barnard

His Excellency Benning Wentworth Esq a Tract of Land to Contain Five Hundred Acres as Marked B: W: in the Plan which is to be accounted two of the within Shares One whole Share for the Incorporated Society For the Propagation of the Gospel in Foreign Parts one whole Shaire for a Glebe for the Church of England One Share for the First Settled Minister of the Gospel and one Share for the Benefit of a School in said Tound—

Province of New Hampshire May The 18th 1763 Recorded in the Book of Charters Page 399 &c T Atkinson Junr Secry

The Proprietors at once went to work to assign each owner his "right" or "share." The Town was divided into sections. First, came the meadow lots of one hundred acres each; then the division of one hundred acre lots; next, the eighty acre lots, and last the north and south divisions of forty acre lots. But before any division of the land was to be made, a section in the centre of the Town was to be set apart for house lots of one acre for each grantee.* All shares were drawn by lot, except in the case of a few persons who were privileged to "pitch" their "rights," and several also were allowed to have their entire "right" in meadow lots. Capt. Hazen and Col. Jacob Bailey were allowed such privilege, and a few others who doubtless had something to do in getting the charter. Gov. Wentworth's "right" of five hundred acres, rated as two shares, was in the north-west corner of the Town, where Woodsville is situated, and next south of him was the "right" of his Secretary, Theodore Atkinson. All numbering of lots was from north to south, but the meadow lots were numbered according to the meadow the lots were in. For example, Upper meadow had nine lots which were numbered from one to nine as situated in that meadow; Horse Meadow had twenty lots and were numbered from one to twenty in that meadow, and so on.†

Some of the grantees of Haverhill were also grantees of Newbury, Vermont. Of many of the names given in the list little or nothing is known. Probably some became Proprietors simply as a matter of speculation. We learn from the Proprietors' records that quite early "rights" were sold at public auction for the payment of taxes. These rights belonged to persons who in all probability did not come to the new settlement, and their lands remaining un-

---

*The object it would seem was to have a village street run through the centre of the town, on which the dwellings were to be built, with each grantee's land running back from the street. But the house lots in Haverhill were laid out along the high ground of the meadows.

†The names of the meadows beginning at the north were as follows: Upper Meadow, Horse Meadow, Wheeler Meadow, Ox Bow, Morse Meadow, Bailey Meadow, Oliverian Meadow.

improved gained little in value, and as a consequence were allowed to be confiscated for taxes.

Of these grantees of prominence who were also grantees of Newbury, and whose interests were more in Newbury than in Haverhill, foremost must be mentioned Gen. Jacob Bailey. He and Capt. Hazen were warm friends, and acted together in the settlement of the Cohos Country. Gen. Bailey became a very conspicuous man in the history of this region, and held a high commission during the Revolutionary War, being Commissary General of the Northern Army. The Baileys of Newbury and of Haverhill are descendants of Gen. Bailey.

Jacob Kent was also a prominent citizen of Newbury, and was the ancestor of the Kents of that Town. Hon. Henry O. Kent, the present Naval Officer at Boston, is a grandson of Col. Jacob Kent.

Moses Hazen was a brother of Capt. John Hazen, but went to St. Johns, Canada, before the Revolution. At the commencement of hostilities, however, he joined the revolutionists, and took a prominent part in the struggle for independence, coming out of the contest with the rank of Brigadier General. He died in Albany, N. Y., in 1785.

Of the grantees of Haverhill whose interests were more particularly with the development and progress of the Town, notice is taken in another place so far as anything could be learned of them.

CHAPTER V.

EARLY SETTLEMENT BEFORE THE CHARTER.

Two remarkable men—Michael Johnston and John Pattie the first settlers, 1761—Wintered at Ox Bow—Indians then in possession—Johnston and Pattie return to No. 4—A tragic end—Capt. Hazen comes to Cohos in 1762 with men and material for saw-mill and grist-mill—Leading position—Death—Moses Hazen and John Hazen confounded—William Hazen-Joshua Howard—Jesse Harriman—Simeon Stevens—Thomas Johnson—Col. Timothy Bedel and family—Capt. John Page and family—First Marriage—First Family—First Birth—First Death—Morse Meadow.

In the early settlement of the Cohos Country there were two men of remarkable energy and force of character. They were men of large experience in those stormy times, and occupied prominent positions in the communities where they lived. One was Jacob Bailey of Newbury, Mass., and the other was John Hazen of Haverhill, Mass. Both had taken a leading part in the French and Indian war, and were in excellent favor with those in authority. Their gallant and brave services in the war which had just closed, would naturally give them special claim to consideration, and when the tide of emigration set into the Connecticut Valley, these men directed their energies to the Cohos Country, and took early steps for occupancy and possession. They worked in harmony. Capt. Hazen was the first to send forward men who took possession of the east side of the Connecticut river in the summer of 1761, two years before a charter of the Town was granted. No doubt there was a good understanding between these leaders and the authorities at Portsmouth in reference to the occupancy of this part of the Connecticut valley. The names of Hazen and Bailey stand at the head of the list of grantees of the Township of Haverhill.

The men whom Capt. Hazen sent into the Cohos Country in the early summer of 1761, were MICHAEL JOHNSTON and JOHN PATTIE, both from Haverhill, Mass. They were the first white persons who set permanent foot on the soil of Haverhill. They came first to No. 4 and then up the Connecticut river, and brought with them some cattle. Before the winter set in they built for themselves and their cattle shelters at Ox Bow where they found clear intervals, as Capt. Powers seven years before had stated in his Journal when he and his party passed through the country. This cleared land which at some time had been cultivated by the Indians in raising corn, was now covered with a heavy growth of grass which the two white occupants gathered in the fall and fed to their cattle during the winter. Indians were then dwelling on these intervals, but they were friendly and made no opposition or threatening protests to the occupancy of these lands by strangers, as they had done in 1752 when preparations were made at that date to take possession of the country.

Johnston and Pattie after their long winter in the wilderness, embarked in a canoe on the Connecticut river in the early summer with the intention of returning to No. 4 and their friends. In their journey they met with a sad accident. A little above the mouth of White river, in an angry plunge of the Connecticut over rocks at a point afterwards known as Olcott Falls, the canoe was capsized and the two voyagers were thrown into the water, Johnston losing his life. The body was washed ashore on an island just below the Falls where it was found soon after by a stranger coming up the river, and by whom it was buried in the sand. The island now bears the name of Johnston's Island. Pattie escaped the fate of his companion by superior skill in swimming, and afterwards reached No. 4 in safety. Of his after history nothing is known. Michael Johnston was a brother of the distinguished Col. Charles Johnston who a few years afterwards came to Haverhill, and took a prominent part in the affairs of the Town.

In the spring of 1762 Capt. Hazen joined Johnston and

Pattie with a new force of men, and with material for building a grist mill and a saw mill which he erected on Poole Brook, on the site where afterwards stood the Swasey mill.

JOHN HAZEN was born in 1731, his father's name being Moses Hazen, and his mother's Abigail White of Haverhill, Mass. He was a man of great force of character and full energy and enterprise. The Township of Haverhill was granted to him and seventy-four others. By the charter he was intrusted with the duty of warning the first Town meeting, and he was also named in the charter to be the first moderator. He was also moderator of the first Proprietors' meeting. In Town affairs he took a foremost part, and held various positions of trust, serving either as moderator, selectman, Town-clerk during his residence in the Town.

Previous to coming to Haverhill he was active, it is said, in the settlement of the town of Hampstead, and at one time he was a citizen of Plaistow, from which town he was enrolled in the New Hampshire militia. He was a brave and gallant soldier in the French and Indian war, and faced many dangers and saw hard service in the Canadian expedition especially before the walls of Quebec. He held a Lieutenant's commission in Col. Meserve's regiment in the expedition against Crown Point in 1757, and a Captain's commission in Col. Hart's regiment in 1758. He also had a like rank in 1760 in Col. Goff's regiment for the invasion of Canada.

At the close of the war he returned to Haverhill, Mass., and soon after undertook with others the settlement of the Cohos Country. He was a large land-owner in Haverhill, and built as above stated the first saw-mill and grist-mill in the Town.

Capt. Hazen's leading position in the early settlement of the Town is indicated in the fact that he was allowed to select meadow lots Nos. 2, 3, 4, 5, 6, in Ox Bow, and house lots Nos. 31, 32, 33, 34, 35. Mill privileges were reserved for the use of the Proprietors. All other persons were required to draw for their lots.

Capt. Hazen's name which appears repeatedly both in the Town and Proprietors' records till 1773, suddenly disappears after that date, and he is supposed to have died about that time. No record is found of his death or burial, but he was undoubtedly buried in the grave-yard at Ox Bow. No stone marks the resting-place of the founder of the Town. John Hazen and Moses Hazen have been confounded. The latter was a gallant officer of high rank in the Revolutionary War. Capt. Hazen married Anne, daughter of John Swett of Haverhill, Mass., whose name appears amongst the grantees of Haverhill, N. H. She died in 1765. They had four children, Sarah, John, and two who died in early life. John went with his uncle William to New Brunswick, and married Priscilla, daughter of Dr. William McKinstry, and had a numerous family. Sarah became the wife of Maj. Nathaniel Merrill, and was the mother of a family of twelve children, eleven of whom were daughters. Capt. Hazen married a second time,—a daughter of Rev. Josiah Cotten,—and she after Capt. Hazen's death, became the wife of Henry Hancock of Lyman. This fact determines the date of Capt. Hazen's death approximately. He was supposed to be a man of large property, but it is said after his estate was settled there were only $12 left, which were given to his daughter Sarah, and with this money she bought a large family Bible that is now in possession of Benjamin Hibbard of Piermont.

Capt. Hazen was a man of great courage. One Oliver Willard according to Powers, undertook to thwart his plans in regard to the grant of Haverhill, and for this purpose he sent some men to take possession of the territory. But Hazen had anticipated them, and being in excellent favor with the governor of the Province, and having as his ally Gen. Jacob Bailey, a brave and resolute man, he had little difficulty in gaining a complete victory over his rival. Willard was furious at his discomfiture, and threatened to take vengeance upon his opponent if he ever caught him outside the settlement. The parties soon after met at No. 4 when the attempt was made to carry out the threat, but the doughty Captain it is said was more than a match for his rash assailant.

WILLIAM, brother of John and Moses Hazen, was a proprietor in the original grant of the Town. He went early to New Brunswick, and had a family of sixteen children, several of whom became connected by marriage with some of the first families of the Province, and some held high official positions.

JOSHUA HOWARD.—Of those who came with Capt. Hazen in the spring of 1762 to put up his mills and begin the settlement of the Cohos Country several afterwards became prominent. One of these was Joshua Howard, a young man from Haverhill, Mass., who lived to the very advanced age of 99, dying in 1839. He was one of the grantees of Newbury, Vt., and was a townsman of Hazen's in Massachusetts. With two others he was the first person that came direct from Salisbury to Cohos, the usual route being by the way of No 4. This was in April, 1762. His companions were Jesse Harriman and Simeon Stevens, with an old hunter as guide who led them through the wilderness. They accomplished the journey in four days, travelling up Baker's river and crossing the height of land into what afterwards became the town of Coventry, now Benton, thence followed down the Oliverian. They were probably the advance force of the men whom Capt. Hazen brought to Cohos as already stated.

Col. Howard lived for some time on an island in the Connecticut river which bears his name. At one time he kept a hotel where the County Poor House now stands. He was a leading man in the community in his day. In 1787 he was one of the selectmen of the Town with Charles Johnston and Ezekiel Ladd. He was also on the committee of safety for the Town in 1776, and served as a lieutenant in a company of rangers in the Revolution. When the Union Convention met at Windsor, Vermont, for the purpose of organizing a state government that should include towns on both sides of the Connecticut river, Col. Howard was a representative from Haverhill in that convention. Little is known of his family. The oldest son, Joshua, died at the homestead on Howard's Island. Benjamin went to Ohio, and a younger son, Rice, was a sporting man, and spent much of his time away from home, chiefly in the South. Col. Howard was a man of intelligence, energy, and strict integrity, and in religious sentiment would be called a Universalist.

JAASIEL HARRIMAN, one of Howard's companions, came from Haverhill, Mass. He was commonly called "Jesse," and was a grantee of Haverhill, Bath, and Newbury. He remained in Haverhill only a few years and then moved to Bath. His was the first family that settled in that town. A daughter, Nancy, married Jesse Carleton and afterward lived in Haverhill. She was the grandmother of Chester M. Carleton.

SIMEON STEVENS, another of Howard's men, is probably the same person as Simon Stevens whose name appears as one of the grantees of Haverhill. A Simeon Stevens was also a grantee of Newbury. Simeon Stevens was a captain in Col. Bedel's regiment in 1778. The Stevens family became quite prominent in Piermont in later days.

Two other persons appear in company with Capt. Hazen in the early settlement of Haverhill, and afterward became conspicuous in the history of Cohos. One of these was THOMAS JOHNSON, a young man in the service of Gen. Bailey. He first lived in Haverhill for a short period, and then purchased land in Newbury and became a citizen of that town. The name of Johnson is found in the list of Newbury grantees. Col. Johnson was an ardent patriot during the Revolutionary War, and made himself very obnoxious to the British authorities on that account. He was at the taking of Ticonderoga, and acted as aid to Gen. Lincoln. Afterward in 1781 he was taken prisoner at Peacham, Vt., by a party of British soldiers and carried to Canada, but was allowed to return on parol to Newbury at the end of seven or eight months.

TIMOTHY BEDEL was the other person. He was from Salem, and after remaining in the employ of Capt. Hazen for a year or two, he moved his family to the newly organized Town, and settled on Poole brook. He and his family were a valuable accession to the population, and added to the substantial character of the new settlement. Col. Bedel was one of the original Proprietors of Haverhill and also of Bath, and was a man of large influence and prominence in the Town. Previous to the Revolution he lived for a short time in Bath. In 1775 he was a member of the Provincial Congress of New Hampshire, which met at Exeter, but at the breaking out of the War of the Revolution, he entered the military service, first as captain of a company of rangers, and afterwards as colonel of a regiment. During the long struggle he raised several regiments, one of which he led to Canada in 1776 in the army of Gen. Schuyler when that officer made the attack on Montreal. In this campaign Col. Bedel's regiment which was stationed at a place called "the Cedars," disgracefully surrendered to the enemy, and Col. Bedel suffered much in reputation; but subsequent revelation of the facts in the case completely exonerated him, as at the time he was on his way to Montreal for reinforcements, and his regiment was in command of Maj. Butterfield. The pay-roll of his regiment for 1776 is now in possession of his grandson, Hon. Hazen Bedel of Colebrook. He was also in the army of Gen. Gates at the battle of Saratoga when Gen. Burgoyne and his army were captured.

The first regiment Col. Bedel raised was for the defence of the Cohos Country in 1775. This was a body of rangers. Afterwards, in 1777, he was in command of a regiment for service in the Cohos Country and for the defence of the western frontier on the Upper Connecticut river. He also raised a regiment in 1778 for a like service when the time of the regiment of 1777 had expired, and he was for most of the time, after his return from Canada till the close of the war, in command of troops stationed in the Cohos Country and vicinity. After the Revolutionary War he was appointed Major-General of the Second Division of New Hampshire Militia.

He was a man of large endowment and great force of character, and was admirably fitted to be a leader of men in stirring times. A purer patriot did not engage in the Revolutionary struggle. He took a prominent part in the early history of Haverhill, in the development of its resources and in the advancement of its prosperity, and was a valuable citizen of the Town. He was repeatedly called by his fellow men to various trusts of honor and responsibility in Town affairs.

Col. Bedel had a family of six children, of whom Gen. Moody Bedel was the oldest and most distinguished. One daughter, Ruth, married Jacob Bailey, son of Gen. Jacob Bailey of Newbury, Vermont. Anna became the second wife of Samuel Brooks of Haverhill; her first husband was Dr. Thaddeus Butler. Another was married to Dr. Isaac Moore. Drs. Butler and Moore were early physicians of Haverhill. Col. Bedel died in 1787.

Gen. Moody Bedel was born in 1764, and like his father was a very prominent citizen of Haverhill. He was married twice, first to Ruth Hutchins, and they had a family of nine children, all of whom are now dead, but the descendants of some of these are numerous in the northern section of the state. For his second wife he married Mary Hunt of Bath, and by this marriage there were also nine children, some of whom are still living. Moody resides in Peoria, Ill., and Lonisa is the wife of Warren J. Fisher of Haverhill; Hazen and John Bedel (see Chap. XIX.); and Maria L. married Rufus Dow. Their son, Charles Dow, was in the War of the Rebellion, and now lives in Portage City, Mich., where he is post-master.

Gen Bedel lived at one time in the old toll house at the foot of Powder House Hill, and also in a small brick house half way up the hill near the old brick yard. He was a man of excellent education. At the age of twelve he was present with his father, Col. Timothy Bedel, at the battle of Saratoga, and later he enlisted as a private in Capt. Ezekiel Ladd's company in his father's regiment. When the War of 1812 broke out he commanded the Sixth Brigade of New Hampshire Militia, and was put in charge of the "District of New Hampshire for recruiting." Afterwards he was Lieutenant-Colonel of the 11th Regiment U. S. Infantry and was stationed at Burlington, Vt., and Plattsburg, N. Y., but for much of the time, contrary to his wishes, he was kept on detached duty on account of his great executive ability. In the memorable sortie at Fort Erie he led his regiment with conspicuous gallantry and success against the British forces, and for his bravery on that occasion he was promoted to be Colonel of the regiment.

At one time he was the possessor of a large property, owning not only some of the best meadows on the Connecticut river in Haverhill, but also large real estate in Bath, in Burlington, Vt., and in Plattsburg N. Y. He with others as early as 1798 purchased from the St. Francis Indians an immense tract of land in northern New Hampshire known as the "Philip Grant," from the fact that an Indian called "King Philip" signed the deed. They began a settlement called the "Indian Stream Settlement," but the War of 1812 called Gen. Bedel away. After the close of the war he returned to the settlement, but the legislature through the influence of speculators refused to confirm the "King Philip" title, and he became greatly embarrassed, dying in 1841 a poor man, "owning," as one who knew him well says, "not an inch of land." "Gen. Bedel," says the Adjutant General's Report, "had faced the cannon's mouth at the 'Sortie of Erie,' but he could not successfully face the speculators and interested parties about the legislature."

Whilst Gen. Bedel lived at Pittsburg he and his family endured many hardships. The mother with three of the youngest children returned to Haverhill, and after suffering much privation, the family was once more united in one home in Bath.

Gen. Bedel was one of the foremost citizens in Haverhill, and took an active and leading part in the affairs of the Town. He was distinguished for his enterprise, liberality, and ability. The first bridge across the Connecticut river at South Newbury was built by him, and the present bridge is known as "Bedel's Bridge." He also built a large brick building at the Brook which was afterwards used as a tavern.

JOHN PAGE came to Cohos in the early fall of 1762, and brought with him only an ax and a small bundle of clothes. But he had what was more than gold,—courage and industry. He bought a tract of land which has remained in the Page family to the present time.

The first winter he was in the employ of Gen. Bailey at the Great Ox Bow in Newbury and continued in his service until he could pay for his tract of land. His first house was built of logs on a knoll on the meadows, which is still pointed out. The house and barn were afterwards burnt, and he built the frame house in which he lived to the close of his life. The house is now owned and occupied by Mrs.

John Webster, and has been much changed from its original style and form.

The following memoranda, copied from the old family Bible of Capt. Page, give the exact facts of his early history :

John Page born in Lunenburg, Mass., 1741, and moved with his father's family to Rindge, N. H., and helped to get a log house built, and performed "sutler's duty" and thereby got a lot of land in said Rindge. He came to Coos meadows in September, 1762, wintered in the Great Ox Bow, took the charge of Gen. Bailey's cattle with one other man and boy, worked for Gen. Bailey and paid for a right of land in Haverhill, went to the Upper Coos [Lancaster], worked for his uncle David Page, and paid for another right in Haverhill. Came back to Haverhill, built a log house on the meadow, married Abigail Sanders, daughter of Master Sanders of Haverhill, lived with her about twelve years. She died of consumption, without children.* Married a second wife, Abigail Hazeltine of Concord, N. H., out of a good family, and an excellent woman, who died in child-bed of her first-born who also died, and both were buried in the same grave. Married a third wife, widow Hannah Green, daughter of Rev. Samuel Rice of Landaff, unto whom were born four sons, viz., John, William G., Samuel, and Stephen R.

Capt. Page belonged to a numerous family. Two of his brothers older than himself lost their lives at the taking of Louisburg in the French War. He was a man of medium height, but powerfully built. He lived on friendly terms with the Indians of Cohos, over whom he seems to have had very great influence. When they were going to have a "high time" on "fire-water," they would put their weapons in his hands, so as to avoid the danger of hurting each other in their drunken revelries. They had the highest opinion of his physical strength and prowess which were taught them by an incident that illustrates his keen mother-wit. On one occasion when he was cutting wood the Indians chal-

---

* The marriage of John Page and Abigail Sanders is the first marriage recorded in the Town records, and occurred Dec. 18, 1766. James Woodward and Hannah Clark were married Dec. 30, 1766, according to Town records, and were not, as Grant Powers says, the first couple that were joined in wedlock at Cohos.

lenged him to a trial of strength which he declined, but shrewdly waiting his opportunity he cut off a log as large as he could lift at one end, and then promptly and with apparent ease placed one end against his breast. Then he challenged any one of them to raise the other end, which of course none were able to do. Their untutored minds did not understand that to raise the end on the ground whilst the other was resting against his breast was equivalent to lifting the weight of the entire log. It is said he could lay his hand on the back of one of his yoke of oxen and vault over both at a single leap.

Mrs. Edward L. Page who owns and lives on the old Page homestead has in her possession the gun which Capt. Page used for protection the first winter he spent in the Cohos Country. Originally it was about six feet in length, but is now a little shorter, the barrel having been cut off several inches, and a cap-lock has taken the place of the old flint-lock. Mrs. Page has also in her possession four silver spoons which came into the Page family through Mrs. Hannah Green at the time of her marriage to Capt. Page. They are desert-size, and are said to have been made from some French coin and bear the initials W. G. H.—the G. stands for Green, the sur-name of her first husband, the W. for William, his Christian name, and H. for Hannah her own Christian name.

What little is known of Mrs. Hannah Green Page distinguishes her as a woman of great superiority of mind and character. Her influence in moulding the moral and intellectual bent and habits of her children was an important factor in their training, and left its impress upon their lives and character. "In the early history of Haverhill," writes a worthy descendant of the family, "I think my grandmother Page was a very important member of that family, and a very bright woman, exceedingly smart and energetic. Her house, I have heard my father say, was the house of the educated people of those times. Her father was the Rev. Samuel Rice, and I believe the education and advantages which her sons received were achieved mainly through her influence and exertion." In religious belief she was a Baptist, and a woman of great exemplariness of life.

Of Capt. Page's children two died in early life, John and Samuel lived to a good and honored old age. John attended school regularly in his early years, but at the age of fifteen his education was interrupted, and he was compelled to relinquish it. This was owing to the financial embarrassment of his father, and it was a great disappointment to the son, though he cheerfully aided his father in redeeming the homestead from debt. He became a prominent citizen in town and state, and held many places of trust and honor, selectman, representative, register of deeds, councillor, United States senator to fill ex-Gov. Hill's unexpired term, and governor in 1839–41. Gov. Page was engaged chiefly in farming, and took an active part in securing the building of the Boston, Concord & Montreal Railroad. He married a daughter of Maj. Nathaniel Merrill, and they had a family of nine children. In the War of 1812 he held a Lieutenant's commission, and served a short period on the northern frontier of New Hampshire. He was strongly attached to the Methodist church, and at his death he bequeathed the sum of $1000 for the use of the church at Haverhill Corner. Gov. Page died in 1865.

John A., second son of Gov. Page, (see Chap. XIX.) Several of the sons moved to the West. Nathaniel M. lives in Haverhill where the old Towle tavern stood. He is the only representative in Haverhill of the Gov. Page family. Edward L. lived till his death on the old homestead, and was a man of bright mind and of pleasing manners. He died of consumption.

The only daughter, Sarah H., married Dr. Dickey of Lyme, who died a few years ago. She was a woman of most noble and generous character, and an unselfish and devoted Christian. A young man from Lyme, a member of Dartmouth College, who was trying to work his way along, got discouraged and finally concluded he would quit school. Mrs. Dickey heard of the case and sent for the discouraged student. "John," she said, "I learn you intend to quit college. What is the reason?" "I have no money." "We have concluded that it is our duty to let you have what you need." The young man went through college, and is now a most useful man, having taught with distinguished success for seventeen years in a western city.

Samuel Page, brother of Gov. Page, was born in 1793, and lived and died in Haverhill. He was married twice. His first wife was a daughter of Maj. Nathaniel Merrill, and by this marriage there was one child, Louisa M., now Mrs. Babcock, (see Chap. XIX.) His second wife was Eliza Swasey, daughter of Obadiah Swasey of North Haverhill. They had a numerous family. William H., the oldest, has always been a citizen of Haverhill, with the exception of a few years when he lived in Piermont. He is a man of excellent business judgment, and has been very successful both as a farmer and as a merchant. He is now the senior member of the firm of W. H. Page & Son, which does a large general mercantile business. Mr. Page is one of the first citizens of the Town, though he has never taken a very prominent part in public matters. Whilst living in Piermont he represented that town for four years in the legislature, and was a member of the committee on finances. He is a deacon in the Congregational church. His wife was Mary E. Poor of Piermont, and they have two sons, Charles P. and Fred W., the former in business with his father.

Of Samuel Page's other children, Elizabeth, a largehearted and intelligent woman, married Jonathan S. Nichols, and Samuel lives on the old homestead. Harriet married Simeon C. Senter of Thetford, and is a woman of superior

Christian character. One of the daughters, Josephine, resides in Kansas. Hannah, who became Mrs. Bowen, died a few years after her marriage, and Ellen who married Milo Bailey, is also deceased. Mary, a lady of attractive manners, makes Haverhill her more permanent home. The youngest daughter, Emily, is the wife of Rev. C. N. Flanders of Newport. The youngest son, Moses S., (see Chap. XIX.)

Mr. Samuel Page was a man of sterling integrity and pure character, unostentatious, and of plain manners. He represented the Town in the legislature, and served a number of years in the board of selectmen. He and Mrs. Page died in 1877, only a day or two apart, and were buried at the same time.

The first family that came to Cohos was Uriah Morse and his wife, in June, 1762. They were from Northfield, Mass., and settled near the mouth of Poole brook. It was with Uriah and his wife that Capt. Hazen and his men boarded in that year, and their house may be considered the first tavern in the new settlement, as it was the stopping-place for strangers who came to Cohos. At this house in the spring of 1763 the first English child was born, but the little stranger survived its advent only a few days. Here also occurred the first death in the new settlement. It was that of a Miss of eighteen summers, and it would seem that Polly Harriman had made a very favorable impression on the sturdy pioneers of the Town, as her name comes down to us in this fragrant eulogy: "her death was much lamented," a memorial worth more than granite shaft. "Morse meadow" got its name from that of Uriah Morse, who also at a Proprietors' meeting in 1763 was allowed to have "pitch" No. 1 in that meadow. This was probably due to the double fact,—first, being the head of the earliest family in the new settlement, and second, because he made himself especially valuable in boarding Capt. Hazen's men.

CHAPTER VI.

EARLY SETTLERS AFTER THE CHARTER.

Character and energy of the men—Their training and education—Rapid settlement—Jesse Johnson—John White—James Bailey—Elisha Lock—Johathan Sanders—James Woodward—Uriah Stone—Jonathan Elkins—John Taplin—Ezekiel Ladd—Moses Little—Haywards—Timothy Barron—James Abbott—William Eastman—John Hurd—Maxi Hazeltine—Joseph Hutchins—Simeon Goodwin Jonathan Hale—Thomas Simpson—Ephraim Wesson—Charles Johnston—Asa Porter—William Porter—Andrew S. Crocker—Nathaniel Merrill—William Merrill—Joseph Pearson—Samuel Brooks—The Morses—Joseph Bliss—Joshua Young—Amos Kimball—William Cross—John Osgood—The Carrs—The Swans—Obadiah Swasey—Moor Russell—The Gookins—Asa Boynton—John Montgomery—Ross Coon—Glazier Wheeler—Parker Stevens—William Tarleton.

After the charter of Haverhill was granted to Capt. Hazen and his associates, settlers poured into the territory, and those who came were generally young and enterprising men. In this as in a former chapter I shall note such of the more prominent in regard to whom anything of public interest can be learned. Of some only the name is preserved, whilst of others a few facts or traditions have floated down on the tide of the years to tell their life and character. As a class, the early settlers were picked men whom ambition or love of achievement brought into the new settlement. They were brave and sturdy men and women, not afraid to encounter hard labor and vexations delays in their endeavor to found new and prosperous homes. The opening was one of the most inviting and promising in all the Connecticut valley, so that the Cohos wilderness was rapidly settled.*

The sketches are given, as far as can be learned, in the order of time when these earlier settlers came into the Town.

JESSE JOHNSON has the honor of standing at the head of the list of town-clerks. He was chosen to that office in Plaistow, June 13, 1763. His name appears in the list of Newbury grantees.

---

*The population as early as 1767 was 172 persons,—99 males, 73 females, 3 slaves, no widows, and only one person over 60 years of age.

JOHN WHITE was the first selectman in 1763, and was a grantee of the Town. He served as First Lieutenant in Col. Bedel's regiment in the Revolutionary War.

JAMES BAILEY was also a selectman in the first board, and took a very active and prominent part in the affairs of the Cohos settlement. In 1763 he was one of the committee to "bound out" the Town. He was the first treasurer of the Town, and often aided in various positions in the management of Town matters. In the French and Indian War he was a brave and energetic officer, and held the rank of major. He also took an active part in the Revolutionary struggle, having charge of several scouting parties that were sent out from Haverhill in the early part of the war. In 1777 he was a member of the Provincial Congress at Exeter, and with Col. Johnston and others he served as committee of safety, and of correspondence for Haverhill.* In the Proprietors' records he is styled "James Bailey, Esq." Soon after the Revolution he removed to Newbury, Vt.

ELISHA LOCK was one of the pioneer business men of Haverhill, who early began to develope the resources of the Town. He built and owned mills at the Oliverian falls, and was associated in these enterprises with Col. Timothy Bedel. He was moderator in 1765, and also served as selectman and town-clerk. The records show that he was not a skilled penman, but he was a man of enterprise and energy, and exerted much influence in business matters.

JONATHAN SANDERS came from Hampton in 1763, and settled on a tract which in after years was the late Samuel Page place. His was the first settlement south of Capt. John Page's. Mr. Sanders like his neighbor Eastman was greatly annoyed by the long controversy between the Town and Piermont in regard to the disputed boundary. He

---

*These committees were chosen in many of the towns, one for purposes of safety, and the other to gather information concerning the situation of things during the period of the Revolution.

served in the board of selectmen in 1766. One of his daughters became the wife of Capt. John Page, and another married a Mr. Fifield, and was the maternal grandmother of Dea. Grove S. Stevens. Two of Mr. Sander's sons enlisted in the Revolutionary War. Mrs. Ethan Brock is a descendant of Jonathan Sanders.

JAMES WOODWARD also came in 1763 at the age of twenty-two, and was for a long term of years a very prominent citizen of the Town. He was from Hampstead. His first house was built on the meadow near the river, and the foundations or stones which formed the foundations and chimney, are still visible at low water, the bank of the river having been carried away in flood-time in the course of years of abrasion. The great flood of 1771 drove him back upon the high ground where he built his second house. This house or part of it is still standing, and is the second north of James Woodward's present residence, and is known as the old Judge Woodward place. For several years he lived alone in his primative house on the river's bank, clearing away the trees and walking to what afterwards became the Dow farm where he took his meals. This, however, grew monotonous in time, and the young pioneer looked about for a companion to share with him his home. Marriageable young women were not numerous in those frontier-days, but Woodward's opportunity soon presented itself, and he was sagacious and brave enough to accept it.

It was in this wise. A year after Woodward came to Haverhill Judge Ladd moved into the same neighborhood, and with him was a winsome young Miss whom Judge Ladd brought to the new settlement for a purpose of his own. Young Woodward in becoming acquainted with the fair newcomer also conceived a purpose of his own, which however was not the same as that of the Judge's, but which he nevertheless on suitable occasions aimed to carry out. Hannah Clark and the gallant young farmer soon came to a tacit understanding in the matter of their feelings, and the latter when this became known to Judge Ladd's family, was given to understand that his presence was not as agreeable to them as his room. But for "ways that are dark" and tricks that were not in vain, the brave young suitor and his blooming love were "too many" for the Ladd household. So on a fine afternoon according to previous arrangement, just as the sun was in his last hour before setting, Hannah and a friend took a walk down the path toward the river, and coming to Woodward's little house they quickly turned in, and the young lovers were immediately united in marriage by the obliging clergyman from Newbury, who with a friend of the happy couple were awaiting the arrival of Hannah at that point. Immediately after the ceremony Hannah returned to her home at Judge Ladd's, and continued in the service of the family, whilst the victorious husband kept on toiling at his work. But soon the secret got out, and Mrs. Ladd with motherly wisdom and kindly feeling told Hannah that she might go and live with her husband. So she made haste to get to the little house on the river-bank.

Judge Woodward was married twice. His second wife was Elizabeth Pool of Hollis, who lived till 1846. Of his large family, all children of his first wife, one son was a physician in Barnstead, and the other sons were generally farmers. Joshua remained on the old homestead, whose son James is now living on Ladd Street.

Judge Woodward was prominent in Town matters, holding positions of trust and honor, and was the Town's first representative to the legislature. He was appointed one of the justices of the Court of Sessions, and held the office a number of years. He was a man of character and influence, and left behind him an honorable record. He died in 1821.

The early settlers on the meadows when they cleared their lands drew or rolled the logs into the river as the easiest way to get rid of them. Timber was valueless at that time, and burning logs did not seem to be the custom. Samuel Ladd had a lot a little away from the river, and spoke to Judge Woodward of his perplexity about getting the logs off of his ground. The Judge engaged to do the job, and drew the logs into heaps preparatory to burning them, but Mr. Ladd not understanding the object of piling the logs remonstrated with him, and told him that that was not the agreement he made. The Judge becoming impatient with Mr. Ladd's interference threatened to administer to him some birch bark, whereupon Mr. Ladd thinking discretion the better part of valor withdrew, and the Judge finished the job.

Uriah Stone deserves mention not for any influential part he had in the history of the Town,—for he moved away too soon for that,—but because of his relation to a subsequent prominent historical event. He with his young wife came to Haverhill from Hampstead in 1763 or 1764 amongst the first settlers, and built himself a log cabin not far from where Bedel's bridge now stands. This house was washed away by high water, and Uriah went down the river to Piermont and built a log house just west of the present Benjamin Hibbard place. He was a German, and his original name was Stein, the German word for stone. In his youth he was a soldier in the old French War, and he is said to have been a man of excellent character and of much energy and activity. There were, of course, as yet no bridges in those days over the Connecticut, and Uriah Stone conceived the plan of running a ferry across the river at his place for the accommodation of the public. Saw-mills there were none near by to cut out the plank for the boat, but the energetic and broad-shouldered German was equal to the emergency, and with his own stout hands he hewed the logs and built his boat, and here for years promptly answering the "Ferry-Ho," he lived and ferried people across the river between Piermont, Haverhill, and Moretown, then the name of Bradford.

He also cleared and cultivated a large farm and carried on a tannery. After a few years he built the present Hibbard house which is now about a hundred years old. Meantime a large family of thirteen grew upon his hands, and the years rolling on this sturdy pioneer was carried in 1819 to his last resting-place in the old Piermont grave-yard. On the stone that marks his grave is one of those quaint inscriptions which were common a century ago, and which may be found in many an old grave yard,—

"You may go home and dry your tears,
I must lie here till Christ appears."

Mr. Stone was very ingenious and skillful. His wife having broken the only sugar bowl she had, and not being able to replace it in the new country, her husband carved her one from a knot, which is now in possession of a descendant of the family, Mrs. A. P. Webster of Plymouth, and is said to be really beautiful in form and workmanship.

In those earlier days the people depended a good deal on wild game for their meat. The forests abounded in deer and the streams were alive with fish. One day a deer came down to the river on the further bank and quenched its thirst, and then plunging in swam to the opposite shore just in front of Uriah's house within easy reach of the rifle. Mrs. Stone who had been taught the use of the rifle by her husband, put her skill into practice and shot the animal. The antlers of the deer are now in possession of the only descendant of the Stone family living in Haverhill.

As illustrating the religious ideas of the times the following incident in the Stone family is given. The Sabbath was kept with great strictness, and as the family was rather numerous it was necessary to divide the children into two sections, each going to church on alternate Sabbaths. Those remaining at home were solemnly commanded not to play out-doors, nor hunt eggs in the barn, nor pick berries by the road-side, and in addition to these prohibitions they were required to commit portions of the catechism to memory. But the hours were long in the warm days of Summer, and when the children got through on a certain Sabbath learning the parts assigned them, they set themselves to making rhymes and parodies on some of the declarations of that ancient religious document. They were so highly pleased with their success in this new departure of life that they enthusiastically vociferated the parodies and rhymes in the ears of their reverent and devout parents on their return from church. This was such a sore grief to their pious hearts that they sent for the minister to come and administer an appropriate reproof to those young sinners. The good man came, and arrayed before him were the wicked rhymesters. One by one he read the parodies, but the quick eyes of the little culprits detected a lurking smile in the countenance of the benignant dominie, so that when he came to the couplet,—

"Job felt the rod
Down by Cape Cod."—

the ludicrousness of the thing was too much for even a decorous minister of the olden times, and bursting into an open laugh he dismissed the transgressors with a gentle admonition.

But to return to the "historical event." One of Uriah's sons, George Washington, a child of the Revolutionary age as his name indicates, went to Canada, and a daughter of his, Melvina, became the wife of Rev. William Arthur, D. D. and their son, Chester A. was the late Chester A. Arthur, President of the United States.

There is still one person in Haverhill who is a lineal descendant of Maj. Uriah Stone,—Miss Hattie C. Rogers of Court Street, in whose possession are the deer antlers above mentioned, and she and the late President Arthur were in blood second cousins.

JONATHAN ELKINS and family were a valuable acquisition to the new settlement. They came from Hampstead in

1764, and settled near the Dr. Carleton place. Mr. Elkins remained in Town about ten years, and then moved to Peacham, Vt. He has been called the "father" of that town. His wife, before her marriage, was Elizabeth Rowell of Chester. They had a large family, and their son Harvey was the first white child born in Peacham. Theirs was also the first house which was built in that town. Owing to the disturbed condition of the Cohos Country, and the dangers from Indians during the Revolution, the family was compelled to move back to Haverhill once or twice. At one time Dea. Elkins was a scout or pilot in Col. Bedel's regiment. He was a man of great excellence of character, good judgment, large ability, and influential and prominent as a citizen both in Haverhill and in Peacham. In the formation of the Congregational church at Peacham he was a prime mover and its first deacon.

Dea. Elkins' son Jonathan had a prominent career. He was captured by the English and Indians in an attack upon Peacham in 1781, and carried to Quebec, from whence he was taken to England, and with others cast into prison, where he remained till near the close of the war, when he was exchanged and returned to his native country. Previous to his capture he was a scout in Col. Hazen's regiment which was stationed along the military road from Haverhill to Peacham.

Col. Elkins after his return from capture lived in Peacham till 1836, when he moved to Albion, N. Y. He was married twice. His second wife was Mrs. Eunice Stoddard Sprague, the widow of lawyer Sprague of Haverhill, of whom the tradition comes down that she was a woman of elegant manners and brilliant mind, and of great worth. Of the children by this marriage Henry who married a daughter of Obadiah Swasey of Haverhill, is a prominent lumber-merchant of Chicago. A grandson of Dea. Elkins went to New Orleans and became very wealthy.

JOHN TAPLIN was a grantee of Haverhill, and was town-clerk at a special meeting in 1765. He was active in the developement of the Town in the first years of its settlement, but seems early to have gone to Newbury, Vt., where before the Revolution he held official position under the appointment of the Governor of New York which at that time claimed jurisdiction over Vermont. During the Revolution he with others was involved in a conspiracy to hand the Cohos Country over to the British. He was a man of standing, notwithstanding his sympathy with the royal cause.

EZEKIEL LADD moved to the Cohos Country in 1764. He and his wife were from Haverhill, Mass., and were in comfortable circumstances, with social standing, and accustomed to the refinements of life at that day. Mrs. Ladd relates that on the first Sabbath after their arrival in the new settlement when they went to church at the Ox Bow, she and her husband thought it would be only proper that they should appear in their best clothes. But the people were rather plain in their dress and looked upon the new comers as aristocratic, whose presence was studiously avoided. Appearing the following Sabbath in a plainer garb, she and her husband found the people most cordial and sociable.

Judge Ladd's house was situated on the east side of Ladd street between the school-house and the Azro Bailey place, where he lived for fifty years until his death in 1818, dying at the age of eighty. He was one of the very earliest tavern-keepers in the Town, was also engaged in the tannery business, and was a man of prominence in the settlement. He served as selectman for a number of years, and was also treasurer of the Town and one of the judges of the Court of Sessions.

Judge Ladd's wife was Ruth Hutchins before her marriage, and they had a large family. The oldest daughter married Joshua Young, and another became the wife of Jacob Bailey of Newbury. Ezekiel, Jr., who married Elizabeth Swan, was the father of Caroline and of Horatio Nelson Ladd who died a few years ago. Moody Ladd lived in a house opposite Mrs. Azro Bailey's, which afterwards was moved and became the kitchen of the Bailey house.

With Judge Ladd, or soon after, came five of his brothers, and later still a sister, all of whom settled on Ladd street. Samuel Ladd lived where James Woodward now resides; John Ladd who married into the Eastman family of North Haverhill, built the Henry Bailey house; David Ladd lived in the Clifford house; James Ladd lived across the road from the Cross house, and Jonathan Ladd's house was the old grist-mill house, and is part of the house now occupied by Mr. A. W. Lyman.

Of the eighty or more Ladds whose names come down to us, who either moved into Haverhill from Massachusetts, or who were born here, not one now remains of that name. Miss Caroline and Horatio Nelson Ladd were the last of the family in Haverhill.

Samuel Ladd, mentioned above, had a son Samuel who lived in a house just south of James Woodward's residence, a little back of the large willow which is standing at the road-side. Samuel, Jr., was a bright and handsome innkeeper in 1790, and was in the early years of widowerhood. This willow has a very romantic story connected with it. In this same year Dr. Jonathan Arnold of St. Johnsbury, who was a lonely bachelor, went to Charlestown to spy out a wife, in which mission after some entreaty he was successful in winning the heart of Cynthia Hastings, and arrangements were immediately made for their marriage and return to St. Johnsbury. The journey was made on horse-back, and on the morning of their start a roguish cousin of the young bride handed her a willow stick with the request that she might use it to urge on her horse when his spirits needed quickening, and after she got through with it for that purpose, she might plant it by the door of her second husband.

The last words were a sly hit at the Doctor's age which was considerably above that of his young bride. The willow stick, however, was accepted in good part, and the journey was begun. On the evening of the second day they arrived at Haverhill, and stopped at the inn of Samuel Ladd, Jr., for the night. The next morning as they were ready to proceed on their way the gallant landlord presented Mrs. Arnold with a new stick, and the old one was left behind. After Dr. Arnold and his bride had started out the willow stick was planted in the door-yard, and came to be the large tree now standing on the site of the Samuel Ladd tavern. Dr. Arnold died within a few years, and his young widow on her way to Charlestown to visit her friends, had occasion to spend the night in Haverhill at the Ladd tavern. Being invited to make her home at the Ladd inn whenever she had occasion to pass that way, she accepted the courteous invitation, and afterwards became the wife of the friendly young landlord, and saw the willow stick which her cousin presented to her on the morning of her first marriage, grow to be a large tree, and his good natured mock-words turned into a prophecy.

Cynthia Hastings Arnold by her first husband had two children, Lemuel Hastings and Freelove who came with their mother to Haverhill when she married Samuel Ladd, Jr. Lemuel Hastings Arnold in after life became prominent in Rhode Island, and was governor of the state and a member of Congress. Freelove married Noah Davis of Haverhill, and became the mother of the distinguished Judge Noah Davis of New York. She was tall and graceful whilst her husband was correspondingly short. Both the Arnold children were educated at Haverhill Academy. When Lemuel Hastings Arnold ran for governor of Rhode Island, one of the points made against him was that he was born in Vermont.

One of Samuel Ladd's daughters by his marriage with

Mrs. Arnold became the wife of Jeremiah G. Farman, son of Dea. Chester Farman of Haverhill. Another daughter whose maiden name was Martha H., now Mrs. M. H. Goss, is still living in Waterford, Vt., at the age of 87.

MOSES LITTLE.—A person by this name took an active part in the Proprietors' matters. The name also appears amongst the grantees of Newbury. Whether the Moses Little of Haverhill was the same as the Col. Moses Little of Newbury, Mass., a brave officer in the Revolution, is not clear but quite probable. Moses Little was one of the principle grantees of Littleton and other towns. He purchased the Gov. Wentworth "right" of 500 acres on which Woodsville is built, and which remained in the family for many years. He was appointed in 1773 one of the first justices of the Court of Sessions for Grafton County, but he declined the honor on account of "other business out of this [New Hampshire] Province." Indeed, it does not appear that he was a citizen of Haverhill for any considerable length of time. He seems to have been a large land owner.

THE HAYWARDS were active in the early history of the Town, Joshua being a selectman. When the Courts were established in Haverhill, 1773, he was one of the first jurors. He also did honorable service in the Revolutionary struggles, and was Major of the 12th Regiment N. H. Militia. Jonathan Hayward's name appears as one of a committee of the Town called the "committee of inspection," and was associated with Col. Charles Johnston and other prominent citizens.

TIMOTHY BARRON held a captain's commission in 1775 in Col. Bedel's regiment, and took an active part in the Revolution. He was one of a committee to "see that the results of the Continental Congress were observed in Haverhill," and was also on the committee of safety. He served as selectman.

JAMES ABBOTT was moderator in 1767. He was active

in public matters, and held various positions of trust and honor. In 1777 he was appointed one of a committee by the Town to confer with similar committees from other towns in reference to the safety of the Cohos region at that time. After the Revolution he moved to Groton, Vt., and was one of the first settlers in that town. His name appears in the Town records of Haverhill as " Dea. Abbott."

WILLIAM EASTMAN came to Haverhill about 1766, and lived for a short season on Ladd street. Afterwards he moved to Bath. His mother, Harriet Eastman, was carried away by the Indians to Canada when they made their attack on Haverhill, Mass., in 1697, and was kept there three years. Her husband found her with a friendly French family in concealment from the Indians.

Of William Eastman's children, Obadiah lived for many years in Haverhill, but died in Littleton, and a daughter of his, Rebecca, married Nathaniel Rix, a prominent man of that town. James purchased the Maj. Merrill farm, and lived to be 99 years old. His son Eber came into possession of a part of it after his father's death, and still resides on it living with H. L. Woodward who now owns the farm. He relates that his father in the early history of the Town hunted moose along the Ammonoosuc. Eber's brother Joel had an inventive turn of mind.

Eber Eastman in early life devoted himself to teaching, and for six or eight years was superintendent of schools in Haverhill. He also represented the Town in the legislature in 1843–4, and is at the age of 84 of bright and quick mind, a man of gentle and refined manners, and a most estimable citizen. He published some years ago an account of his great-grandmother's capture and rescue. He sent the author a few years ago the Lord's Prayer as a souvenir, written on a card about the size of a postage stamp, in a beautiful hand, so fine that it can be read only with glasses, but each letter is perfectly formed.

Four of the sons of William and Rebecca Eastman were soldiers in the War of the Revolution. James was the first one to bring the news of the surrender of Cornwallis to Haverhill, on which occasion Col. Johnston brought out the little field piece and fired a salute in honor of the great event. Mrs. Geo. E. Eastman and Herbert Eastman of North Haverhill are great-grandchildren of William and Rebecca Eastman.

John Hurd became a citizen of Haverhill at an early period of its settlement, and lived at Horse meadow. He came from Portsmouth, and was a man of great prominence and influence in all this section. Previous to his living in Portsmouth he was a lawyer in Boston, and after he moved to the former place he became secretary to Gov. Wentworth. His name was inserted in several of the charters in this vicinity, and the county records show that he was much interested in lands in the new country, owning tracts in many of the towns of Grafton county. It was through his influence that the courts were brought to Haverhill. He acted as agent of the Town in the matter, and was to receive as compensation for his services if successful a tract of one thousand acres in a " square pitch " of unoccupied land. Afterwards some difficulty arose, and it would seem that he did not receive the full reward of his success in securing the courts at Haverhill. This doubtless had something to do with his leaving Haverhill, between whose citizens and himself there had sprung up " mutual disaffection."

Col. Hurd was a man of large public spirit. In 1774 he petitioned the General Court for aid to complete a road " from the lower country to Haverhill." It would seem that before that date a road had been granted, but had not been finished. This unfinished road is described in the petition as " expensive and dangerous to man and beast, miry, rooty, and narrow, with bad pitches." And further it was "tedious and hazardous" for the judges to travel on to and from Haverhill.

He took a deep interest in the Revolutionary struggle, and was in command of a regiment, but on account of physical infirmity he was prevented from taking an active part in the field, writing in 1777 to the committee of safety at Exeter, thus: "I am extremely chagrined that my infirm limbs will not permit me to share the toils and dangers of the field with my countrymen." However, he was an influential man in advancing the cause of the patriots, and was in constant communication with Gov. Weare, the president of the Provincial Congress of New Hampshire. He had the general charge of troops—a sort of war minister—at Cohos, to "fix them off" for Canada, and was one of the Town committee to direct scouting parties. Whilst a member of the Provincial Congress he served on various important committees,—to draft a declaration of independence, to draw a plan for the government of New Hampshire, to prescribe an oath for the Provincial Congress,—and was a prominent and influential member of that body.

He also held other important official positions. When the Court of Sessions was organized he was appointed one of the justices of that court, and held that office till 1778. He was also Chief Justice of the Court of Common Pleas, though this last court, on account of the Revolution, did not hold sessions till the close of that struggle. In addition to these positions he was county treasurer and the first register of deeds for Grafton county, a member of the governor's council, and receiver of quit rents.

Col. Hurd went from Haverhill to Boston at the close of his official term as register of deeds, which was in 1778. Nothing is known of his characteristics except what can be gathered from his public career. He was a man of undoubted ability and great force of character, full of energy and enterprise, and exerted a wide influence in the early history of this region. He was noted for his beautiful hand-writing, and was a man of culture, having graduated from Harvard College in 1747, and received the honorary degree of A. M. from Dartmouth College in 1773.

Of his family nothing is learned except that some of his children went to Ohio, and it is a little singular that Rev. Grant Powers, in his History of the Cohos Country, says nothing concerning Col. Hurd except that a valuable cow which he brought from Portsmouth to Haverhill, by way of No. 4, returned safely to her old home in a direct course alone through the forest!

MAXI HAZELTINE was a grantee of Haverhill, and as early as 1770 a selectman. He took a prominent part in Town affairs, and was on a committee whose duty it was to "see that the results of the Continental Congress are duly observed in that [Haverhill] town." After the Revolution he moved to Bath.

JOSEPH HUTCHINS came to Haverhill at an early date, and was a selectman for several years. He was also a representative of the Town for two terms, and in 1791 his name appears in the records with that of Moses Dow as a representative for that year. He was one of a committee to "see that the results of the Continental Congress were observed in Haverhill," and was a member of the committee of safety in 1775-6. He also took an active part in the Revolutionary War, being in command of a company of rangers in 1780. In 1788 he was a delegate to the convention that adopted the Federal Constitution and voted in the negative, and in 1791 he was in the convention to revise the constitution of New Hampshire. Of his family nothing is learned, and the Hutchins of Bath do not claim immediate relationship with it. He was evidently a man of affairs, and was often associated in public matters with the leading men of Haverhill, and the fact that he was a member of the convention that adopted the Federal Constitution would seem to indicate his character and ability and importance as a citizen of the Town.

SIMEON GOODWIN'S name appears early in the history of Haverhill as a man prominent in affairs. He was repeatedly called to posts of responsibility, and was on the committee of safety, and on special committees of conference with other committees for the protection of the Cohos Country during the Revolution. He was also appointed a coroner for Grafton County.

JONATHAN HALE took an active part in the Revolutionary War, and was a member of the committee of safety during that struggle. He with others was also in general charge of the scouting parties which were sent out during the Revolution from Haverhill. In the great alarm of 1776, when the American forces were defeated at Ticonderoga, and when it was thought that the enemy would take immediate possession of the Cohos Country, Maj. Hale was sent to Exeter to give the alarm and to ask for aid. He also secured arms and powder for the Town on several occasions.

THOMAS SIMPSON was a captain of rangers in the Revolution, and was prominent in that struggle. He was also active in Town affairs, and held positions of trust and honor. He was something of a rhetorician. In a petition for a pension on account of loss of eye and other wounds, he closes his request with these glowing words: "That he may express in strains of gratitude the liberality of that country in whose service he had spent the best of his days, and in whose defense he more than once shed cheerfully the crimson flood of life." Thomas deserved a pension.

EPHRAIM WESSON came to Haverhill some time before the Revolution from Pepperell, Mass. He saw much hard service in the Old French War. In 1755 he was in the expedition against Crown Point, entering the army as a lieutenant. Subsequently he was at the taking of Louisburg and in the attack on Ticonderoga, and served in all the battles of note at that period. During his residence in Haverhill he was a very prominent citizen of the Town, and took a leading part in all public affairs. He was called to many positions of responsibility, being moderator and selectman a number of times. He also was a member of the Provincial Congress at Exeter, and a special delegate to that body for the procurement of arms for the settlers of Haverhill. In the Revolution he was intimately associated with Col. Charles Johnston and others in the stirring events of that period, serving on the committees of safety and correspondence for the Town. At the close of the Revolution Capt. Wesson moved to Groton, Vt. His oldest daughter, Sally, married Capt. Edmund Morse, and their daughter was the first child born in Groton. Capt. Wesson was a brave and conscientious officer, and was highly esteemed and trusted by his superiors, a man of excellent character and of Puritan mould and principles. He died in Groton at the advanced age of 93 years.

CHARLES JOHNSTON was undoubtedly the foremost citizen of Haverhill in point of character, ability, and influence, and this too in view of the fact that he had as associates in life such marked men as Col. Bedel, Col. Asa Porter, Andrew S. Crocker, Esq., Col. John Hurd, Gen. Moses Dow, and Alden Sprague, men who would have made themselves felt in any community. He came to Haverhill in 1769 and settled at the Corner, and at once took a leading part in all the affairs of the Town. He had a far-seeing mind. When felling the trees on the Park which he gave to the village, he would tell his wife in apparent jest that he should have a court house, an academy, and a church fronting on the Park, and Haverhill would be a flourishing place, all of which came to pass in his day. Haverhill was the most noted place north of Concord.

The good people of North Haverhill may never have thought much about it, but it was the fine hand of Col.

Johnston that brought the court house and jail to the Corner after they had been located at the Plain for nearly a quarter of a century. To this end he with others of the more enterprising citizens of the Corner, erected the old Academy building and offered it free of charge for the use of the courts. With the growing importance of the South End and its easier access, the courts would hardly be disposed to decline such an offer, and accordingly they were held in that building, and in its successor after the first one was burnt, till the present Court house was erected on Court street. Meantime a jail was also erected at the Corner. The excellent water-power of the Oliverian contributed also largely to the more rapid building up of the South End, and when the Cohos turnpike was constructed to Haverhill, and stage lines centered there, the early glory of the Plain was transferred to the Corner. In all this no hand was more influentially felt than Col. Johnston's.

Col. Johnston was the owner of the land on which Haverhill stands, and the land which constitutes the beautiful Park around which the village is built, was his gift to the place. He also gave the land for the old Court house and that of the Academy, evincing not only his generosity and public spirit, but also his forethought and faith in the future of the Town. His guiding hand and wise counsels were everywhere seen. United with his confidence that Haverhill must some day be the center in these northern limits was the gift of a genius to do. He was laborious and persevering in pushing on his plans. It was he that led in the building of the old Court house and the Academy, and toward the close of his life he was a leading spirit and one of the incorporators of the old Cohos turnpike. He was also one of the incorporators of the Social Library of Haverhill. In the records of the Town his name appears repeatedly on committees for carrying out various enterprises. No man was so prominent in Town affairs. No one held more various public positions of honor and responsibility. Twenty-four times during his active life he presided in Town meeting.

His military record is honorable, even conspicuous for bravery. At the age of twenty-four he was commissioned for the Old French War, and was quarter-master sergeant in Col. Goff's regiment. This was in 1761. Afterwards he took an active part in the Revolution. He was Lieutenant-Colonel of the 12th Regiment N. H. Militia, and was engaged in the battle of Bennington in 1777, in which he gained prominence for distinguished bravery. Col. Johnston was detailed by Gen. Stark to carry an order from one division of the American forces to another division. In order to execute the task he was compelled to pass through a woods which was made dangerous by the enemy having his scouts there in ambush. Col. Johnston pressed forward with only a stout staff which he had cut, when suddenly he was commanded to halt by a Hessian officer with drawn sword. In an instant the sword was struck from the enemy's hand and in Col. Johnston's possession, and pointing it at the Hessian's breast he commanded him and his companions to surrender as prisoners of war on peril of death. The Hessian ordered his men to throw down their arms, which they did, and he and his scouts were led captive into the American lines. The sword was brought to Haverhill and presented to his son Capt. Michael Johnston, with the request that it should descend in the line of the oldest male heir. It is now in the possession of Charles Sanford Johnston of Ovid, N. Y., great-grandson of Col. Johnston.

The following is a minute description of the sword by one of the Johnston descendants, Edward Sanford Burgess of Washington, D. C.

"The sword is adorned with a tassel, silvered and gilded, a brass hilt, a silver corded handle with brass attachments; the blade is double-edged, and on one side bears the words, DEI GRATIA DUX BRUNSV: ET LUNEB: (By the grace of God Duke of Brunswick and Luneburg.) These are engraved lengthwise of the sword, and surrounded by gilt scroll-work, in which appear casques, banners, halberd, a drum, trumpet, spear, etc. A warrior in armor completes the upper part of the figure, represented from the knees upward, and clad in complete coat of mail, with plumes in the helmet; below, toward the hilt, is a crown; below that, an ornamental letter C, followed by scroll-work, under which is engraved transversely and next to the hilt the name JEAN JULION. From most of this engraved work the gilt has worn out.

"Nearly all of the preceeding figures and ornamentations are repeated on the other side, with the following differences: the words, A BRUNSVIC, are engraved transversely, and the motto, NUNQUAM RETRORSUM, longitudinally. The same scroll-work is seen along its sides as before, the same warrior above, the same crown below; in place of the letter C is a prancing charger, mane and tail flying, fore-feet rearing.

"The blade of the sword is about three and a half feet long; it is accompanied by a leathern scabbard and is provided with a steel tip."

Had Gen. Stark listened to Col. Johnston, it is claimed that the battle of Bennington would have been more fruitful in results than it was. In De Puy's "Ethan Allen and The Green Mountain Heroes," the historian says, "We chased them till dark. Col. Johnston of Haverhill wanted to chase them all night. Had we done so, we might have mastered them all, for they stopped within three miles of the battle-field, but Stark saying he would run no risk of spoiling a good day's work, ordered a halt, and returned to quarters."

After the battle of Bennington Col. Johnston returned to Haverhill and took no further active part with the armies in the field, but he was deeply interested in matters at Cohos, which was a point of great importance during the Revolutionary struggle, and constantly exposed to attack from the British forces in Canada. In 1778 we find him appointed to the command of two companies of sixty-five men each to rendezvous at Haverhill for special service, and in the following year he commanded two companies of rangers. He was also active in the organization and direction of scouting parties, and served on various Town committees during these stirring years in providing for the safety of Cohos against enemies from within and from without, and was untiring and patriotic in the service of his country.

Col. Johnston's civil service in responsible positions extended over a number of years. The commission by which he was appointed Judge of Probate for Grafton county bears date Nov. 22, 1781, and from then till he was disqualified by age, a period of twenty-six years, he held that office and faithfully discharged its duties to universal satisfaction. He also was elected to the office of county treasurer in 1795, and continued to be chosen for many years without opposition. He was one of a commission appointed by the governor to administer the oath of allegiance and of office to civil and military officers within the county of Grafton. His colleagues on this commission were such well known persons as Samuel Livermore, Samuel Emerson, Moses Dow, Elisha Payne, and Bezaleel Woodward. In 1784 he was commissioned a justice of peace for Grafton county " during good behavior, for the term of five years," and this commission was renewed from time to time, the last renewal being in 1810, a few years before his death. At that time the office of justice of peace was a more important and responsible position than it is now, since the justices constituted a court called the Court of Sessions. He was also a councillor in 1780–2.

In addition to these more prominent public duties he took an active and foremost part in local matters, holding various offices in Town and Church, and serving on various committees, and his wise counsels and influential hand can be traced in all the growth and progress of the community. An obituary notice of Col. Johnston at the time of his death presents his position and character as it was in the community : " A rare assemblage of virtues concentrated in this remarkable character. He was a colonel of militia, judge of probate, county treasurer. But his principal excellence consisted in professing and exemplyfying the religion of

Jesus. He embraced the gospel in early life, and with singular constancy observed its precepts as his rule of life to the end. His liberality to the poor, his hospitality to strangers, and his aid to public institutions, will be long remembered among his works of faith and labor of love. No death in Coos was ever more sincerely lamented. The public feeling was expressed by a very numerous and deeply affected audience honoring his funeral with their presence on an intensely cold day. Military officers from the adjacent towns on both sides of the river, in their uniforms, formed a part of the procession. A sermon was preached by the Rev. David Sutherland on the occasion, from the appropriate words of the Psalmist, "Mark the perfect man and behold the upright, for the end of that man is peace."

Physically Col. Johnston was a very powerful man. On one occasion finding two men in a quarrel he separated them, but in turn for his kindness they both set upon him. Taking them by the shoulders with one hand hand each, he held them apart, and then brought them violently together, handling them as if they were dolls. He was a man of great kindness of heart, ever ready to give a helping hand to the worthy needy, even though it cost him sacrifice and inconvenience. At one time it is said he divided with a very poor man and his distressed family his two cows. When remonstrated with by Mrs. Johnston who said they could not spare the cow, the Colonel replied that they could do with one cow better than the poor man and his needy family could do without any, and so the cow was allowed to go. As justice of the peace he had occasion to exercise his gift of peace-making, and sometimes mounted his horse and rode miles to see parties who were intent on litigation, and counseled with them if something could not be done to prevent strife amongst neighbors. He was a man of large and quick sympathies and generous impulses, united with the best of judgment and good sense. Some of his neighbors, not as bountifully endowed with these traits as he was, were annoyed by the depredations of boys upon their orchards, and these depredations were made more frequent from the fact that the owners of the orchards were selfish and stingy, and if a boy was found looking over the fence at the tempting fruit beyond, they were sure to be ordered off with harsh and angry words. Col. Johnston was not troubled in this way. When he saw a group of boys near his orchard he would walk out and pick up a hat-full of the choicest fruit and carry it to the fence, and in kind and winning words invite the boys to eat all they wished. The boys would take the apples with thankful hearts and go away, and whilst they were eating the Colonel's apples with many an enthusiastic praise of his kindness and generosity, they were sure to lay plans to raid the orchard of some snarling and stingy neighbor.

In the later years of his life when past labor, he was accustomed to walk out in pleasant seasons to the Johnston woods for exercise and pastime. A small house by the wayside had some beds of bright flowers in front of it, and he would stop to admire these and pass a friendly word with the good woman of the house. He was social and neighborly, and enjoyed life all the more if he saw others in prosperity and happiness.

In those days books were scarce, and knowledge derived from such sources was not very great, but Col. Johnston was a man of much intelligence for the times. He appreciated the value of knowledge, and was foremost in the organization of a village library. His contact with the best and most intelligent men of the times was large and frequent, and his official position gave him many advantages with persons of culture and experience. He was also better trained and equipped by education than the average person of his position in society, and was deemed qualified to take the charge of Haverhill Academy for a term during a vacancy in the principalship. His hand-writing is a marvel of beauty as it stands to-day on the Town and county records, and is almost as perfect as script.

Probably no part of Col. Johnston's character was more marked than his religious character. He was the first deacon of the Congregational church at its formation, and was a most steadfast friend of all that was good and true. His example was a daily call to duty and righteousness. No man in the community exerted a greater influence as a christian. Around his christian character grouped every other trait, and shone through this as the light shines through a pure atmosphere. The kingdom of God was uppermost in his thoughts. From a letter written by his grandson, Michael Johnston Gray, dated Rotherham, Eng., Sept. 12, 1811, where he was studying for the ministry, we learn Col. Johnston's deep interest in the cause of christian education:

" * * *   I am glad that the Academy of which we had thought is likely to be established.   *   *   *
I hope that by this time you will have procured a charter to secure its safety. I am glad that the ministers object to its being connected with Dartmouth College. I don't think that it would do at all. For my part, I never entertained the least doubt but that a sufficiency for its support might be obtained in America, by subscriptions, donations, etc., etc. Christians in America have warm hearts as well as christians in England; and with a little exertion, nay, without almost any, I was going to say, the Academy might be carried on and prosper. A few pence from each lover of Jesus would, I doubt not, be amply sufficient.   *   * "

Col. Johnston's letter, to which this is a reply, is unfortunately not preserved, but from the extract of Mr. Gray's letter it would seem that there was a project at that time to connect with Haverhill Academy, or enlarge its scope, a school for the training of ministers. The endowment of this school was one of the things to be secured.

Col. Johnston's name has lingered more distinctly in public memory than that of any other man in the Town. He was of Scotch origin, and was born in Hampstead in 1737, the fifth child of Michael and Mary (Hancock) Johnston. He married Ruth Marsh of Londonderry, whom tradition says was a person of delicate mould and of womanly diffidence. They had a family of eight children, two of whom died in early life. Michael was the oldest, and remained on the homestead. He was a captain of militia, and served for two years as a private in the Revolution. He also held civil office in the Town. His wife before her marriage was Sarah Atkinson of Boscawen, and of their children Sarah married Capt. Stephen Adams; Charles and Hannah (see Chap. XIX). Michael succeeded his father on the homestead, and married Anna Atkinson of Boscawen; George Whitefield and a sister, Betsey, married Atkinsons of the same place. Hale Atkinson (see Chap. XVII).

Of Michael Johnston's family, son of Michael, the only one living in Haverhill is Kate McK. Johnston, a cultivated lady and an accomplished singer, as was also her sister, Mary, who died a few years ago. A son, Harry A., recently deceased, was a man of keen, bright mind and more than average intelligence. Edward P. lives in Washington, D. C., and is a graduate of Dartmouth College. The Johnston homestead was in the family till within a few years, when it passed into the hands of Amos Tarleton who now lives on it.

Ruth, one of Col. Johnston's daughters, married Ebenezer Gray, and their son Michael (see Chap. XIX). Abigail married Israel Swan, and Betsey married Lawson Dewey who became a judge of a county court in Ohio. The other daughters were Polly and Sarah.

Asa Porter. — The date when Col. Porter came to Haverhill is not known, but early he appears as a man of affairs and enterprise. Before 1772 he owned and operated a ferry across Connecticut river at the Porter place. Owing to his position in the Revolutionary War he was never a favorite with his fellow-townsmen, and it is said he had no near neighbors with whom he associated. His sympathies were with the Tories, and a road at Horse meadow and the woods along it are still known as "Tory road" and "Tory woods." In 1776 he with others was charged with conspiracy in giving information to, and asking aid of, the enemy, and Porter was taken to Exeter for trial. This conspiracy extended to Bath and Newbury and down the river, and was discovered by a young Indian. Porter was tried by the General Court and voted an enemy. Subsequently he made his escape, but was captured at Newburyport, Mass., and afterward he was allowed to return to Haverhill on parole. In later years Col. Porter held official positions in the Town. He lived in a large frame house at the south end of Horse meadow. The farm, now owned by Samuel F. Southard, extended down the river to Major Merrill's farm and back toward Briar Hill. The ferry at his place was kept up till the "Middle Bridge" was built. He was also owner of large tracts of land in Corinth and Topsham, Vermont.

Col. Porter introduced the "Lombard poplars" into Haverhill. He had a field-nursery of these trees on his farm, and when they were large enough for transplanting he set out two rows close to the fence on both sides of the road the entire length of the meadow. This road was called "Horse Meadow street." The poplars soon grew to be tall trees, straight and trim, and had the appearance of two lines of soldiers with heads erect and arms close to their sides. They did not furnish much shade on account of their slender shape, and after they attained their growth, which was quite rapid, the limbs began to decay, and the trees looked ragged and ill-shaped, and soon died out, so that there is not one left to tell the tale of their origin and life.

Col. Porter married a sister of Andrew S. Crocker, and a daughter of theirs became the wife of Mills Olcott, Esq., of Hanover, a very influential and prominent man at that time, and whose family, mostly daughters, attained distinction in their marriages. One was the wife of Joseph Bell, the famous Haverhill lawyer, another married Rufus Choate, the great advocate, and a third was the wife of the late William H. Duncan, Esq., of Hanover, one of the most accomplished men of New Hampshire. One of Col. Porter's sons lived in South Newbury, John (see Chap. XVII). The Porter family became early extinct in Haverhill.

Col. Porter was familiarly known as "Migin Porter" from the habit he had, when expressing his opinion, of saying, "I migin," which was a shorter and perverted form of "I imagine." On one occasion when about to punish his negro girl, he tied a rope around her body, and then fastened the other end to himself, so that the girl could not get away whilst he laid on the lash. But the girl being a very large and powerful person, and he being to an equal degree a small man, ran down to the river bank intending to drag the Colonel in, but seeing his danger he called out frantically for help, and on being delivered from the impending bath, he said, "I migined the creatur would drown me."

Col. Porter was a man of aristocratic and select tastes, and belonged in his social habits to the aristocracy of his day. He had the advantage of a liberal education, being a graduate of Harvard College, and filled a large place in the early history of the Town.

WILLIAM PORTER, a younger brother of Asa Porter, lived near him at Horse meadow for a time and later he moved out on the "Turnpike." "Porter Hill" gets its name from him. He was a selectman, and came to Haverhill about 1779. His wife's maiden name was Mary Adams, and they had a large family of children, one of whom, Sarah, became the wife of John Osgood, the famous clockmaker of Haverhill, whose daughter married the late Daniel Blaisdell of Hanover. Mr. Porter's son William, familiarly known as "Uncle Billy," lived on the homestead on "Porter Hill," and a grand-daughter of his, Mrs. John C. Burbank, is still living there. A sister of Mrs. Burbank was for many years the lady-like cashier of the ladies' department of the Parker House restaurant, Boston. A great-grandson of William Porter, Albert E., is an esteemed and active business man of Ashland.

ANDREW SAVAGE CROCKER came from Hollis, and was amongst the earlier settlers of Haverhill. His name appears in the Town records as early as 1771, when he was chosen one of the selectmen, and served in that position twelve years. He was also Town clerk for a number of years. In the early development of the Town he took an active and leading part, and was one of the most influential citizens of its pioneer history. He bore a royal commission as justice of the peace from the British government in Colonial times, and went by the name of "Squire Crocker." This commission was formerly in possession of his grand-daughter, Mrs. Hiram Carr of Boston, but is now in the keeping of Alvah Crocker of Fitchburg, Mass. In 1776 he was appointed by the General Court coroner of Grafton county, but he declined the appointment on the ground that he "was not in sympathy with the form of government then in vogue." There is a hint in this refusal to accept office of the difference of opinion which prevailed in those times. Men were divided into royalists and revolutionists, oftener called "Tories" and "Patriots" according as censure or praise was intended.

Mr. Crocker's wife was Shua Thurston, and their home was at Horse meadow. Their only child, Edward Bass, married Elizabeth Gibson of Hillsboro', and their six children were Andrew, Giles, Edward, Moses, Frederick, and Mary. One died in infancy, Andrew, Giles, and Edward died in the same year, 1840—Andrew in Cuba, Giles in Mobile, Ala., and Edward in New Orleans. Edward was a lawyer, and read with Joseph Bell. Andrew was the only son, except Frederick that married, and his wife's maiden name was Sarah Carr of North Haverhill. Their only child, Miss Hannah Crocker, is still living in Plainfield, N. J. Mary, the only daughter of Andrew Crocker, married Hiram Carr and is now living in Boston. Frederick (see Chap. XIX).

Mr. Crocker was a man of high character and social position, and above the average of his townsmen in intelligence and knowledge. He with others of that time constituted the aristocracy of the Cohos settlement. In stature he was of medium height with rather slender form, and he commanded respect and influence by his worth and ability.

NATHANIEL MERRILL came to Haverhill quite early from the vicinity of Haverhill, Mass., and settled on a farm at the Plain. The Merrill house is still standing, and is now occupied by Herbert Eastman, but has been changed. He was born in 1754, and married Sarah Hazen, daughter of Capt. John Hazen. They had a family of twelve children, eleven of whom were daughters, all of whom, tradition says, were comely, and some even handsome. The son died in early life. Sally married Aaron Hibbard of Bath, Elizabeth married Moses Swasey, Polly married Nathaniel Runnels of Piermont, Nancy married Obadiah Swasey, Charlotte married Isaac Pearson who lived at the Brook, Lucinda married Abner Bailey of Newbury, Ruth and Hannah were twins, the former married James Morse, the latter John Page.

The grandchildren of Major Merrill were numerous. Miss Priscilla Morse, who lived at the Corner for many years, was a daughter of Thomas Morse who married Hittie Merrill, and Mrs. Babcock of San Francisco is a daughter of the late Samuel Page who married Louisa Merrill.

Major Merrill was a prominent citizen of the Town, and

held many public positions. He was selectman for many years, and represented the Town in the legislature several terms. He was a man of energy and public spirit, and is said to have owned the first chaise in Haverhill. In 1816 he moved to Piermont, where he died in 1825. He was a man of strong character and influence and large common sense, somewhat blunt, but practical and honest, full of fun and quite a favorite. He was also quite eccentric, writing receipts with a quaint humor, using in them the phrase, "from the beginning of the world up to this date." Rev. Ethan Smith said of him, "He knew more than any man who hadn't more education than he had."

As illustrating his character, a young man visiting one of the daughters, and staying as was the custom in those days till, if not "broad day-light," at least early dawn, when about to mount his horse to ride away, Major Merrill stopped him and said, "Abner, stay to breakfast and then go home." The bashful youth not wishing to ride home in day-light, replied, "No, I'll go now." "Well," was the unconditional answer, "if you're ashamed to go home in broad day-light, you needn't come to see my daughter."

On another occasion when two men were working for him whose honesty needed looking after, he observed that they seemed disposed after work to linger around the premises till dark. The lights were extinguished, and Maj. Merrill took a position at the window for observation. Pretty soon the loiterers approached the cellar window. Going to the window Maj. Merrill found one of the men holding a bag, who at once beat a hasty retreat. When the other man came with his hands full of salt pork, Maj. Merrill was holding the bag, and after bringing several lots the man asked if he hadn't about enough, to which Maj. Merrill in his usual vigorous English, replied, "I should think so, by ———." The thief undertook to get out by the window, but was prevented, and was compelled to go up through the house where the Major met him. "I want you and the other man to come to my house to-morrow at twelve o'clock and take dinner with me." The man could do no more than promise. At twelve the two appeared, and a most bountiful boiled dinner awaited them. They sat down and were generously helped, and the Major carried on a lively conversation with them. Dinner over he leaned back in his chair and said to the two men, "When you want pork again come to my house and you shall have all you wish," and then kindly dismissed them. They were ever after Maj. Merrill's most devoted friends.

We do not wonder that being asked to give money to civilize the heathen, he replied, "I'll give $20 to civilize the heathen within five miles of my house." Maj. Merrill in physical aspect was a man of more than medium size, broad shouldered, strong head, and weighed about one hundred seventy-five pounds.

Mrs. Merrill was a woman of rare character and most amiable disposition. She came of gentle blood. One of her grandchildren says of her, "My own remembrance of her is one of the warmest, sunniest spots in my early life and memory. I was not more than five or six years of age when I visited at her home in North Haverhill, and I yet seem to feel her soft hand upon my head, and to see anew her sweet, smiling face as she gave me, to my great satisfaction, a slice of bread."

WILLIAM MERRILL.—A person by this name, tradition says, lived in Haverhill in its early history; that a son, Joshua, enlisted in the War of 1812; that after the war Joshua went to Ohio, and that soon after that period he endeavored to open correspondence with the Haverhill part of the family, but received no answer, the family either having moved to parts unknown, or may have become extinct by the fearful spotted fever that swept over this region in 1815. A son of Joshua has risen to great prominence, being the distinguished Bishop Stephen M. Merrill, D.D., of the Methodist Episcopal church, and now resides in Chicago. Some circumstances make it probable that William was either a brother of Maj. Nathaniel Merrill or belonged to the Warren Merrills.

JOSEPH PEARSON was one of the earlier settlers, and came from Boscawen. The exact date is not known, but as early as 1779 he was the owner of a fulling mill at the Brook. Later, he carried on the lumber business, and was a man of much energy and enterprise. He took a prominent part in developing the resources of the Town and in building up its prosperity. He was an upright and worthy citizen, and highly esteemed. Physically he was large and broad shouldered. His wife's maiden name was Hannah Johnston, daughter of Col. Charles Johnston, and they had a large family. One of their sons, Samuel A., was a graduate of Dartmouth College in 1803, and studied law with Alden Sprague. He practiced his profession in Lancaster, but did not gain special distinction. In his later life he seems to have been unsuccessful. He held the office of post-master for many years at Lancaster. A daughter, Nancy, became the wife of Christopher Marsh, a clergyman in Massachusetts.

Mrs. Pearson was a woman of superior character, and was one of the original members of the Congregational church in Haverhill. She possessed a bright and quick mind, and was especially attractive to the young, to whom she would tell Bible stories in a singularly entertaining and instructive way, and won their love and esteem by her kindly and gentle manners.

Isaac was their oldest child, inheriting much of his father's energetic and enterprising nature, and became his successor in the lumber business at the Brook. He owned large meadows on the river and also considerable land on the east side of Ladd street. He was generally known as "Major"

Pearson, his father as "Captain" Pearson, and was a man of esteemed character and good standing. He married first Charlotte, daughter of Maj. Nathaniel Merrill. They had two children, Merrill and Caroline. Merrill Pearson who died recently in Bloomington, Ill., married a daughter of Dea. Henry Barstow of Haverhill. Maj. Pearson's second wife was Charlotte Atherton, and a daughter by this marriage, Mrs. James M. Chadwick, lives in Saginaw, Mich. James Henry (see Chap. XIX).

This family illustrates the genius for business in one direction. Four of the sons of Maj. Pearson engaged in the lumber business,—James, George, Charles, Isaac,—and this has been the principal occupation of the Pearson family for four generations.

None of the Major Pearson family or their descendants are now living in Haverhill. The old Pearson house is still standing on Ladd street on the left hand side of the road after leaving the Oliverian bridge.

SAMUEL BROOKS came to Haverhill about the close of the Revolution a young man. His father was a prosperous citizen of Worcester, Mass. His mother's name was Hannah Davis before her marriage. Young Brooks when he came to Haverhill opened a store at the Corner, and was also the owner of an oil mill at the Brook, but he was not very successful in these ventures. Later, he went to Quebec and contracted with the governor of the Province for a tract of land in the township of Chester, then an unbroken wilderness, and two of his brothers began lumbering operations in this forest. A year or two later, 1812, he took his family to Canada, but owing to a change of governor in the Province the plans which he had marked out were defeated, and leaving Chester he came to Stanstead where he lived to the close of his life.

Mr. Brooks during his residence in Haverhill was one of the most influential citizens of the Town, and took an active part in all public matters. He represented the Town in the legislature, was a selectman, and also Town clerk. Besides these positions of trust he also held the office of register of deeds for Grafton county for a number of years. He is represented as a man of gentle manners, and is said to have been very ingenious and skillful.

He married a daughter of Col. Timothy Bedel, the widow of Dr. Thaddeus Butler. Of their family one of the daughters, Hannah, married for her first husband Capt. William Trotter of Bradford, Vermont, and afterwards Col. William Barron of the same place. Both, it is said, were famous in their day for their fondness for the chase, and were accustomed to hunt for deer back of Mt. Gardner. Mr. Barron was a gentleman of the olden school, tall, somewhat slightly built, and very dignified and commanding in person and speech. Another daughter married Asa Low of Bradford, Vermont, and a third became the wife of Judge Nesmith of Franklin. These daughters were women of great excellence of character, ornaments in home, church and society. Samuel and Edwin (see Chap. XIX); George Washington, another son, is worthy of mention as bequeathing to his country twenty children, and in this respect may be said to be the father of his country. He was rightly named.

The old Brooks house in Haverhill stood on the South Park near where the pump now is. The house and barn were afterwards moved to Court street, and remodeled, and are now the residences of Judge Westgate and the late Mrs. Barstow.

The Morses have been numerous in Haverhill during most of its history.

Stephen Morse came to the Town from Massachusetts, probably near the close of the Revolutionary War. He was born in 1757, and died in 1843 at the age of 87. His wife's name was Sally Kay. His lived on "Morse Hill," on the old Coventry road from North Haverhill to Coventry, now Benton. By trade he was a blacksmith, and had a family of twelve children, all sons. It is said he would ride on horseback from his home to Horse meadow and to the Corner, and sleep most of the way. He was also very deaf, and used a tin trumpet to aid his hearing.

Of his children, Bryan was the oldest, born in 1781, and married Susannah Stevens, and like his father, he was a blacksmith and also a cabinet maker, but afterwards he became a Methodist clergyman and lived at the Corner in the house opposite the Col. Johnston place till 1833, when with his family he moved to Lowell, Mass., where he engaged in mercantile business for some years. Later, he lived in Groveland, Mass., and died there in 1863 at the age of 82.

Bryan Morse's family, some of them, became prominent in professional and other walks of life. Horace B., the oldest, was a graduate of Dartmouth College in 1823, and lost his life by drowning at Portsmouth.

Peabody A., George W., Isaac S., (See Chap. XIX).

Caleb, the second son of Stephen Morse, lived on a farm near his father. One of his daughters, Ruth, married Charles G. Smith. Caleb Morse died at his home in 1842, and during his life he was prominent in town matters, and also represented the Town in the legislature. John C., followed the occupation of his father, Stephen, and lived at Horse Meadow. In his later life he kept a tavern in the house now occupied by his son, John N. Morse, a prominent citizen of the Town.

Robert, another son of Stephen Morse, (See Chap. XIX).

Joshua was a merchant at North Haverhill, and then the proprietor and keeper for many years of the stage tavern in Rumney, a hostilery noted far and near under his and his wife's care for its excellent service to the travelling public. One of Stephen Morse's children was a physician in Northern Vermont; Hiram lived on the old homestead, and Caleb's son Caleb is the only representative of the Morse family occupying the old ground.

EDMUND MORSE was a younger brother of Stephen Morse, and was born in 1764. He came to Haverhill about the time his brother did, but after a few years he moved to Groton, Vt., and was the pioneer settler of that town. He married Sally, daughter of Capt. Wesson of Haverhill, and their daughter Sally was the first child born in Groton. He was a man of excellent character. It is said his first blacksmith shop in Groton consisted of a fire-place and a stump to put his anvil on, and thus he began business. He was full of energy and enterprise.

A DEACON MORSE lived on Briar Hill, and was for a number of years tax collector. He was very persistent, and on this account he got the name of "Pincher Morse." There was also a Stephen Morse, a deacon in the Congregational church at the Corner in 1813, and he may have been the same as the Briar Hill deacon.

JOSEPH BLISS took a leading part in the earlier history of the town. He was one of the number that built the first Academy building. He lived in the house where George W. Leith now lives, and for many years it was kept by him as a tavern. It was the aristocratic head-quarters in its day for the judges and the lawyers. Mr. Bliss was a trustee of the Academy, a man of influence, but quite small of stature. He was the first post-master in Haverhill, being appointed under Washington.

Mrs. Bliss is spoken of as very much of a lady, of a refined and cultivated mind. She always observed the proprieties of social life with great exactness. And she was equally punctilious when at church. She was a woman of much spirit, and there is a story that on one occasion whilst on a visit at her daughter's, Mrs. Judge Livermore in Holderness,—the Judge in his day being one of the prominent lawyers in the state,—he and Mrs. Bliss had a sharp passage of words just as they were going to leave Holderness for her home in Haverhill, and that they made the ride of forty miles without speaking a word. Mrs. Bliss after the death of her husband kept a ladies' store in the east room of the old tavern.

JOSHUA YOUNG came to Haverhill in the early history of the Town, and was the son of John and Susannah (Getchell) Young. He was born in Haverhill, Mass., in 1755, and died in 1797. His parents were persons of high character and social standing, who moved to Lisbon before or during the Revolutionary War, and afterwards to Hanover, where the father died in 1785. Whilst in Lisbon, John Young, the father of Joshua, was prominent in civil and military affairs. He married for his second wife a daughter of Pres. Eleazar Wheelock, the founder of Dartmouth College, and his daughter, Tryphena, married John Wheelock, the second president of Dartmouth College. Joshua Young married Abiah, the oldest daughter of Judge Ezekiel Ladd, and of their children, Stiva became the grandmother of Judge Charles R. Morrison of Concord. Joshua Young was a bright and capable man, and was, it is said, at one time on Gen. Stark's staff. In the late years of his life he was overtaken by a sad infirmity, the slave of appetite, which finally ended in a very tragic death. Tryphena Young who became the wife of President John Wheelock, was noted for her beautiful and sweet voice, dying whilst singing the hymn of Watts,—" Show pity, Lord, O Lord forgive." Joshua Young lived where Mr. Peter Flanders now lives, and part of the present house was the original Young house.

AMOS KIMBALL was one of the earlier settlers in Haverhill, and lived on Ladd street in a log house at the foot of the hill near the little brook that runs by George Wilson's place. His wife's maiden name was Abigail Corliss, and they had a large family of eleven children. Several of the sons and daughters went to the West and to Canada. A grandson, Francis D., living in Ohio, became quite prominent as a lawyer and politician. He was elected secretary of state on the ticket with the late Chief Justice Chase, when the latter ran for governor of that state, and died whilst in office.

The youngest son, Amos, lived on the farm now owned and occupied by Ezra S. Kimball. Amos Kimball was somewhat active in Town affairs, and was a selectman a number of times.

John, the eldest son of Amos, was a prominent man in public and church matters. He was a deacon of the Congregational church at Horse meadow, and colonel of the 13th Regiment State Militia. He also represented the Town in the legislature for several years, and served in the board of selectmen for a number of years. Of his numerous family, John (see Chap. XIX). Dudley C. died recently in Newbury, Vt., Benjamin F. lives in Newbury, Vt.

Isaac B. resides in Concord. Only one of the seven daughters is living, Mrs. E. T. White of Washington, D. C. Dea. Porter Kimball and Mrs. Lyman Southard are children of the late Dudley C. Kimball.

WILLIAM CROSS is worthy of mention, if for no other reason, from the fact that he so well and faithfully filled a position in which few attained success. He was a brother-in-law of Judge Ladd whose sister Abigail he married, and came to Haverhill in 1788. He was from Haverhill, Mass., and lived in the house lately owned and occupied by Eliza Cross. Mr. Cross was for many years the faithful and trusty sexton of the Ladd street meeting house, and was punctual all that time in ringing the nine o'clock evening bell, the signal for putting out the old candle lights and preparing for rest, as was the custom in early times in New England. Mr. Cross lived to the extreme old age of one hundred years and a few months.

Miss Eliza Cross, his daughter, born in 1790, lived to

nearly her father's age, ninety-seven, and was up to the time of her death, in the enjoyment of remarkably good health and of her reason. She was the last connecting link in Town with the generation of earliest settlers, and has furnished many a fact and incident for these pages, showing a most commendable interest in the progress of the work and in the preservation of the earlier period of the Town's history. Miss Cross was at one time superintendent of the Sabbath school on Ladd street. In those days a bright colored card was given to each scholar for committing to memory a certain number of verses from the Bible. Afterwards a cent was paid for every ten verses committed. The first library for the use of Sabbath schools in Haverhill, she says, was one hundred books each to the school on Ladd street, at the Corner and at East Haverhill. Miss Cross died suddenly, Sept. 2, 1887, aged 97 years and some months.

Jeremiah Cross, brother of Eliza, was a man of more than ordinary ability, but of somewhat limited education, and was very prominent as a Free Mason, holding the very highest position in that order. He lectured all through the country on Masonry, and was regarded as the best authority on the practical workings of the system. He died in 1866.

John Osgood was born in Andover, Mass., in 1770, and became a citizen of Haverhill as early as 1795, dying here in 1840. He was a maker of the old style high clocks which were common in those days, many of which are still in use in this region bearing his name. They are now much sought after by the lovers of the ancient, and command fancy prices, such that if their maker had sold them originally for the sums they now bring, he would have become a money-king. Mr. Osgood was quiet and unobtrusive in his manners, and much esteemed by his fellow citizens. For several years he was a member of the board of trustees of Haverhill Academy, and also served as town treasurer and clerk for a number of years. He had an infirmity of lameness. He lived at one time in the west end of the house where Mr. Nathaniel Bailey lives, afterwards in the house now owned and occupied by Dr. Watson. He married Sarah, daughter of William Porter, and of their children a daughter, Charlotte, married Daniel Blaisdell, Esq., of Hanover, and of their two children, Alfred, a graduate of Dartmouth College, is head draftsman at the Brooklyn navy yard, and Charlotte married Prof. Ruggles of Dartmouth College. Mrs. Blaisdell lives at Hanover with her daughter.

THE CARRS.—Capt. Daniel Carr and his brother, Dea. John Carr, came to Haverhill from Newburyport, Mass., near the close of the last century. John settled on a piece of land now the farm of his son, Joshua. His wife was Hannah Work of West Newbury, Mass., and they had a large family. John Carr's son, Joshua, was selectman in 1861–62, and John E. Carr, a grandson, filled the same position in 1873–5–6, and was representative in 1878–80–81. He has also been a member of the state board of agriculture for Grafton county.

Capt. Daniel Carr settled on the farm where D. E. Carr now lives. He married Elizabeth Work, sister of Dea. Carr's wife. He was a captain in the state militia. His eldest son, Daniel, was a deacon in the Baptist church at North Haverhill, and was a selectman for several years. The Carrs have been prominent citizens of the Town from the first, and were connected by marriage with the Crocker family,—a son and daughter of Dea. John Carr married a daughter and son of Edward B. Crocker. The late Maj. Samuel Carr, an esteemed citizen of the Town, was a selectman in 1854–5.

THE SWANS came to Haverhill at an early date, and were more or less prominent in the history of the Town.

JOSHUA was the oldest, being born in 1767. William

Swan, the hatter, was connected, it is said, with Joshua. William lived where the Exchange hotel now stands, and his son, Col. Charles Swan, built the original hotel. Afterwards Col. Swan went West. He was an active, enterprising, and influential citizen. Joshua Swan was moderator in 1803.

ISRAEL SWAN was born in 1768, and was a brother of Joshua. He married for his first wife Abigail Johnston, daughter of Col. Charles Johnston, and was one of the petitioners for the charter of Haverhill Academy. He was active in Town matters, and held various positions of responsibility. His son, Charles J. Swan, who married Elizabeth Ladd, moved to Ohio, where his family grew up and held honorable positions in society. His wife is still living at LeRoy, Ohio.

PHINEAS SWAN came to Haverhill near the close of the last century. He was not related to the Swans named above. He first lived on Ladd street where Henry S. Bailey now lives. Afterwards he built a wooden house at the Buck place. His wife was a Miss Webster before her marriage, and a daughter became the wife of Ezekiel Ladd, Jr. Benjamin, their son, married Grace Carr of Piermont, and of their children, Henry and his son and daughter are the only descendants of Phineas Swan now living in Haverhill.

OBADIAH SWASEY was born in Haverhill, Mass., in 1775, and came to Newbury, Vt., near the close of the last century. At first he lived with an older brother for a short time as an apprentice to the carpenter trade. He married Nancy, daughter of Maj. Merrill, and moved from Newbury to North Haverhill about 1808, and lived on the old Hazen farm till his death in 1836.

Mr. Swasey was a prominent and successful business man, and built and owned the grist mill and saw mill known as the "Swasey mills" at North Haverhill, where for many years he was extensively engaged in the manufacture of lumber and transporting it to the towns and cities on the Connecticut river in Massachusetts and Connecticut. He died at the age of 61, having enjoyed the esteem and confidence of his fellow townsmen.

Of the numerous family of Obadiah and Nancy (Merrill) Swasey, Mary Ann married John L. Woods; Samuel in later years lived in Belvidere, Ill., and died in 1887, at the age of 82. He fitted for college at Haverhill Academy, and graduated from Dartmouth College in the famous class of 1828, having as classmates the late Prof. Ira Young, and Pres. Labaree of Middlebury College. He studied law and was admitted to the bar in Portland, Me., but did not practice his profession. Soon after his admission he went West where he remained a few years, and then returned to Haverhill.

He was chosen by his fellow citizens to represent the Town in the legislature for five years in succession, and during this time of service he was elected speaker of the House in 1842-3. He again represented the Town in the legislature in 1850, and was also the same year a member of the constitutional convention. For a number of years he served as selectman and for ten years he was Register of Probate for Grafton county. During the administration of President Pierce he was inspector of customs at Portsmouth. At the close of his term of office he moved to Belvidere, Ill., where he continued to live to the time of his death. Mr. Swasey married Edith A. Holmes of Peterborough. Of his surviving children Charles J. is a merchant in Fort Worth, Texas, Edith A. who married Alson Keeler, resides at Cedar Rapids, Iowa, and Edward H. is a promising lawyer in Chicago.

Mr. Swasey was a man of large ability, but was not very ambitious. He was highly esteemed, a man of integrity and high character, and was a prominent citizen both in his western home as well as in his native town.

John Hazen Swasey began mercantile business in Portland, Me., and afterward moved to Boston where he now resides; Louisa became the wife of Ephraim Sprague Elkins of Kenosha, Wis., Nathaniel lives on the old homestead, and married a daughter of Dr. John Angier of North Haverhill. Their only child, Mrs. Brooks, lives in Montpelier. Jane became the wife of Charles James, a lawyer of Wisconsin, and now lives in Chicago; Nancy married Dr. Leonard of North Haverhill; Sarah married a son of Dr. Angier and lives in Chicago, and Mehitabel became the wife of Henry K. Elkins of Chicago.

Moor Russell came to Haverhill in 1792. In 1799 he was elected a representative to the legislature and also served in other official positions, being selectman in 1800 and moderator in 1801. He was born in Litchfield, then called Derryfield, but came to Haverhill from Plymouth, and after a residence in the former place of nine years, he returned to Plymouth in 1801, where he spent the remainder of his life, dying at the advanced age of 94 years, the result of an accident. He was a soldier in the Revolutionary War, and took part in the battle of Bunker Hill. He married Betsey, daughter of Col. David Webster, and they had a large family. Only two of his children, Catharine and Eliza, were born in Haverhill.

The oldest daughter, Nancy, married John Rogers, a merchant of Plymouth, and two of their sons, John P., and Walter M. are merchants in Boston, another, Edward P., is a railroad man in Portland, Oregon, and a daughter, Charlotte H., became the first wife of Prof. William J. Tucker of Andover, Mass.

David Moor Russell, second son of Moor Russell, married Mary Flint of Reading, Mass., and lived in Gainesville, Ala. They had two children,—one a prominent business man in Lawrence, Kansas, the other a large planter in Mississippi. The third child of Moor Russell, Catherine, married Samuel C. Webster, a lawyer of Plymouth. Two of their children were merchants in Plymouth, and two others were merchants in Boston and New York. Eliza, the fourth child of Moor Russell, married Benjamin G. Edwards, and is still living in Brooklyn, N. Y. William W., the fifth child, married Susan Carleton Webster of Salisbury, and of their children, Alfred is a prominent and successful lawyer in Detroit, Mich., and graduated from Dartmouth College in 1850. Two of his brothers, William W. and Frank W., are enterprising merchants in Plymouth, men of character and influence, successors of their father in the business which he carried on so extensively for many years, and which was established by their grandfather nearly a century ago. The other children of Moor Russell were Mary, who married Eliza M. Davis of Barnet, Vt.; Walter W. went South and died at Gainesville, where he was a prominent merchant for nearly half a century; Jane A. married Milo P. Jewett of Plymouth, and is now living in Milwaukee, Wis., where Charles J. also lives and has been engaged for many years in mercantile life. He married Catherine Wells Merrill of Plymouth. The youngest, Julia A., married Dr. Samuel Long of Plymouth.

The genius of merchandising was a marked characteristic in the Russell family, and all who engaged in that business have been successful in a more than usual degree.

Mr. Moor Russell was a man of excellent character, who had gained the esteem and confidence of the community, and possessed much energy and enterprise. He was prominent in church and religious matters, and was a most uncompromising temperance man. The story runs that he cut down his orchard because the fruit of the apple tree was made into cider and used as a beverage.

THE GOOKIN FAMILY.—Samuel Gookin was born in 1742 and lived in Dedham and Boston. His business was that of a merchant. Afterwards he moved to Haverhill and died in 1823. His son Richard was a prominent man in Haverhill, and was born in Boston in 1769. He came to Haverhill in 1799, and with his brother Samuel was the first person, it is said, who manufactured watch and hair springs in America. For a time he was foreman in the first cut nail factory at Amesbury, Mass. Subsequently he and a person by the name of Standrin introduced from England the wool-carding machines into the United States, for the improvement of which Mr. Gookin obtained several patents, and he and his partner manufactured in Boston the first wool-carding machines ever used in the United States. Previous to this wool was carded by hand. Afterwards, 1799, they moved their business to Haverhill, and manufactured wool-carding machines which were sold in all parts of our country and in Canada. He was interested in woolen factories in Bath and other places, and was a man of uncommon energy and enterprise. He lived on Ladd street, and with Obadiah Swasey was owner of the famous "Fisher farm." There is a tradition that on account of the carding-machines being brought from England, an attempt was made on the lives of Mr. Gookin and his partner. A hat was sent the former armed with a secret deadly spring, but was discovered before the hat was worn. It was put on a dog and instantly killed the animal. To his partner was sent a trunk that was intended to explode when unlocking.

He died at Haverhill in 1826. His wife's maiden name was Rebecca Demman. One of their daughters married John L. Bunce, a son, Warren Demman (see Chap. XIX). Mr. Gookin left a strong impression on the community.

ASA BOYNTON was a prominent and influential citizen of Haverhill in the latter part of the last century and the first of the present. The name also appears in the Piermont records. He was a selectman in 1802-3-6, and moderator in 1806. He was one of the petitioners for the charter of Haverhill Academy, and also at a later date, 1805, for the charter of the Cohos turnpike. It was said he was the keeper of the tavern that afterwards became the famous Towle tavern,—at least his name appears amongst those who were licensed as a "taverner to sell spirituous liquors." He went from Haverhill to New York where his descendants, it is said, are active and enterprising people.

JOHN MONTGOMERY was of Scotch origin, and was born in 1764. His father came to America in 1749 and settled in Londonderry. The son it would seem moved to Haverhill from Andover, Mass., toward the close of the last century. He was moderator of town meeting as early as 1796, and was one of the pioneer merchants at the Brook. He took an active part in public matters, and was an influential and leading citizen of the Town, being often honored with positions of trust and responsibility. He represented the Town for three years in the legislature. When the War of 1812 broke out he was Lieutenant-Colonel of the 13th regiment N. H. Militia, was appointed Brigadier-General of the N. H. Militia that were stationed at Portsmouth for the defence of the harbor. Afterwards he was promoted to be a Major-General. He married Betsey Ring of Haverhill, and in the marriage record he is recorded as from Andover, Mass. Of his large family none are now living in Haverhill. One of the daughters became the first wife of Jonathan Nichols, and a granddaughter is now Mrs. E. H. Rollins, whose husband was a representative in Congress and also served a term as United States Senator. Gen. Montgomery, it is said, was noted for his singing talents, and in appearance was a fine looking man. He was highly esteemed, and had extensive influence in the northern section of the state, and was a man of great energy and force. The old Montgomery place is still standing—a large, square, two-story house—at the Brook.

ROSS COON was one of the characters of Haverhill, and on one occasion, in 1802, served as moderator. He lived in a wooden house which stood where the Bank house now stands, and was kept as a tavern, called the "Coon tavern." This house was moved away afterwards, and it is said part of it formed the house now belonging to Mr. L. B. Ham, and the other part was the Whitney house. Coon was called "Doctor," and in addition to the duties of a landlord he added also those of a physician. He was quite illiterate, and when prescribing for people of a bilious state he would say the medicine was for clearing out the "bilery dux." He afterwards lived in a large brick house at the Brook, which was also known as the "Coon tavern." Tradition says he was a faithful practitioner at the Coon bar. Landlord and Doctor Coon, it is said, combined still another profession. He preached as well as practiced. He was a man in poor health and was confined to an arm chair, but of immense size, weighing about four hundred pounds. He was famous for his mirth and story-telling, and did little else than "laugh and grow fat," and made others laugh also. He was the author of the saying. "A thousand lies are told every day and not half of them are true.'

GLAZIER WHEELER was another character of Haverhill. He was a very skilled worker in the fine metals, and was employed, it is said, by certain persons in Haverhill who were willing to make a cheap dollar go as far as a true one, to get up such a coin, in which there was only one-half as much silver as in the genuine coin dollar. Wheeler got into trouble by his counterfeiting and suffered the consequences of his misdeeds. According to the customs of the times he had his ears cropped as a part of the penalty. He afterwards told some of his customers, for whom he had been operating, that they were not satisfied with having two dollars for one, but asked of him three and four for one, and in this way their adulterated dollars were discovered. It is said he was subsequently employed in the mint at Philadelphia on account of his great skill.

EARLY SETTLERS—CONTINUED.

RICHARD FRENCH, familiarly known in his day as "Dick" French, was an early settler in the direction of Briar hill, and was famous for his skill as a trapper and a disciple of Isaak Walton. What he did not know of the habits of the "speckled trout" and of wild animals was not worth knowing. Pool brook above the Swasey mills was noted for its fine trouting, and French pond, the chief source of the brook, abounded in trout. Alas, that long ago its waters should have been given over to the deadly pickerel, so that now only a stray trout can be found. Descendants of the famous hunter and trapper are still living in the neighborhood of French pond.

There are two other persons with their families that may appropriately be given a place in this chapter, since all their business and social relations were with Haverhill, although their homes were not within the limits of the Town.

PARKER STEVENS came to Haverhill from Hampstead in 1787, and settled on a tract of land in Piermont on the edge of Haverhill. This tract was the generous lot of 500 acres. He brought with him a family of seven children. The sons became farmers, and the original tract was parcelled out to them. The youngest child, Caleb, born in 1782, remained on the homestead till quite late in life, when he moved to Concord and lived with his son, Lyman D. Stevens, and died in 1870. Mr. Parker Stevens was an enterprising man, of some force of character and soon after coming to Piermont he petitioned the General Court to be allowed to run a ferry across the Connecticut river on his farm. Caleb Stevens married Sally Dewey, daughter of Dea. Dewey of Piermont, and they had two children. A daughter, Cynthia, married Isaac H. Healey and lived in Piermont. The son, Lyman D., (see Chap. XIX.)

WILLIAM TARLETON lived in Piermont on the Turnpike near Tarleton lake, a beautiful sheet of water about two miles long and nearly a mile wide at its greatest width, to which he gave name. The exact time when he came to the Cohos Country is not known, but earlier than 1774. He was a young man just turned of twenty-one, but a man of force and energy, and soon took a prominent part in public matters. He came from Newmarket or from that vicinity, at least the name is found in the Portsmouth and Newmarket Town Papers, and his bearing was such as to indicate parentage of social standing. He was a man of large ability, intelligence, and influence, and held many positions of trust and honor in town, county, and state. He was also a man of high character and is said to have been quite aristocratic in his tastes and ideas. He held a captain's commission in Col. Bedel's regiment in the Revolution and subsequently he was appointed Col. of the 13th N. H. Militia. He was active in Town matters, and represented Piermont and Warren in the legislature, and was one of the most widely known citizens of Grafton County. He was also a member of the committee in 1791–2 to revise the Constitution of the State. In 1804 he was a Presidential elector, and again in 1808. He ran as a candidate for Senator in 1805 and in 1807, and was a member of the governor's council in 1808. From 1808 to 1813 he was high-sheriff of Grafton County. All these positions at that time were the prizes of the first men of the Country, and rarely could a man without possessing ability and character attain them.

We find Col. Tarleton associated in various ways with the prominent men of this section of country in all matters of enterprise. He was one of the leading spirits in procuring the charter of and in pushing to an early completion the Cohos turnpike, and was one of the proprietors of that thoroughfare.

From 1774 when travel was pouring into the Cohos Country he kept tavern at Tarleton lake, and gave fame to that early hostelry where the traveller was sure to find not only excellent service, but a host who in intelligence and genteel bearing was the peer of his guests. The old sign is still preserved. It is made of a single oaken board beautifully painted. On the top on one side is the name "William Tarleton," at the bottom the date, "1774." Between the name and the date is a painting of Gen. Wolf with drawn sword and full uniform. Washington had not yet come into view. Wolf was the great hero. On the other side was a representation of "Plenty." The sign is now in possession of Amos Tarleton of Haverhill, a grandson of Col. William. For two generations it swung in the free winds which swept over Tarleton lake, and could it speak of all that took place during that time, what a strange tale it could tell of the days of old.

Col. Tarleton was tallish, but not heavily built, erect in bearing, and gave the impression, it is said, of superiority and force. He wrote a beautiful hand. He was married twice. His first wife before her marriage was Betsey Fisk of Piermont, a woman of excellent qualities of heart and mind. By this union there were five children. For his second wife he married Polly Melville of Derry, and they had nine children. She outlived her husband some years, and was remembered by the older people as a woman of culture and society. Of the large family of children, Amos, the eldest, succeeded his father in the old homestead. He represented the town of Piermont for several years. Most of the other children went South and West, (see Chap. XIX.) Col. Tarleton died at his home in 1818 at the age of 66, and his death is said to have been hastened by troubles which came upon him whilst sheriff, through the unfaithfulness of some of his deputies, but which in no way tarnished his honorable reputation, for which he is said to have been very jealous. He lies buried in the Ladd Street Cemetery where a beautiful and appropriate monument marks his resting place. When the funeral procession reached Haverhill Corner the coffin lid was removed, and many who could not go to the house were given an opportunity of looking upon the face of one so well-known in the community and who had filled so many and important places of honor and trust.

CHAPTER VII.

SETTLERS FROM 1800.

Division-line between early and late Settlers—River and back Settlements—Briar Hill—Along Oliverian—East Haverhill—Woodsville—Biographical Sketches—Noyeses—Websters—Barstows—A character—Wilsons—Towles—Ephraim Kingsbury—Merrills—Timothy A. Edson—Bells—Noah Davis—Morses—Chester Farnam—Perley Ayer—The Jeffers—Timothy Wilmot—Michael Carleton—Woodwards—Hosea S. Baker—StClairs—The Pikes—Russell Kimball—James P. Brewer—Southards—Charles C. Kimball—Jos. B. Niles—Mansons—John McClary—Rixes—John L. Bunce—Stowes—Reding Brothers—Jonathan Nichols—William C. Marston—Haywards—Warrens—Jonathan B. Rowell—Elliotts—Timothy K. Blaisdell—Cuttings—Clarks—Salmon Fish—Smiths—Alonzo W. Putnam—Cummings Brothers—Caleb Hunt—Jackson Brothers—Timothy R. Bacon—Daniel Batchelder—John Vose Bean—Bailey Brothers—Charles A. Gale—Darius K. Davis—Levi B. Ham—Currier Brothers—Augustus Whitney—The Stevenses—The Weekses—J. G. Blood—William H. Nelson—Joseph Powers—Meaders—Charles B. Griswold—Andrew J. Edgerly—Caleb Wells—Charles H. Day—R. D. Tucker.

I have made the division-line between early and later settlers at 1800, which in one sense is purely arbitrary, and yet that date may be said to indicate a transition period. The early settlers were fast passing away from the stage of active life at the beginning of the present century, and a new generation of men were stepping into their places. This date may also be the division-line between the period of the river-settlements and the settlements in the central and eastern section of the Town. Up to 1800 population was mainly along the river road, at North Haverhill and Ox Bow and at the Corner and the Oliverian falls. A few openings were early made in the direction of Briar hill, and still fewer to the east, and along the Oliverian, but for the most part the territory of the Town east of the river road was an unbroken forest at the opening of the present century. As long ago as 1830 there were only two or three clearings at East Haverhill, and the expanse on which that village stands was covered with primeval forest. Indeed the population in and around East Haverhill village has chiefly grown since the railroad came in. From 1830 population moved in the direction of the east and north-east sections of the Town, though prior to that date openings were made in all parts of the Town. The growth of Woodsville has been quite recent, mainly within twenty-five years.

And thus with the growth and development of the Town from 1800 on, I continue the biographical sketches of those who were most active in its public history and in its moral, educational and material advancement. Some names perhaps deserving a place here may have escaped notice. Generally the line has run along those who have been active in public matters, though others have been recognized on account of some special circumstance or characteristic.

TIMOTHY NOYES came to Haverhill from Portland, Me., and lived near the old Isaac Pike place. The exact date is not known. He had a large family,—fifteen daughters and one son. Timothy Noyes and his son Person were the discoverers of the whetstone on Cutting hill, and were the first manufacturers of scythe-stones in Haverhill. One of Timothy Noyes' daughters married Capt. Henry Noyes,—no relation,—who lived where Alonzo F. Pike now lives. Person Noyes' widow became the wife of Isaac Pike, and his son Person, (see Chap. XIX), Horace E. and R. H. Noyes of East Haverhill are great-grandchildren of Timothy Noyes.

BENJAMIN NOYES came from Landaff in 1828. He was born in 1813, the son of David Noyes, and his mother was a daughter of Col. Mark Fisk who commanded a regiment in the War of 1812. He married Mary C. Wheeler of Haverhill, and they had six children: one, George, was killed at the battle of Gettysburg, and two sons are living in California.

DAVID WEBSTER was born in Plymouth, and was a son of Col. Webster of that town. He was high-sheriff of Grafton county from about 1783 to 1809. He lived in Haverhill for a few years about the beginning of the present century, and is said to have built the Samuel T.

Page house. His sister Betsey married Moore Russell. He was known as "Capt. Webster."

SAMUEL C. WEBSTER, son of the above, was also high sheriff of Grafton county. He graduated from Dartmouth College in 1808, and was admitted to the bar at Plymouth, and practiced there for many years. It does not appear that he practiced his profession after moving to Haverhill. He was Speaker of the House of Representatives of New Hampshire in 1830, and was a man of ability and influence. He married Catharine, daughter of Moore Russell. He died in Haverhill in 1835.

STEPHEN P. WEBSTER became a citizen of Haverhill about the beginning of the present century, and built the Henry Merrill house. He was a graduate from Harvard College and taught the Academy for a time. From 1805 to 1835 he was clerk of the court for Grafton county, and held many other public positions. He was moderator for many years, selectman, representative, and councillor in 1829. He was a man of much culture and urbaneness of manners, and of high character. Mrs. Webster was a woman of refinement, and was intimate, it is said, by the second marriage of her father, with Mrs. President John Quincy Adams. She was a most devoted Christian, and tradition says that she could always be seen going down Court Street on prayer meeting evening with her lantern in hand. Literally, she "let her light shine." She got up the Cent Society in Haverhill, and instructed the collectors to "be sure and get the fifty-two cents, especially the *two*." She knew the weakness of some very good people to cut off, if they could, the two cents. She gave $500 as a permanent fund to Haverhill Academy, but the money, it is said, was lost through negligence of the trustees.

JAMES P. WEBSTER was a son of Col. Moses and Sarah (Kimball) Webster. His father was a leading citizen of Landaff, and a brother of Stephen P. Webster.

He was prominent in public affairs, serving twelve years in succession as moderator, for which position, like his father, he had a natural talent. He was a representative for two years. He married Rebecca M. English. Their only child is Mrs. Eliza W. Kellum.

JOHN V. WEBSTER, brother of James, was for many years engaged in business in Haverhill. He carried on a tannery at the Brook in company with James A. Currier, and afterwards was the agent of the Haverhill Paper Company. He married Sarah Perkins of Lyme. Mr. Webster died a year ago. Mrs. David Quimby is a sister of the brothers Webster, and the only survivor of Col. Moses Webster's ten children.

CALEB WEBSTER came to Haverhill from Gilmanton and was a merchant at North Haverhill for a number of years. He married Hannah Peaslee. One of their sons, Sydney, married the daughter of Hon. Hamilton Fish, Secretary of State under President Grant, and Warren is a surgeon in the U. S. Army. Mrs. Webster is still living.

HENRY BARSTOW was born in Campton in 1787, and came to Haverhill about the beginning of the present century. He married for his first wife Harriet, daughter of Capt. David Webster, and their daughter Lydia married Merrill Pearson. His second wife was Frances Pierce of Woodstock, Vt., and of their family, Frances is now Mrs. Benjamin F. Labaree of Hartland, Vt. Alfred, Anson and Gardner, (see Chap. XIX). Ellen married Henry M. Ketchum of Chicago. Dea. Barstow was prominent in town and church, and was a man of sterling worth in the community. He was a deacon in the Congregational church for many years, and was one of the earlier merchants of Haverhill. In 1840 he moved from Haverhill, going first to Claremont, and a few years later to Lowell, Mass., where he died.

WILLIAM BARSTOW, brother of Henry, was a clerk in

Gen. Montgomery's store for a time, and then became a partner with his brother at the old Brick Block. He was appointed postmaster in 1841. Of his large family, James is the only one now living in this vicinity. George W. and Charles W., (see Chap. XIX.) James represented the town of Piermont in the legislature.

THOMAS BARSTOW, a younger brother of the above, was a clerk in their store. He married a Miss Tarleton, sister of Amos Tarleton, and a daughter of theirs, Mrs. Jesse R. Squires, is now living with her mother on the Col. Johnston place.

EZEKIEL H. BARSTOW became a resident of Haverhill about 1860, and died soon after. He had retired from the active duties of a minister and was engaged in teaching in Newton, Mass., before moving to Haverhill. He was a man of superior worth of character. Mrs. B. survived him some years, and was a woman of most gentle and winning manners, of trained mind and excellent Christian influence. Of their children, Mary and John, (see Chap. XIX). Another son, William, is in business in Nebraska, and a younger daughter, Sallie, is a teacher in Portland, Me.

AMOS HORN was a genius and a character, a shoe-maker by trade, and lived where Dr. Moses Carbee's house stands. His shop stood near the side-walk on the opposite side of the street. He was fond of dispute, with strong likes and dislikes, and was full of dry humor. He went by the name of "Judge," and was in the habit of referring to his neighbors by sarcastic epithets. He was heavy and fat. In those days the shoe-maker furnished none of the stock. Dr. Carleton, after getting some shoes made at Horn's shop, sent his son for the "waxed ends." Horn knowing the Doctor's great carefulness in "gathering up the fragments," and not willing to aid him in his economical purpose, unraveled the bristles before handing the "waxed ends" to the boy, saying, "Your father did not furnish the bristles." On another occasion he bought some salt pork of the Doctor, and when Horn's son went for it, the Doctor said, "Tell your father this pork was killed on the full of the moon, and it will swell in the pot.". Horn sent the boy back to ask the Doctor if he thought it would "bust the pot." Horn came on the stage near the beginning of this century. He was married in 1803.

NATHANIEL WILSON came to Haverhill in 1801 from Pelham at the age of twenty-four, and was the son of Jesse and Ruth (Merrill) Wilson. His mother was a sister of Maj. Nathaniel Merrill, from whom he was named, and he was the ninth of a family of sixteen children. His wife was Sarah, the eldest daughter of Capt. Joseph Pearson, and they had three children, Isaac P., Ann Maria, and Nathaniel. Isaac married Rhoda Brainard, and one of their sons is Geo. L. Wilson of Ladd street, and another is Edward B., (see Chap. XIX). Nathaniel, the youngest son of Nathaniel and Sarah (Pearson) Wilson (see Chap. XIX).

SIMON TOWLE was born in Hampton in 1759. He afterwards moved to Chester, and married Eleanor Hall of that town, and came to Haverhill in 1805. Their children were Edward, Henry, Charles, Elizabeth, and Frederick. Frederick (see Chap. XIX). Elizabeth married Samuel Brooks and lived in Canada; Charles married Lucy Bellows, a cousin of the late Chief Justice Bellows, and also lived in Canada; Henry married Susan Pierce, and lived in Haverhill, and of their children Antoinette became the wife of Horace Hunt, Simon married first Rebecca Parkhill of Florida, and then Harriet Hunt; James H. (see Chap. XIX). Susan Emily, the youngest, said to be a person of uncommonly lovely character, died early.

Edward, the oldest child of Simon Towle, was a selectman in 1819. He was a large man, of commanding presence, and for many years after the death of his father he kept the famous Towle stage tavern, the headquarters of the court and lawyers after the days of the Joseph Bliss tavern. He married Nancy Elliott of Chester, and of their children Elizabeth married Dr. Hiram Morgan, Eleanor H. became the wife of George W. Chapman, Ann E. married George S. Towle, a lawyer and editor in Lebanon; Charles S. died in Canada. Emily H., like her cousin Susan Emily, died young, and like her was said to be a person of rare character.

Simon Towle died soon after he came to Haverhill. He was a soldier of the Revolution, a colonel of militia, and represented the town of Chester for several years in the legislature before coming to Haverhill. He was a man of unusual size, tall and of large frame, and weighed it is said four hundred sixty pounds. His ancestors were persons of massive size. Col. Towle was a much esteemed citizen of the Town, and was the successor of Asa Boynton in keeping tavern.

EPHRAIM KINGSBURY, called "Squire Kingsbury," was a man of importance in the Town. He held numerous public positions, being town clerk and treasurer for a number of years, and was also a selectman. He was a member of the board of trustees of Haverhill Academy, and at one time principal of the school. He graduated from Dartmouth College in 1797, and afterwards read law, but it does not appear that he was in active practice whilst living in Haverhill. He moved from Town about 1834, and went to Connecticut and thence to New York where he died in 1855. He was a man of much ability, but somewhat eccentric, and was noted for extravagant speech and conduct. Once whilst the Methodists were holding tent-meetings on the park, and were more than usually demonstrative, Kingsbury went to the tent door and read to the meeting the riot act. At another time when a piece of road on the Oliverian, which had some stone wall in its construction, was to be accepted by the Town authorities, he said in describing the character of the stone used in the wall, "I can put any three stone in it into my eye and wink with perfect ease."

DAVID MERRILL moved to Haverhill in 1804, and settled on a tract of land north of Pool brook, which afterwards was the Town farm. He was at one time a selectman. He had a large family and one of his sons, David, was also a selectman. The oldest daughter, Abigail, was the mother of Chester M. Carleton, and Schuyler is still living at the age of eighty-six. Two of the latter's sons were in the War of the Rebellion.

BENJAMIN MERRILL came from Warren in 1814. He was born in Plaistow, and married Sarah Haynes of Rumney, who was distinguished when a young lady for her remarkably fine voice. Capt. Merrill, as he was usually called, was a country merchant in Warren before he came to Haverhill, and continued in that business for many years after he moved into Town. He was a man of much sagacity and good judgment, with a large amount of quiet humor, and could be very reticent. On one occasion when keeping store in Haverhill, as he locked up to go home, he took a ham for family use. After going a few steps he found he had forgotten something, and laying the ham in a feed-box he went back. When he returned the ham was missing. He said nothing, but some months after a man asked him in his store, "Captain, did you ever find out who took your ham?" "Yes, you are the very fellow; walk up and pay for it."

Capt. Merrill took an active part in public matters, was justice of the peace, a director in the Grafton County Bank, a selectman for several years, and pension agent. Of his children, Abel K. was the oldest. He fitted for college at Haverhill Academy, and was a member of the class of 1828, but was compelled to quit his studies at the end of the junior year on account of his health. He intended to devote himself to the ministry. He was town clerk for some years, a director of the Grafton County Bank, and was also engaged in mercantile business. For nearly fifty years he was superintendent of the Sabbath school of the Congregational church, and a deacon for nearly fifty years. He was a prominent and influential citizen of the Town, and one of its most esteemed and well-known citizens. He was also widely recognized in the county and state in church matters, and was a delegate from New Hampshire to the National Council of Congregational Churches in 1855, which met in Boston. He was a man of great purity of character, and a most kind and steadfast friend. Dea. Merrill was married twice, his wives being sisters, the Misses Leverett of Windsor, Vt., and their children, Lizzie and three brothers (see Chap. XIX).

Henry Merrill was educated at Haverhill Academy and also spent one year at Phillips Academy, Andover, Mass. He was postmaster for thirteen years, beginning his term of service under President Lincoln. His first wife's maiden name was Mary J. Weeks of Salisbury, Vt., and his second wife was Helen C. Currier before her marriage. Three of their children are living in Haverhill. Mr. Merrill is a prominent citizen of the Town, and a member of the board of trustees of Haverhill Academy. He is now engaged in farming.

Arthur was educated at the Academy, and afterwards went to Boston in the life insurance business. His health failing he afterwards returned to Haverhill, and died of consumption. His wife was Sarah Merrill of Plymouth before her marriage, and their children are all living in the West. The youngest, a promising young man, died in Montana a few years ago.

Harriet married Timothy K. Blaisdell. Another daughter became the wife of Rev. Alfred Goldsmith. Louisa married John L. Bunce. Charlotte was the wife of Dr. Phineas Spalding. William (see Chap. XIX).

JOHN MERRILL was born in Warren, and was educated

at Haverhill Academy. He was a real estate broker in Boston for nearly fifty years. He married Mary C. S. Wells of Plymouth, and of their children three are living, Mrs. Preston of Medford, Mass., Charles H., a merchant in Boston, and a son who lives with his mother in Haverhill in the Bell house. Mr. Merrill moved from Cambridge to Haverhill in 1874, and died suddenly a few years ago in Boston. He was of fine personal presence, and a most companionable man.

DANIEL F. MERRILL was born in Stratham in 1812, and fitted for college at Hampton Academy. He entered Dartmouth College in 1832, and graduated in course. After leaving college he was principal of Haverhill Academy for two years, and then his health failing he went to Mobile, Alabama, and was a successful teacher in that city for twenty years. During the last year of this time he was superintendent of public schools of Mobile, and also for several years he was school commissioner. After his retirement from teaching he was superintendent of a copper mine in northern Georgia. In 1860 he returned to Haverhill, and again was at the head of the Academy for several years, and also filled the office of school superintendent for the Town. He then went to Washington and was a clerk in the treasury department from 1865 to 1886. He married Luella B., daughter of Jacob and Laura (Bartlett) Bell, and they had a family of six children. Mr. Merrill is a man of the highest character, and has filled a most useful and honorable life.

TIMOTHY A. EDSON was a leading citizen of Haverhill in the earlier years of this century. He was a selectman in 1807, high-sheriff of Grafton county from 1813 to 1818. In 1824 he moved to Littleton where he died. His wife is said to have been a woman of much character, bright in intellect and elegant in manners. Mr. Edson was at one time the owner of the Hazen farm and lived there for a while.

BELL BROTHERS—JOSEPH (see Chap. XVII).

JACOB BELL came to Haverhill in 1811, at first engaging in teaching in the northern part of the Town, and then was a clerk in a store of Gen. Montgomery, and with his brother JAMES, who came to Haverhill about 1830, engaged in mercantile life, and did a very extensive business. They were also the owners of a large tannery and a potash factory as well as a saw mill and a grist mill. James was the financial manager of the firm. South American hides were brought from Boston in large quantities in exchange for leather and potash. About 1840 James Bell moved to Bolton, Mass., and died there in 1864. He was married twice and had a family of thirteen children, seven of whom are living. Two daughters married McPhersons of Boston, distinguished decorators, who learned their art in London and Edinburgh. James W. and John (see Chap. XIX).

Mr. Jacob Bell continued to live in Haverhill till his death. Of his children, J. Leroy Bell, lives in Haverhill, and is a merchant. He enlisted in the War in 1862, and saw hard service in the campaign against Richmond from the battle of the Wilderness till the early autumn of 1864. He was wounded several times, and was mustered out of service at the close of the war with the rank of captain, having risen to that position from a private. Capt. Bell's present wife is the daughter of Moses M. Weeks. The daughters of Jacob Bell, one married Hon. Ellery A. Hibbard of Laconia, a prominent lawyer and formerly a Congressman, and the other is Mrs. Daniel F. Merrill of Washington.

NOAH DAVIS was born in Connecticut about 1787, and came to Hanover where he was apprenticed to a druggist and learned that business. Afterwards he settled in Haverhill, and was engaged in selling drugs and medicines, and also dry goods. He remained in Haverhill till 1825, when he moved to Albion, New York. Mr. Davis built the house now owned and occupied by George W. Chapman, Esq., and the little store where he sold goods stood on the south side of the lot. He married Freelove Arnold, and had a large family of children. His eldest son, Noah, (see Chap. XIX).

MORSES.—Two brothers, JOHN and DANIEL, came to Haverhill about 1806 from Plymouth. A son of John is Rev. Joseph B. Morse (see Chap. XIX). A son of Daniel, Lafayette, lives on the homestead at Horse meadow; another Daniel, father of Luther C. Morse (see Chap. XVII), lived at North Haverhill. The two Daniels were not related. Mr. Osgood Morse was the youngest son of John Morse of Horse meadow. Charles O. and Edward B. are sons of Osgood.

Other MORSE BROTHERS came from Hebron in 1824, and settled in the eastern part of the town which was then an almost unbroken wilderness. It is said there were five brothers. JACOB is still living, and was a selectman and a representative in the legislature. ISAAC was also a selectman and represented the Town several years. One of Jacob's daughters is the wife of George Wells of North Haverhill.

STEPHEN ADAMS was born in Lexington, Mass., and came to Haverhill in the early part of the present century. His second wife was the sister of the late Michael Johnston. His oldest son, Charles J. (see Chap. XIX). Another son, Stephen, was a Methodist minister, and Abbie married Henry H. Wilder, a prominent business man of Lowell, Mass. Capt. Adams was a large man, tall and well built. He was captain of a horse company of militia, and was very fond of having himself addressed by his military title. The boys who were accustomed to go to his store to buy candies, would sometimes forget this point of civility, whereupon the Captain would disregard their wishes. When, however, they remembered to call him by his proper military title, he was sure to reward their politeness with an extra sugar-plum and a pleasant manner.

CHESTER FARMAN came to Haverhill in 1810 from Strafford, Conn., and settled near Pool brook. He was engaged in lumbering and mill building. In manners and speech he was plain and unassuming, with a quaint humor that agreeably spiced his conversation. He possessed great excellence of character, and was a man of strictest integrity. For many years he was a deacon in the Congregational church, and took an active and genuine interest in its welfare and support. On one occasion the church being in financial distress, he said, " I wish I was rich, I would do so and so," and then repeated what the good Scotch woman said, " but I suppose the Lord don't trust me." He married for his second wife Lucy Stearns of Haverhill. Their only son, Jeremiah Gordon, married Cynthia Hastings Ladd, and lived in Haverhill till 1852, when he moved to Hartland, Vt., and afterwards to Claremont. The daughters of Dea. Farman were Miriam Sargent, and Anne Watson. A daughter of the former is the wife of William B. Stevens of Bradford, Vt. Of Jeremiah Gordon Farman's children, one married Sheron Howard, a lawyer of St. Johnsbury, Vt., Cynthia Hastings became Mrs. Fulton of Bradford, Vt., Elinor Louisa married Leonard Cady of St. Johnsbury, Vt., and Samuel Ladd was for many years connected with the Claremont Paper Co., and is now living at White River Junction engaged in the paper business. He is the last of Dea. Farman's descendants bearing the Farman name.

PERLEY AYER was born in Piermont in 1798, and came to Haverhill in early youth. He was for many years the owner of what is now the county farm. He moved to the Corner in 1853. He married Mary E. Worthen. A son, Phineas, graduated from Dartmouth College in 1852. A grandson, Perley, is living with his aunt, Miss Eliza Ayer, on the homestead.

JEFFERS—JAMES, JOSIAH, JOHN—came to Haverhill about 1810, and settled in the eastern part of the town. A neighborhood in that section is now known as the "Jeffers neighborhood," where some of their descendants still live. Several members of this family held public positions in Town. They have been farmers, and Sylvester Jeffers has for many years been a lumber manufacturer.

TIMOTHY WILMOT came to Haverhill in 1815, and of his large family Harvey B. (see Chap. XIX). Haron lives in Haverhill. Mary (Mrs. Daniel Sargent) in Cambridgeport, Mass., and Betsey (Mrs. Henry Tower), and Harriet (Mrs. Charles Snow) in Hudson, Mass.

MICHAEL CARLETON was born in Newbury, Vt., and came to Haverhill in 1812. He married Betsey Putnam of Newbury. They both died within a year, in 1875-6. The oldest child, Michael, is living in Haverhill, and married for his first wife Louisa B. Rodgers of Newbury, Vt., and for his second Susan Cone of Guildhall, Vt. They had three children, Charles, Annie, and Bessie. The daughters married, one as his first, the other as his second wife, Frank D. Hutchins, cashier of the national bank, Lancaster, and a graduate of Dartmouth College. Sally Putnam married William H. Burbeck, and of their children, Edward C. and George (see Chap. XIX). James lives in Concord; Walter, who married Abbie, daughter of Ezra S. Kimball, lives in Binghamton, N. Y.; Mary and William O. are with their parents. The latter married Carrie A. Blanchard, of Cumberland, Me., and was educated at Lancaster Academy. A daughter of William H. Burbeck by his first marriage lives in Boston. Mehitabel B. married Levi Rodgers of Guildhall, Vt., and their children are Levi and Michael C. (see Chap. XIX), and Harriet C. Betsey married Stephen J. Roberts and lives in Claremont. Mary and Martha were twins, the former dying in 1856, the latter marrying Eben L. Rowell of Newport. Harriet Newel died young. Horace D. married Mary Eliza Mahurin, a woman of gentle manners and winsome character.

C. B. M. WOODWARD lived for the greater part of his life in Town, and was an esteemed and most worthy man. In the early part of his life he was a Methodist minister, and took a deep interest in temperance reform. In his later years he was engaged in the manufacture of patent medicines. He married Sophronia Mudgett, a woman of superior mind and worth. Mr. Woodward died a few years ago, and Mrs. Woodward is living with a daughter in Orange, Mass. Another daughter married Dea. Samuel S. Shepherd, Salem, Mass.

GEORGE WOODWARD came to Haverhill from Springfield, Vt., about 1836, and purchased a farm at Horse meadow. His wife's maiden name was Nancy A. Lake. Of their children George J. lives on the homestead, and Henry L. is a farmer at North Haverhill.

HOSEA SWETT BAKER was a young man less than twenty years of age when he came to Haverhill about 1817, and was a descendant on his mother's side of Capt. John Lovewell the famous Indian warrior. His mother died when he was an infant, and he came to live with an uncle in Piermont. Before he was of age he attended Haverhill Academy, earning money for that purpose, and fitting himself for teaching which he pursued for several years in Haverhill and in Rumney. Afterwards he engaged in the lumber business on the Oliverian. In 1825 he moved to the Corner and carried on for many years the meat business, and was also engaged in the shoe and leather trade and general merchandise with Blaisdell & Co. The last thirty years of his life he followed farming at East Haverhill.

Mr. Baker was a man of excellent ability and good judgment, and of large intelligence. He was well known in all this section of Grafton county, and was noted for his genial nature and love of conversation and anecdote. He was probably the best informed man in Haverhill in its local and personal history, and took a deep interest in these pages, for which he contributed many facts and incidents. He was full of energy and enterprise, and was always ready to engage in whatever was for the good of the community.

Mr. Baker held many places of trust and honor,—deputy-sheriff, captain of militia, postmaster, justice of the peace for forty years, selectman, representative, and trustee of Haverhill Academy. He helped to organize one of the earliest Sabbath schools in Town, and was its superintendent for a time. He was also often in requisition in the settlement of estates, and in all these positions he acquitted himself with credit and fidelity. He was a member of the Masonic fraternity, and in religion a Methodist. He died in 1885 at the age of eighty-six years.

He married Fanny Huntington of Hanover, and of their six children three are living. Peyton Randolph was a graduate of Dartmouth College in 1848, and practiced his profession in Maine. He died in 1873. Oliver Randolph Baker, a clothing merchant in Bradford, Vt., is a son of Peyton Randolph. Solon H. lives at East Haverhill. Oliver is in business in Kansas, and the daughter is married to Rev. Moses T. Runnels, a Congregational minister.

St. Clairs sometimes pronounced Sinclairs.—Jonathan and Samuel came to Haverhill about 1818, perhaps earlier. Jonathan kept tavern very soon after moving to Haverhill in the three-story brick house now owned and occupied by Dr. Spaulding. A daughter married Ezra Hutchins who became a prominent merchant in Boston.

Samuel Sinclair lived on the turnpike about one mile from the Corner.

Moses H. Sinclair was a nephew of Jonathan and Samuel. He was at one time jailor, and also served as moderator of

town-meeting, and was known as "Major Sinclair." He married Mary Burnham of Rumney, and they had four children, two of whom are living in Concord,—Henry and Nelson. As illustrating Maj. Sinclair's humor, a person of rather large feet wanted a pair of shoes made,—Maj. Sinclair was of that trade,—and asked to know how soon he could have them. The Major replied, "That 'll depend on the weather." "What," said his customer, "has that to do with it?" "Why," was the waggish answer, "I shall have to build them on the commons, as there is n't room enough in the shop."

ISAAC PIKE was born in 1799 in Cockermouth, now the towns of Hebron and Grafton, and was the fifth child of Moses and Mary (Bell) Pike in a family of thirteen children. The Pike family came to this country as early as 1635, and settled on a farm in Salisbury, Mass., which is still in possession of descendants of the name. An early member of the family was a graduate of Harvard College, and was the first minister of the Congregational church in Dover. Nicholas Pike, author of the Pike arithmetic, very generally used in schools fifty years ago, was also of this family. The New Hampshire branch of the Pike family, consisting of several brothers, came to Cockermouth about 1785 from Dunstable, Mass, and the late Hon. Austin F. Pike, a senator in Congress, was a grandson of the youngest of these brothers. A brother of the late senator lives at the Brook.

Isaac Pike came to Haverhill about 1818, and settled in the east part of the Town, where, at the age of twenty, he cleared a piece of land and built himself a house. This house is now owned by Royal H. Noyes. Mr. Pike was married twice. His first wife was Irene Dole, and a grandson, Samuel P. (see Chap. XIX). His second wife was Sally M. Noyes, and they had seven children, of whom four are living.—Mrs. John L. Ayer, Alonzo F., Isaac, and

Edwin B. Sarah M. married Henry Smith, and a son, Frank A. (see Chap. XIX).

Mr. Pike was engaged in farming, lumbering, and in the manufacture of scythe-stones, and till near the time of his death he was one of the most active business men in Haverhill. He also was a merchant, and at one time lived at the Corner, keeping store in the building afterwards used for the same purpose by Samuel F. Hook.

In early times the timber and lumber of the upper Connecticut was taken down the river in rafts. Mr. Pike ran large quantities of logs and lumber from Haverhill to Hartford, Conn. He also transported whetstones on his rafts, and hauled large quantities of them to Burlington, Vt., and then shipped them to New York by water.

Mr. Pike was a man of great energy and enterprise, and was esteemed a strictly honest man. On several occasions he became much involved financially, but he always refused the offer to settle for less than the full amount. Courage, perseverance, and industry were prominent traits of his character, and his impulses were kindly and generous. He gave the ground on which the first church in East Haverhill was built, and he was a willing and constant supporter of its services. In personal appearance he was somewhat more than medium in size, with dark eyes and thick, black hair, broad shouldered, erect in form, and weighed about two hundred pounds. He died of apoplexy.

Alonzo F. Pike is the fourth child of the above, and was born in 1835. He is a self-made man, and early displayed the same business energy and courage of his father. Before he was of age he bought out his father's store and carried on the business for himself. At the time of Isaac Pike's death the whetstone business was in a very unsatisfactory condition, and the estate being very much entangled, Mr. Pike, at the earnest solicitation of the mother and family, consented to act as administrator of the property, and by careful and wise management he succeeded in unraveling the entanglement, and settling the estate. Although his plans had been formed to engage in business in the city, he now abandoned his purpose and entered into the business of his father. At that time the whetstone business was comparatively limited, but by great energy and industry it has now grown to be one of the most extensive plants in the state. Mr. Pike has been an earnest, indefatigable worker, and by close attention to his affairs, careful and prudent direction of his plans, and punctuality and integrity he has risen from a meagre beginning, and in the course of twenty-five years of his business life finds himself one of the most successful business men of the state. He has a sound and trustworthy business judgment. He is president of the A. F. Pike Manufacturing Company, and one of its principal owners. He resides at Pike Station, in a beautiful and sightly home which looks to the east on one of the finest scenes in all this region, having for the fore-ground the charming valley through which the Oliverian winds, with the foot-hills of Benton beyond, and back of these the grand outlines of Moosilauke.

Mr. Pike married Ellen M. Hutchins, and has a family of five children living, and he owes much to a thoughtful and faithful wife for the large measure of his success. He takes a deep interest in all matters of public concernment, and is a generous and public-spirited citizen. He is a trustee of Haverhill Academy, and a liberal supporter of the church. In looks he resembles his father, dark complexion, black eyes and hair, stocky in build, square shouldered, strong and firm mouth, full head, the whole man in his physique indicating energy and force of character. He is a most kindly and genial man, and hospitable in his home, still in the prime of life, turned a little of fifty-three years.

Isaac and Edwin B. are brothers of Alonzo F., and in business with him. Edwin B. lives at the Corner. His wife, recently deceased, before her marriage was Addie A.

Miner, and of their children two are living. Mr. Pike is a courteous and large hearted citizen, and a member of the Congregational church.

Charles W., son of Samuel Pike, has been a selectman of the Town, and Burns H., Charles J. and Oscar B. are sons of Drury Pike.

A family of PIKES came to Haverhill in 1830, and were engaged in the manufacture of bricks at North Haverhill. Newhall was a selectman.

RUSSELL KIMBALL was born in Kingston in 1799, and came to Haverhill about 1818. He served as a clerk in Capt. Merrill's store for ten years and then became a partner with his employer. Their store was on Court street. He married Louisa Bean of Lyman, a sister of Samuel V. Bean who was at one time principal of the Academy, and a niece of Stephen P. Webster. Of their family only one child is living, Peabody W. Mr. Russell Kimball gave himself strictly to his business and was successful in that direction, having accumulated at the time of his death a large property. He was an esteemed citizen.

Peabody W., son of the above, was born in 1834, and was educated at Haverhill Academy and at Newbury Seminary. He married Jane Pearson, and their two children, a daughter and son, are living at home. Mr. K. was a clerk in his father's store for some years and then became a partner with him. After the death of his father in 1862 he retired from active business. He is a man of excellent ability, safe judgment, and sound sense. Being left with a large property which he has carefully managed, he is now one of the wealthiest citizens of Haverhill. His extreme diffidence has stood in the way of accepting public trusts for which his ability and integrity especially qualify him. He was, however, a representative in the legislature for several terms, and has been for many years a trustee of Haverhill Academy. He is a deacon in the Congregational church and has been superintendent of the Sabbath school, in both of which he has always taken a deep interest. As a citizen and neighbor he is highly esteemed, and though a man of ample fortune he is entirely free from pride or ostentation. With his more intimate acquaintances and friends he is social and genial, and has a quick sense of the humorous. He is thoroughly devoted to his family.

CHARLES C. KIMBALL came to Haverhill in 1843, and of his five children four are living in Town,—John G., Geo. F., Albert F., and M. E. Morris E. Kimball was postmaster at North Haverhill for twelve years. Charles M. lives in Newbury, Vt.

JAMES P. BREWER (see Chap. XIX).

SOUTHARDS, MOSES and AARON, came to Haverhill in 1822 from Walpole and settled on the Col. Porter farm which was divided between them, and which has remained in the Southard name ever since. They are descendants of an old family that came to New England in the Mayflower. They were twins and were often taken for each other on account of their striking resemblance. Both were married before they came to Haverhill. Lyman M. is the only one of Moses Southard's family living, and he resides on the widow Currier farm. He married for his first wife Jane Bachup, and for his second a daughter of Dudley C. Kimball of Newbury, Vt.

Aaron Southard's children were Samuel F., who occupies the old Porter homestead, Joseph who died at nine years of age, Eliza, Ann Jane, and Kate. Two of the daughters married sons of Gov. Page, and one became Mrs. John N. Morse. The mother of these children is said to have been a very superior woman.

Moses and Aaron Southard were very successful in business, and were amongst the leading agriculturalists of Grafton county. They were highly esteemed citizens of the

Town. Aaron was a Congregationalist and a generous supporter of that faith.

Samuel F. was only nine years of age when his father moved to Haverhill. He received part of his education at Haverhill Academy, and is an intelligent citizen. He takes laudable pride in his beautiful and productive farm, and gives to it his entire attention, and like his father before him, he is a prominent agriculturalist. He enjoys the friendship of the leading citizens of the Town, and is a man of integrity and character.

JOSEPH B. NILES lived in Benton before he moved to Haverhill about sixty years ago. Two sons, Alonzo F. and Horace L. (see Chap. XIX).

ALEXANDER MANSON came to Haverhill about 1825, and was a blacksmith. Several of his sons followed the same trade. Two, Alexander and Charles, live in Exeter; Mary and Lucy F. married Boswells, and Elizabeth, Mrs. George Kimball, lives in Black River Falls, Wis. Mrs. Shepardson of East Haverhill is also a daughter. Mr. Manson had a brother die in California a few years ago who amassed a large fortune.

JOHN McCLARY came to Haverhill in 1832 from Bristol where he was engaged in the tannery business with Gov. N. S. Berry. He was born in Newburyport, Mass., in 1792, and lived some years in Lisbon. Maj. Andrew McClary, who was killed in the battle of Bunker Hill, was an ancestor of his. At the breaking out of the War of 1812 young McClary enlisted for one year, and at the expiration of that time he enlisted "for the war." In 1814 he was commended by officers to the attention of the War Department as a suitable person to hold a commission in the regular army, having been sergeant major in the 45th Reg. of Vols., where he showed himself an efficient and faithful soldier. At the close of the war he returned to Lisbon, and afterward moved to Bristol. When he came to Haverhill he entered into partnership for five years with the Bells at the Brook in the tanning business, and before the expiration of that time he was elected register of deeds for Grafton county, which office he held for five consecutive years. He also served one year by appointment of the county commissioners to fill the vacancy caused by the resignation of B. F. Dow. He was a representative in the legislature in 1834-5, and took an active part in Town matters, being selectman and town clerk.

Col. McClary was of Scotch origin, and belonged to the McClarys who settled in Epsom before the Revolution. He married twice, first Rebecca Dodge of Lisbon, and afterwards her sister. Mrs. Silvester Reding is a daughter by the first marriage. He was colonel of the 13th Regiment N. H. Militia, a man of intelligence, high character, public spirited, and much esteemed by his fellow-townsmen.

RIXES. — "Maj. Rix," as he was called, moved to Haverhill about 1825, and was a man of strong will and vigorous mind. He was noted for his facility in amplifying news, and had a very imaginative conception of things.

John L., his son, was a prominent man in Town. In build he was slender, but active and wide-awake. He was a merchant, and was regarded as a man of integrity. He represented the Town in the legislature, and was a selectman, and had much to do with local politics, of which he was a shrewd master, and kept the run of details. He was also intelligent in regard to political movements. He was for many years a member of the Republican state committee. As a citizen he was public spirited, and of generous impulses, fond of story, and a radical temperance man. Mr. Rix was a director in the B. C. & M. Railroad.

NATHANIEL RIX came from Littleton and was prominent in that town, having been a representative in the legislature from 1821 to 1827, and also a member of the governor's council in 1832-3. He moved to Haverhill about 1840, and took an active part in public matters, serving as selectman and representing the Town in the legislature. He was also register of deeds.

JOHN L. BUNCE came to Haverhill from Hartford, Conn., about 1825 to take charge of the Grafton county bank as its cashier. Previous to this he held a subordinate position in the Phœnix bank of that city. After a service in Haverhill of some years he returned to Hartford as cashier of the Phœnix bank, and continued in that position for many years until he retired and accepted the presidency of the bank in 1860. He was a man of scrupulous integrity and a careful financier. As a family man he was social and full of geniality, and fond of his friends. He had a special passion for fishing, and after banking hours whilst he lived in Haverhill he often drove out to Tarleton lake to try his hand at the rod and line for pickerel. He married for his first wife Louisa Gookin, and for his second Louisa Merrill. His children are living in Hartford, Conn., one son following the business of his father.

STOWES.—Amos Stowe came to Haverhill from Springfield, Vt., in 1825. He was born in Concord, Mass., and was a Revolutionary soldier. He died in 1829, and is buried at East Haverhill.

JOSEPH STOWE, son of the above, came to Haverhill at the time his father did, and married for his second wife Priscilla Page of Landaff, and of their seven children William Page (see Chap. XIX). Joseph Stowe settled on the North Branch of the Oliverian about a mile from East Haverhill village, where he built a saw mill. Quite a story connects itself with the latter. Mr. Stowe was a staunch temperance man, and refused to have rum at the raising. After the first section of the frame was up the gang of men wanted rum, and being refused they propped the frame and quit work. For several days the country round was scoured before men enough could be got to finish raising without rum. A part of this frame was afterwards used for the building where George W. Richardson keeps store at East Haverhill. The class teacher remonstrated with Mr. Stowe for his fanaticism, telling him that he would "ruin the church and break up the Democratic party." Mr. Stowe was crier of the court and also a selectman, and whilst holding this latter office he came near losing his life on account of prosecuting the license law and posting the names of forty common drunkards in Town. He moved from Haverhill in 1842, and settled in Wisconsin.

REDING BROTHERS—JOHN R. REDING was born in Portsmouth in 1805, the son of a ship-master, and received what school education he had in the common school. After leaving school he served in a grocery store for a year and then entered the office of the New Hampshire Patriot, owned and edited by Hon. Isaac Hill, to learn the "art preservative," where he remained till 1826 when he became foreman in the Boston Statesman office, afterwards changed to the Boston Post. He held that position for two years, and then came to Haverhill in 1828. In July of that year he issued the first number of the Democratic Republican, and was its sole proprietor and editor till 1841. The paper was vigorously edited and influential. In 1840 Mr. Reding was elected to Congress, and served four years. He took his seat in the extra session called by President Harrison at the beginning of his presidential term. The Democratic Republican continued to be published by his brothers, Messrs. Warren and Silvester, till the paper was suspended in 1863. Mr. Reding was appointed postmaster in 1831, being the fourth postmaster of Haverhill, and held the office for ten years. He was also chosen to various town offices, serving as selectman, overseer of the poor, and town agent for building the Town house. In 1840 he was a delegate to the National Democratic Convention in Baltimore that nominated Martin Van Buren, and in 1852 he served in the same capacity in the National Democratic Convention which placed in nomination Gen. Pierce. For five years he held the office of naval store-keeper at Portsmouth, and in 1860 he was elected mayor of that city, but declined a second term. He was a member of the legislature for three years from Portsmouth, and was chairman of the committee to select a site for the county buildings and to build the same for Rockingham county. He also engaged in farming, building, and other lines of business, in all of which he displayed energy and enterprise, and achieved large success.

Mr. Reding moved to Portsmouth in 1853, where he now resides at a green old age, erect, quick of step, and with mental powers unimpaired. He married Rebecca, the youngest sister of Hon. Isaac Hill, who died in Washington. His second wife before her marriage was Jane Martin of St. Johnsbury, Vt. They have no children.

SILVESTER was engaged for many years in the publication of the paper his brother founded. He was register of deeds and represented the Town in the legislature. He married Ellen D., daughter of Col. John McClary, and they have four children. John (see Chap. XIX), Mary R., Mrs. George F. Putnam; Ellen, Mrs. George Butler, and William, now a clerk in the Naval Office, Boston. Mr. Reding was an intelligent and esteemed citizen of the Town.

WARREN was also connected with the Democratic Republican. He married Amelia C. Chandler, a woman of very superior character, and their only child, Harry, is a graduate of Washburn College, Kansas, to which state Mr. R. moved about 1870. He was postmaster at Centralia, Kansas, at the time of his death.

JONATHAN S. NICHOLS came to Haverhill in 1828, and engaged in the manufacture of carriages. He was also for twenty years agent of the Fairbanks Scale Company of St. Johnsbury, Vt., and traveled mostly in the South and West. He married for his first wife Myra, daughter of Gen. Montgomery. George E., Nellie P., and Clara I., (see Chap.

XIX.) Mr. Nichols is one of Haverhill's most intelligent citizens.

WILLIAM C. MARSTON is the son of Capt. David Marston who was a prominent and energetic citizen of Benton. William C., has been a selectman and a representative in the legislature. A daughter, Mrs. Edward Brainerd, lives in Piermont.

HAYWOODS, BENJAMIN and NATHANIEL. This is probably the same name as Hayward which appears in the early history of the Town. The Haywoods came from Vermont. Nathaniel's son, Alvah E., married a daughter of James Jeffers, and of their six children five went West, and one is Mrs. Solon H. Baker. Alvah E. was selectman and town clerk, justice of the peace, and captain of militia.

WARRENS, LUTHER and GEORGE.—The former was largely engaged in the lumber business. A daughter married a Congregational minister, and a son married a sister of A. F. Pike. The daughter of George Warren is prominent as a revivalist, and is a woman of much power and success as a speaker. She lives in Montana.

JONATHAN B. ROWELL came to Haverhill about 1830, and was a prominent citizen of the Town, being selectman for several years. He was a man of much energy. In 1846 he moved to Illinois, and of his large family some have made their mark in the world. Jonathan H., Chester, (see Chap. XIX).

ROSWELL ELLIOTT'S great-grandfather was one of the first settlers in Benton, and signed the call for the first town-meeting of that town. Roswell Elliott was a selectman of Haverhill in 1862.

TIMOTHY K. BLAISDELL was an uncle of the late Daniel Blaisdell, and came to Haverhill about 1835. He built the cottage parsonage house as it was before the recent alterations, and was a merchant. He was town clerk in 1838, and postmaster in 1841. Mr. Blaisdell married Harriet

Merrill, daughter of Capt. Benjamin Merrill, and they had five children. A son, Timothy, served in the War of the Rebellion, and died at its close. One of the daughters became the wife of William Blanchard of Chicago, a successful lumber merchant. Another married Charles H. Cram of Chicago, a graduate of Dartmouth College, and an accomplished gentleman, and fond of literature and rare books. He was engaged in the shoe trade, and died a few years ago. Mrs. Cram lives in Haverhill. Her oldest son, Nathan, a graduate of Dartmouth College, is supervisor of a division of the public schools of Washington, D. C., a daughter, Bessie, has spent two years in Germany, pursuing her education, a married daughter lives in Chicago.

CUTTINGS. — JAMES and ABIJAH came to Haverhill in 1834 from Hanover, and settled near Pike Station. Of James' family John W. has been a selectman and a representative in the legislature. Abijah's family moved to Iowa, and one of the sons, James A., (see Chap. XIX).

WILLIAM R. CLARK married a daughter of Josiah Colburn who was an eccentric man. Being asked about his religious hope, said, "I've nothing to brag of." On another occasion during his last illness, when a neighboring minister called to see him, and after prayer at the bed-side, remarked that he must put his trust in the Saviour, Mr. Colburn replied, "I'd sooner trust Him than an Injun."

HENRY H. CLARK came to Haverhill from Bath, and was register of deeds four years. He was born in Lyman. His education was pursued at Bath and at Newbury and Montpelier, Vt., fitting for college in 1871. Being prevented by sickness from entering college, he took a special course at Tilton Seminary. In 1872 he was appointed head master of Seabury Institute, Saybrook, Conn., serving till 1876 when he resigned on account of health. Later he was principal of Bath Academy. He also served for several years as superintendent of schools in Bath, and was town clerk. He is now instructor in mathematics in Dow Academy, Franconia. Mr. Clark has taught with much success, and was one of the most efficient registers of deeds the county ever had. He married Annie E. Babcock of Granville, Vermont, and they have two children. Politically a Democrat, religiously a member of the Congregational church.

SALMON FISH came to Haverhill from Charlestown in 1838. His name was changed to Fremont. Of the four children only one survives, Mrs. Osgood Morse. One of the sons, Sewall Lawrence, was a graduate of West Point. His early education was received at Haverhill Academy. He saw military service in the Seminole War, and afterwards took part in the Mexican War, coming out of it with the rank of captain. In 1855 he resigned his commission and engaged in building railroads in North Carolina. During the Rebellion he held high position in the engineer department of the Confederacy. At the close of the war he engaged in civil pursuits, and later he was employed by the government in superintending the construction of public buildings. He died suddenly a year or two ago whilst in charge of the buildings in Memphis, Tenn. Col. Fremont was a man of fine presence and high character.

SMITHS — ELEAZER SMITH was born in 1797 in Washington, Vt. His father lived to be ninety-three years old. Eleazer moved to Haverhill in 1838, and was for twenty years the proprietor of Exchange hotel, but which under his management and that of his son was known as Smith's hotel. He afterwards moved to Wentworth and kept a hotel there for thirty years. In early life he was one of the drivers on the Concord and Haverhill stage line. He married Anna Peters, whose father was a prominent and honored citizen of Bradford, Vt., having held the office of town clerk for over forty years. They had two children, Charles Goudy and William Peters. The latter was killed by the over-turning of a stage coach. Charles G. lives in Haverhill. In boyhood days he spent several years in Lyndon, Vt., and also for a few years he was a clerk in a store in Charlestown, Mass., after which he returned to Haverhill and was associated with his father in the hotel business. In 1853 he was appointed a clerk in the Portsmouth Navy yard, and held that position for three years, when he purchased the hotel of his father and continued in that business till 1881.

Mr. Smith has taken a prominent and influential part in public affairs in Town and county. At twenty-one years of age he was chosen town clerk, and he was a representative in the legislature for two years. In 1868 he was appointed by the legislature one of a committee of five to act in conjunction with the county commissioners in purchasing a county farm for Grafton county. Later, in a town meeting called for the purpose of relieving the Town from financial embarrassment, he advocated a plan for funding the Town debt, which was adopted, and he was chosen trustee of the sinking fund to meet the bonds as they became due. He has repeatedly been chosen a selectman and moderator, and for six years he was county commissioner, during which time he had the immediate superintendence of rebuilding the poorhouse buildings which were burnt in the last term of his commissionership.

In addition to these political positions of trust and honor, he was also a trustee for twelve years of the Bradford savings bank, and for a time its president. He has been for many years a trustee of Haverhill Academy, and at one time president of the board. In all these positions he has brought to the discharge of his duties faithfulness, good judgment, and commendable prudence. His manners are plain and reserved, and his mode of life unostentatious. He is a man of few words. In all proper matters for the improvement of society he is public spirited and always ready to join his fellow-townsmen in such matters. He is often called upon for advice by those who distrust their own judgment in regard to practical matters, and has proved himself a safe and prudent counsellor. He has the confidence of his fellow citizens.

Mr. Smith married for his first wife, Ruth Morse, a descendant of one of the early settlers of the Town. His second wife was Charlotte S. Dow, a daughter of the late B. F. Dow. There are two children by the first marriage, William P., and Anna M.

ALONZO W. PUTNAM came to Haverhill from Hanover in 1839. He was an uncommonly active man. His son Parker and another son live in the West. The home farm is now owned by Mrs. Putnam and two of the sons.

CUMMINGS BROTHERS—WILLIAM H. CUMMINGS was born in 1817 in New Hampton, and is a descendant of the old Cummings family of Dunstable. He received his education in the common schools. For a few years he was a clerk in a store in New Chester, and later he became a partner in the store. Afterwards he went to Lisbon and was a clerk in a store for a year, and then about 1840 he came to Haverhill and was in company with John L. Rix. He lived in Haverhill about eight years, and then returned to Lisbon, where he engaged in the business of merchandising and lumbering in the firm of Allen & Cummings, and has lived there ever since, being closely identified with the growth and commercial interest of the place.

Mr. Cummings is a prominent citizen of Lisbon, and has held public positions, being a representative in the legislature, a state senator, a delegate to the national convention that nominated Gov. Tilden for the presidency. He has been president of Wells River national bank since 1873, is a sound and careful financier, and has been very successful in business. He is a man of industry and energy. He married Harriet Sprague Rand, sister of the late Judge Rand, and of their three children a son is dead, and the daughters live at home.

STEPHEN H. CUMMINGS, brother of the above, came from Lisbon, as register of deeds in 1871, and held that position for three years. He was postmaster, town clerk, and superintendent of schools in Lisbon, and also selectman for five years in Haverhill. Only one of his own children is living, Mrs. Worthen of Brooklyn, N. Y. A son of his second wife, Arthur Mitchell (see Chap. XIX). An older son was eminent in his profession in the Sandwich Islands, and physician to the king and queen. He died a few years ago in Florida. Mr. Cummings is an intelligent and esteemed citizen.

CALEB HUNT came to Haverhill about 1840. He was a man of strong mind, but his educational advantages in early life were limited. He married a Miss Poole, and they had five children. For Caleb, Horace, Prescott and Helen, (see Chap. XIX). Louisa married James Woodward of Ladd street.

JACKSON BROTHERS moved to Haverhill from Coventry about 1840. Samuel Jackson, the grandfather, was a soldier in the Revolution before the organization of that town, and was its first selectman. He was a well educated man. Two of his grandchildren, Thos. B. and John W., settled in Haverhill. Both were educated at Newbury Seminary, and the former has represented Haverhill in the legislature.

TIMOTHY R. BACON came to Haverhill in 1840. An older brother, Asa, came earlier. Several of the former's children have been prominent in business, (see Chap. XIX).

DANIEL BATCHELDER was born in Corinth, Vt., 1803, and lived for many years in Benton, where he was a prominent citizen, representing that town in the legislature for seven years, from 1833 to 1839. He was captain of a company enlisted for the Mexican War, but resigned before the company went to Mexico. He was a captain in the 13th Reg. N. H. Militia. About 1840 he came to Haverhill, and was a deputy sheriff, and pursued the business of an auctioneer, in which he displayed tact and talent, sometimes making sharp hits at the expense of others.

JOHN VOSE BEAN was Principal of Haverhill Academy during the time it was run as a ladies' school in 1849. He was a graduate from Dartmouth College in 1832, and was a man of ability and high character. Whilst living in Haverhill he was a deacon in the Congregational church. His wife's name before her marriage was Caroline Graham, and of their children Ellen (Mrs. Baker) alone is living. Isabel married Hon. Otto Kirchner, a distinguished and able lawyer of Detroit, Mich., who for four years was attorney general of that state and also a lecturer for a time in the law school of the University of Michigan. The oldest daughter of the Bean family, Caroline, married Dr. George Page, son of Gov. John Page. Mr. Bean moved from Haverhill in 1854, and died in 1861. Mrs. Bean survives him, and with her daughter, Mrs. Baker, lives in Detroit, Mich.

BAILEY BROTHERS. — Five brothers, descendants of Gen. Jacob Bailey of Newbury, Vermont, came to Haverhill, three of them about 1850, and two later. Albert and Nathaniel were merchants at the Brook and did a large business. They followed the same occupation at Topsham, Vt., before coming to Haverhill. Nathaniel afterwards engaged in farming on Ladd street. Albert moved to Bradford, Vt., and became one of the most successful, and prominent citizens of that town. He died suddenly in Boston. He married Isabella Blake of Topsham, and their only living child is Mrs. Chamberlin of Bradford. Milo was at first a clerk in the store of his brothers and afterwards a partner. He was also a merchant at the Corner. He married a daughter of Samuel Page. Azro and Allen came to Haverhill later, and were farmers on Ladd street, the latter afterwards engaging in mercantile business with his brother Milo. Nathaniel Bailey married the widow of his brother

Allen. Azro married Hannah Lang of Bath, and of their large family some remain in Haverhill, others have gone West, one of the sons lives in Boston, and one is a railroad engineer in Mexico. Nathaniel was a selectman and a representative in the legislature. Albert also was a representative. Mr. Nathaniel Bailey is a man of means and lives in retirement, and is an esteemed citizen of the Town.

CHARLES A. GALE came to Haverhill from Gilmanton in 1850, and has lived on his present farm since that time. He was a representative from Haverhill in the legislature in 1875-6. A son, Charles A., lives at Woodsville.

DARIUS K. DAVIS moved to East Haverhill form Northfield in 1856. He was a partner in mercantile business with two of his brothers, and continued in trade with them or by himself for over twenty-five years. At different times he was interested in stores at Warren, Tilton, Pike Station, and at Indianapolis, Ind. He was a selectman in Benton for two years, and is now a member of the board of education. He has been successful in the bee and honey business.

LEVI B. HAM came to Haverhill in 1851 and was engaged for about twenty-five years in the stove and tinsmith business. He has been deputy sheriff, representative in the legislature, town clerk, and selectman. He has two children living, a son in Boston and a daughter at home.

CURRIER BROTHERS moved to Haverhill in 1852, and carried on the tanning business at the Brook. James A. was a selectman during the War. F. P. Currier has a family of three daughters.

AUGUSTUS WHITNEY came to Haverhill as register of deeds about 1855. Afterwards he was mail route agent for eight years between Springfield, Mass., and Newport, Vt. Mr. Whitney was a professional vocal music teacher, and was one of the best drill masters in that art. He was a man of intelligence, and catholic in his views. He married a

Miss Currier of Wentworth. A daughter lives in Winnepeg, Manitoba, and devotes herself to music.

GROVE S. STEVENS came from Piermont to Haverhill in 1856. He is a deacon in the Congregational church, and was for ten years high sheriff of Grafton county, and previous to that he was deputy sheriff. Of his family of five children the son is a lawyer in Littleton, and three of the four daughters married lawyers — Mrs. Charles A. Dole of Lebanon; Mrs. J. L. Foster of Lisbon, whose husband is a graduate of Dartmouth College, and Mrs. Morrill of Contoocook. A daughter, Mary, is at home. She was formerly a successful teacher in Arlington, Mass.

GEORGE W. STEVENS lived just south of the Piermont line. He was a deacon in former years in the Congregational church in Piermont. His son George H., lives on the homestead, and a daughter married Luther Holt of Lowell, Mass., a retired iron manufacturer.

ENOCH R. WEEKS came from Warren about 1874, and has been a merchant at North Haverhill. He has held the position of town clerk for a number of years, and is now postmaster at that place. One of his daughters is Mrs. Charles P. Page of the firm of W. H. Page & Son.

MOSES M. WEEKS moved from Bath in 1877. He married Sally Minot of Bath, and of their two children living one is Mrs. J. LeRoy Bell, and a son carries on the farm. Another son, a young man of most excellent traits, died a few years ago.

J. G. BLOOD came to Haverhill about twenty-five years ago, and is engaged in the manufacture of prepared lumber and shingles at the old Swasey mill. He married Elizabeth Wetherbee.

WILLIAM H. NELSON first moved to Haverhill about 1860, and was a merchant at North Haverhill for ten or twelve years, when he went to Lawrence, Mass., and engaged in the same business there. After a few years he returned to Haverhill, and carried on the business of general merchandising till his death about a year ago. He had a large family of children, most of whom are married. Mrs. W. H. Brock of South Newbury, Vt., was a daughter; another married Charles F. Bailey of Minneapolis; one became Mrs. Scott Sloane of Wells River, Vt.; another, Mrs. Hazen of St. Johnsbury, Vt.; a daughter married, and until her recent decease, lived in the Sandwich Islands; a son is in California, and a younger son in Dartmouth College. Mrs. Nelson now lives in Lawrence, Mass., and is a woman of much ability and noble character.

JOSEPH POWERS was born in Groton, the son of William and Mary (Thompson) Powers. In early life he was a teacher. Subsequently he moved to Plymouth, and whilst there he was appointed high sheriff of Grafton county. He lived in Haverhill after he became sheriff. From 1871 to 1873 he was a member of the governor's council, and in that position he served with much acceptance. He was a member of the constitutional convention in 1876. He owned the farm at North Haverhill where his niece, Mrs. Filley, now lives, and on this farm the first Jersey cows in Haverhill were kept, and in later years the herd was one of the finest in the state. (See Chap. XXI.) He was a man of strong character and large ability, and was held in high esteem by those who knew him. He was a staunch temperance man. He married Betsey Blood. Mr. Powers died in 1879.

MEADERS came from Warren where the family was numerous. Daniel W. went to Pennsylvania and was engaged with a brother in constructing railroads. Afterwards he lived in California. He returned to Haverhill in 1865, and engaged in the manufacture of starch. He was a selectman.

CHARLES B. GRISWOLD came to Haverhill as register of deeds in 1867, which office he held for five years. After the expiration of his term of office he was engaged for several years in the cotton and lumber business in Texas. Since 1874 he has been the efficient clerk of the supreme judicial court for Grafton county. He married Alzina M. Sawyer, of Malone, N. Y. They have one child, a graduate of Dartmouth College, who has just been admitted to the bar.

ANDREW JACKSON EDGERLY was born in Barnstead in 1828, and worked on a farm till he was sixteen years old, when he entered the Amoskeag manufacturing company's works at Manchester to learn the machinists' trade. He also continued at this business in Boston, and in Biddeford, Me., and then returned to Manchester. In 1861 he enlisted men for the 3d Regiment N. H. Vols., and again for the 4th Regiment, in which he was appointed second lieutenant of Co. E. He was in the expedition against Port Royal, S. C., and soon after was promoted to be first lieutenant. Whilst inspecting the picket line he received a severe wound by the falling of his horse, and was sent home on recruiting service. In March, 1863, he was dishonorably discharged "for circulating copperhead tickets and doing all in his power to promote the success of the rebel cause in his state." He rested under this stigma for a number of years, but the case being carefully investigated by the military committee of the House, a bill passed both branches of Congress fully exonerating him, and giving him an honorable discharge from March, 1863. Lieut. Edgerly was a representative in 1874, but declined a renomination. He also held the position of adjutant general of the state under Gov. Weston. He married twice, first, Ann Eliza Williams of Mansfield, Mass., and then Sarah Crocker Carr of Haverhill. A daughter by the first, and a son by the second marriage, who is a senior in Tufts College. Lieut. Edgerly secured his education at the common schools, is a Mason, and came to Haverhill in 1863.

CALEB WELLS came to Haverhill from Benton in 1868, where he held the position of school superintendent for seventeen years. He was also a representative in the legislature from that town, and served as selectman and as a justice of the peace. He has been a selectman of Haverhill, and is now a member of the board of education.

CHARLES H. DAY came from Bristol as register of deeds in 1878. He held that office for four years. Before moving to Haverhill he was deputy sheriff for a short time.

R. D. TUCKER came to Haverhill in 1880, and the year following he built the handsome Tucker house on South Main street. Before moving to Haverhill he was engaged in the manufactory of axletrees in Philadelphia, and previous to that he was superintendent of the New York & Flushing railroad. He was a man of thorough business habits, and was enterprising and public spirited. He died suddenly in 1883. His wife before her marriage to him was Mrs. Morris Locke of New York.

The influx of population at the extreme north-west corner of the Town, Woodsville, has chiefly taken place since the Boston, Concord & Montreal railroad was built to that point, and both population and valuation have rapidly increased within a few years. But as early as 1830 JOHN L. WOODS began the manufacture of lumber near the mouth of the Ammonoosuc, and carried on an extensive business for many years. He married Mary Nancy, daughter of Obadiah Swasey, and their son John L. (see Chap. XIX).

LUTHER BUTLER settled in this part of the Town about the same time. His early years were spent in Bath. He was a stone mason by trade, and worked on the Quincy market, Boston. He also built the Ammonoosuc bridge at Woodsville. He was a selectman and justice of the peace. His wife's maiden name was Abigail Chamberlain of Bath, and three of their children are living—Mrs. Maria Hibbard of Brooklyn, Iowa, and a son, George C., lives on the homestead. Mr. Butler died in 1885. The youngest daughter, Alice, married and lives in New Jersey.

CHARLES B. SMITH manufactured shovel handles for some years, when in 1878 his plant was carried away by a freshet. He gave the lot for the Episcopal church, and was postmaster from 1873 till 1880. A son, George F., is a railroad conductor.

JOHN L. DAVIS was one of the builders of the Mt. Washington railroad, and ran the first engine to the summit. He built the Mt. Gardner house and kept it for several years.

IRA WHITCHER came from Benton where he was a prominent man in business and in town matters. He was a representative for six years, county commissioner for a like term, and a member of the constitutional convention in 1851. He has been extensively engaged in the lumber business since he came to Woodsville, and has been a selectman. He married Lucy Royce, and of their four children a son (see Chap. XIX), and a daughter, Mrs. Chester Abbott of Woodsville. David Whitcher of North Haverhill, and Daniel Whitcher of Bath are brothers of Ira.

C. M. WEEKS came from Vermont about 1858, and took an active part in Town matters. He was a merchant; represented the Town in 1868–9, moderator a number of times, county treasurer in 1883. He was a man of much energy and force. He now lives in Lowell, Mass.

ENOCH G. PARKER came from Newbury, Vt., in 1873, and engaged in the hotel business. Mr. Parker is an energetic man, and was selectman and moderator. He now lives in Wells River, Vt.

Other active and enterprising men worthy of more extended notice have come into Woodsville from time to time, and have given impulse to the growth and business of the place.

EZRA B. MANN has been a representative. Came from Benton; druggist.

EDWARD F. MANN, brother of the above, now assistant superintendent of B. & L. R. R. Has been a state senator and represented Benton in the legislature; passenger conductor on B. C. & M. R. R. for twelve years.

GEORGE S. CUMMINGS came from Ashland, druggist. now the oldest male resident in the place.

JOSEPH P. KIMBALL, EZRA S. KIMBALL, GEORGE C. BUTLER, and HENRY F. KING were born in Town. Mr. Butler has a stock farm of high grade Durhams. Mr. Joseph P. Kimball has a large dairy of high grade Jerseys. Henry F. King is a wool grower, and has been selectman.

BENJAMIN DOW came from Lyman, dealer in live stock, stock breeder of cattle and Norman horses.

LANGDON BAILEY came from Lisbon, carriage maker.

GEORGE A. DAVISON whose sudden death recently has been such a sad loss to business and social circles, came from Sutton, Canada. He was station agent, and clerk and treasurer of Woodsville Water Co., a prominent Odd Fellow, and was district deputy for this portion of the state.

SAMUEL B. PAGE (see Chap. XVII).

GEORGE F. SMITH came from Belfast, Me., passenger conductor.

DAVID A. FRENCH came from Warren, teacher of music.

CHARLES R. GIBSON came from Alstead (see Chap. XVIII).

OLIVER D. EASTMAN came from Topsham, Vt. (see Chap. XVIII.)

CHESTER ABBOTT came from Bath; in Woodsville lumber company.

EDGAR B. MILLER came from Ryegate, Vt.; merchant.

SETH P. STICKNEY came from Lyman; merchant.

TRUMAN W. GLOVER came from Newbury, Vt.; merchant.

GEORGE EMERY came from Ashland; assistant postmaster.

ISAAC K. GEORGE came from Bristol; proprietor of Hotel Brunswick; formerly superintendent of county farm.

MELVIN J. MANN came from Benton; in employ of railroad for twelve years, passenger conductor for the last five years.

G. H. MANN in employ of railroad fifteen years, freight and passenger conductor for last twelve years.

WILL H. MOORE came from Northfield; one of the oldest engineers on the road.

GEORGE E. CUMMINGS, son of George S., passenger conductor on B. C. & M. R. R. for three years, wood agent two years, agent for White Mountain Division B. & L., and now train master at Woodsville.

D. L. HAWKINS came from Bath, leased the Parker House in company with S. E. Nutting, and kept it for two years. House is now owned by O. D. Johnson, and kept by Johnson & Hawkins.

A. H. LEIGHTON & Co.—Albert H. Leighton and Quincy A. Scott. Mr. Leighton came from Bath; Mr. Scott was conductor on Passumpsic railroad, rose from train boy. Firm established 1875. With the exception of the drug store, the oldest store in the village. Mr. Scott also manufactures society uniforms and regalias.

The population of Woodsville is mostly composed of young and middle-aged persons, wide-awake and full of push, who have given to the place its live and energetic character, and placed it on the highway of still greater prosperity. And with the splendid water-power at this point, which is unlimited, and the fine railroad facilities, few places in New England are more hopeful of becoming great manufacturing centers than Woodsville. Her citizens are well deserving the gratifying success which has followed their enterprise and public spirit.

CHAPTER VIII.

TOWN AND PROPRIETORS' RECORDS FROM 1763 TO 1800.

First Town and Proprietors' Meeting—First Town Officers—Committee of Survey—Laying out of Lots—Drawing Lots—First Annual Town Meeting—First full List of Town Officers—Town Expenses—Pound—Wages for Town Work—Record Book—Danger of Wild Animals—Small Town Expenses—First Treasurer—Deer Reaves—Grant of Mill Privilege—Taxes Abated—Care of Imbecile—Census—Burial Places—Law suit—Town Meeting Places—Waif—First Town-order for Aid—Legal Tenders—First Vote for Congressman and Presidential Electors—First Representative—First Vote for Governor and State Senator—Troublesome Persons—Special Choice of Selectmen—Question of Conscience—Traveling on the Sabbath—Small Pox—Old Debt—Care of Poor.

The first Town meeting was to be held on the second Tuesday of June, which as we learn from the Proprietors' Records was June 13th. This date was fixed by the charter which also directed that the meeting was to be "notified by Capt. John Hazen" who likewise was appointed to be its moderator. From the Proprietors' Records it appears that a Proprietors' meeting was held at the same time and place. This meeting like the Town meeting was appointed by the charter, and was also to be "notified" and presided over by Capt. John Hazen. The Proprietors chose Town officers as follows:—Jesse Johnson, clerk; Stephen Knight, constable; and Capt. John White, James Bailey, Esq., and Maj. Edmund Morse, selectmen. The only other business which was transacted at this meeting was the choice of a committee "fully authorized" to "bound out" the Town, and "lay out one lot to each proprietor's share in the interval, and one other lot of upland, so as to commode [accommodate] the settlers." This committee consisted of Capt. John Hazen, John White, James Bailey, Esq., Robert Peasley and Benjamin Morse, and they were directed to enter upon their duty at once after the town of Newbury was laid out." From this it may be inferred that the committee had something to do with laying out Newbury as well as Haverhill, which was quite likely the fact, as the two leading spirits in securing the charters of these towns were Capt. Hazen and Gen. Bailey, and a number of the proprietors of both towns were the same. Accordingly the same committee and surveyor would answer for both towns. At a subsequent meeting the committee made their report which was accepted by the Proprietors, and we learn that William Whiting who seems to have been the surveyor, was voted "4 shillings per day for his services in laying out the Town of Haverhill in Cowass." [Cohos.]

The Proprietors subsequently appointed a committee whose duty it was "to lay out 100 acre lots to each right," and also another committee for the purpose of drawing these lots. During the next few months there seems to have been some difficulty in transacting the business of the meeting, as repeated adjournments took place, and the records close with these despairing words,—"At which time [Jan. 1764] said meeting was dropped without any further transaction ever done at said meeting." The drawing as we learn from a subsequent record was not finished at the meeting when the clerk entered the above note of despair, but was completed afterwards, since we find in the records a "list of the Proprietors of Haverhill with the number of their house and meadow lots annexed to each proprietor's name, as said lots were drawn at the several Proprietors' meetings of the said Town of Haverhill."

The annual meeting of the Town as well as the first meeting was also fixed by the charter, and was directed to be held on the second Tuesday in March. The first annual meeting of which any record is made, was held March 13, 1764, in Plaistow at the house of John Hall, inn-holder. James Bailey was chosen moderator, after which it was adjourned to "Haverhill at Cohos, to the house of John Taplin to June 13." Of this June meeting no record is preserved.

The first full list of Town officers, of which any record is found, was chosen at the annual meeting in 1765. These fathers of the Town government were as follows,—moderator, Elisha Lock; clerk, John Hazen; selectmen, John Hazen, Elisha Lock and Jonathan Elkins; constable, Edward Bailey; surveyors of high-ways, James Woodward, Joshua Hayward; fence-surveyor, Jonathan Sanders; hogreave, Uriah Morse; tithing-man, Jonathan Goodwin. According to this list it would seem that the Jonathans were a popular class in the infant settlement of the Town.

The Town records inform us that in 1766 £10 was voted for Town expenses. This was the first appropriation of money by the Town, except that which was voted for preaching the previous year. It was also ordered that a "pound" be built, and John Ladd had the honor of heading the long list of pound-keepers for the little Republic. The location of this pound was most likely at the "Plain," as afterward, 1793, the Town voted that two pounds be built, one "at the North end at Col. Howard's," near where the County Poor House now stands, and the other "at the South end on land owned by Moody Bedel, in the corner where the road leads to Maj. Joshua Young's." This road turned off just south of the Eliza Cross house, and led to where Peter Flanders now lives. The present pound opposite the residence of James Woodward was built in 1802. Also at this meeting it was voted that "all labor done for the Town should be at fifty cents per day."

In the following year a book of records for the Town was bought, which fact may account for the imperfect condition of the records in the first and second years of the Town's organization.

The exposed condition of the settlement is indicated by the fact that in 1769 an article was put in the warrant to see if the Town would provide a "stock of ammunition." It was also voted at the same time that "20 shillings be paid for each wolf-head catched or killed." These bounties in the interest of protection against wolves were frequently renewed in subsequent years, as well as bounties against other wild depredatory animals.

In 1770 the amount of money voted for Town expenses was £6, and in the following year the first treasurer was chosen, and James Bailey had the honor of being entrusted as treasurer with the keeping and the disbursing the Town's funds. Previous to this time the selectmen discharged the duties of that office.

Our fathers seem to have grown economical as the early years rolled on; for in 1772 only £4 were voted for town expenses. This small sum was doubtless for the ordinary charges of the Town, perhaps mainly expended for the salaries of officers. The selectmen received for their duties and responsibilities three shillings per day.

In the following year a new office was created, demanded it would seem by a new emergency. The occupant was styled a "deer-reave." When the country was first settled deer were found in great abundance, and were the most valuable of all the wild animals of the forest. Being killed in large numbers by the settlers it became necessary to protect them against an indiscriminate slaughter that threatened their early extinction. In Massachusetts before the close of the seventeenth century it was unlawful to kill deer between January 1st and August 1st. For this reason an officer was chosen whose duty it was to inform against those who killed deer out of season. The first mention of this officer in the records of Haverhill is found as above, and was designed for the protection of deer. This year, also, the one hundred acre lot reserved on Hazen (Poole) brook was given to John Fisher for a mill privilege, if he would "saw for the proprietors for one-half."

Taxes were abated in certain cases as early as 1771, and in the same year the Town was asked to see what it would do in reference to David Swain, who is described as "non compos mentis." What the Town did for the unfortunate David does not appear. Also in this year Edward Bailey was voted "3 shillings for one day in numbering the people in 1767." The population at that time is given on page 57 in foot note.

As early as 1774 the burial of the dead was cared for by the Town, and two places for this purpose were set apart in that year for public use. Also a "burial cloth" was provided at the public expense. Private corporations were as yet unknown in the infant settlement. One of these burial places is the present cemetery at Ladd street, the other the old graveyard at Horse meadow.

The first ordained and settled minister in the Town, as was the custom in those times, was granted by the charter a "right of land." From the records it would seem that this "right" was brought into controversy. One "Ranna Cossit"—the name looks as if he thought he ought to be the Town cosset—seems to have been the person who wished to disturb the minister's right of glebe, and the authority of the Town was interposed to defeat his unfriendly purposes: for in 1775 it was voted to defend the "minister's right of land" against the said "Ranna Cossit." It would seem from a document entitled "Haverhill and Newbury Covenant," dated January 28, 1775, that Cols. John Hurd and Asa Porter were the instigators of this plot, and were accordingly censured by their fellow citizens as "acting contrary to the society of Haverhill and Newbury," in trying to foist an Episcopal minister upon the community, and claiming for him the "right of glebe," when they knew that Rev. Peter Powers had been an ordained clergyman for a number of years. The affair stirred the community to its very depth, and in the "covenant" Cols. Hurd and Porter were declared to be "public enemies to the good of the community." The signers of this "covenant" "carried the war into Africa," and pledged themselves "not to have any communication with either of them, not so much as to trade, lend, borrow, or labor with them ;" and further, that they would "not hold any correspondence, nor have any dealings with any that hold with Cols. Hurd and Porter, until they shall willingly make public satisfaction for what they have done in the premises." Evidently the boycott was abroad in those days.

In early times the meetings both of the Town and of the Proprietors were held either at private houses or at innholders. The records of 1776 speak of a meeting which was adjourned to the "state house." This "state house" was the court house which was built a few years before.

About this time a child of Susanna Hadley was a constant care of the Town, and finally ten shillings were paid for a sort of "underground railroad" service in regard to said child.

In 1786 the Town voted unanimously to emit a paper currency as follows :

"That one hundred thousand pounds be emitted,—twenty thousand pounds to be in suitable bills to defray the charges of government, and to exchange for such public securities as may be offered at their current exchange, which is to be ascertained, and to carry no interest but to be receivable in taxes and all demands of government and a tender in all cases equal to silver and gold, and to be called in by taxes annually,—the residue to be made in different bills expressing their import, and to be loaned to individuals at five per cent. on landed security of double the value, and to be paid into the treasury at proper times, which shall carry an interest of two and a half per cent., and so receivable in all demands of government and a tender in all cases as above—with the interest due on said bills at the time of payment."

The action of the Town, with similar action in other towns, being brought before the legislature, it was voted that there was no authority to "make paper bills of credit a tender to discharge private contracts made prior to the passing such act." And thus this earlier "greenback" scheme to pay debts with irredeemable paper came to a sudden end.

The Town cast its first vote for congressmen and presidential electors in 1787. Moses Dow, a prominent lawyer and distinguished citizen of Haverhill, was one of the persons voted for for congressman, and received the vote of Haverhill. This vote was a sort of popular nomination, and from the list of persons voted for, the legislature chose the three persons who had the largest popular vote in the state as the representatives to Congress. Previous to this, in 1784, the legislature had appointed Mr. Dow a congressman, but he declined the honor for reasons chiefly which do not now burden men's minds.

At a special meeting in 1783 the Town voted to send its first representative to the General Court. The person who received the honor of the first appointment to that office by the suffrages of his fellow townsmen was James Woodward, a prominent and worthy citizen, and the qualifications of the person who should be decreed fit to be chosen for this position were set forth in the warrant as follows : " A reputable freeholder and an inhabitant of said Town, and qualified as the law directs to represent said Town in the general assembly of said state." Our forefathers had no friendly side for political tramps. They believed in the "best," and evidently thought that a man who could not or would not become a property holder was not a suitable person to have the care of the commonwealth. They were sound statesmen and true patriots, who did not believe in committing the infant state to the nursing of doubtful persons. Also in this year the Town cast its first vote for governor and state senator, and Moses Dow received the vote of the Town for the latter office.

In 1783 the warning of a special meeting had this article : " To pass some votes as said inhabitants [Town] shall see fit concerning tories, absentees, or persons who had left the United States of America, and voluntarily taken residence within the lines of the enemies of said United States, and have returned or may return into this Town." And a committee was appointed to execute this article, viz., "That no such persons be suffered to reside in this Town." Some of these persons it would seem returned after the war was over to their homes, since the Town directed the constable to warn sundry persons that they must "leave their country for their country's good," under the pains and penalties of the law "in such case made and provided."

At a later period the Town seems again to have been troubled with persons whose presence was not as agreeable as their room, and the records tell of two votes, one of thirteen shillings to Capt. Ephraim Wesson for warning thirteen of these unwelcome people out of Town, and another of twenty-seven shillings for warning twenty-seven others of the same character.

Also in the year after, the following episode garnishes the Town records: It was the first marriage in Town by a magistrate, and the parties were Joseph Clowd and Nancy Frazier. Those were the days of "publishments," and Joseph and Nancy were unfortunate, as their publishment was torn down, and the record is marked "void." So Joseph and Nancy had to put off and be "put up" again, before "they twain" could be made "one."

The selectmen were chosen at a special meeting in 1790, for what reason does not appear, and in the year following a question of conscience appears upon the records in a vote to excuse the selectmen from taking the oath of office "so far as it respects the Sabbath act." The act referred to here required the selectmen to inform against all persons who traveled on the Sabbath between sun-rising and sun-setting, except to "attend to public worship, visit the sick, or do works of charity." This law was vigorously enforced, and many persons, it is said, who were found traveling on the Sacred day, were compelled by the vigilant tything-man to "lie to." Capt. John Page once spent a quiet day in Warren at the invitation of one James Dow who was very jealous for the observance of the Sabbath. After paying fines and costs the next day he was allowed to go home in peace.

Another article at this meeting, 1791, read.—"To see if the Town would consent to have the small-pox in said Town by way of inoculation," which however was rejected at first. Was it under the impression that the Town preferred not to have the small-pox at all? But afterwards this vote was reversed, and the Town took its small-pox homeopathically.

In the interest of patriotism a long-standing debt was discharged in 1798. In that year the Town voted to pay Capt. Ebenezer Sanborn $10 for "fetching two hundred pounds of balls, fifty pounds of powder and a quantity of flint from Exeter." This service was rendered in 1775. A vote was also passed to take care of the poor as the law directs. This was a vote to enforce the law which allowed towns to have "houses of correction or work-houses in which to set their poor to work;" and towns were also empowered to use these for the "keeping, correcting, and setting to work of rogues, vagabonds, common beggars, lewd, idle and disorderly persons."

CHAPTER IX.

TOWN RECORDS FROM 1800 TO 1886.

Town in Relation to Condition of Country—War of 1812—Bounties for Soldiers—Small-pox—School Trouble—Town Farm—Town House—Fire Proof Vault—War of the Rebellion—Money Voted for Soldiers' Families—Bounties—Sum Total of Money Voted during the War for War Purposes—Funded Debt—Duty of Town to Needy Soldiers—Monument—Party Struggles—Character of Early Officers—A Memorable Contest—Improved Order.

Already as early as 1809 "coming events were casting their shadows before," and we find the Town, through a committee appointed for the purpose, expressing its feeling in regard to the condition of the country. This committee declared that the country was in a "truly interesting and alarming condition," and called upon the government to abandon its policy in regard to the "embargo laws."

At a town meeting in 1812 the question of bounties for drafted soldiers was considered, and a motion to vote such bounties was defeated by a very decided majority. At the same time resolutions were passed condemning the national authorities on account of the war. A strong "states rights" doctrine was assumed, and it is very evident that the "peace party" of that day was largely in the ascendant in our goodly Town. This meeting declared the War of 1812 to be "unnecessary and impolitic," and expressed a willingness to join other towns in convention to secure the rights of the people. A convention for this purpose was to be held at Orford, and Joseph Bell, George Woodward, and John Smith were appointed delegates to represent Haverhill in that convention. Feeling ran high, and not only was the petition for giving soldiers of the War of 1812 additional bounty to that which was offered by the general government promptly voted down by the "peace party," but also a proposition to allow militia men compensation for powder and ball expended by them, was rejected by an equally decisive vote. The Town was thoroughly in the hands of the Federalists.

In 1822 the Town was afflicted with the small-pox, and Dr. Simeon Woodward engaged to vaccinate the inhabitants of the Town for thirty dollars, provided they would assemble for that purpose as far as possible in the school houses. The disease seems to have raged with much force and destruction, as a committee appointed at that time in regard to the matter reported one hundred sixty-nine dollars "expense incurred" in meeting this enemy of the people.

In this same year we have revealed the school troubles of Mr. William Ladd, who was a resident of district No. 7, but who wanted to get into district No. 8. The people of No. 8, however, voted in the negative "almost unanimously," and gave as their reason that when said Ladd was in No. 8, the district was kept in "constant broil and discord," and when he was disannexed to No. 7, "harmony and unanimity prevailed." But the Town took compassion on Mr. Ladd, and allowed him the opportunity of keeping No. 8 in "constant broil and discord," on condition of the payment of fifteen dollars.

The matter of a poor-farm first came up in town meeting in 1831, but nothing definite was done till 1838, when a committee was appointed to consider the question of buying a poor-farm. Subsequently a poor-farm was purchased, and was held by the Town till the county system was adopted in 1868. This farm was the David Merrill farm, situated north of Poole brook west of the river road bridge which spans that brook.

In 1848 a committee of five was appointed to consider the "cost and expediency" of building a town house. Up to that time town meetings were held at hotels or in churches at the north and south ends of the Town. This committee reported at a subsequent meeting, and fifteen hundred dollars was voted for a town house. The place of location was to be near the Union church, and a committee was appointed to select a site, John R. Reding being chairman of this committee. The house was occupied the first time in 1851. The building committee greatly exceeded the amount of money appropriated for the town house, and there was a disposition on the part of the Town not to accept the building. The matter, however, was finally adjusted by arbitration, John R. Reding acting as agent for the Town. Another account of this affair is that pending the settlement of the dispute between the Town and the builders, the selectmen, without thinking of or knowing the consequences of their action, posted a warrant for a town meeting on the door of the town house, and called the meeting at that place. This action of the selectmen was a tacit acceptance of the building at the hands of the committee, and made the Town liable for its cost. This house was a large stone building at the centre of the Town a little south of the Union church, and was used for town purposes till 1883, when it was voted to build a new town house at North Haverhill in order to accommodate the citizens of the Town more conveniently. This last building is a wood structure, neatly and well built, and answers the purposes of the Town very well, though a more commodious edifice built of permanent material, with a fire-proof vault, and of public architectural character, would have been more in keeping with the wealth and standing of the Town. The present building cost about two thousand dollars. They also at a subsequent meeting voted twelve hundred dollars for a vault to keep the records in, and which has since been built.

The War of the Rebellion laid upon the Town heavy burdens in men and money. The first money appropriated for war purposes was five hundred for soldiers' families; this was in 1861. In the following year eight thousand dollars was voted for bounties. There were two votes of money for bounties in 1863, one of ten thousand dollars and the other of fourteen thousand dollars. The large sums voted in the year following for the enlistment of soldiers, shows how reluctant those were who were liable to do military duty, to respond to the country's call without the stimulus of tempting bounties, for in this year the extraordinary sum of forty-five thousand dollars was voted for this purpose, making a total during the four years of the war for bounties and soldiers' families of seventy-seven thousand nine hundred dollars. In 1864 the Town voted to fund the floating debt in a sum not exceeding twenty thousand dollars. The entire debt of the Town, or sixty-five thousand dollars of it, was funded to be paid in five, ten, fifteen, and twenty years, and a sinking fund was provided to meet these obligations at maturity. The first payment of the funded debt was in 1875, the next 1880, and the third in 1885. The debt reached its highest figures in 1870, and the Town was entirely free from debt in 1885.

In the trying struggle of the nation for integrity and preservation, the Town pursued a patriotic and liberal policy. She furnished her full quota of troops at every call, and spared no means to put her sons into the field. Those who went forth to danger, hardship, and death, have been gratefully remembered by the Town, and the stigma should never rest upon her fair fame that any of those who periled their lives for the nation, should ever through old age or infirmity be allowed to come to want. The Town also owes it to herself—may I be permitted to make the suggestion—to erect a soldiers' monument at some commanding point, on which should be inscribed the names of all soldiers who fought for their country from the War of the Revolution to the War for the Union inclusive. The sum of twenty-five hundred or three thousand dollars for such a monument would perpetuate to coming generations the memory and deeds not only of those who won our liberties, but also of those who were the preservers of our goodly heritage. The time of the dedication of such a monument might be fitly made the occasion of a grand gathering of the sons and daughters of the Town from far and near, a revival of patriotic feeling and fraternal good-will amongst all her citizens, and a deeper sense of the obligation of each one to the good of the country. Such an event would be an honor to her historic record and her noble founders.

In all these years there have been some quite warm contests when party feeling ran high and when good neighborly relationships were at times strained; but generally these earnest contests for political supremacy were waged in good part, and when they were over they left little or no rankling behind. The Town has been held in turn by Jeffersonian Republicans, Federalists, Whigs, Democrats, Republicans, and in the main has been well managed in its public affairs. In the earlier history of the Town men of unquestioned character and ability were as a rule called to official trust and position; but a change has come in, and now there is danger that almost every one is tempted to think himself qualified to manage the concerns of the Town. As a consequence incompetency and assurance sometimes take the place of merit and capacity for public affairs.

A long contest in town meeting occurred in 1879. It was chiefly for political control, and some warm blood was stirred up on this occasion. This was the time when the Greenbackers came into existence, and although not very numerous they were still strong enough to hold the balance of power in many places. This was the case in Haverhill, and as a consequence they made terms for the offices to suit themselves. Over these the contest was waged for six successive days before the matter was ended. This contest served the occasion for some smart and spicy speaking, and it was said that "soiled linen" was freely aired. But the struggle ended in good nature, and soon passed out of the minds of most. "All's well that ends well."

To the honor and good name of the Town it ought to be said that greater order and quiet has prevailed in later years in town meeting than in former times. This is no more than is due the time and place when every citizen is called upon to exercise his highest and most sacred privilege and trust.

CHAPTER X.

HAVERHILL IN THE REVOLUTION.

Prominence in the Revolution—Geographical Position—Able Leaders—Compact—Cohos well known to Enemy—Col. Johnston's Letter—Forts in the Upper Cohos—Rangers at Haverhill—Haverhill the Rendezvous for Troops and Scouting Parties—Character of the Ranger—Haverhill in constant Communication with Exeter and the Northern Army—Col. Wyman's Regiment—Four Stockades—Alarm from Indians in 1776—Retreat of our Army from St. Johns—Great consternation at Cohos—A Second Alarm in 1777—Again after the fall of Ticonderoga—Military Road from Cohos to St. Johns—"Block Houses"—The Alarm of 1780—Town Authorities wide-awake—Frequent votes of Powder, Lead and Fire-arms—Efficient Committee of Safety Men—Conferences with other Towns—Vigilant eyes on Home-enemies—The Conspiracy of Col. Porter and others—Strong feeling—Persons who were obnoxious to the British—Rev. Peter Powers—Col. Johnson captured—Gen. Bailey's Escape—Dea. Elkins' Alarm—Quotas of Beef and Flour—Transportation of Grain from Cohos prohibited—Money. Patriots—Disastrous effects of the War—Rapid increase of Town Expenses—Sale of Rights—Decrease of Population during the War.

In the stirring events of the Revolution Haverhill took a conspicuous part. Her citizens were generally full of patriotic zeal and enthusiasm for the cause of freedom, and responded with promptness and brave hearts to the calls of their country. Some of the most eminent citizens held honorable rank in the patriot army. Her prominence in the great struggle for independence was due to several causes; partly on account of the geographical position of the Town, and partly also to the fact that amongst her citizens were those who had taken active part in the French and Indian War, and being men of ability and character they were especially well qualified to assume important parts in the new drama that was opening. Then, too, being the most populous town north of No. 4, she was able to send a large quota into the service of the country.

By the kindness of Gen. A. Harleigh Hill, who wrote the history of Groton, Vt., I give the following document which presents in a very vivid light the war-like atmosphere that prevailed in Haverhill and in the neighboring towns at the beginning of the Revolution, and which extended through to the close of that struggle:

HAVERHILL, May 2d, 1775.

We, the subscribers, do solemnly declare by all the sacred ties of honor and religion, that we will act at all times against all illegal and unconstitutional impositions and acts of Parliament, made and enacted against the New England governments and the continent of English North America. And we do believe that shutting up the port of Boston, Quebec bill, and sundry other bills and acts, to be illegal and unconstitutional, and also the declaration wherein the New England governments are declared in a state of rebellion, etc., are unconstitutional and unjust; and we do engage to stand in opposition to all force come or coming against us, by order of the present ministry, for supporting of the present measures, while our *lives* and *fortunes* last, or until those notorious unconstitutional acts are repealed and the American Colonies re-established in the privileges due to them as English subjects.

At a meeting of the committee of the several towns, Voted for Lime [Lyme], Lieut. Charles Nelson; from Orford, Daniel Tilleston, Esq.; from Piermont, Lieut. Jona. Chandler, Lieut. John Weed; from Haverhill, James Bayley, Simeon Goodwin, Timo. Brown [Barron?], and Charles Johnston; from Bath, Timothy Bedel, Esq., Capt. Oliver Sanders, William Eastman; from Gunthwen [Lisbon], Mr. John Young; from Lancaster, Capt. Edward Bucknam; from Northumberland, Joseph Peverly, Esq. Convened at the house of Lieut. Joseph Hutchins, inn-holder of Haverhill, on Tuesday, the 2d day of May instant, passed the following votes:

First—Chose Timo. Bedel chairman.

Second—Chose Charles Johnston clerk.

Voted: Daniel Tilleston, Ebenezer Green, and Lieut. Charles Nelson, be a committee for Lime [Lyme] and Orford, to send men to Canada if need be.

Voted: Lieut. Jonathan Chandler, Lieut. John Weed, Lieut. Joseph Hutchins, Lieut. Ezekiel Ladd, and Charles Johnston, to be a committee to send a scouting party to Canada, or elsewhere, as they shall think proper.

Voted: Captain Oliver Sanders, Mr. Nathaniel Hovey, Mr. John Young, Capt. Edward Bucknam, Joseph Peverly, Esq., be a committee to send scouting party to Canada or elsewhere as they shall think proper.

Voted: That the several towns in this county, within this regiment, shall choose their officers, namely: captain, lieutenant and ensign, annually.

Chose Timothy Bedel to be colonel of this regiment.

Chose Charles Johnston to be lieutenant-colonel.
Chose Jonathan Childs 1st major.
Chose James Bayley 2d major.
Chose Simeon Goodwin adjutant.
Chose John Young quartermaster.
Chose Samuel Hale, Esq., to be the surgeon of the regiment.
Voted: To adjourn this meeting until to-morrow morning at eight o'clock.
Met on [according to] adjournment at time and place.
Voted: That the officers that shall be [appointed] by the several towns, see that their respective companies be equipped with arms and ammunition as soon as may be.
Voted: That the committee from the several towns are empowered to call the company together in those towns where there are no officers, in order for the choice of officers.
Voted: That this committee do adjudge it absolutely necessary as representatives for each particular town, that each and every person, belonging to our said towns do put themselves under command, and submit themselves unto such commanding officers as is and shall be chosen by this committee, and each particular town.
Voted: That a true copy of the proceedings of this committee be transmitted by the clerk of this committee unto the honorable committee appointed by the Provincial congress to be convened at Exeter on the seventeenth day of May, instant.
Voted: That Ezekiel Ladd be a delegate to represent this committee in the Provincial congress.
Voted: To adjourn the meeting unto the first Tuesday in June next, unless the chairman think it necessary to meet before.

         CHARLES JOHNSTON, *Clerk.*

The Cohos Country was well known to the enemy through the French War, and being, as it were, the door-way of entrance from the north to eastern New England, Haverhill was constantly in danger of being attacked by forces from Canada. The importance, therefore, of holding the Cohos Country was early seen, and was set forth in a letter from Col. Charles Johnston to the New Hampshire congress, June, 1775: "Now, gentlemen, as to the situation of these parts, how near the borders of the enemy we are, everyone knows who is acquainted with the boundaries of our own Province. As to the position of defence, we are in want of both arms and ammunition, and have not a sufficient number of men to defend our frontiers without some assistance from the lower towns." The committee of safety at Exeter at once directed Col. Bedel to proceed to Upper Cohos and "erect a garrison" at Northumberland, and to "assist in building garrisons in such other places on the frontier as you [he] shall judge most necessary."

On this account troops known as rangers were early stationed at Haverhill and in the Upper Cohos, also at Newbury, and Moretown [Bradford], Vt., to keep a sharp lookout toward the north and west. At one time two hundred and fifty troops were ordered to Newbury. Col. Bedel was in command of the first company of rangers in this section in 1775, and from that time on to the close of the war Haverhill was made a rendezvous of troops.

In 1776 the Provincial congress at Exeter voted "that there be but one place of rendezvous in this [New Hampshire] colony for the troops destined to Canada, and that it be at Haverhill on the Connecticut river." And in the same year Col. John Hurd "was authorized to fix off all the companies from Cohos [Haverhill] with ten days' provisions."

Accordingly, from here scouting parties were constantly sent out towards St. Johns and Lake Champlain to ascertain the number and position of the enemy, and they often brought in spies and deserters in their long and swift marches.

These scouting parties or rangers were composed of men of great daring and bravery, who shunned no danger if need be, and declined no service however perilous and exacting. They adopted the Indian mode of warfare, and were trained to wonderfully quick marches and secret movements. It was their duty to ascertain the condition and intentions of the enemy, and watch his motions. They hung upon his skirts and harrassed his scouts, lying in ambush for days along Indian trails to administer to the savages in the enemy's service the same cruel warfare which these savages employed. They swam swollen streams, crept stealthily through tangled undergrowth, scaled rugged mountains, and waded through dangerous swamps, in order to accomplish their purpose.

Haverhill, through her committee of safety was in daily communication with the Provincial congress at Exeter and the patriot army acting against Canada. The Town was more or less in constant alarm from invasion from Canada. In June, 1776, a regiment under command of Col. Isaac Wyman of Keene was ordered to rendezvous "at Haverhill on the Connecticut." Four stockade forts were built in 1776 to secure the people against sudden attacks. Two of these were at the Corner, and two at the "Plain." One at the Corner was built around the Col. Johnston place, and the other was on Ladd street. On one occasion during this year the people north of Haverhill were gathered into these stockades in fear of an attack from the Indians. There was also about the same time great alarm from an anticipated invasion from Canada after our army retreated from St. Johns. The committees of safety of Haverhill and Newbury sent messengers to headquarters in Massachusetts and New Hampshire to inform the authorities of the dangerous situation these parts were in, and unless immediately supported, the inhabitants would be compelled to abandon this door-way to Canada. Arms and ammunition were loudly called for, and the utmost anxiety prevailed for the safety of Cohos.

In March, 1777, Cohos was threatened a second time by an Indian invasion, and Col. Bedel was ordered by Gen. Schuyler to Haverhill to observe their motions, and get what intelligence he could about affairs in Canada. Through a scout sent to St. Francis it was learned that a large body of Indians had engaged with the British troops, and that it was thought an early attack would be made upon Cohos. Col. Bedel asked for immediate assistance in order to guard this section from devastation.

In the same year, after the fall of Ticonderoga, the Cohos Country was again thrown into the greatest consternation, and was hourly expecting an attack from the victorious enemy. Col. Hurd wrote from Haverhill, July 21, 1777, to Gov. Weare at Exeter:—" Now we may most surely expect a visit from the enemy;" and Gen. Bailey, of same date, says:—" Sundry expresses have arrived from Windsor informing of the enemies passing toward No. 4 and Cohos."

In order to facilitate the easy and rapid movement of troops from Haverhill in the direction of St. Johns, whilst our army was operating against Canada, a military road was begun from the Cohos Country and was built as far as Peacham, Vt., and various points on the line were garrisoned. The forts were called "block houses," and were safe against an enemy carrying only small arms. This road was begun by Gen. Bailey in 1776, and was intended to extend to St. Johns, but after the surrender of Burgoyne the war was transferred chiefly to the South. Afterwards, in 1779, the road was completed by Col. Moses Hazen to Montgomery, Vt., about fifty miles beyond Peacham, and the gap in the Green Mountains through which it passed is called Hazen's Gap, and the road was known by his name. Col. Hazen's regiment was stationed along this road, and the principal points were Haverhill and Peacham.

In 1780 there was again general alarm in regard to the safety of the Cohos Country. A committee was called at Dresden [Dartmouth College] to "consult what is best to be done for the protection of these frontiers." Gen. Bailey of Newbury wrote to Gov. Weare of New Hampshire that the British forces were strongly posted at Crown Point and on Onion river, and an immediate attack on Cohos was expected. "I wish," he writes, "you would give orders that the mightiest regiment in your state [would] come, so one [we] might be in readiness." And again later:—" This frontier is the only one for five hundred miles west remaining [exposed]. It is near the enemy. It is of great importance to you [New Hampshire], and the other New England states."

The Town records during this period show that the authorities and the people were wide-awake to the urgent demands of the hour. Frequent votes are found for powder, lead and fire-arms for the purpose of arming the people and furnishing them with the means of defense. The spirit of the camp breathes all through these records from the beginning of the war till its close. As early as 1774 £20 were voted for ammunition for Town protection; and at a special meeting in the following year it was voted that a committee be chosen "to see that all the results of the Continental Congress are duly observed in said Town [Haverhill]." It was also voted to appropriate £10 to Capt. Ebenezer Sanborn for "fetching 200 pounds of ball and 50 pounds of powder and a quantity of flint from Exeter." Other appropriations of money were made from time to time for "fetching up ammunition for the Town," for "running 90 weight of lead," for "gunpowder for the Town," for "the payment of scouting parties and for furnishing horses for the use of the same." The Town also voted supplies to the families of those who were serving in the army.

Various sums of money, too, were paid to the Town by order of the "Provincial Congress" for supplies of ammunition and provisions to the troops stationed at Haverhill. In 1781 Timothy Barron received certain moneys for troops, £49 for beef; and in the same year Col. Johnston was paid £363 for beef. In 1782 100 pounds powder, 200 pounds balls, 300 flints and 825 pounds beef were furnished soldiers at Haverhill.

During all this time energetic and able men were appointed a committee of safety for the Town, whose duty it was to communicate with the provincial committee of safety at Exeter. Also special conferences were appointed to devise ways and means for the defence of the frontier.

In 1777 the Town "chose a committee to meet a committee of the several towns at Lebanon." The object of this meeting we learn in a subsequent town meeting, when 33 shillings were voted to Capt. Wesson, James Bailey and Dea. Abbott for the journey to Lebanon to "converse with a committee sent by the General Court." The town committee of safety had the general direction of the scouting parties, and to this committee the scouts reported on their return from their beats. Here were sent arms and ammunition for distribution to the troops coming and going.

Our forefathers in these stirring times were also vigilant in regard to those whose sympathies were with the mother country. We read of votes in town meeting of £9 to Daniel Stevens for "committing Edward Picket to jail as an enemy to his country, and of £5 for "warning five persons out of Town." Some of the leading men of the Town were in a conspiracy to betray the Cohos Country to the enemy. Col. Hurd, Aug. 7, 1776, writes to Gov. Weare:—"In my last I hinted to you that we had our eyes upon those persons who were propagating the notion of the expediency of sending into Canada for protection." The leading persons in this plot were Col. Porter, Col. Taplin of Newbury, Jacob Weeks of Bath, and Jacob Fowler of Newbury. The plan was divulged by a young Indian hunter, and Col. Porter was secured and sent to Exeter for trial. It would seem that the plot was known to the enemy in New York, and those in Haverhill and vicinity who were in the conspiracy were in communication with persons in New York, and were only waiting for news from that point to make the strike. The party which was to go to Canada was to set out "under the pretence of moose hunting," and they were to guide Burgoyne and his troops into the Cohos Country, and aid him in taking possession of it.

The feeling between this class and the patriots ran very high, so that neighbors would not speak with each other. In a letter to the committee of safety at Exeter, 1777, the conspirators were referred to in this vigorous language: "We are entirely laid open to the sudden attack of our British and savage enemy, and the more infernal race of enemies amongst ourselves, who are secretly and unweariedly plotting our destruction."

There were those in Haverhill and Newbury who had become especially obnoxious to the British authorities on account of their loyalty to the patriot cause. Rev. Peter Powers, who came early from the Vermont side of the river to Haverhill for safety, and Col. Johnson, who had taken an active and prominent part in the struggle, were in constant danger of their lives. Col. Johnson was captured in 1781 and carried to Canada, and Gen. Bailey a year later only escaped capture by a timely warning, and by crossing the river to Haverhill, which on account of its position east of the river, was less exposed to sudden attacks of scouting parties from Canada.* Col. Johnson was captured at Peacham, Vt., in the house of Dea. Elkins, and after the scouting

---

* A British and Indian scout had come into the neighborhood for the purpose of capturing Gen. Bailey, and were lying in ambush upon the heights back of Newbury. Col. Johnson, who was captured the year before, was now at home on parole, and according to the conditions of his parole he was under the directions of the British officers. The officer in command of the scouting party signaled Col. Johnson to come to their hiding place, which he did, and he was informed of their intention to capture Gen. Bailey in the evening. Johnson was in great perplexity about his friend, but at last resolved to inform Gen. Bailey of his danger. He wrote on a slip of paper: "The Philistines be upon thee, Sampson," and gave it to a trusty person who was to cross the meadow where Gen. Bailey was plowing, drop the slip as he passed near the General, and go on to the river. When Gen. Bailey came to the slip he carelessly picked it up and read it, and then plowing around once or twice, said to his boys, "Take care of yourselves," whilst he crossed the river to Haverhill. The attack was made that night.

party had carried him to their camp. Dea. Elkins sent an alarm to Gen. Bailey and to the inhabitants of Cohos that the British and Indians were on their way to the Connecticut river, and were threatening to burn the settlement at Cohos. I copy Dea. Elkins' letter, the original of which is in the possession of the "Historical Society of Vermont," and was found amongst Gov. Weare's papers in 1843. The Johnson mentioned in the letter was Col. Thomas Johnson of Newbury, and must not be confounded with Col. Charles Johnston of Haverhill:

PEACHAM, 9 March, 1781.

SIR:—We were surprised yesterday morning, about three hours before day, by four Tories; the officer's name was Patterson: one was Smith, and two Crosses, who came in when we were all in a sound sleep; had Daniel Davis for a guide. They called us all up, and told us we were their prisoners, and ordered lines to bind us, but did not. They took Mr. Johnson, Mr. Page and my two sons. They told me they had burnt the upper block house, and that they had four or five hundred at the lower block house and at Mr. Davis', and that there was another party at Onion River, fifteen hundred in the whole, and that Cohos would be burnt the night following; and that the road between my house and Cohos was waylaid, and that Mr. Bailey's fort had surrendered, and that I must keep clear or else myself and family would be killed by the savages. Daniel Davis said that both their houses were full of men, and a great number of Indians camping abroad. This is what account I can give.

JONATHAN ELKINS.

To Gen. Bailey or the inhabitants of Cohos.
(A true copy).

During these years of Revolutionary struggle the committees of safety in the several towns were directed to furnish their quota of beef and flour for the troops in the field. Haverhill with her rich and extensive meadows was able to do much in this line. This was then a great wheat-growing section, hundreds and thousands of bushels being harvested annually. In 1780 a meeting was called to " consult upon measures to be taken about the transportation of grain from this place," [Haverhill,] and then the Town voted to " take efficient measures to stop all the grain in said Town for the use of the public." Gen. Bailey was directed in 1779 by the General Court to " pay to Col. Charles Johnston $2400 which he has in his hands, for forage supplied on the farm of John Fisher."

It is also handed down in tradition that there were those in this section, whether Haverhill made any contribution to the enterprising company does not exactly appear, who were willing to turn a penny in furnishing beef without too close a scrutiny as to where it was going or who might eat it. In a quiet way cattle were brought from secluded pastures, through the woods, and then after nightfall they were driven to the mouth of the Oliverian, and at an opportune time, of which these patriots were apprised, they swam the cattle across the Connecticut river and delivered them to British guards who were in waiting to drive them to the enemies' lines in Canada.

The disastrous effects of the Revolutionary war are seen in the rapid apparent increase of town expenses. In 1766 the amount voted for this purpose was £10, whilst in 1780 it rose to £1880, 10s., and in the year following $34,150 was voted for the Town's " quota of beef." The troubled state of the settlement is also indicated in a vote in 1780 to release certain parties from fulfilling contracts for building mills on account of the " difficult times," and at the close of the Revolution there was a sale of original and other rights belonging to persons who were embarrassed. These rights numbered almost fifty. Population also increased very slowly during this period, and at one time actually decreased. In 1773 the population of the Town was 387, whilst in 1775 it was only 365, many persons removing to " more safe and central parts of the state," as the cloud of war began to threaten. This was especially the case of such as were not land-owners. But after the close of the Revolution population again rapidly increased, and the Town became one of the most prosperous ones in the state.

CHAPTER XI.

ENTERPRISES AND BUSINESS.

First Saw-mill and Grist-mill—General Progress—Liberal Offer for Blacksmith—First Saw-mill and Grist-mill at Hosmer Brook—Second Saw-mill—Other Mills—Fulling Mill—Side Light—Flax Mill—Water Power—Rafting Lumber—First Tannery—Cloth and Carding Mill—Potash Factory—Paper Mill—Other Mills and Shops—Pulp Mill—Swasey Mills—Other Factories and Shops—Woodsville Lumber Co.—Marble Works—Other Enterprises—A. F. Pike Manufacturing Co.—Stores and other business at Corner, North Haverhill, East Haverhill, Pike Station, Woodsville.

The Proprietors of the new settlement at Cohos went promptly and vigorously to work to develop the resources of the country, and used diligently the facilities and means at hand for this purpose. According to an early entry in the Proprietors' records, 1764, Haverhill and Newbury had joined in interest in a common ownership of some mills which were situated on Poole brook. These mills were located on the sites or privileges which were exempted when Capt. Hazen was allowed to select his house and meadow lots before any of the other proprietors drew theirs, and were the two mills which Hazen erected in the spring of 1762 when he came to Haverhill with his workmen. The joint ownership of these mills by the two Towns or Proprietors was of short duration, as within a year after their erection they were offered at public sale, March 13, 1764, "agreeable to the vote of the Towns of Haverhill and Newbury,"* and were bid off by Hezekiah Hutchins for the sum of $520. This sale took place, no doubt, at Plaistow, as the date of sale is the same as that of the town meeting which was held at Plaistow, March 13, 1764. Something, however, seems to have been wrong about the matter, and the sale was adjourned to April 2d at Hampstead, "when said mills were set up anew," and bid off by Jesse Johnson, John Hazen

---

* This vote, although called a vote of the two Towns, was undoubtedly a Proprietors' vote.

and Jacob Bailey for $297, "After," as we are informed by the Proprietors' clerk, "very many bids were made."

The general prosperity and the material interests of the settlement were also diligently looked after by the Proprietors in another way. They offered liberal inducements to industry and capital in order to develop the resources of the Town, and to turn its great natural advantages to speedy profit and usefulness. William Wheeler was voted, 1764, "One right of land" on condition that he would "follow the business of blacksmithing for ten years, or some one else for him." And he was required to "work for the people of Haverhill before any others," and "sufficient bonds" were demanded of him as a guarantee that he would carry out his part of the contract. The Town's blacksmith was not given much time to "turn around in," as he was to begin work on or before November of the same year, so that he had only about fifteen days in which to "set up shop." This shop was at the Plain or Ox Bow.

The Proprietors also had a meeting, 1764, and voted to "give to Timothy Bedel and Elisha Lock the whole privilege of the lower falls on Hosmer brook,* together with the whole lands laid out for said privilege, provided they complete two mills by the 20th of November, 1765," or within a year. One of these mills was to be a saw-mill and the other a grist-mill.

"A perpetual privilege" was given, 1768, to build a saw-mill "on one-half the land laid out for that purpose on Hosmer's brook," on condition that the owner should put up a mill "fit to saw boards by the 4th day of April, 1769;" and for a term of five years he was to "deliver 400 of boards out of a 1000 to the man that draws the logs," after which he was to "deliver one-half of the boards." Johnston & Sanders were granted a privilege for a saw-mill at the Brook in 1772, and in the following year the 100 acre lot, reserved

---

* This was the name of the Oliverian brook in early times.

on Hazen's (Poole) brook for mill privilege, was voted to John Fisher, Esq., on condition that he would build a grist-mill and saw-mill, and would saw for half the boards for the Proprietors and keep the mill in good repair. Also, in the same year a privilege for a grist-mill and saw-mill was granted Reuben Foster at the falls on Oliverian brook. This is the first mention of the Brook by that name in the records.

Here is a side light thrown upon the character of our forefathers. They were practical and thorough men. A privilege was granted in 1779 to build a " fulling mill," on condition that the mill was to be put up to do work in six months, and to do it in a " workmanlike manner." Joseph Pearson was the man that " pitched " for this mill, the site of which was designated as at the " falls about three rods above the great bridge, and opposite a little island." A plan of this privilege is found in Proprietors' records. We also learn that a " flax mill " was erected at Hosmer falls as early as 1779, as in a grant of that year to Timothy Bedel, giving him the privilege of building two mills; one of these was to be opposite the " flax mill." Joseph Hutchins was also granted the same year a privilege to build a grist-mill on Hosmer brook.

The Brook was from the first a busy place. Few clearings had been made at the beginning of the present century along the Oliverian, and its heavily-shaded banks in summer shielded it against rapid evaporation, whilst the densely wooded country served to hold in store the water-fall. As a consequence the water-power at the Brook was ample and steady. Here for many years Capt. Pearson, and afterward his son, Isaac, manufactured lumber and carried on milling. The manufacture of lumber was easy in those days, as the forests came close home to the mills. At first the logs were run down the Connecticut river, but in later years, from the early part of the present century, the lumber was sent in rafts after the river was equipped with a series of locks around the falls. At an early date Samuel Brooks ran an oil factory at the Brook, and Richard Gookin made carding machinery. Later, Mr. Herbert also manufactured machinery. Ezekiel Ladd was the owner of a tannery in the last century, which was continued by others to a recent date. Cloth and carding mills were early established, and later the Bell potash factory did an extensive business. Uriel Ward was a hatter and quite a military man. Blumly & Sturtevant ran a woolen mill. Paper making was begun by Hutchins & Co., and continued by the Haverhill Paper Co., till it passed into the hands of P. F. Litchfield. Also, Joshua Blaisdell manufactured shoes, with George W. Miner as head-workman. At present A. W. Lyman runs the old Pearson grist-mill. Michael Carleton has a carriage and repair shop, John L. Cook a shingle and cider mill, and Robert Jenkins, now a dealer in carriages, was formerly in the marble business. Archibald's marble works are here. Jonathan Nichols also manufactured carriages. Some fifteen years ago the Pulp Mill was built, but it was never successfully operated, and has recently passed into the hands of P. F. Litchfield, who intends to use the lower part for a paper-mill, and has offered inducements to the money-men of Haverhill to put into the two upper floors machinery for the manufacture of woolens, but the offer has not been accepted.

Along the Oliverian, as clearings opened, saw-mills were built at several places, the first at a point now called Pike Station, the only one at the present time in operation on the Oliverian above Brook village. The water-power is uncertain and in dry seasons inadequate for continuous work. However, it is said that at very moderate expense a sufficient storage of water could be secured on the North Branch to tide over the dry season and furnish ample supply for all the mills and shops on the Oliverian; the new growth of forest which is fast taking the place of the old that was cut away in the earlier days of railroads, is increasing, it is thought, the steadiness of the water-power on the Oliverian, so that in the course of years the old-time water-power may be restored.

At North Haverhill in early times, after the first saw-mill and grist-mill were built by John Hazen, mills were operated by Obadiah Swasey, chiefly in the manufacture of lumber, of which large quantities were gotten out, as the plain at North Haverhill was then covered with the finest of pines. This lumber was mostly sent to Hartford, Conn. The old Swasey site is now occupied by J. G. Blood as a shingle and planing mill. Here also are Sleeper & Co.'s bobbin mill, Eastman's carriage shop, Spencer's grist and flouring mill and Getchell & Co.'s carriage manufactory. Mr. Sleeper is also engaged in the manufacture of corn-planters.

Woodsville has always been a lumber point of considerable importance. It was first occupied by John L. Woods, and since the incorporation of the Woodsville Lumber Co., large quantities of rough and dressed lumber have been shipped from their plant. They do an extensive business in laths and clapboards. Smith's shovel-handle manufactory was here till 1878, when it was washed away by high water. C. C. Smart has a large brick-yard, and W. H. Hill's marble works are here.

In addition to these business enterprises are the Jeffers and Chase saw-mills, Bacon's carriage and wagon shop and Lewis' wood-pump shop. Few of these establishments are extensive and they are so scattered over the Town as to make no great show, yet in the aggregate they do a large amount of business, and if concentrated at a single point would present much outward activity.

But there is one extensive plant in the Town that demands a more particular notice—the A. F. Pike Manufacturing Co., which was organized in 1883, just sixty years after Isaac Pike began the manufacture of whetstones in Haverhill, and is the direct successor of A. F. Pike who continued the business of his father from 1860 to 1883. The company consists of A. F. Pike, E. B. Pike, Isaac Pike, Charles J. Pike, and Charles G. Smith. A. F. Pike is president and general director, E. B. Pike is vice-president and has the active management of the business outside the office, Isaac Pike is treasurer and has the general oversight of the manufacturing at Pike Station, and Charles J. Pike is superintendent of the quarrying and cutting of the stone before they are taken to the mills to be ground. The capital of the company is seventy thousand dollars. They manufacture all kinds of scythe-stones and whetstones for sharpening edge tools. Their principal quarries are in Haverhill, Piermont, and Lisbon, and their ledges contain a stone which is better adapted, it is claimed, for sharpening scythes and edge tools than anything else ever found. The stone is of a sharp, gritty character, lying in rifts, and is broken out with the grain without impairing its strength, and makes a strong, durable sharpener, hard enough to cut any steel. These whetstones do not glaze, the layers being so thin that one after another wears off in using and a new, fresh surface is all the time exposed.

The various kinds of whetstones and scythe-stones of this company are used in all parts of the United States and in Canada, and many car-loads are sent annually to Europe. The company also have quarries and mills in Vermont and New York, where they manufacture other grits of stone. Besides these they receive and handle stones in large quantities from Ohio, Michigan, Indiana, Arkansas, Nova Scotia, England, Germany, Belgium, Turkey, and from other parts of the world. They have their agents in New York, Chicago, St. Louis and Baltimore. In their different quarries and mills they employ a large force of workmen, and are converting barren ledges into articles of indispensible usefulness, which to them and to the Town of Haverhill are a constant source of revenue. Their business is annually enlarging, and if capital, industry, energy, wise business plans are rewarded with success, the "A. F. Pike Manufacturing Co." must stand at the front in this line of business. They are also largely interested in soap-stone both in New Hampshire and in Vermont.

Stores were established in Haverhill as soon as roads would permit the transportation of goods to the new settlement. This was not till about the close of the Revolution. In early times heavy goods were brought from No. 4 on the ice, and lighter articles found their way to Cohos on pack-horses. This continued till about 1790. From that date, or perhaps a few years earlier, stores began to be introduced. Probably the earliest store at the Corner was kept by Samuel Brooks. Other merchants were the Barstow Bros., Stephen Adams, Benjamin Merrill, Russell Kimball, Timothy K. Blaisdell, Rix & Cummings, S. F. Hook, William H. Page, Bailey Bros., Poor & Westgate. Noah Davis kept a drug store about the beginning of the present century, and Mrs. Joseph Bliss about the same time had a ladies' store. The present drug store is kept by John W. Merrill, and Charles N. Miner is jeweller. Henry Merrill preceded John W. Merrill in the drug store, and also dealt in jewelry. The early jewellers were John Osgood and Henry Towle. The former also manufactured the old-fashioned high clocks. Mrs. M. D. Buzzell serves the ladies in bonnets and fancy goods. Other business—George W. Leith is a merchant tailor; James A. Page, harness maker; Edwin J. Facey deals in stoves and tinware as successor to L. B. Ham, and previous to that R. N. Brown was tinman, better known as "Tinker" Brown. Nathan H. Batchelder, manufactures carriages and sleighs; Moses B. Carpenter has a wheelwright and repair shop; John O. Gifford, carpenter and joiner; W. R. Clark, repairer; W. E. Pike keeps a meat market. The lawyers at the Corner are Geo. W. Chapman,

Samuel T. Page, William F. Westgate. The doctors, Samuel P. Carbee, M. D. Carbee, Henry P. Watson.

At the Brook the earliest merchants were John Montgomery, Bell Bros., afterwards Blaisdell Bros., Bailey Bros., A. M. Bowen, W. H. Nelson. Also, quite early Mrs. Gookin and Miss Eliza Cross kept ladies' stores; later Mrs. Cook. The present merchants are F. T. Kiernan & Co., J. LeRoy Bell; Miss H. F. Morrison keeps fancy goods, and George Whipple is tailor.

At North Haverhill the merchants were John and Thomas Hall, Joshua Morse, the Hibbards, Caleb Webster, Morse & Celsey, Samuel B. Rodgers, Joseph B. Cotton, W. H. Nelson, E. R. Weeks; and at present, Morris E. Kimball, N. C. Wright, C. H. Wetherbee and W. W. Millen.

The merchants at East Haverhill were Wheeler & Aiken, Davis & Abel, Arthur L. Page; then later, Park & Davis, Richardson & Merrill, G. W. Richardson, H. D. Gannett.

At Pike Station, Isaac Pike was the first merchant, then his son A. F. Pike, Pike & Davis, C. J. Ayer.

At Woodsville the following have been or are now in various branches of business.

John L. Wood, general merchandise; Edward Child, general merchandise; Ezra S. Kimball, general merchandise; John Hale, general merchandise for Hutchins & Buchanan; C. M. Weeks, general merchandise; Lewis Barter, flour and grain; C. B. Drake and G. S. Cummings, drugs and medicines; A. H. & J. Burton, general merchandise; E. B. Mann and G. S. Cummings, drugs etc., W. K. Wallace, jeweller; S. L. Estabrook, groceries; J. H. Cutting and Frank Smith, general merchandise; E. B. Miller, groceries; A. H. Leighton and Q. A. Scott, clothing, boots and shoes; George Emery, tin shop and hardware; H. E. Fletcher & Co., flour and grain; H. W. Ramsey and I. K. George, general merchandise; Mrs. E. Batties, millinery and fancy goods; George A. Davison and Langdon Bailey, flour, grain, lime; S. P. Stickney and T. W. Glover, general merchandise. Mulliken & Davis, stoves, tin and hardware; F. L. Moore, grain, coal, hair, cement.

Other business not mentioned—Andrew Moulton, Dewey & Young, house painters; Ai Willoughby, D. Mitchell, meat, provisions; Chester Abbott, insurance; George W. Lyons, Michael Stevens, masons; Geo. A. Davison, western tickets; Geo. H. Newell, locksmith; Jos. Martel, Kimball Marshall, blacksmiths; Joseph Willis, carriage and repairs; D. A. French, music teacher; T. H. Aulis, barber; L. E. Collins, Woodsville Bottling Co., bottlers; Woodsville Aqueduct Co.; Page & Shurtleff, lawyers; C. R. Gibson, O. D. Eastman, physicians.

CHAPTER XII.

ROADS AND BRIDGES.

Roads and Civilization—First Roads little more than Bridle-paths—First Ox-team from Haverhill to Plymouth—Course of the Road—Road from Portsmouth to Cohos—First mention of Town Roads—Road from the "Plain," to Coventry line the Earliest Town Road—Ingress to Cohos—A suggestive vote—The Road from Piermont to Bath—Along the side-hill—The Oliverian Road—Highway Taxes and Labor—Public Ferry—County Road—Roads built before 1800—Roads extended and built as Population settled in eastern part of Town—Character of Roads—Cohos Turnpike—Corporators—Improvement in Roads—Room for further Improvement—Permanent material—Grades—Road Engineers—Railroad—Canal—Bridges.

Roads are both a sign and a necessity of civilization, except where water-courses serve the purposes of roads. The savage uses only a trail which answers all his needs of travel and transportation. His means of subsistence are either near at hand, or can be transported without roads to meet the limited necessities of his condition. But civilization has numerous demands, and draws her subsistence from near and far. Ancient Assyria had national highways reaching from one end of the empire to the other. Along these passed her immense traffic and war-chariots. Rome was like the centre of a wheel, from which in every direction radiated her magnificently-paved roads to all parts of her vast dominions. Over these for centuries she marched her numerous legions and by means of these she drew to herself the treasures and products of remote provinces.

Before the Revolutionary War there were few, if any, roads in the Town that could be used except for horseback travel. Indeed, in the earlier years what were denominated roads were little more than bridle-paths. Ingress into the territory was through unbroken forests, which were "blazed" to indicate the direction of the path. Over these the pioneer settlers in winter-time dragged on sledges or carried on horseback at other seasons, the provisions and whatever else was necessary for their living until land could be cleared and crops could be raised. Heavy goods were also brought from No. 4 on the ice. Judge Woodward and Mr. John Page related to Rev. Grant Powers how they, with others, dragged from Concord on a sled the crank for a saw-mill for the new settlement in Cohos.

According to Mr. Powers, who had his information from persons living at the time he wrote, the first ox-team that went through from Haverhill to Plymouth was some time after 1772, and the event excited a great deal of public interest. It was an expedition sent out by a company of persons and was more like a construction party than an ox-team passing over a road already prepared. The people of Cohos had had little hope of a wagon-road being constructed in the near future between these two points. Accordingly, when the ox-team and the men in charge of it returned to Haverhill after accomplishing the trip to and from Plymouth, the citizens of Haverhill were so rejoiced at the event that they went out to meet them, and the men in charge of the team were conducted to their homes in state, whilst the oxen were rewarded with an extra feed for their part of a successful achievement.

This was the original road from Plymouth to Cohos at the Corner, and was at first only a bridle-path. The general course of this road beginning at Haverhill was as follows: It commenced just south of the Whitney place running east to StClair hill, thence over the low part of the summit east of Day's, keeping on the line of the turnpike till it bore off south-east past Putnam's, thence east to Putnam mill and past Tarleton Lake, over the Height-o'-Land to Warren. The points are given as they now are. This road became a great thoroughfare from Haverhill to " down country," and traces of it can still be seen.

As early as 1765 Gen. Jacob Bailey petitioned the General Court at Portsmouth that a road might be built at public expense from that city to Cohos, and an act for that purpose was passed and signed by the governor; and in 1774 Col. John Hurd petitioned the governor to have the road leading to Cohos improved and made safe. So that up to 1774 highways in Haverhill were in a very imperfect and infant state.

The first mention of Town roads appears in the Proprietors' records as early as 1763, when it was voted that " the Proprietors of Haverhill join with the Proprietors of Newbury to look out and clear a road through Haverhill." This vote was reversed in the following year, and in the records of that date this road is described as " a road through Haverhill so as to meet the road that leads to Portsmouth." This " Portsmouth " road was the bridle-path leading from the " Plain " to the Benton (Coventry) line. The road, therefore, which was to be " laid out " by the Proprietors of Haverhill and Newbury to " meet the road leading to Portsmouth," was probably a road from the " Upper meadow " or Porter place to the Coventry road at the " Plain." Afterwards the Proprietors voted to " cut out a road from North Haverhill court house to Coventry line," which was merely an enlargement of the bridle-path.. But it is doubtful if this vote was carried out, since a few years later the Town records inform us that the Town voted to " lay out a road from the court house eastward four rods wide." This vote was probably intended to carry out the Proprietors' vote above, after the Town assumed the care of the Coventry road. This road is the one that passes over " Morse hill," and comes in upon the Oliverian brook a little east of the Benton (Coventry) line. The " Portsmouth " road and the " Coventry road " are one and the same.

This road was undoubtedly the earliest road in the Town, and was used by the first settlers in coming into the Cohos Country through Coventry, as this was the nearest course in reaching the settlement at the " Plain " or Ox-bow. The settlement at this point was the earliest in the Town. It was here that Capt. John Hazen and his men built the grist-mill and saw-mill in the spring of 1763.

An early mention of roads is found in the Town records in connection with a very suggestive vote. The road surveyor was directed not to "call on those who had done the most work till the others had done their part." From this it would seem that there were even in those heroic and self-sacrificing days patriots to be found who were perfectly willing that "their wives' uncles and brothers" should do all the road-making and road-mending of the Town.

There was also another road described as running "through Haverhill from the Bath line to the Piermont line." At a later date this road was given to the Town on condition that its course should not be changed from the original road, or to use the Proprietors' own language, the road was to be maintained "as it is now trod." The grant of this road to the Town by the Proprietors was made in these words: "To give the road, as it is now trod, from the Bath south line south-westerly to Lieut. Hayward's, thence south to north side of ministerial house, thence south-easterly to Capt. Hazen's, thence south-easterly a little over Mill [Poole] brook, thence in a general south-westerly line to Piermont." At the time of the Town's assuming this road it was little more than a bridle-path, along which the early settlers had built their houses, and which it would seem they did not wish varied from the original course on this account, so as not to be left off the road. This road from Bath to Lieut. Hayward's ran east of what is now Woodsville, and was the original of the present river road from Bath to Piermont.

The section of road at the Corner between Col. Johnston's and Bedel's skirted at first along the west side of Powder House Hill, where the old Page log cabin stood, and crossed the Oliverian at Jonathan Ladd's house below the grist-mill, and thence ascended the hill from that point, traces of which, it is thought, can still be seen on the Oliverian near Mr. Lyman's house. The change to the present road from the Corner to the Brook was made in 1795.

In 1789 the Town ordered the completion of a road on the south side of the Oliverian bridge in lieu of a road between house lots Nos. 65 and 66, which was on the north side, and this south side road was afterwards extended farther east " along the Oliverian brook to the bridge." This bridge was probably not far from the high railroad bridge.

Highway taxes were allowed in 1791 to be paid " in labor at three shillings per day, or other articles in proportion." The Town seems to have gone into a sort of " produce exchange business." Also, this year the public ferry at the lower end of the Town was sold at auction to Moody Bedel for £30, who obligated himself to keep a good road from the main or river road to the ferry; and at the same meeting which ordered the sale of the south ferry, a road was authorized to be laid out to the upper ferry from the main or river road, " at the convenientest place, without being very expensive to the Town."

In 1798 the Town ordered a road built from " Greenleaf's mill in a straight course as the land would admit, till it strikes the south-west corner of James Woodward's 100-acre lot, and to be in range line of said lot till it strikes the road to Horse meadow, thence by Ephraim Wesson's and Samuel Gould's to Bath line." In the same year a road which is described as " turning off at the mills on the Fisher farm," was ordered to be carried to the east boundary of the Town, and each person along its course was directed to give land on his premises.

From the first settlement of the Town till the beginning of the present century the only roads of any extent that were built, were the river road running the length of the Town, the original Coventry road from North Haverhill over

Morse hill, and the road which came into the Corner from Plymouth. The road along the Oliverian was pushed out as fast as population settled in that direction, but until about 1818 there were few settlements beyond the old Pike mill, the present site of the A. F. Pike manufacturing company's plant.

The road described as leading from Greenleaf's mill to the Coventry road, 1798, is now called the county road, and the road from the mills on the Fisher farm, is probably the same as the road to the Centre from North Haverhill. Other roads were built or old ones were enlarged from time to time as the population settled back from the river and filled up the east sections of the Town. Indeed, before the beginning of the present century few settlements were made away from the river road, except in the direction of Briar hill, and there were also several openings on the Morse hill road and on the Oliverian.

At this date the roads were imperfect in places, as for example the road from Ayer's hill to Poole brook in 1810 was ordered to be made "passable." The river road originally went by the Dow-farm house, and ran east to the foot of the hill, a little south of the Powers place, now Mrs. Filley's. When the road was voted to be changed, in 1810, Gen. Dow was much incensed at the contemplated movement, and carried the matter before the court in a long remonstrance, setting forth the inconvenience and injury which the change would inflict upon him and his property.

In matters of roads the most important as affecting the prosperity of the Town, though not a town road, was the old Cohos Turnpike which took the place of the old Cohos road from Plymouth through Warren to Haverhill above described. The Cohos Turnpike was chartered in 1805, and was built in a direct course from Warren to Haverhill Corner, so as to shorten the distance between these two points, and was mainly accomplished through the enterprise and public spirit of Haverhill people. Alas, that this enterprise and public spirit has so largely departed! The road was surveyed by Gen. John Duffee, who in those days was famous for his accomplishment in that line of engineering. The corporation consisted of Gen. Moses Dow, Absalom Peters, Joseph Bliss, David Webster, Jr., Asa Boynton, Charles Johnston, Alden Sprague, Moody Bedel, Col. Wm. Tarleton, John Page, and Stephen P. Webster, all of them men of ability and large influence. The road was completed in 1808, and for more than a generation was the great thoroughfare for travel and teams in northern New Hampshire, and made Haverhill during these years the most important and lively town north of Concord.

The roads of Haverhill will average in passableness and comfort with the roads of neighboring towns, and there has been a steady improvement from year to year. There is, however, yet much room in this direction. The theory of road-making and road-mending is all wrong as now practiced, and although the Town votes money liberally for keeping its highways in repair, and in altering them for the greater convenience of the public, it does not get the benefit of the large yearly outlay. There is too much road-making and road-repairing of such a superficial and shiftless character that the same work must be done over year after year at a cost that if doubled or trebled at the start would give not only more permanent results, but in the end would be far more economical. Bridges and culverts should be built with scientific thoroughness and of the most durable material. Rome built bridges two thousand years ago that bid fair to stand two thousand years longer. Stone or iron should in all cases be used. Grades should be so made that little change would be wrought upon the road-bed by the most violent rain, and at unavoidable points of steep grade macadamizing should supercede the present method of merely dragging on earth to be washed off by the first June shower.

And the present method of meeting hills by direct cuts should in every case where practicable be avoided. Hills should be flanked as a rule. Were this method pursued with engineering skill and knowledge, at least seven miles out of every ten of what is now hill road, could be reduced to almost level grade. The roads of Norway and Sweden are carried through a hill country more abrupt than ours, but they are so skillfully built, winding in and out, flanking steep barriers, that the carrol—the Norway and Sweden stage coach, corresponding to our one-horse express—is dragged over these roads hour after hour at the rate of seven to ten miles an hour. They are kept as free from loose stones as a barn floor. Such roads when once built require little outlay to keep them in a high state of service. Thorough work is always cheapest in the end, and every town should have the service of a trained and scientific road engineer, as much as railroads have, whose business it should be to secure to the public the best and safest of highways.

Haverhill was favored with railroad facilities in 1852—the " Boston, Concord & Montreal "—which enters the Town on the east border, and runs west to the Connecticut river, and thence north to Woodsville, traversing through the Town a distance of nearly fifteen miles, and having within that course five stations which furnish convenient means for travel and freighting.

In the time when canals were introduced into the country the project of a canal occupied the attention of the people of New Hampshire, and a highway of this sort was contemplated to be built from Dover at the head of tide-water, to the Connecticut river. Its course was to be from Dover to Lake Winnepiseogee, thence from the head of the Lake to the Pemigewassett river, up Baker's river to Warren, and then across the summit to the head waters of the Oliverian, and down that stream to the Connecticut. Elaborate surveys were made, but the project failed, it is said, on account of the difficulty of getting sufficient water to supply the canal in crossing Warren summit except at enormous expense. The United States government sent an engineer to assist in the survey of the canal. Gen. John Duffee was the chief engineer.

The bridges of the Town have never been very expensive, as the streams which are crossed by highways are not large. The bridge at the Brook is the largest wholly owned by the Town, and was formerly an open bridge. A young man, it is said, who was leaning against the railing which had become very rotten, fell off into the stream. In former times the Brook bridge was farther up stream near where the Pulp mill now stands. The bridges across the Connecticut are owned by corporations. The "middle bridge" was built about 1795. A charter for Bedel's bridge was secured in 1802, and the bridge was completed in 1806. This bridge has been built four times, once being swept away by a violent wind. Wells River bridge was chartered in 1803.

CHAPTER XIII.

MAILS, STAGES, TAVERNS.

Early Communication—First Mail—John Balch—State Routes—Postage—Haverhill Office—National Mails—Dutch Mail Wagon—Col. Silas May—Post Horn—Express—Bi-weekly Mail—First stage line—William Smart—Second stage line—Robert Morse—First Trip—Col. Silas May driver—Entrance into Haverhill—Almost an Accident—Tri-weekly Mails—Daily—Extras—The Drivers—Hanover Route—Six-horse Coaches—Haverhill a great stage center—Travel—Stage Lines—Famous Drivers—Their Character—Responsible Positions—Some Successful Men—Drinking Habits—Taverns: Bliss', Coon's, Towle's, Exchange, Sinclair's, Second Coon tavern, earliest tavern, Richardson's, Ladd's, Howard's, Morse's, Cobleigh's, Swan's, Morse Hill tavern—A great thoroughfare—Teams and Teamsters—Provisions—Lodgings—Large Teams—Crouch Tavern—A famous hostelry—The old-time tavern—Haverhill's stage-tavern—News Center—Barroom—Fire-place—Flip—Mental training—The Landlord.

Communication of frontier settlements with the parent populations is one of the first things to be secured. At first letters are sent back and forth by chance travelers going into the new settlements or returning from them. This for some years was the only means of communication between the "Cohos Country" and the towns in New Hampshire and Massachusetts from which the early settlers came. At the beginning of the Revolution the State Committee of Safety appointed one John Balch a post-rider for the term of three months, who was to start at Portsmouth and ride to Haverhill by way of Conway and Plymouth, thence down the Connecticut river to Charlestown and back to Portsmouth. This service was to be performed every two weeks, and for which the pioneer post-rider was to receive the "sum of seventy hard dollars, or paper money equivalent." This service faithful John Balch performed during all the stormy years of the Revolution.

The only United States mail service as early as 1791 was that of a post-rider along the sea-board. But in the same year the legislature of the state passed a law establishing "four routes for posts, to be thereafter appointed to ride in and through the interior of the state." These routes were performed once in two weeks, and the postage on a single letter was six pence or twelve and one-half cents for each forty miles, and four pence or eight cents for any number of miles less than forty. Post-masters were also allowed two pence or four cents for all letters that passed through their offices. Amongst the inland post-offices established at that time was one at Haverhill. The national government assumed the carrying of the mails to Haverhill soon after 1793. Mails were light and consisted chiefly of letters, and the era of newspapers and periodicals had hardly yet dawned.

This state of things continued till the beginning of the present century, or indeed till the building of the turnpike, when the post-rider was displaced by the Dutch wagon in which the mail was carried. Col. Silas May was the mail-man then, and had been for some time before. As he drove his first mail wagon into Town he blew harder and oftener his old horn. It was a great event, and marked also the beginning of a new business, the carrying of bundles for twelve and one-half cents, in fact an incipient express. Every house he passed on the route was awakened by the blast of his horn, giving them warning of bundles to be left or taken. The mail was carried twice a week, and twice a week Col. May was seen coming down over the long turnpike hill leading into Haverhill, his old horn heralding the mail-carrier's approach, and equally often in the week he started out on the return trip.

But this lasted only a few years. The spirit of innovation and progress had taken possession of the Cohos settlement. The stage coach was in fashion "down below," and a stage line was projected as early as 1811. Col. William Tarleton was one of the owners; but alas! good and faithful May, post-rider for many years, and the jolly driver of the Dutch mail and express wagon, was not the Jehu of the new enterprise. The driver was William Smart, and the line soon came to grief, and it was not till 1814 that a permanent stage line ran into Haverhill. It was organized by Robert Morse, a Haverhill boy then of Rumney, who afterwards became famous as a stage proprietor, and enlisted the interest of all towns along the route between Haverhill and Concord. The first trip was made in the spring with Morse and some invited guests as passengers, and the faithful post-rider, Col. Silas May, was the happy driver. He is said to have been a great horseman, and never did man see a prouder day than Col. Silas did as he came down the long St. Clair hill with his four-in-hand, blowing his horn in wild blasts and wheeling his coach with its grand load of passengers up to the Towle tavern. A great and eager crowd was in waiting when the trusty driver laid down his reins, and gave him a loud and enthusiastic welcome. It is said that just before reaching the Corner a linch-pin was lost from one of the wooden axles, but by May's skillful driving the wheel did not come off, and the coach reached its destination without serious accident.

Soon the trips were increased to three per week each way, and next a daily coach was run, and in the height of travel two or three coaches going and coming were necessary to meet the demands of the public. Other drivers were Caleb Smart, Peter Dudley, Sanborn Jones, Eleazer Smith, James F. Langdon, afterwards a large owner in this and other stage lines, William W. Simpson, known better as "Wash" Simpson, Seth Greenleaf who became also famous in the days when the great stages rolled in and out of Haverhill Corner.

About the same time that the line from Concord to Haverhill via Plymouth court house was put on, another stage came into Haverhill from Concord via Hanover. This was a two-horse coach at first, and connected with the stage line to New York. The driver was Wait Gould. Subsequently six-horse coaches were driven on all the important stage lines that centered in Haverhill.

Haverhill very early became the stage center in northern

New Hampshire. In the height of travel and before the railroad invaded these limits, there were six or eight stage lines that brought the mails and passengers from all sections. Usually they came in in the evening and took their departure in the morning. Reliable authority states that the number of persons who were set down at the different taverns in Haverhill ranged from seventy-five to one hundred fifty daily. Extra coaches were run on the main routes in order to meet the urgent demands of travel. The chief lines were those to Boston, New York, and Stanstead, Canada; whilst lesser lines came from the White Mountains, Montpelier, and Chelsea, Vt., and other points. Most of these were dailies, and used four and six-horse coaches of immense strength and capacity for carrying passengers.

Some of these stages had famous drivers. Dan Field, who drove in the Stanstead line, was noted for the wonderful skill with which he blew his bugle announcing his coming as he entered the village, and would land his passengers after making a graceful curve with his team in front of the tavern. Another driver was "Wash" Simpson. He was a jolly old Englishman, a sort of Sam Weller, and had a proprietory interest in the line he drove in. Then there were the Morses, father and son, who also were large owners in the Boston line; Seth Greenleaf of the White Mountain stage, the two Simonds brothers, Joshua and Jehiel; the Henry brothers, Timothy and Charles; James F. Langdon, better known as "Jim," Bill Fuller, and many others who had wide fame as skillful and experienced drivers. They were a hardy set of men, frequently exposed to perils, cold, and storm, and held very responsible positions. In their hands was the safety of mails and passengers. In the fall and spring of the year when the roads were heavy, and many points of danger were to be passed, these weather-beaten men with a rough exterior perhaps, and homely speech, were found true and faithful to their responsibilities. Often at such seasons they met with many delays, and brought in their fatigued teams and passengers at late hours. As a rule they were favorites and justly popular with the traveling public. "They were also regarded," says a writer in a sketch of James F. Langdon, "as important men of the community, and a nod of recognition from the driver on the box was enough to make the ordinary man happy through the day." They had a pleasant word for the children, and were patient with and considerate of the ladies who happened to be put into their care, and were proud of the immense loads of passengers which daily they set down at the taverns. Some of these drivers were also proprietors in the stage lines, and not a few of them were men of ability and enterprise, who, after the stages were displaced by the railroads, were successful in other lines of business, like Nathaniel White and James F. Langdon.

In those days of almost universal drinking habits the stage-drivers were no exception to the general rule, and their exposed life and exacting work were a constant temptation for them to indulge their appetites. They usually occupied rooms in the attic of the tavern for lodging, and many were the gay and lively times they indulged in as they got together and recounted the incidents of their trips, and not seldom did the marks of hilarity tell of these jolly men of the reins. Let their names be embalmed in history as a strong feature of the olden times, when they filled a place and did a service which is worthy of mention.

Haverhill, in the glory of the stage era, was full of taverns. The "Bliss tavern" was one of the first that was built, and was owned and kept by Joseph Bliss, an early settler in the Town. This house is still standing and bears marks of its early construction in the finish and carving over the front entrances and in the wainscotting and panelling of the interior. It is now owned and occupied by Mr. George W. Leith, and stands on the corner of Court street fronting the commons. This tavern was the aristocratic headquarters where the judges of the court and the lawyers stopped in early days.

Another old tavern stood on the spot where afterwards was built the Grafton county bank house, now known as the "bank house." The tavern was called the "Coon tavern," and was kept by Ross Coon. It was cut in two and moved from the premises, one part forming, it is said, the house in which Mr. L. B. Ham lives, and the other part forming the house owned and occupied by the late Augustus Whitney.

The great stage tavern was owned and kept by Col. Simeon Towle, and was known as the "Towle tavern." It stood where now Mr. Nat. Page's house stands. Col. Towle's son Edward succeeded his father, and later Mr. Edward Towle's widow continued to keep the house. This was a large three-story house, the headquarters of the stage lines, and was a famous hostelry known along all the stage routes leading into Haverhill.

The present brick hotel was at first a private house and then enlarged for a tavern. It was kept by a Mr. Williams, and afterwards by Eleazer Smith who was succeeded in its ownership and management by his son, Charles G. Under these last two proprietorships it was known as Smith's hotel, and was kept by them for nearly half a century. It is now owned and managed by Scott Fellows, and is called the "Exchange hotel," which was its earlier name before the Smiths kept it. Mr. Chas. G. Smith improved and enlarged it by adding the present new wing. It has also undergone changes under the present management, and is and always was a well kept house.

The large brick house on Court street, now the residence of Dr. Phineas Spalding, was originally built for a tavern, and was kept as such by Capt. Jonathan Sinclair for many years.

There was also a brick tavern in early days three stories high situated on the level plot between Mrs. Chandler's house and the stone house at the Brook. This house was burnt and was never rebuilt. It was kept by Ross Coon after he left the old "Coon house."

Besides these taverns at the Corner there were taverns in other parts of the Town. Probably the first tavern, or at least what served the purposes of a tavern, was Uriah Morse's on Poole brook. Capt. Hazen was an inn-holder as early as 1766 in the same locality a little north, and Luther Richardson kept a public house in 1774 at the "Plain." Another very early tavern was kept by Samuel Ladd on Ladd street. This house stood just south of where Mr. James Woodward lives, and the site is marked by a large willow tree still standing, with which is connected a very romantic story. There was also a tavern in early times on Ladd street where Mrs. Osgood Morse's house stands. Col. Joshua Howard kept a tavern near the site of the county poor-house. Also a little later there was a tavern at Horse meadow known as the "Morse tavern," and was kept by John Morse, and a mile north of this was the "Cobleigh tavern," where the fast men of the day met and drank and handled cards. This house is still standing though somewhat changed. The Buck house on Ladd street was once a tavern, known as the "Swan tavern." In later days it was kept by Capt. Lyman Buck.

The old "Morse tavern" on Morse hill was a famous stopping place in earlier days for teams that came down from northern Vermont and New Hampshire on their way to Portsmouth and Boston. It was a one and a half story house, standing just east of the present Dearborn house, traces of its location are still visible, and contained four large rooms below and two in the attic. One of the lower rooms was used as the bar-room, and the other opposite was a sort of reception room. Back of these were the kitchen and dining room. In the attic were rooms for the family. This was a common style of tavern-house in those days.

The road from North Haverhill to "down country" was a great thoroughfare, more than rivaling the road from the Corner to Plymouth in the number of teams that passed over it. Often long trains of pungs and pods could be seen on this road, and the "Morse tavern" would house these teams and their drivers over night, sometimes to the number of thirty or more. The drivers generally carried their own provender and food. Few regular meals were got for these teamsters, except for the more well-to-do. Some took a cold "bite" as it was called, but as a rule they spent little for food and oats on the trip. Their provisions consisted of cold meats, sausages, bean porridge, brown bread, pies, cake, and cheese. These in the cold winter days would freeze, and when the driver, with the aid of the hostler, had seen to their teams, they brought in their provisions and thawed them out by the great blazing fire in the bar-room, and thus ate their suppers, which they washed down with a glass of cider or other drinks. Perhaps before lying down to sleep they indulged in the famous mug of flip. Their beds consisted of robes which they spread on the bar-room floor, and for pillows they used their fur coats, and then with their feet toward the fire they stretched themselves in a semi-circle around the immense hearth on which was piled great quantities of wood. When the number was too large for the bar-room the reception room was used for the overflow.

Here in the early hours of the evening they told stories and sang songs, and had a merry good time. In the morning they took their breakfast very much as they did their supper, and after paying for their lodgings and indulging in another glass of cider or flip, they continued their trip to market with the same experiences at the next night's stopping place. For a lodging ten cents was charged, twelve and a half cents for a bite, and twenty-five cents for a regular meal, and with what was left at the bar, the landlords managed to collect quite a revenue in those days.

The grade over Morse hill was too great for the large six and eight-horse teams of a later day, and to avoid this long heavy pull they went, after the road was built, by " Brushwood" road along the Oliverian. This was about 1838 or '40. A tavern was kept in the early part of this century at East Haverhill in the house now owned and occupied by A. L. Warren. This house became the stopping place for teams after they ceased going over Morse hill.

Another tavern deserves mention here, perhaps the most noted tavern in the early history of Cohos. Though not situated within the limits of Haverhill, it properly belongs to the history of the Town. This was the famous Tarleton tavern at Tarleton Lake on the old road from the Corner to Plymouth, and was first kept by Col. William Tarleton as early as 1774, and afterwards by his son Amos. The stages as they pulled out from Haverhill over the steep hills, or over the Height-o'-Land from Warren, were sure to give their horses a breathing spell and a sip of water with a handful of salt in it, whilst the passengers were equally sure to make a friendly call at the landlord's well supplied bar of all kinds of drink. The driver was always invited by the passengers to take a drink, was the testimony of a famous driver and proprietor—James F. Langdon—" and if he was so disposed he could get drunk twenty times a day." Tarleton's was also a great place for teams to stop at.

The tavern of the olden time was distinguished for its home-like hospitality. Blazing fires burned in the open fireplace in the bar-room and in the reception room to welcome the weary traveler, and a substantial and appetizing meal was sure to greet him as he responded to the call of the dinner bell. Many of these hostelries became famous for their excellent tables, and the traveler who had occasion to go over the road often, looked forward with pleasure to the hour when the coach would draw up to their hospitable doors. At breakfast he was sure of a delicious cup of coffee, and in the evening after a long and tedious ride, often over rough and heavy roads, he sat down to a tender and smoking steak, such as would gladden the heart of an epicure.

As the great northern stage center, Haverhill had its famous stage tavern which was known far and near. Its excellent cheer and plentiful board went through all the routes, and mine host was an important personage. Many have been the sighs of a generation of men fast passing away for the good old days of the stage taverns. Modern cooking may be more elaborate and artificial, and abound in delicacies and more numerous tid-bit dishes, but the aroma of beef, and mutton, and fowl from the old-fashioned baking-ovens, steaming before you in ample quantities and stimulating the appetite, can never be excelled by the butter and grease of later times.

The stage tavern was the great center of attraction in those days, and when the stages came in from various points bringing in their passengers and news, the village people were accustomed to gather at the tavern to learn what was going on in the outside world. Here reputable citizens congregated and talked over the happenings of the day. Newspapers were infrequent in those days, and the tavern with its new-comers became a sort of literary exchange where everybody that had any thing to relate could always find eager listeners. The bar-room, as it was then called, with its bottles of whiskey and gin, was a large room with benches and settees on all sides. This was filled with a crowd of men and boys who spent the greater part of the evening there. The open fire-place was a conspicuous feature, and the flip-iron and mug were inseparable concomitants of the bar-room. Treating was an universal custom in those days, and the mug filled with steaming flip was passed around amongst the crowd, and everybody took a sip of the favorite beverage.

When the news was all talked over, and the hours were speeding toward midnight, especially when the coach happened to be late, the crowd dispersed for the night only to renew its gathering on the following evening. Those stage villages where the mails lay over night were busy little centers, and manifested all the attributes of a small metropolis. These populations retired at night with a general knowledge of the doings and happenings of the great outside world, and awaited with undisturbed self-possession the coming of the next coach. And so life rolled on in those earlier days with a satisfaction and success which now to our swifter means of locomotion and faster ways of living seem tame and abortive. Information and knowledge were gained then more by hearing and talking than by reading, but the people were quite as intelligent on general matters as they are to-day, and the peculiar discipline of those times developed many a hard-headed man of shrewd common sense and large experience. Those attritions of mind and interchange of information and opinion had a flavor of their own. What an educational force the old stage tavern was!

In olden times the first families kept tavern, and it has often been remarked why this was so. The explanation is easy enough. Only those went away from home who as a rule belonged to the wealthy and intelligent class, and the tavern-keeper was brought into closer social relations to the traveling public than is the case at the present time. He was expected to entertain his guests not only with good eating and drinking, but also it was expected of him that he would make himself agreeable and companionable by his ability to engage in intelligent conversation. He was the depository of a vast amount of current information which was dropped at his house by the coming and going of guests, and this he was expected to pass over to each new-comer. As a consequence he was generally found to be a man of intelligence and of social standing. Many of these tavern-keepers were the most influential men of the times. They came into larger contact and closer relationship with the leading spirits of society, politics and business, and had opportunities of mental growth and insight into the ways and character of men that made them exceptionally intelligent and large minded. Mine host held a leading place in all affairs and movements. This was especially the case along the great thoroughfares of travel and business.

CHAPTER XIV.

EDUCATION—ACADEMY.

Early Education—School lots laid out—School money—Earliest School Districts and School Houses—Second Class of School Houses—Re-districting—Districts and Schools increase with population—Town system—First Board of Education—Town liberal in maintaining Schools—School Centres—The Corner and Woodsville Schools—Dartmouth College Grant—Incidents—Haverhill Academy.

The matter of education early engaged the thoughts of the first settlers of the Town. At the beginning probably little was done in the way of schools except in individual families, and as the inhabitants were largely composed of new families and single persons, the school population did not come into prominence in the first years of the settlement.

In 1772 we find an article in the Proprietors' warrant to see if they will "lay out a tract of land for the use of the school in Haverhill," and a school was probably in existence before that date. A few years later school money was ordered to be "paid in specie." On the first page of the Town records are found several receipts for money paid for teaching, amongst these is one given by Timothy Curtis for £8, 19s., 6d. for teaching school five months and twenty days. This receipt bears date 1774.

Although money was appropriated for school purposes as early as 1774, no mention is made of school districts till 1786, when the Town was divided into four districts. The first district extended from the Piermont line to the Oliverian, the second to the south side of the Fisher farm, the third to Col. Howard's bridge near where now are the county poorhouse buildings, and the fourth to Bath line. In the following year four school houses were ordered to be built, and the sum of £100 was appropriated to carry this purpose into effect. No. 2 was known as Ladd street district on account of the number of persons of that name, who lived within its territory.

At a later period, 1805, one thousand dollars was appropriated for building school houses in the different districts. These houses were to take the place of those built about twenty years before, which were crude structures. In 1811 it became necessary to increase the number of districts, and accordingly a vote was passed for that purpose, but it does not appear that this vote was carried into immediate effect, since in 1815 the matter was brought up again, and a vote was passed to re-district the Town. A committee was appointed to report upon the matter, and their recommendation that the Town should be divided into nine districts was adopted. From that time on the number districts has multiplied as the increase of population and the settlement of the eastern section of the Town made it necessary. There was no re-districting of the entire Town as on the two former occasions, but new districts were formed by the division of old districts, or by forming new ones out of parts of old ones as was most convenient for schooling, until the number rose to twenty-one.

Meantime as the graded system became better understood and more fully appreciated there was a growing demand, especially at the Corner, for better schools, and in 1875 the matter of realizing such a school began to be agitated in Nos. 1 and 17. There was much opposition to the movement on account of prejudice and misinformation, to which was added a fear of cost, and it was only after several school meetings and the utmost exertions of the more public-spirited of the community, that a vote was secured to unite Nos. 1 and 17 in one school district of two grades, primary and grammar, for a single year. But notwithstanding, two most excellent teachers were employed for the year, school-time increased several weeks, and by the admission of all great improvement of the schools was perceptible, the voters of No. 17 refused to go on another year, and the people of the two districts were compelled to accept the old order of things for a little while longer. A plan, however, to resuscitate the Academy having been suggested in 1880, and the plan being favorably received, Nos. 1 and 17 were by contract between the districts involved and the trustees of the Academy, united into a single school with three departments,—academic, grammar, and primary,—and since that time the schools at the Corner have been in a most prosperous condition, and have largely met the expectations of the people.

In Woodsville a graded school of two departments, primary and grammar, has existed since 1872, and has greatly added to the efficiency and success of the schools in that village. In the same year the present school building, which affords convenient accommodations for the schools, was erected.

In 1885 the Town system went into operation. The law authorizing a change from the old district system was intended to reduce the number of districts and increase the efficiency of the schools. It provides a board of education which has charge of all the schools, and the Town constitutes a single school district with schools at such points as the board may prescribe. Few changes were made in the old districts during the first year two of the new law—Nos. 9 and 20 only were discontinued in that time—but further changes were promised "as soon as the schools could be accommodated in other places." The first board of education chosen under the new law consisted of Caleb Wells, Samuel P. Carbee, M. D., and Darius K. Davis, and the opinion is expressed by a member of the board, Dr. Carbee, that the change has worked well thus far in the interest of education, and that the "law of 1885 has come to stay."

The Town has always been liberal in the maintenance of schools, and these have been as efficient, and have served their purpose as well as could be expected under the difficulties of a sparsely settled population in parts of the Town and the constant diminution of school children. Usually the Town has voted a definite sum to be distributed equally amongst the several districts, and thus districts of less valuation were enabled to have longer terms of schooling without burdensome taxation.

In the present distribution of centers of population, which will not be likely to be changed in the near future, a system of graded schools could very easily be established, and the entire school population could be put into reasonably convenient communication with the centers. These centers are four—one at the Corner including Ladd street, another at East Haverhill, a third at North Haverhill, and a fourth at Woodsville. It might be necessary to establish at a few intermediate points single schools for parts of the population too remote from the centers, but for those more advanced in their studies a system of graded schools, as above indicated, is entirely feasible, and should be gladly welcomed by all who have the interests of our schools at heart. Adequate compensation could be made for instruction, thoroughly trained teachers could be secured, and the Town, at even less expense than under the present arrangement, would afford its school population the means of an excellent education, equal to that of large villages and cities.

As an indication of the deep interest which our forefathers felt in education, for many of them were men of considerable mental training, an article was put into the Proprietors' warrant of 1770 to " see if they would give anything to Dartmouth College, Dr. Wheelock, or Col. Phelps, or either of them, as an encouragement for said college being fixed in said Township." And it was a wise forethought and public spirit worthy the founders of the Town that they voted to " give to Revd. Elitzer [Eleazar] Wheelock, D. D., fifty acres of land in Haverhill lying on Capt. John Hazen's mill [Poole] brook, where there is a convenient water-fall for a mill, provided Dartmouth

College should be erected in Haverhill." There is no blame to be attached to the founders of the Town that Dartmouth College did not come to this fair spot.

Few controversies have sprung up in the history of our schools, and none of these have left any serious marks behind. But there were those of a rather humorous side. In one of the districts the question whether to repair or to rebuild the school house came up for discussion and decision. Those in favor of repairing the old house were in the majority, but the minority were not disposed to rest the matter in such way, and resorted to violent measures, and tore down the old house. The matter became quite serious, and was already in the earlier stages of a law suit, but by the friendly intervention of outside counsels, those who tore down the old house were persuaded to put up a frame at their own expense, equal in value to the old house, and the district was then to complete the building. This compromise prevailed and the matter was amicably settled. One person, however, whose sense of justice was rather strongly tinctured with vindictiveness, was not so easily mollified, and when counselled with in regard to the plan of adjustment, said, "No, they must be punished."

On another occasion at a school meeting for the purpose of uniting two districts into a graded school, those present were treated to an exhibition of a very ludicrous character. The people were nearly equally divided, and feeling ran quite high. The debate on the proposition was warmly conducted on both sides, sharp hits were given and received, and the fire flew. The chiefs in this discussion were two of the most esteemed and respected citizens of the district, of advanced age, and both happened to be school teachers in their younger days. Both also claimed to bring superior knowledge to the discussion of the question in debate, which led to a challenge of their respective qualifications to be judges. "Mr. A. considers himself a proper judge of what is best for our schools, but I wish I could show you his letter to me asking for a school, and see the spelling." This was a dead shot, and the speaker's eyes flashed and an air of satisfaction mantled his face, as the audience smiled audibly. Then his opponent replied, "Yes, I wish you could see a certain document which Mr. B. sent to Washington, and which was returned to have the bad spelling corrected." This was too much, and the audience broke forth in violent demonstration. The combatants had each fired a red-hot shot, and both were struck in a vulnerable spot.

In addition, however, to the provision which was early made by the first settlers of Haverhill for the education of their children, they also felt the need of furnishing facilities for more advanced studies than could be provided for in common schools. Accordingly steps were early taken for the erection of a building for the purpose of establishing an academy at a date previous to 1793. In June of that year an edifice which the Proprietors styled a "commodious building" was offered to the Court of Sessions and to the Court of Common Pleas for their use and convenience free of charge, in which the owners, however, reserved the right to hold a public school at any time when the courts were not in actual occupancy of the building. This building is described as situated near the corner of the road leading from Haverhill to Plymouth, and was south of the spot where now stands the present Academy building. The Academy was incorporated in 1794 on petition of Charles Johnston, Esq., and others, who state in their petition that they had employed "a young gentleman of liberal education, eminently qualified as a preceptor, and that about thirty pupils had already engaged there in pursuit of an education in the arts and sciences." The name of the institution was given in the charter as "Haverhill Academy," and its object was set forth to be "to promote religion, purity, virtue, and morality, and for teaching the youth in English, Latin, and Greek languages; in writing, music, and the art of speaking; in geography, logic, geometry, mathematics, and such other branches of science as opportunity may present and the teachers shall order and direct." The trustees who were named in the charter were the " Honorable Charles Johnston, the Rev. Ethan Smith, Messrs. John Page, Samuel Bliss." The number of the board was limited to ten, of whom a majority constituted a quorum. They were empowered to receive and hold in the name of, and for the use of the Academy, real, personal, and mixed property, but the net income of real estate should at no time be allowed to be in excess of seven hundred dollars, whilst the net income of personal and mixed property could not be made to exceed one thousand dollars. It was also provided that when the real estate amounted to more than $3,333.33⅓ all of such excess should be liable to taxation. The act of incorporation was approved February 12th, 1794, and bears the signature of Josiah Bartlett who was the president or governor of the state.

As is seen in the aim of the Academy, which is set forth in the charter, our forefathers regarded religion and education as inseparable, and in accordance with that sentiment religion and morality were made foremost features in the training of the school. A belief in God and our obligation to Him were considered prime articles of faith. The union of religion and education was emphasized in the government of the school in its requirement of teachers and pupils that they should attend public worship on the Sabbath and also daily prayers during term time at the Academy.

The manners and deference which the young of that day were expected to observe toward their superiors, is illustrated by one of the earlier by-laws. It required "students to respectfully notice their teacher when they pass him on the street; also the trustees of the Academy, and all public characters." It is feared that both these features in the early education of youth—religion and politeness—have somewhat fallen into decay in these undeferential modern times.

The Academy had its struggles in the earlier years of its career, and sacrifices were demanded of our fathers to keep it alive. The trustees and others were assessed for the support of the school. Trouble also seems to have come upon it, as in 1807 a committee was appointed to "investigate the situation of the school," and the frequent adjournments of the board of trustees without accomplishing anything, show that its history was marked by many fluctuations and uncertainties.

Its endowment early occupied the attention of its friends, and in 1803 a committee was chosen whose duty it was to petition the General Court for a grant of land. It does not appear, however, that anything was accomplished in this direction, and with the exception of about five hundred dollars, the gift of Mary P. Webster, the school has never been endowed, but has been maintained by tuition and the voluntary aid of interested friends. For this reason its career has been less successful and prosperous than it otherwise would have been. Nevertheless it has filled an honorable and serviceable place in the educational facilities of a large surrounding country, and has been the educational home of many graduates who have filled stations of usefulness and prominence in the various walks of public and private life. Its most distinguished graduate was the late Justice Nathan Clifford of the United States Supreme Court.

In earlier years pupils in District No. 1 attended school at the Academy, and this district as well as No. 17 had certain rights in the building. The county held an interest in the Academy building from 1793 for the use of the courts which were held in the second story. In 1841 an agent of the board of trustees was chosen with a view to transfer the Academy's interest in the building to the county, and also to obtain from the state the land on Powder House hill for a site for another building for the Academy. But after the new court house was erected on Court street the interest of the county in the building passed into the hands of the trustees who are now the sole owners of it.

The first Academy building was constructed of wood and was burned in 1814. It was voted to rebuild with stone; the material of the old building was sold in 1816 to Israel Swan except the stone and bell, and reservation of the old building was made till the new one could be finished, from which it would appear that the destruction by fire was not complete.

Moses P. Peyson, afterwards a prominent lawyer in Bath and a very accomplished gentleman, was the first principal of the Academy, 1794. The income of the school for that year was £78, which would be about $375 of our money. Tuition for English branches was seventeen cents per week, and for languages twenty cents per week.

In 1801 the trustees fixed the salary of Stephen P. Webster, who was the second principal, at $336.36. The records show that he occupied this position until 1805, at least. They also inform us that Isaac Patterson was principal in 1813, but how long before that time, if any, he filled the place is not known. Mr. Patterson was afterwards a lawyer in Bath for many years, and lived to an extreme old age, dying in 1883. He was a very gallant man and was distinguished for his immense shirt collar.

Joseph Bell, the famous Haverhill lawyer, taught the Academy for one year after he graduated from college in 1807, and Col. Charles Johnston filled a vacancy later. Cyrus Grosvner was principal in 1819 but did not seem to have been successful either in teaching or in his government of the school, and a committee was appointed to investigate the matter and to rectify the difficulty if possible, or to dismiss the principal as the committee should see fit. Jesse

Kimball succeeded Mr. Grosvner, and in 1821 Mr. Mack became principal, and continued so till 1828. Ephraim Kingsbury followed him. Peter T. Washburn was principal in 1836. He afterwards became a distinguished lawyer in Woodstock, Vt., and was also governor of that state. Joseph C. Bodwell followed next; he afterwards was prominent as a clergyman. He was succeeded by Daniel F. Merrill who continued in that position for a number of years, afterwards going South, but again took charge of the school in 1862 and continued to be its principal for some time. John P. Humphrey taught the Academy from 1839 to 1841, and Hermon Rood was the head of the school for a number of years previous to 1849, when he resigned. From this date John V. Bean opened a Female Seminary in the Academy building, which continued for several years. At the close of this school, however, there was more or less interruption until 1880 when it was reorganized under the charge of Joseph H. Dunbar, who taught the Academy for four years with much success.

When the school was reorganized in 1880 the Academy was thoroughly repaired at an expense of about one thousand dollars. The philosophical and chemical apparatus was enlarged at the same time, and since, and the school is now well equipped for furnishing a complete Academic education in English and classical studies. There are also Encyclopædias and other needed books of reference.

The present principal is D. Otis Bean, a graduate of Dartmouth College, and the school is in a prosperous condition. It has been an active force in the educational appliances of the Town and surrounding country, and offers to all who are seeking an education excellent facilities at reasonable cost. It pays special attention to fitting the young for college, and has regular classes organized for that purpose. The school has a long and honorable history, and is worthy of the patronage not only of Town, but of a wide region of territory which is poorly provided with higher schools of learning. All that is necessary to give it a still wider usefulness, and place it upon a par with the foremost schools of the land, is an ample endowment. No spot in New England has so many facilities and advantages of pure air, healthfulness of location, cleanliness of population, and safe social, and moral surroundings as the village of Haverhill in which the Academy is situated.

CHAPTER XV.

RELIGION AND CHURCHES.

Religion and the founders—Early vote to call Rev. Peter Powers—Salary—Temporary preaching—First meetings at Newbury, Vt.—Parsonage Lot—Extent of Parish—Minister paid by Town—Protest—Certain Persons excused—Meeting House—Meetings in Houses and Barns—Union Meeting House in Newbury—Coming of Mr. Powers—People worshipped part of time in Newbury—Crossing river—Mr. Powers' Parish—Town divided into two Parishes—Propagating the Gospel—Church organizations—First Congregational Church—Pastors: Ethan Smith, John Smith, Grant Powers, Henry Wood, Joseph Gibbs, Archibald Fleming, Samuel Delano, Moses C. Searle, Edward H. Greeley, John D. Emerson, John Q. Bittinger, Eugene W. Stoddard—Methodist Episcopal Church: North Haverhill, Corner, East Haverhill—Baptist Church, North Haverhill—Free Will Baptist Church—Union Church—Advent Church—Protestant Episcopal Church, Woodsville—Methodist Episcopal Church, Woodsville.

Our fathers being strongly impressed with the importance of religion took steps early with reference to their needs in this respect. In 1765, at a special town meeting, it was voted to "join with Newbury to give Mr. Peter Powers a call as their Gospel minister." Haverhill's part of the salary was "£35, 6s., —d., and one-third part of Mr. Powers' installment." In addition to this sum of money Mr. Powers was to have "thirty cords of wood at his door, cut and corded, a year." These were the days of immense fire-places and large chimneys which consumed such generous quantities of wood.

This was the first vote of money by the Town. The committee chosen to carry out this vote were Timothy Bedel, John Taplin, and Elisha Lock, who were also directed to ask the co-operation of the Proprietors in what they were pleased to call "this affair." It would seem from the Town records of Newbury that each town was to be a separate parish, and afterwards Mr. Powers claimed that he was "installed pastor of Haverhill equally as of Newbury."

But previous to this, as early as 1763, at a Proprietors' meeting a vote was passed that "the Proprietors of Haverhill join with the Proprietors of Newbury in paying for preaching for two months this fall;" and again in the following year the Proprietors voted to join Newbury in "having preaching for six months next ensuing." It was stipulated that the preaching was to be at Newbury. The meeting at which this vote was taken was the last meeting of the Proprietors that was held away from the settlement. Afterwards they met at Haverhill. The first of these meetings convened at the house of Capt. John Hazen, where in the early days of the Town the pioneers were wont to gather, and devise ways and means for the government and progress of the settlement. At this meeting in Haverhill the first article acted on was that " two hundred acres of land be laid out as a parsonage [lot] for this parish, next to the river." This lot was at Horse meadow north of the Hazen farm. In early times in New England the parish extended over the whole Town, and it was customary for each town to set apart a ministerial right or lot of land for the first settled pastor.

In colonial times under a statute enacted in Queen Ann's reign, towns were empowered to hire and settle ministers, and pay them a stipulated salary from the public treasury. Each town could employ a minister of such persuasion as it chose, and every taxable citizen was compelled to contribute toward his support, unless he could prove that he belonged to a different persuasion and regularly attended worship on the Sabbath; and this condition of things continued practically until the toleration act was passed in 1807, notwithstanding the bill of rights declared " that no person of any one particular sect or denomination shall ever be compelled to pay toward the support of the teacher or teaching of another persuasion, sect, or denomination." The established church of the early history of the Town was the Congregational church, and all persons were taxed for the support of it.

As already noted the Town voted in 1765 to unite with Newbury in giving Mr. Powers a call, and appropriated money for his support. Against this method of providing for the gospel there was at first no opposition, at least it did not manifest itself in public; but as diversity of religious sentiment grew more marked, and religious sects began to multiply, an uneasy spirit gained possession of many minds and made itself heard in public protest against what was considered a hardship and an injustice. This spirit was embodied in a notice which was served upon the Town in 1805 and was in these words: "We are not of the same sect or denomination on matters of religion with Mr. Smith, the minister of the Town. We do not attend on his ministry or meeting, nor do we consider our polls or estates liable to be taxed or to pay any part of his salary." This notice was signed by sixteen persons.

In the previous year Moses Dow protested in town meeting against the payment of the minister's salary from the public treasury. Other persons about this period,—showing that the toleration act of 1807 was the outgrowth of a general protest against the support of religion by taxation,—were excused from paying minister's taxes in Haverhill, on the ground that they belonged to other denominations and contributed for the support of the gospel in them. One Thomas Nichols was thus excused because he was "sentimentally a Baptist."

There was no meeting house in Haverhill for some time after the advent of the pioneer settlers, and the matter of building a place of public worship was first put into the warrant in 1769. The size of this building, according to a vote of the following year, was to be forty by fifty feet, and it was ordered to be built within a year. But this vote was not fulfilled, at least the building was not completed, and the size was afterwards voted to be changed from the above dimensions to that of thirty by thirty-six feet. This house was at Horse meadow and was afterwards enlarged. It was taken down in 1882 and converted into a barn by Lafayette Morse.

However, as early as 1767, the Town voted to join Newbury in building a meeting house in the center of that Town on the road next to the river, and the house erected at that point was long used by the people on both sides of the river for public worship. At first, meetings were held in private houses or in barns. Even as late as 1776 meetings were held in barns on the Haverhill side, for in that year the Town " voted to pay Rev. Peter Powers £37, 10s., provided he preached one-half the time in Haverhill, and to meet the first six months in Mr. Kay's lower barn." It would seem from this vote that at that date the meetings on the Haverhill side were held half the time at the south end.

Rev. Peter Powers came to the New Settlement in 1764 to look after the religious interests of the inhabitants. The settlers of Haverhill attended church in Newbury part of the time, and continued so until the organization of the First Church of Haverhill in 1790. Those at the south end of the Town crossed the river near where the middle bridge now stands,—a path from Judge Woodward's led down to the ferry which in the earliest days was a log canoe,—and after crossing they followed a path along the west bank to the meeting house at the Great Ox Bow. Those living at the Plain or North Haverhill crossed the river at the Dow farm and at the Porter place. In those days everybody attended church, and it was deemed disreputable without valid excuse to be absent from worship on the Sabbath. Some of the inhabitants had to go five miles or more. Often parents were seen carrying their children in their arms the entire distance going and coming. The church was plain and without the comforts of modern sanctuaries. The people sat on rude benches, joining reverently in long prayers, and listening patiently to still longer sermons, and at the close of the service they walked back to their homes.

The church at the Great Ox Bow was for some years the

only church north of Charlestown, and Mr. Powers was frequently called upon to officiate at funerals and at weddings up and down the river, going as far south as Hanover, and north to Wells River. These journeyings were at first performed in a canoe.

Grant Powers tells a story in connection with bringing up Rev. Peter Powers' goods from No. 4, which illustrates the sort of discipline that prevailed in the church at that time. It was in early spring. A person by the name of Way had charge of a sled, and at the mouth of the Pompanoosuc river the sled broke through the ice. Way, seeing the danger he had escaped, exclaimed, "That is a cussed hole." Mr. Powers admonished his parishioner for this misdemeanor, but Way, being somewhat eccentric, held to his position, saying that he could prove what he said. "How so?" asked the minister. "Why, didn't God curse the earth, and do you suppose he excepted that little hole?"

In 1788 it was voted to divide the Town into two parishes, and the line was to run on the south side of the "Fisher farm," but this vote was not at once carried out, and by a subsequent order of the Town the vote was rescinded. Some difficulty seems to have arisen, and a committee was appointed to settle all disputes between the two ends of the Town. It was not till 1815 that the Town by vote of the legislature was divided into two parishes, and Samuel Morey of Orford, Jonathan Merrill of Warren, and Samuel Hutchins of Bath, were appointed a committee to run the line. The second parish church was organized at Horse meadow after the organization of the church at Ladd street.

By the charter of the Town one share was to be laid out "for the propagation of the gospel in foreign lands," but a record of 1773 informs us that the Proprietors refused to lay out the share.

CHURCH ORGANIZATIONS.

THE FIRST CONGREGATIONAL CHURCH.

The First Congregational Church of Haverhill was organized Oct. 13, 1790, with an original membership of twenty-three. Previous to this members of the church in Haverhill were connected with the church at Newbury. The religious condition of the people of Haverhill was much depressed at the close of the Revolution, and continued so for some years after, when a powerful religious interest was awakened, out of which grew the organization of the First Church. The first church building was on Ladd street, and was occupied about forty years, when the present brick church was bought from the Methodists in 1830.

PASTORS.

ETHAN SMITH.

In 1792 the church called Ethan Smith to be its pastor,—born in Belchertown, Mass., in 1762, and a graduate from Dartmouth College in 1798,—and he was ordained and installed, 1792, over the infant church, remaining till 1799. For some reason he was not settled by the Town. He was afterwards pastor of the church in Hopkinton, Hebron, N. Y., Poultney, Vt., and Haverhill, Mass., and ended his ministerial career as city missionary in Boston. He died at the age of 87, and during his life he was highly esteemed as a man and as a minister, and was unquestionably a person of strong mind and character. When he left Hopkinton where he was pastor for many years, the whole town turned out and escorted him several miles on his way. He was an early advocate of temperance, and a friend of the slave, and was progressive in all his thoughts and purposes. Daniel Webster, who knew him well,—their wives being intimate friends,—regarded him as one of the ablest and most godly men in New England. Mr. Smith was an author, publishing works on the Prophecies and on Revelation, also an ingenious book maintaining that the North American Indians were the lost tribes of Israel, a work on Baptism, and a hand-book on the Trinity. All these had wide sale in their day.

He married Bathsheba, daughter of Rev. David Sanford of Medway, Mass., an uncle of Mrs. Alden Sprague of Haverhill. They had ten children. The sons were born in Haverhill, and attained distinction, (see Chap. XIX). The daughters were born in Hopkinton. Grace Fletcher and Sarah Towne became, one the first and the other the second wife of Rev. J. H. Martyn, a well-known minister in New York City. Sarah Towne was a gifted writer, and was elected one of the earliest principals of the female department of Oberlin College. She wrote "Women of the Bible." Harriet married Rev. William H. Sanford, and Ellen Chase was the first wife of Hon. C. B. Sedgwick, a member of congress from Syracuse, N. Y., during the War of the Rebellion. Mrs. Sanford of Worcester, Mass., is the only child of Mr. Smith now living.

JOHN SMITH

Was settled by the Town in 1802 and was dismissed and deposed in 1807. He afterwards continued to live in Haverhill, and pursued farming. Two of his sons, it is said, were graduates of Dartmouth College.

GRANT POWERS

Was born in Hollis in 1784, fitted for college at Phillips Academy, Andover, Mass., graduated from Dartmouth College in 1810, studied theology with Rev. Asa Burton, D.D., of Thetford, Vt., and was ordained and settled as pastor over the church in Haverhill in 1815, where he remained till 1829. Afterwards he became the pastor of the Congregational church, Goshen, Ct., dying there in 1841. He was a successful minister, a man of strong mind, and left his impress on the Town. He wrote the "History of the Coös Country."

His wife's maiden name was Eliza Howard Hopkins, and they had eight children. Of these Elizabeth Abbott, Mary Webster, Henrietta Mumford, and George Carrington (see Chap. XIX). Mrs. Powers died recently in Washington, and was very active during the Rebellion in ministering to sick and wounded soldiers. In Mr. Powers' day Methodists were regarded by Calvinists as not orthodox, and Mr. Powers, it is said, got into a controversy with Bryan Morse. Both men were somewhat pugilistic in their opinions.

HENRY WOOD

Was born in London in 1806, and was one of eight children of Eliphalet and Elizabeth (Tilton) Wood. His father was from Boxford, Mass., and his mother from Chester. The Wood family came from the Isle of Wight early in colonial times, and within thirty years after the arrival of the Mayflower records of death are found in Boxford, Mass. His grandfather was at Bunker Hill and saw Warren fall; Burgoyne surrender; with Arnold at Quebec: at Trenton, Princeton, Valley Forge: saw Andre hung, and was one of Washington's life-guards.

Mr. Wood's early education was in the common school, at Gilmanton Academy, and in a printing office in Concord. Then fitting for college at Meriden he entered Dartmouth College, working his way by teaching, and graduated in 1822, being valedictorian of his class. He was a good linguist, and had mastered during life seventeen languages which he read with fluency. Choate and Marsh were contemporaries with him in college. After graduation he remained one year as tutor in the college and then studied theology at Princeton Seminary. He was subsequently for two years tutor and for a like time professor of Latin and Greek in Hampton-Sydney College, Va. Before coming to Haverhill in 1835 he was settled at Goffstown, and after leaving Haverhill he became pastor of the college church, Hanover. For a time he edited the Congregational Journal at Concord, then in 1853 was appointed by President Pierce consul at Beirut, and afterwards was a chaplain in the navy till his death in 1873 in Philadelphia. Whilst in China and Japan he became much interested in missionary work.

He married Harriet Frances McGaw of Bedford, and of eight children the eldest daughter, Ellen, became the wife of Capt. Thornton who commanded the Kearsarge when that vessel sank the rebel cruiser Alabama. The eldest son was at one time literary editor on the Philadelphia North American, and now lives in Washington. A younger daughter married Prof. A. S. Hardy of Dartmouth College. Mr. Wood was a man of ability and much independence of thought. He received the honorary degree of Doctor of Divinity from Hampton-Sidney College in 1867.

JOSEPH GIBBS

Was installed over the church in 1835. He was a Scotchman and educated in London. His ministry, on account of ill health, was brief, dying within two years after it began. He was a man of much promise.

ARCHIBALD FLEMING.

Archibald Fleming settled in 1838, dismissed in 1841. He was also a Scotchman. It was in Mr. Fleming's pastorate that the anti-slavery feeling came into the church.

SAMUEL DELANO

Became pastor of the church in 1842. He was a man of imperious will, much vigor of mind, and quite eccentric. Being remonstrated with by one of the sisters of the church on this account, he replied in characteristic style: "I must be Sam Delano or nobody." He was a graduate of Dartmouth College in 1823, and a trustee of that institution for thirty-two years. He died in 1877 aged 82. Mr. Delano after dismission from Haverhill was acting pastor of the

Second Church for a time, and then went to Hartland, and afterwards to Strafford, Vt.

MOSES C. SEARLE.

Mr. Searle was acting pastor from 1847 to 1849.

EDWARD HANFORD GREELEY,

Son of Edward and Hannah (Eaton) Greeley, was born in Hopkinton in 1817. He fitted for college at Kimball Union Academy, and graduated from Dartmouth College in 1845. For one year after leaving college he was principal of Atkinson Academy, and then went to Andover Seminary, from which he graduated in 1849. The same year he was ordained pastor of the church at Haverhill. After remaining nine years he was called to the Pearl Street Church, Nashua, then to Methuen, Mass., and afterwards, 1868, he returned to Haverhill. In 1874 he was elected secretary of the New Hampshire Home Missionary Society, which position he now holds.

He married first Jane Jewett Richards of Rowley, Mass., who lived only two years after marriage, then Louisa Maria Ware of Needham, Mass. They have four children living, three sons and one daughter. The sons are graduates of Dartmouth College, and the daughter of Andover, Mass., Female Academy.

Mr. Greeley is a man of excellent judgment, of decided ability, and takes large views of things. He has filled the position of secretary of the New Hampshire Home Missionary Society with distinguished faithfulness and success. He received the honorary degree of Doctor of Divinity from his Alma Mater in 1884.

JOHN D. EMERSON

Was born in Candia in 1828, educated in common schools and at Pembroke Academy, and graduated in 1853 from Dartmouth College. For two years he was principal of Pembroke Academy and then studied theology at Andover,

Mass. In 1858 he was settled over the church at Haverhill, remaining till 1868, when he became pastor of the Second Church, Biddeford, Me. Afterwards he was pastor of the church at Underhill, Vt., and also taught in the Academy at that place, and since 1883 he has been pastor of the South and North Churches, Kennebunkport, Me.

Mr. Emerson married first, Sarah Jane Dudley of Candia, and their only child Edward D. is a graduate of Dartmouth College; second, Mrs. Elizabeth French Bell of Chelsea, Mass., and a son, Stephen Goodhue, is a graduate of Dartmouth College and a student now at Oberlin Seminary; third, Leha Florence Kendall of Biddeford, Me., and by this marriage there were four children.

Mr. Emerson has written much, and published a number of discourses and memorial addresses, of which " History of York Conference," " Memorial of the Pilgrims," " History of Second Church," Biddeford, Me., " Ideal in Character," are amongst the more important. His style is graceful and original at times, and full of imagination and poetry.

JOHN QUINCY BITTINGER

Is the eighth child of Joseph and Lydia (Bair) Bittinger, born in 1831 in Berwick township, Adams county, Penn., early education in common schools and printing office, began to fit for college at Oxford Institute, Adams county, Penn., two years at Phillips Academy, Andover, Mass., graduated from Dartmouth College and from Andover Seminary. Settled at Yarmouth, Me., St. Albans, Vt., where health failed, one year supplied Broadway Church, Norwich, Conn., five years at Hartland, Vt., twelve years at Haverhill, resigning January, 1886, and editor of New Hampshire Journal two years and a half, resigning February, 1888.

Mr. Bittinger has written much for the secular and religious press, and has published " Address on Ephraim Jewett Hardy," a classmate senior year in college ; " Cairnes' Slave Power," North American Review ; " Christian Miracles and

Physical Science," Presbyterian and Theological Review; "Preaching and Architecture," Congregational Review; "Address on Benjamin H. Steele," a judge of the Vermont Supreme Court; "Address on Elias Bates;" "Centennial Discourse;" "History of Haverhill."

Married Sarah Jones Wainwright of Hanover, and of their children three sons and one daughter are living, two sons being educated at Haverhill Academy and Dartmouth College.

EUGENE W. STODDARD

Was born in Milford, Mass., in 1860, the son of Lorenzo and Jane (Fisher) Stoddard. Was educated in the common and high schools of Milford, graduated from Amherst College in 1882, and from Andover Seminary in 1886. He was ordained and installed in 1886. His wife's maiden name was Lillie A. Mitchell, and they have one child.

METHODIST EPISCOPAL CHURCH, NORTH HAVERHILL.

Methodism was introduced into north-western New Hampshire about 1800, at which time the Landaff circuit which included Haverhill was organized. The new doctrine spread rapidly. One of the first to preach it was a Haverhill boy, Laban Clark, born in 1778, but in his infancy his family moved to Bradford, Vt., when young Clark about the age of twenty, being dissatisfied with the ways of Calvinism, became interested in the "New Departure," of those days. A year later, 1800, whilst on a visit to Wentworth, he went with a local preacher, John Langdon, on a preaching tour, making two appointments in Landaff. Clark afterwards became very prominent as a Methodist preacher in the denomination and held many leading positions, including New York, Troy, Hartford, and New Haven.

The exact time when Methodist preaching first commenced in North Haverhill cannot now be ascertained. The old Landaff circuit originally embraced the Town of Haverhill, and probably Methodist preaching began in the Town as early as 1800.

In the old minutes we find some historic names connected with Landaff circuit, such as Elijah Sabin, Martin Ruter, Asa Kent, John W. Hardy, Jacob Sanborn, Lewis Bates, Samuel Kelley, Abram D. Merrill and Benj. R. Hoyt. These men were among the pioneers of Methodism in New Hampshire, and probably the foundation of the Methodist church in North Haverhill was laid by them.

The oldest accessible records of church membership is that of 1836. In 1842 at a camp-meeting held in Landaff under the superintendence of Rev. Chas. D. Cahoun, Presiding Elder of Haverhill District, a great revival began, which spread all over Landaff circuit. There were many additions to the M. E. Church at North Haverhil'. Up to this time, the Methodists had no house of worship at North Haverhill, but meetings were held in the Congregational Church at Horse meadow. This great revival so increased their strength, that they resolved to build a house of worship. Eber Eastman, Newhall Pike and James Glynn, were chosen a building committee. This house of worship was erected in 1843, on the site now occupied by the M. E. Church. In 1865 it was destroyed by fire.

It was rebuilt in 1866. John W. Jackson, Hubert Eastman, N. P. Rideout, James Glynn, Jefferson Pennock were the building committee. Both houses were dedicated by Rev. Elisha Adams, a former pastor. A year or two later, a fine parsonage property was added, located beside the church.

This church has not been without its trials and reverses, meeting with many losses by death and removals; yet it has exerted a great influence for good in this part of the Town. It has enjoyed the services of some eminent men, who have filled the pulpits of our largest churches. Among the preachers stationed at North Haverhill the following have filled the office of Presiding Elder, viz.: Benj. R. Hoyt, Reuben Dearborn, Newell Culver, Chas. R. Harding, John Currier, Silas Quimby, Elisha Adams, Chas. U. Dunning, M. T. Cilley.

The following are the appointments of the Haverhill circuit, which included North Haverhill, from 1830 to 1845:

1830, Caleb Dustin, William Peck,
1831, Caleb Dustin, Chas. R. Harding, Jas. W. Mowry,
1832, N. W. Aspinwall, C. R. Harding, S. A. Cushing,
1833, Caleb Lamb, Daniel I. Robinson,
1834, D. I. Robinson, C. Granger,
1835, M. G. Cass, R. Dearborn,
1836, J. Gould, D. Blodgett,
1837, S. Quimby, J. Gould,
1838, S. Quimby, J. Dow,
1839, E. B. Fletcher, W. Johnson,
1840, D. Wilcox, E. B. Morgan,
1841, Geo. W. Stearns, C. W. Lovering, Elisha Brown,
1842, E. Adams, J. W. Wheeler,
1843, E. Adams, J. W. Wheeler, T. P. Brigham,
1844, D. Lee, H. H. Hartwell,

Appointments at North Haverhill:

1845, H. H. Hartwell,
1846, Newell Culver,
1847, Benj. R. Hoyt,
1848-9, Kimball Hadley,
1850, Charles H. Lovejoy,
1851, D. W. Barber,
1852, Richard Newhall,
1853, O. H. Call,
1854, Nelson Martin,
1855, A. C. Dutton,
1856-7, C. U. Dunning,
1858-9, A. K. Howard.
1860-1, Silas Quimby,
1862-3, Geo. S. Noyes,
1864-5, L. W. Prescott,
1866-7, S. P. Heath,
1868-9, H. A. Matteson,
1870-1, W. C. Robinson,
1872-3-4, John Currier,
1875-6, Joseph Hayes,
1877-8, J. H. Knott,
1879, I. J. Tebbetts,
1880-1, James Cairns,
1882, S. P. Heath,

1883–4–5, J. H. Brown. 1887, M. T. Cilley.
1886, J. H. Hillman.

METHODIST EPISCOPAL CHURCH, HAVERHILL.

The date of the organization of the Methodist Episcopal Church at the Corner is not certainly known, but is supposed to be the year 1822, when the Rev. Mr. Bliss labored there. Amongst the earlier prominent members of the church were Ex.-Gov. John Page, George Woodward, the lawyer, Jonathan St. Clair, Samuel Smith, William Ladd, Abba Swift and C. B. M. Woodward. In 1828 the Methodists built the Brick church, but soon after sold it to the Congregationalists, and later, in 1836, they erected the present church edifice, the ground on which it stands being given by Gov. Page. It is a neat wood structure, and answers well the wants of the congregation. The present membership of the church is fifty-four, and a flourishing Sabbath school of one hundred is connected with it. A parsonage has recently been added to the church property. It also owns a cottage at the Weirs.

The following are the names of the pastors from its organization to the present time:

1826, Haverhill and Orford, Ebenezer Ireson, Nathan Howe.
1827, Haverhill, E. Ireson, Moses Merrill.
1828, "   E. Wells, John J. Bliss.
1829, "   Schuyler Chamberlin.
1830, Orford and Haverhill, Caleb Dustin, Wm. Peck.
1831, Haverhill and Orford, Caleb Dustin, C. R. Hareling, Jas. W. Mowry.
1832, Orford and Haverhill, N. W. Aspinwall, C. R. Hareling, Samuel A. Cushing.
1833, Haverhill, C. Lamb, D. I. Robinson.
1834, "   D. I. Robinson, C. Granger.
1835, "   M. G. Cass, R. Dearborn.

1836, Haverhill, J. Gould, L. D. Blodgett,
1837,   "   S. Quimby, J. Gould,
1838, Haverhill and East Haverhill, S. Quimby, J. Dow,
1839,   "   "   E. B. Fletcher, J. W. Johnson,
1840, Haverhill, D. Wilcox,
1841, Haverhill and East Haverhill, Geo. W. Stearns, Chester W. Lovings, Elisha Brown,
1842, Haverhill and East Haverhill, E. Adams, J. W. Wheeler, T. B. Bingham,
1843, Haverhill, E. Adams,
1844, Haverhill and East Haverhill, R. H. Spaulding, D. Lee, H. Hartwell,
1845, Haverhill, East Haverhill, North Haverhill, Wm. Hewes, G. W. H. Clark, H. H. Hartwell,
1846, Haverhill, Piermont and Orford, Wm. Hewes, Geo. S. Dearborn,
1847, Haverhill, Mission and Piermont, Lewis Howard,
1848, Haverhill, Mission and North Haverhill, Kimball Hadley,
1849, To be supplied,
1850, Haverhill and North Haverhill, Chas. H. Lovejoy,
1851, Haverhill and Piermont, to be supplied,
1852–3, Haverhill, Piermont and North Haverhill, R. Newhall,
1854, Haverhill, East Haverhill and Piermont, A. C. Dustin,
1855, One to be supplied,
1856–7, Not mentioned.

From 1858 to the present time, Haverhill had pastors alone, with the exception of one year, 1878, when Piermont was united with Haverhill.

1858, Chas. U. Dunning.   1860, Geo. C. Thomas.
1859, Probably   "   1861–2–3, Chas. H. Chase,

1864, Richard Harcourt,
1865–6–7, J. M. Bean,
1868, John Gowan,
1869, H. S. Ward,
1870–1, H. A. Matteson,
1872–3, J. Hooper,
1874, J. Hayes,

1875–6, J. T. Davis,
1877, T. Winsor,
1878–9–80, G. N. Byrant,
1881, C. E. Rogers,
1882, A. C. Hardy,
1883–4, Wm. Ramsden,
1885–6–7, J. H. Trow.

METHODIST EPISCOPAL CHURCH, EAST HAVERHILL.

A Methodist society was organized at East Haverhill in December, 1833, by Henry Noyes, Moses Mead, Caleb Morse and Roswell Elliot. Long, however, before this time there was Methodist preaching in this part of the Town, the meetings being held in barns and houses. A church edifice was built in 1834, and has been remodelled several times since. The ground was given by Isaac Pike. There is also a neat parsonage near the church.

The following are the names of ministers who preached at East Haverhill previous to 1838, some of whom were local preachers, others were on the circuit:

Elder Britten,
Charles Baker,
Elder Emory,
Caleb Lamb,
Caleb Dustin,
Newell Culver,
Moses Cass,
Reuben Dearborn,
J. W. Mowry,
Joseph Peck,
Daniel Robinson,
J. Gould,
Samuel A. Cushing,
C. W. Lovings,

D. W. Barker,
W. Hemenway,
J. N. Moffett,
Daniel Wise,
W. B. Leighton,
J. English,
Charles Harding,
C. Granger,
Elder Smith,
N. W. Aspinwall,
Bryan Morse,
Brazzilia Pierce,
Moses Merrill,
Elder Savage

From 1838 the church had pastors as follows:

S. Quimby,	Kimball Hadley,
J. Dow,	Charles H. Lovejoy,
E. P. Fletcher,	John M. Blake,
J. W. Johnson,	Richard Newhall,
E. P. Morgan,	Orick W. Watkins,
Elisha Brown,	Calvin F. Bailey,
Charles Lovejoy,	Charles H. Chase,
J. W. Wheeler,	H. Montgomery,
T. P. Brigham,	A. B. Russell,
George W. Stevens,	Josiah Hooper,
D. Lee,	A. W. Brown,
H. H. Hartwell,	I. J. Tebbetts,
G. W. H. Clark,	C. W. Dockrill,
C. L. McCurdy,	L. W. Prescott,
Benj. R. Hoyt,	C. E. Rogers,
George W. Bryant,	W. A. Loyne.

This church and society is now in a prosperous condition and has just raised $1,000 for a vestry. It also owns a neat cottage at the Weirs.

BAPTIST CHURCH, NORTH HAVERHILL.

A Baptist Society was organized at North Haverhill, Dec. 22, 1836, composed of Oliver Davidson, Asa Thing, Elijah Blood, George Warren, Joshua Blaisdell, Jacob Morse, Asa Baron, Aaron P. Glazier, Daniel Carr, Jr., George W. Bisbee, Zebulon Cory and Clark Baron. The following year the society built a brick church costing $1,533.87, which is still standing. The first minister was Rev. D. Burroughs, and from the society's records it does not appear that it had any other, and the organization does not seem to have existed long, as February, 1846 is the last entry in the record of the society. Incidentally we learn that Oliver Davidson and Daniel Carr, Jr., were deacons in the church.

FREE WILL BAPTIST CHURCH.

A church of this order was organized in the eastern part of the Town in 1831. There was a religious meeting held in June of that year in the barn of Josiah Jeffers, and a number of persons being baptized, a church was organized on the occasion. Elder George W. Cogswell preached to this church part of the time for a number of years, and then Abel Wheeler, a member of the church, was ordained and became pastor. But previous to 1831 there was occasional Free Will Baptist preaching by itinerants, the earliest being Elder John Colby, a noted Evangelist, and in 1820 Elder John Davis of East Haverhill preached there and in adjoining towns. In 1842 there was a great awakening in the church, and the preachers after that time were Stedman Cummings, Almon Shepard, Warren Stafford, L. D. Jeffers and J. D. Cross. There is now no Free Will Baptist organization.

UNION MEETING HOUSE, CENTER.

The meeting house at the center was called the "North Haverhill Union Meeting House," and was built in the summer of 1836. There does not appear to have been any church organization connected with it. Religious services have been held more or less frequently by Methodists and Adventists, and at the present time there is a Sabbath school gathered there.

ADVENT CHURCH, HAVERHILL.

The Advent church at the Brook was built in 1875 and was occupied regularly for religious purposes for a year or two. Since 1880 no religious meetings have been held there, and the house was afterwards sold. It is now the creamery building. There was no church organization.

PROTESTANT EPISCOPAL CHURCH, WOODSVILLE.

St. Luke's Protestant Episcopal Church was organized in 1876 by Rt. Rev. Bishop Niles of the Diocese of New Hampshire. The first rector was Rev. W. B. T. Smith. For several years services were held in the school hall, but in 1879 steps were taken to build a church, and the sum of $1,876.00 being raised, a handsome wood structure was erected in 1881, with a seating capacity of two hundred twenty-five persons. The entire church property is valued at $7,900. The society has thirty-five communicants and a Sabbath school of fifty-three. Rev. H. A. Remick is the present rector.

METHODIST EPISCOPAL CHURCH, WOODSVILLE.

This church was organized in May, 1885, by Rev. George W. Norris, Presiding Elder, and Rev. A. Twichell, with a membership of seventeen persons. In 1886 the society built a beautiful church edifice at a cost of $2,500 and a seating capacity of three hundred. Although the church is still small in numbers, it has a flourishing Sabbath school of nearly one hundred. The present pastor is Rev. A. Twichell.

CHAPTER XVI.

HAVERHILL IN WAR.

Her honorable position and officers of highest rank—List of Haverhill soldiers in the several Wars—War of the Revolution—War of 1812—Mexican War—War of the Rebellion—Second Regiment—Fourth Regiment—Sixth Regiment—Ninth Regiment—Eleventh Regiment—Fifteenth Regiment—Eighteenth Regiment—First Regiment Heavy Artillery—First Cavalry.

Haverhill has an honorable place in all the wars in which the country has been engaged. In the War of the Revolution and in the War of the Rebellion she has a conspicuous place and contributed her full share of soldiers. Gen. John Montgomery and Gen. Moody Bedel were her officers of highest rank and served in the War of 1812. In the Revolution she contributed Col. Timothy Bedel, a brave and accomplished officer, and Col. Charles Johnston, one of the heroes of the battle of Bennington. In the War of the Rebellion, though she had no office of high rank, she was bravely represented in minor positions and her sons were in the forefront of the storm and hail of battle. Their names, as far as can be ascertained, are recorded in this chapter and should be inscribed as suggested on a former page, in more worthy and lasting form.

LIST OF HAVERHILL SOLDIERS IN THE SEVERAL WARS.

The following are the names of soldiers who enlisted from Haverhill in the several wars as accurately as can be ascertained:

WAR OF THE REVOLUTION.
1775.

Timothy Bedel, Captain.
Nathaniel Wales, Second Lieutenant.
Joseph Fifield, Corporal.
Joseph Springer,   John Sandburn.

John Tayler,
George Moors,
John Lovering,
James Ladd,
Joseph Hadley,
John Haselton,
Thomas Caprien,
Timothy Curtiss,
John Dodge,
Thomas Simpson,

Joseph Moulton,
David Ladd,
Ebenezer Sanborn,
Mark Sanborn,
Joseph Sawyer,
John Rine,
William Haseltine,
John Tayler,
Thomas Simpson, Jr.

1776.

Charles Johnston, Colonel.
Timothy Bedel, Colonel.
Thomas Simpson, Captain.
Nathaniel Wales, Second Lieutenant.
Jacob Kent, Corporal.
Jonathan Sanders, Sergeant.
George Moors, Sergeant.

Samuel Allen,
Josiah Elkins,
Isaac Stevens,
Thomas Manchester,
John Fifield,
Joseph Fifield,
David Ladd,
John Hodgdon,
Joseph Hadley,
Jesse Heath,
Asa Bailey,
William Abbott,
John Sanborn,
Richard Sanborn,
Benaiah Hall,
Zebulon Hunt,

James Adams,
Amos Heath,
Mark Sanborn,
Moses Duty,
Joseph Sawyer,
Joshua Burnam,
Henry Morgan,
Henry Palmer,
Perley Rogers,
Ebenezer Rice,
Ephraim Wesson,
Samuel Lang,
Alexander Hogg,
Soloman Parker,
William Minor,
Joshua Hayward.

1777.

John White, First Lieutenant.
Thomas Simpson, Second Lieutenant.
Jonathan Sanders, Sergeant,
George Moors, Sergeant.

Joseph Fifield,	John Lovering,
David Ladd,	Daniel Stevens,
John Hodgdon,	Avery Sanders.
Joseph Hadley,	Perley Rogers,
Jesse Heath,	Hezekiah Fuller,
Moses Duty,	Henry Springer,
John Taylor,	Timothy Curtiss,
——— Foster,	John Bishop,
Joshua Burnam,	Gains Niles,
Silas Wheeler,	Antonia Foster,
Henry Palmer,	Robert Simpson.

1778—1782.

Officers and soldiers from 1778 to 1782, but in what year each one served, cannot in every case be exactly determined:

Timothy Bedel, Colonel.
William Tarleton, Captain.
Simeon Stevens, Captain.
Luther Richardson, Captain.
Timothy Barron, Captain.
Ezekiel Ladd, Captain.
James Ladd, Lieutenant.
George Moor, Lieutenant,
Luther Richardson, Lieutenant.

William Locke,	Michael Satter, Drum,
Avery Sanders,	Jonathan Platt, Fife,
Elisha Lock,	Elisha Brown,
Will Lock,	Edward Clark,
Caleb Young,	Ezra Gates,
David Ladd,	Thomas Hazleton.

William Cross,
Andrew Martin,
Jois [Gains] Niles,
Avery Sanders,
Elisha Lock,
Frederick Zilgo,
Jonathan Ladd,
Joseph Young,
Elisha Cleveland,
Noah Moulton,
Joseph Ladd,
Asa Ladd,
Reuben Page,
Michael Johnston,
John Page,
Smith Williams,
Joel Richardson,
Hugh Barnett,
Jonathan Pike,
Daniel Stevens, Jr.,
Elisha Balcom,
John Lovering,
Amos Blood,
William Green,
Ezra Abbott,
Caleb Young,
Michael Salter.

Josiah Pratt,
William Locke,
Jonathan Pratt
Elisha Brown,
Thomas Hazelton,
Jonathan Sanders,
Joseph Fifield,
John Hodgdon,
David Ladd,
Robert Bartley,
John Brown,
Josiah Elkins,
Jonathan Cooper,
Obadiah Eastman,
William Eastman,
Jonathan Eastman,
James Eastman,
John Hackett,
James Gould,
Stephen Morse,
Moses Burns,
Eleazer Danforth,
Daniel Doty,
Ebenezer Whittaker,
Seth Flanders,
Jonathan Morse.

Perhaps in justice to the Town, it ought to be noted that in addition to the above soldiers who volunteered during the Revolution, there were those who doubtless served with Col. Johnston in the 12th Regiment N. H. Militia at the battle of Bennington, as the 12th was made up of the militia forces from Haverhill, Piermont, Orford, Warren and Coventry.

WAR RECORDS.

WAR OF 1812.

John Montgomery, Major General.
Moody Bedel, Brig. General.
George H. Montgomery, Aid-de-camp.
John Page, Jr., Lieutenant.
John McClary, Sergeant.
William W. Bailey, Second Sergeant.
Benjamin Swan, Quarter Sergeant.
John Abbott, Drummer.

Joshua H. Johnston,
Jonas Flagg,
Arad Ford,
Levi Judd,
Robert McKeon,
John Stevens,
Nathan Stevens,
Samuel Woodbury,
Jacob Alls,
Timothy Goodwin,
William Jones,
Joseph Pratt,
Daniel Perkins,
Levi Stafford,
Charles J. Swan,

William Stevens,
Ulysses Young,
Freeman P. Brown,
Samuel Smith,
Amos H. Jones,
Isaac Carleton,
Elisha Hibbard,
Jeremiah Goodwin,
Uriah Ward,
Ezekiel Day,
William Stearns,
Henry Towle,
Ethan S. Ladd,
James Woodward,
E. P. Woodbury.

MEXICAN WAR.

Daniel Batchelder, Captain.
Ezra T. Pike, Third Sergeant,

Henry Albert,
Kinsman Avery,
John Boudle,
John W. Brewer,
George E. Barns,
John F. Glynn,
William Gould, Jr.,

Asa Randall,
George W. Woods,
Nelson B. Woodward,
George Welch,
James Williams,
Albert Knapp,
Charles Ladd,

Joseph E. Little,　　　William W. Welsh.
Arthur L. Pike.

WAR OF THE REBELLION.

Haverhill had soldiers in the following regiments during the War of the Rebellion:

SECOND REGIMENT—THREE YEARS—COMPANY G.

The first enlistment from Haverhill in the War of the Rebellion was in the Second Regiment. This regiment was commanded by Col. Gilman Marston till after the battle of Gettysburg, a brave and able officer. It was in the forefront of danger and service for three years, and participated in twenty-seven battles and skirmishes,—Bull Run, Siege of Yorktown, Williamsburg, Skirmish at Fair Oaks, Savage Station, Peach Orchard, Glendale, First Malvern Hill, Second Malvern Hill, Bristow Station, Second Bull Run, Chantilly, Fredericksburg, in 1862; Skirmish at Manassas Gap, Gettysburg, Wapping Hights, in 1863; Swift's Creek, Drury's Bluff, First Cold Harbor, Second Cold Harbor, Siege of Petersburg, Fair Oaks, Skirmish at Proctor's Creek, Skirmish at Chesterfield, Skirmish at Darbytown, Skirmish at Spring Hill, in 1864.

In the battle of Gettysburg three hundred and thirty-one officers and men went into the fight. The regiment lost two hundred and five men, and out of twenty-three officers, twenty-one were killed or wounded in that terrible contest.

The following are the names of Haverhill men who enlisted in this Regiment:

Lieutenant, Hiram K. Ladd, died at Haverhill, second enlistment, 18th Reg.
Harry B. Casson, died in rebel prison, Andersonville, Ga.,
Samuel Woodward, wounded in action,
William E. Bancroft,
Curtis Hicks, wounded slightly,

Wm. G. Wolcott, second enlistment, 1st Reg. Heavy
  Artillery,
Jowell E. Hibbard, second enlistment, 13th Reg.,
V. B. Glazier,
Samuel E. Merrill.

FOURTH REGIMENT — THREE YEARS — COMPANY I.

This regiment was mustered into the service in September, 1861, and was commanded by Col. Thomas J. Whipple. Its first actual war service was at Port Royal, S. C., and in Florida. It was in the Battle of Pocotaligo Bridge, Oct. 22, 1862, and lost twenty-seven in killed and wounded. Afterwards it was stationed for a time on Morris Island near Charleston. In 1864 the regiment was in the trenches in front of Petersburg, Va. It was engaged in the frequent skirmishes, and was in the charge on Fort Gilmore, a strong earth-work on the lines of defence around Richmond, in which the loss was severe for the number engaged. Later in 1864 it was ordered to take part in the expedition against Fort Fisher, N. C., where it skirmished successfully with the enemy. Afterwards it returned to its old place before Richmond. No record is left of its subsequent movement, but doubtless it took part in the final struggle which caused the evacuation of the Confederate capital.

The following are the Haverhill soldiers who enlisted in the Fourth Regiment:
Lieutenant, Henry M. Hicks,
   "   Eben Webb.
First Lieutenant, Andrew Jackson Edgerly.
Sergeant, Jonathan Clark.
   "   John W. Bemis.
Corporal, Dana Fifield.
Corporal, James Wilson.
Corporal, John T. Wolcott.
Alfred T. Hardy.

John D. McConnel, killed in action, Petersburg, Va.,
Jonas E. Haynes,
Joseph Ranney, killed in action,
Daniel C. Randall, died in hospital.

SIXTH REGIMENT — THREE YEARS — COMPANY B.

This regiment was recruited in 1861, and left for the seat of war in December, under Col. Nelson Converse. It was under Gen. Burnside in N. C., and saw its first hard service at the Battle of Camden, and for distinguished bravery it was allowed to enscribe on its banner, "CAMDEN, APRIL 19TH, 1862." The regiment was afterwards in the following battles : — Second Bull Run, Chantilly, South Mountain, Antietam, Annisville, White Sulphur Springs, Fredericksburg, Vicksburg, Jackson, 1862. It also participated in the campaign under Grant against Richmond, from the Battle of the Wilderness till the close of the war, and was often in the thickest of the fight. This was one of the regiments that suffered so heavily at the explosion of the mine at Petersburg, July, 1864.

The following are the names of those from Haverhill who enlisted in this regiment :
Captain, Samuel P. Adams, died at Haverhill.
Sergeant, H. L. Blanchard, killed by accident in the service.
Sergeant, A. J. Randall.
 " E. L. Smith.
A. Stover, missing in action,
George Cass, killed in action at Cold Harbor,
Sumner Hardy,
Hiram H. Pool, died at Lynn, Mass,
John Swift,
C. W. Sherwell, killed at Fredericksburg, Va.,
Nathan W. Wheeler, died at Hatteras Inlet, N. C., March 15, 1862,
John Flavin,

Henry G. Tasker, died in rebel prison.
Horace Holmes,
West Pearsons, died in hospital,
Edward C. Holmes,
Charles P. Pattern, died at Soldiers' Home in Maine.
M. V. B. Randall,
Ira Stowell, died in hospital,
George H. Smith,
Joseph Weed, wounded, died of wounds.

NINTH REGIMENT—THREE YEARS—COMPANY A.

This regiment left the state in 1862 in command of Col. E. Q. Fellows, and within a month after its departure it saw stern war service in pursuit of Gen. Lee, when he invaded Maryland, after the defeat of Gen. Pope's army. It participated in the battles of South Mountain, Antietam, and afterwards engaged with distinguished valor in the Battle of Fredericksburg, where scores of its brave officers and men fell dead or wounded on the field. The regiment went next with Gen. Burnside to Kentucky, and soon after joined the forces around Vicksburg, though it was not in the immediate assault upon that stronghold, joined the column in pursuit of Gen. Johnston, and took part in the Battle of Jackson, Miss. The regiment was then ordered to Kentucky on provost duty, and later to Cumberland Gap in expectation of participating in Gen. Sherman's campaign in Georgia, but it was unexpectedly ordered back to Virginia to take part in the last march against Richmond. It led the advance at Spottsylvania Court House in storming the enemy's works, and suffered a loss of more than two hundred in killed, wounded, and prisoners. In this assault both its Lieutenant-Colonel and Major were severely wounded. A few days later it stormed alone a strong rebel position, and at Cold Harbor in a brilliant charge it captured three pieces of artillery and three hundred and seventy-five prisoners. The regiment was in all the engagements before Petersburg, including the explosion of the famous mine, and distinguished itself for bravery and gallantry. Its subsequent history is not definitely stated, but probably it formed a part of that grand army that finally captured Richmond and caused the surrender of Lee's forces.

Scott Keyser,
William Clark, died in hospital.
George S. Humphrey,
Henry Chapman, died of wounds,
Charles T. Collins,
Joseph S. Willey.

ELEVENTH REGIMENT—THREE YEARS—COMPANY G.

The Eleventh regiment left Concord in September, 1862, in command of Col. Walter Harriman, and joined the grand army of the Potomac under Gen. McClellan. The regiment went into camp near Falmouth, Va., and soon after was engaged in the Battle of Fredericksburg, where it distinguished itself for gallant conduct in the hottest of the fight, losing in killed and wounded, two hundred and one officers and men. In February, 1863, it went to Newport News, Va., and soon after as part of the Ninth Army Corps, it was transferred to Kentucky, and thence to Vicksburg, where it was engaged in the trenches around that stronghold until the city fell. It was also in the Battle of Jackson, Miss., and took a prominent part in the capture of that city. After this, it returned to Kentucky, marching two hundred miles on almost trackless mountain roads to Knoxville, and was engaged in the siege of that city. It formed part of the army that pursued Gen. Longstreet till he left Tennessee and then in 1864 it again joined the army of the Potomac against Richmond and was engaged in all the battles of that campaign. In the Battle of the Wilderness it fought bravely, losing severely in officers and men, including in the former its Lieutenant-Colonel killed, and Col. Harriman taken prisoner. It also lost heavily at Spottsylvania, and was engaged at North Anna, Cold Harbor, Petersburg, and all the series of engagements till the fall of Richmond. The Eleventh saw hard service and always bore itself bravely in every battle in which it took part. By order of the War Department, for meritorious conduct in battle, it had subcribed on its banner, " Fredericksburg, Vicksburg, Jackson, East Tennessee, The Wilderness, Spottsylvania, North Anna, Cold Harbor, Weldon Railroad, Poplar Grove Church, Hatcher's Run, Petersburg."

The following are the names of Haverhill men, an unusually large quota in the Eleventh Regiment :

Captain, J. LeRoy Bell, wounded.
Cyrus Alden.
Levi B. Bisbee.
Frank B. Carr.
D. J. Coburn.
M. V. B. Cady.
W. W. Coburn.
Robert W. Haney, died at Haverhill.
George W. Miller, died in hospital.
Henry Merrill.
J. C. Pennock.
Charles F. Carr.
James W. Sampson, died in hospital.
George C. Swift, killed in action.
George W. Woodward.
Joseph Willis.
W. C. Wetherbee, died at North Haverhill.
Lewis Bean.
Benjamin Bixbee.
Thomas Baxter.
Riley B. Cady, died in hospital.
Hiram S. Carr, died at Woodsville.

Ira B. Gould,
Amos Lund, Jr.,
Moody C. Marston, wounded,
Elias Moulton,
Martin Rogers,
George Southard, died in hospital,
Solon Swift, died at Claremont,
Albert H. Teft,
Orrin M. Whitman,
Albert U. Willey, died of wounds in hospital.
Adion Pike, died of wounds in hospital.

FIFTEENTH REGIMENT—NINE MONTHS, COMPANY B.

This regiment was part of the three hundred thousand nine months men called for by the President in 1862. It was mustered into service in November of that year, and assigned to Gen. Banks' army. Its commander was Col. John W. Kingman. The regiment sailed from New York in December for New Orleans, disembarking and remaining in the vicinity for a short time, and then went to Baton Rouge to form a portion of the forces operating against Port Hudson. It took a gallant and distinguished part in the reduction of that city, being in the hottest of the fight, and making most heroic charges upon the entrenched city. The siege lasted over two months, when on July 9th the rebel forces surrendered. The regiment soon after returned home.

The following are the names of Haverhill men enlisted in this regiment:

Lieutenant, James A. Page.
Sergeant, George W. Pennock.
James Buckland, deserted,
Royal F. Clark,
Charles Carpenter, second enlistment 1st Reg. Heavy Artillery.
R. C. Drown,

James G. Glynn, died in Minnesota,
Ethan O. Harris,
John Hackett,
H. P. Kidder.
Aiken Latherbush,
Lewis Latherbush,
Sylvester W. Marden,
George C. Smith,
Charles G. Perkins, died in hospital New Orleans, La..
Caleb Knight, died at Lowell, Mass.,
John D. Brooks,
N. D. Brooks, died at Lisbon,
E. J. L. Clark,
D. C. Dunklee,
Frank Ferguson,
Hylus Hackett, died in hospital,
N. S. Hannaford,
George F. Keyes, second enlistment 1st Reg. Heavy Artillery,
George W. Leith, wounded, second enlistment 1st Reg. Heavy Artillery,
Calvin Pennock,
John C. Shelley, wounded, died at Haverhill,

EIGHTEENTH REGIMENT—ONE YEAR—COMPANY E.

The Eighteenth regiment was enlisted in July, 1864, under a call for five hundred thousand volunteers. It consisted at first of only six companies, and was under the command of Lieut. Col. Joseph M. Clough till the spring of 1865, when the remaining companies were added, and Col. Thomas L. Livermore assumed command. It was stationed at City Point and on the James river for a time, and then ordered to the front. It took part in the recapture of Fort Steadman after that fortress fell into the hands of the enemy, and was placed in the fort, a position of great importance and danger, as a constant fire was kept up on both sides. Later the enemy again assaulted the fort, but was quickly repulsed by the Eighteenth, but with the loss of Major Brown who fell in the action. Afterwards the regiment was ordered to make a charge on the rebels in front of Fort Steadman, but finding them in full force the attack was abandoned. On the 3d of April after the fall of Petersburg the Eighteenth marched into the city of Richmond, and then soon after went to Washington, where it did guard duty during the trial of the assassins of President Lincoln. The regiment was mustered out at Concord in the summer of 1865. The career of the Eighteenth was short but honorable, and by order of the War Department the names of the following engagements were placed upon the colors of the regiment:

"Fort Steadman, March 25, 1865; attack on Petersburg, April 2, 1865; capture of Petersburg, April 3, 1865."

Sergeant, Harlan S. Blanchard, died at Haverhill.
Frank D. Davis, killed on railroad.
O. S. Hicks,
Don F. Willis,
Levi Bradish, died in Minnesota,
S. H. Butterfield,
Joseph Came, deserter at Concord,
Simeon E. Puffer,
Pearson Wallace.

FIRST REGIMENT HEAVY ARTILLERY — ONE YEAR — COMPANY L.

This regiment began to be recruited in sections in 1863. At first there was only two companies, then four, and after ten companies were raised they were organized into a regiment. Col. Charles H. Long was its commander. The early companies did garrison duty at Portsmouth before the regiment was placed on duty in the fortifications around Washington. Two batteries returned to Portsmouth in the fall and winter of 1864–5. The remaining companies garrisoned a line of works ten miles in extent, and gained great proficiency in artillery drill. The regiment was mustered out of service in June, 1865. The history of this organization is brief and not of startling interest, but it rendered valuable service at a critical time. Most of the men had seen from one to three years service in the earlier period of the war.

Corporal, Orrin Simpson,
Ezekiel Day, died in hospital, Washington, D. C.,
Joseph Deland,
Henry M. Miner, died at Haverhill,
John Stearns,
Patrick Baldwin,
John Day,
Charles Goodwin,
C. J. Pike,
George W. Woods.

FIRST CAVALRY — THREE YEARS — COMPANIES A, C, I.

This regiment was raised in the spring of 1864. Four companies were formerly a part of the First Rhode Island Cavalry, and were raised in 1861. The New Hampshire companies forming a battalion, were commanded by Maj. David B. Nelson. The winter was spent in camp at Concord and at Pawtucket, R. I., and in March, 1862, the regiment was ordered to Washington and later to Warrenton Junction to protect the Capital. Gen. Banks being driven back in the Shenandoah Valley the battalion was ordered there and did valorous deeds before Fort Royal, capturing more prisoners than there were men in the battalion. It was also at Port Republic under Gen. Shields, when Gen. Pope's "Army of Virginia" was acting against Richmond by way of Culpepper Court House, the regiment now united, formed a part of his forces, and was conspicuous in all the battles of that disastrous campaign, South Mountain, Groveton, Second Bull Run and Chantilly, and in the retreat of the army it rendered valient service in protecting the rear, and holding in check the enemy. Afterwards it was active in Virginia, and took part in the engagement at Kelley's Ford, and was with Gen. Stoneman in his famous raid when Gen. Lee started on his Pennsylvania campaign, the regiment was sent to Thoroughfare Gap, where it defeated the enemy, and then attacked Middleburg, but was forced to retreat after a brave and obstinate fight against superior numbers, cutting its way through the enemy's lines. The regiment reached the main body of troops a mere fragment. It was ordered to Gettysburg, and afterwards was in the battles of Bristow Station and Auburn.

In January, 1864, the New Hampshire battalion was permanently detached from the First Rhode Island Cavalry, and the veterans of the battalion re-enlisting, formed the nucleus of the First New Hampshire Cavalry. When organized, it was sent to Washington under command of Col. John L. Thompson, and took an active part in Grant's campaign against Richmond. It was in Gen. Wilson's celebrated raid along the Welden railroad, in which it saw hard service. Afterwards it was with Gen. Sheridan in Shenandoah Valley and fought with great bravery in that campaign. The regiment was mustered out of service in July, 1865.

The later recruits of this regiment were generally bounty-men, and as a class, were worthless, but the first seven companies were composed of the sons of New Hampshire and were brave and soldierly men who reflected honor upon the State.

Lieutenant, George Morrison.
Sergeant, H. H. Morrison.
Corporal, Hiram S. Kellum, died at Haverhill.

Natt Westgate, died in rebel prison Danville, Va., Jan. 7, 1865.
George Cutting,
Byron Carr, lost an arm in action,
J. B. Davis,
Edwin St. Clair,
Simon Cutting,
Simon Elliott,
Jerome Carr, died in rebel prison Danville, Va.

The following Haverhill men enlisted in regiments in other states:
John Chapman, 17th Reg. Vt. Volunteers,
James Boswell, 1st Reg. Vt. Cavalry,
Henry C. Wright, 12th Reg. Vt. Volunteers, died in hospital,
William Dean, 12th Reg. Vt. Volunteers,
Wesley Porter, Mass. Regiment, died in hospital,
Lyford Bailey, 9th Vt. Volunteers, died in hospital,
John Copp, 9th Vt. Volunteers,
George Copp, 9th Vt. Volunteers,
George Perkins, 9th Vt. Volunteers,
Robert Arnold, 9th Vt. Volunteers,
Silas Woodward, 9th Vt. Volunteers, died in hospital,
John H. Day, 9th Vt. Volunteers, second enlistment 1st Reg. N. H. Heavy Artillery,
Chester M. Carleton, Missouri Regiment.

CHAPTER XVII.

THE LAWYERS OF HAVERHILL.

Moses Dow—Alden Sprague—John Porter—Moses Dow, Jr.—George Woodward—Joseph Emerson Dow—John Nelson—Henry Hutchinson—David Sloan—Joseph Bell—Samuel Courtland—Edmund Carleton—Hale A. Johnston—Edward R. Olcott—Daniel Blaisdell—Jonathan Bliss—William H. Duncan—Samuel C. Webster—Nathan B. Felton—David Dickey—David H. Collins—Jonas Darius Sleeper—John S. Bryant—David Page—Charles E. Thompson—George W. Chapman—Charles R. Morrison—Nathaniel W. Westgate—George F. Putnam—Luther C. Morse—Samuel T. Page—Samuel B. Page—William F. Westgate.

From the fact that Haverhill has been a shire town since 1773, she has held a more or less prominent position on account of her lawyers, some of whom have been amongst the ablest and most distinguished in the state. And as the legal profession has always exerted a powerful influence in the community, I have deemed it proper to sketch the lives of all lawyers who have practiced their profession in the Town. Of some only a few facts have been learned, whilst of others of less note the biographies are necessarily brief. Of some, however, the sketches have been made as full as the limits of the chapter would admit, and their character and fame is gladly committed to this keeping.

MOSES DOW.

The exact time when Gen. Dow came to Haverhill is not certainly known, but it must have been previous to 1774, as in that year he was appointed by the Court of the General Sessions of the Peace to act as king's attorney in the absence of the attorney-general. His native place was Atkinson, and his father's name was John Dow. Of his early education we have no information, but his academic course was pursued at Harvard College, from which he graduated in 1769. When and with whom he read law is also unknown. He began the practice of his profession in all probability at Haverhill soon after his admission to the bar, and continued to do so till he was appointed a judge of the Court of Common Pleas, with an interruption of five years at Plymouth. He was also probably the earliest permanently settled lawyer of Grafton county. He was unquestionably one of the strong and leading lawyers in the early history of the Grafton county bar, and held a prominent position not only in his profession, but also in popular esteem. His name occurs repeatedly in the town records as taking an active part in town affairs, and he filled various town offices from 1783 till toward the close of his life. In addition to these more local places of service and honor, he was called into larger spheres of trust. For four years he was solicitor for Grafton county, and from 1774, for a period of thirty years, he was register of probate. In 1780–81 he represented the Town of Haverhill in the legislature, and as early as 1790 he was a member of the state senate, of which body he was chosen president during his term of senatorial service. Previous to this he was a member of the governor's council. He was interested in military matters and was major-general of the state militia. In 1808 he was appointed a judge of the Court of Common Pleas for Grafton county, which office he held till the close of his life. Gen. Dow was also elected in 1784 to the Congress of the United States by the General Assembly of New Hampshire, but declined the honor on the ground that he did not feel himself qualified for the high responsibilities of the position. In his letter to the governor he says: "As I have had no apprehension [no thought of being called to so responsible a position] I had entirely neglected every necessary preparation. * * * The present infirm state of my health, the real conviction of my inequality to the business of the mission, render it extremely difficult, or rather impossible, for me to engage in a trust so arduous and interesting." The average congressman of to-day would vote such modesty and patriotic conscientiousness as blank idiocy.

Gen. Dow was the second postmaster of Haverhill. He took a deep interest in all local matters, and was active in promoting the welfare of the Town. His name appears as one of the incorporators of Haverhill Academy, and he was a heavy subscriber to the stock of a bridge company, for the purpose of building a bridge across the Connecticut river at Haverhill. He was the owner of the " Dow farm," so called in local parlance, a tract of land two and a half miles north of Haverhill Corner, where he resided during the early part of his life, and after he moved to the Corner he lived in the house now owned and occupied by Milo Bailey.

Gen. Dow was a man of great independence of mind, and early led off in a protest against being taxed for the preaching of the gospel. He was fond of discussion, especially the discussion of religious questions. In person he was tall and commanding, with dignified bearing and courtly manners. As a citizen he was enterprising, energetic, a true and earnest patriot, and a man of high character and fine literary attainments. His prominent standing in his profession, and his great abilities, made him not only a foremost citizen of the Town, but eminent in the county and in the state. Dartmouth College bestowed upon him the honorary degree of A. M. in 1785.

Gen. Dow married Phebe Emerson, and they had four children, two sons and two daughters. He died in Haverhill in 1811.

ALDEN SPRAGUE.

Alden Sprague's ancestors came to Plymouth, Mass., from Plymouth, England, in 1623, and were afterwards amongst the prominent people of Rochester, Mass. At what period Alden came to Haverhill is not known, but it must have been earlier than 1796, for in that year he was one of the Selectmen of the Town. He is supposed to have pursued his professional studies in the office of his half-brother, Hon. Peleg Sprague, a prominent lawyer and a member of Congress in 1797–99. Mr. Sprague married twice; first, a cousin of Rev. Ethan Smith's wife, said to have been a very beautiful woman. By this marriage there were two children, Betsy and Harriet. The former became the wife of James I. Swan of Bath, a very able and distinguished lawyer whom the late Isaac Patterson said was the equal of Daniel Webster in eloquence, both of whom on one occasion he heard in an important case at Plymouth. Harriet married Hamlin Rand, father of the late Judge Rand of Lisbon, and Hon. Charles W. Rand of Littleton. Mr. Sprague's second wife was Eunice Stoddard, said to have been a woman of remarkable accomplishments, and they had five children, two sons and three daughters. The eldest, Noah Paul, married Abiah Carleton of Bath, and moved to Buffalo, N. Y., where he engaged in mercantile life till his death. Only one of his children survived infancy, Hon. E. C. Sprague who is now a prominent lawyer of Buffalo and author of the famous Sprague-Clark letter in the Cleveland-Blaine campaign, which refuted the Buffalo slanders against Mr. Cleveland. Mr. Sprague's second son, Alden, became a very eminent physician in western New York. Of the daughters, Mrs. Fenton of Beloit, Wis., and Mrs. Martin of Peacham, Vt., are still living.

Mr. Sprague was a distinguished member of the Grafton county bar in its earlier days, and a man of prominence in Town. He was a trustee of Haverhill Academy. In personal appearance he is described as tall and dignified, genteel and manly in bearing, and was very fond of society, of which he was a great favorite, on account of his brilliant conversations. He died at the age of forty.

The following anecdote was related by one who knew Mr. Sprague. Col. Jonathan Tyler, one of the early settlers of Piermont and a prominent man in its early history, having occasion to consult Mr. Sprague on some matter of law went on to state his case. The young lawyer paid no attention to him, but kept on writing. At length Mr. Tyler took the hint and put a dollar on the table, when Mr. Sprague rubbed his hands in satisfaction, and said he was now ready for business. Col. Tyler had a good memory. Some time after, Mr. Sprague made a bet with some one that he could hunt more partridges than any other person. Col. Tyler had a famous hunting dog and Mr. Sprague secured his services in the hunt, but it was necessary for the Colonel to go with the dog to direct him. Instead, however, of setting the dog on, he secretly by a motion of the hand kept the dog back. After some trudging through the Piermont woods in fruitless search of partridges, Sprague broke out, "Tyler, why don't he hunt?" Whereupon Tyler dryly remarked that his dog never hunted until he got a dollar.

JOHN PORTER

Was born in Haverhill in 1769, and was the son of Col. Asa Porter. He graduated from Dartmouth College in 1787, and read law in Chester. After practising there for some years he returned to Haverhill about 1794 and remained there till 1800, when he moved to Broome, Canada.

MOSES DOW, JR.

Was born in Haverhill and was the oldest son of Gen. Moses Dow. He studied law with his father and was admitted to the bar in 1800, practising his profession from that time till 1838. In 1808 he was appointed register of probate, and continued to hold that office till 1838. He was also for a number of years postmaster, but was removed by Gen. Jackson. He was not a man of much force of character, and took no prominent part in town matters. In the famous Dow-Bell breach of promise case, Attorney General Sullivan in speaking of Dow's testimony, said, "Dow appears pretty well, and generally has a ruffled shirt on, but it isn't always clean."

GEORGE WOODWARD

Was born in Hanover in 1776, and was a grandson of the elder President Wheelock of Dartmouth College, from which institution he graduated in 1793. His father was Judge Bezaleel Woodward of Hanover, and he began the practice of law at Haverhill in 1805, previous to which time he was treasurer of Dartmouth College for two years. He continued at Haverhill till 1816, when he moved to Lowell, Mass., and resumed the practice of his profession in that city. He was married twice, his first wife being the daughter of Capt. David Webster of Plymouth, his second the daughter of William Leverett, a prominent citizen of Windsor, Vt. One of his daughters by the last marriage is the wife of Judge Warren Currier of St. Louis, Mo. Also a son, Henry, is living in St. Louis, and another, William, lives in Brooklyn, N. Y. Mr. Woodward was a man of prominence and high character. He died in 1836.

JOSEPH EMERSON DOW

Was the second son of Gen. Moses Dow, and was born in Haverhill in 1778. He studied at Haverhill Academy and was a graduate of Dartmouth College in 1799. His professional studies were pursued with his father, and he was admitted to the bar in 1802. It is not certain whether he first began the practice of his profession at Haverhill or Strafford, Vt., but in 1807 we find him located at Littleton, the pioneer lawyer of that town. He remained five years and then moved to Franconia. For a few years he lived in Thornton, and was postmaster in that place, but returned to Franconia in 1847, and died there in 1857. After leaving Littleton he engaged in teaching, and faithfully discharged the duties incident to the office of a magistrate. It is said when he was examined for admission to the bar the only question asked him was, "What is the best title a person can have in real estate?" "I don't know." Like his brother he was noted more for negative than for positive qualities. He was gentle and unassuming in manners, and was averse to the turmoil and strife of business. He had little standing in his profession, and practically abandoned it after leaving Littleton.

Mr. Dow married twice. His first wife was a woman of high character and social standing, the daughter of Hon. Jonathan Arnold of Rhode Island, at one time a member of the Continental Congress. Her father dying when she was quite young, she was received into the family of Charles Marsh of Woodstock, Vt., and thus became the adopted sister of the late Hon. George P. Marsh, the eminent scholar and diplomatist. One of their children was the late Moses A. Dow of Boston, founder of Dow Academy in Franconia.

Mr. Dow married for his second wife Nancy Bagley of Thornton, who on one occasion, the story goes, when Mr. Dow was harrassed by the sheriff, stood her ground and made it too warm for the bailiff, introducing him to a sudden baptism of hot water.

JOHN NELSON

Was one of the most prominent citizens of Haverhill during the early part of this century, and was a leading member of the Grafton county bar. He was born in Exeter, in 1778, but his parents moved when he was still a child to Gilmanton. As a boy he early displayed talent and was sent to Dartmouth College, graduating in 1830. Daniel Webster was in college at the same time with him. He read law with Charles Marsh of Woodstock, Vt., and later in Boston, Mass., and then settled in Haverhill.

He married twice, first, Susannah Brewster, daughter of Gen. Ebenezer Brewster of Hanover, and second Lois Burnham Leverett, daughter of John Leverett of Windsor, Vt. The Leverett family came from England in 1633, and was a leading one in Boston, Mass., giving to the colony a governor and to the young college at Cambridge, a president. Mrs. Nelson was a woman of superior intellect, and of unusual literary taste and culture. Of their large family, the eldest daughter, Mary Sewell, a woman of brilliant mind, married Ira Perley of Concord, one of the most distinguished lawyers of New Hampshire and Chief Justice of the Supreme Court.

Susan Brewster became the wife of William C. Thompson of Plymouth ; Martha and Frances, were the first and second wives of William R. Hooper of Worcester, Mass.; Lois Leverett married David Dickey of Haverhill ; Sarah married Samuel H. Goodall of Portsmouth, son of Ira Goodall of Bath, and her sister Elizabeth became the second wife of Mr. Goodall ; Anna Roby married William B. Fox, and afterward George T. Rice, both of Worcester, Mass.; Thomas Leverett, (see Chap. XIX) ; Ebenezer Brewster died in Texas, and William is living in St. Louis, Mo.

Mr. Nelson was an able lawyer and ranked high at the Grafton county bar, but his voice was rather feeble, and he did not possess the physical power of Mr. Bell. He was associated with Hon. Richard Fletcher in the famous Dow-Bell breach of promise case. He was a man of pure character, most highly esteemed in the community, and of amiable disposition. Both he and Mrs. Nelson were strongly anti-slavery in their sentiments, and felt a lively interest in home and foreign politics. He was a man of few words, walked with measured step, so that he gained the title of "Admiral," wore the old-time blue coat with brass buttons, and was tall and well-built.

HENRY HUTCHINSON

Was born in Lebanon in 1785, and was the son of Aaron Hutchinson, a pioneer lawyer of Grafton county. Graduating from Dartmouth College in 1804, he read law in the office of his father, and was admitted to the bar in 1807. He probably began the practice of his profession in Lebanon with his father, and in 1810 he went to Haverhill, remaining there till 1815, when he moved to Hanover, where he continued till 1825, and then settled in New York. He married a daughter of Judge Bezaleel Woodward of Hanover. Mr. Hutchinson died in 1838.

DAVID SLOAN.

Mr. Sloan was born in Pelham, Mass., in 1780, and graduated from Dartmouth College in 1806. He worked his way through college, and earned some money by writing diplomas. His professional studies were pursued with Judge W. H. Woodward of Hanover, and George Woodward of Haverhill, and he began the practice of his profession at the latter place, continuing to do so to the time of his death in 1860. He did a large business, and is said to have been an astute lawyer and a shrewd and practical business man. He acquired considerable property and was prudent in the care of it. In personal appearance he was somewhat indifferent, and was also quite eccentric in manners.

Mr. Sloan married Hannah, daughter of Capt. Thomas Johnson of Newbury, Vt., and two of his sons were educated at Dartmouth College, but died early in life. Miss Lizzie Sloan, a daughter of David Sloan, is the only representative of the family in Haverhill. Scott Sloan, Esq., of Wells River, Vt., is a grandson.

JOSEPH BELL

Was without doubt Haverhill's most distinguished lawyer. He was born in Bedford in 1787, the son of Joseph and Mary (Houston) Bell, and was of Scotch origin. He received his academic education at Dartmouth College, and graduated from that institution in 1807. For a year after graduating he was principal of Haverhill Academy, and then pursued his law studies with Hon. Samuel Bell of Amherst, Hon. Samuel Dana of Boston, and Judge Jeremiah Smith of Exeter. He was admitted to the bar and began the practice of his profession at Haverhill in 1811, and continued there till 1842, when he moved to Boston and entered in partnership with the late Henry L. Durant. In his earlier professional career he was cashier of Grafton Bank, and in later years he became its president. During his residence in Haverhill he held various public positions, was solicitor for Grafton county, and also represented the Town for a number of years in the legislature, and ran for Congress in 1835. After his removal to Boston he was a member of the legislature of Massachusetts in both branches, and at one time he was president of the Senate.

Mr. Bell began his professional life in straightened circumstances, but by great industry, frugality, and careful investment he amassed a large property. In this it is said he was aided by being the administrator of Col. Asa Porter's estate, who owned large tracts of land in Topsham and Corinth, Vt. These lands were sold in bulk and were bought up by a syndicate and afterwards sold out in small lots. The tradition is still handed down that those who were in it made "large money."

He was a close and industrious student, and early won a front place at the Grafton county bar, where for a long time he was its admitted leader. Practice became very extensive and lucrative, and reached into the neighboring counties. At forty years of age he had gained the full mastery of his powers and as the leader of the Grafton county bar, he had to defend this position against such able men in the profession as George Sullivan, Ezekiel Webster, Icabod Bartlett, Joel Parker, Levi Woodbury and Chief Justice Jeremiah Smith. These contests drew forth all the powers of his mind and his skill and learning as a lawyer. He was distinguished for the deliberate preparation of his cases and did not trust to others. In his knowledge of pleadings he was very particular, and did not allow his opponents to escape the consequences of their mistakes or negligence. His great ability and learning in the law did not appear so conspicuously on great occasions as on questions that came up incidentally in the trial of causes. His analysis of facts was keen and exhaustive, and he possessed a wonderfully exact legal language. He was always a master of legal principles, and could cite with great promptness the authorities and cases that were pertinent to questions at issue. In argument he was generally brief, and saw at a glance the strong and salient points in an issue, and seized and dwelt upon these in presenting his case to the jury or to the court. His examination of witnesses was very direct, and he rarely discredited a witness. He was not diffuse and miscellaneous in his knowledge of law, but thorough and exact, and there was little display of his legal acquirements. He was always prompt and orderly, all papers were at hand and carefully marked, and when called for they could be furnished at once. The details of a case were carefully looked after, and nothing was left at loose ends. With clients and associate counsel he was patient and deferential, and listened attentively to all they had to say. Hon. Nathaniel Wilson of Orono, Me., who for a short time was in Mr. Bell's office sums up his standing as a lawyer: "As a lawyer he was clear-headed, keen, discriminating, logical and thoroughly read. His influence with the court and with the jury was very marked, and his services were always in demand."

In manner Mr. Bell was somewhat severe and over-bearing. In the examination of witnesses and in his address to the jury he spoke in loud tones which was due, it is said, to his extreme diffidence, and by a singular mental constitution he seemed to gain confidence as his voice rose. He was less successful before the jury, however, than before the court. This was owing in part to the shock he gave the jury by his imperious manner and forceful speech. He was not distinguished for his persuasiveness with a jury, gently and kindly leading them along over the difficulties of the case, but his manner was such as rather to drive the jury before him by main force. As a consequence he was stronger as a lawyer than as an advocate. He was more learned than Moses Dow, though less brilliant than Alden Sprague. With his brethren he was always honorable and high-minded, and was far removed from low tricks either to gain or to hold clients.

Mr. Bell was a very exacting man and held everybody to the strictest account. He once discharged his butter-man who had agreed to furnish him butter for twelve and a half cents a pound, but in looking over the bill he discovered that the man had carried out one pound at thirteen cents. He said nothing, but informed the man that he need not bring any more butter, without, however, explaining to him the reason. This was his method of treating all persons who presented bills to him. He promptly paid their face, but woe to the person ever after if he detected the slightest error in their accounts. Once in a while he got treated to his own medicine to the great delight of those who knew his exacting ways. He was accustomed when he took gilt-edged paper to file these away and let the interest do its work, whilst he attended more closely to less reliable obligations. It so happened that he held a man's note in Rumney for a large sum, and regarding the paper perfectly good, as was the fact, he overlooked the date of its out-law. Running over his papers one day he discovered that this note had passed the limitation of statute. He got his brother-in-law Thompson to go and see the man, and try if he could not in some way get him to acknowledge the note. But the debtor was an adroit person, knowing full well that if he was in Bell's hands no mercy would be shown him, and after Thompson had felt his pecuniary pulse, he coolly remarked, " Mr. Thompson, if I owe Mr. Bell anything," putting special emphasis on the word owe, "I am abundantly able to pay him." As the money-king of the place most persons feared Mr. Bell, though many were compelled to seek his aid. He always did as he agreed, but he was sure to make a close agreement in the start.

Mr. Bell carried his imperious manner somewhat into social life, but with intimate friends he is said to have been a most agreeable and companionable person. Although he rose from humble circumstances he was a natural-born aristocrat. He was much alone, and rarely spent any time in the same room with his students of whom he usually had two or more in his office, yet he was always ready to impart any information which was sought by them, and was much gratified to aid them in their studies. His office was his throne of empire. He was accustomed to walk to church alone, apart from his family, with his hands folded under his coat tails, and gave the impression of a proud and aristocratic man.

Speaking of Mr. Bell being a proud man the following incident is told of him: As he advanced in years his eyes began to fail him, but he persistently resisted the decline of his sight. So on one occasion in court he undertook to read a paper which was written in rather small style, and he had to hold it out at arm's length. His keen opponent knowing his pride in resisting glasses, said to him: "Brother Bell, you'll either have to get glasses or a pair of tongs."

Mr. Bell was finely connected by marriage, having for his wife a very accomplished woman, a daughter of one of the first families of the times—Mills Olcott's of Hanover. This, however, brought him into serious trouble, and he was compelled to defend himself in court on a charge of breach of promise, which was brought by Miss Dow, daughter of Gen. Moses Dow. The case was tried twice, in the first trial the jury disagreeing, but in the second the jury gave a verdict in his favor.

After Mr. Bell's marriage he concluded to make Haverhill his life-home, but as years of prosperity rolled on and his means began to accumulate, a new pressure fired his heart. He became ambitious of political preferment, in which it is said his wife shared his feelings, and that it was largely due to her urgency that he finally broke up and went to Boston, where the political soil was more favorable to his aspirations than in iron-clad Democratic New Hampshire.

Mr. Bell fought his way up over all obstacles to wealth and distinction. He was a high-priced lawyer for those days, but he is said to have been entirely honorable in his professional conduct. He had just views of the grounds and elements which are necessary in order to give professional success. To his son he said : " Your standing at the bar depends entirely upon your industry, assiduity, and diligence in your profession."

Mr. Bell had a family of five children, only one of whom is now living, Mrs. Dr. Upham of Keene. His son, Joseph Mills, was a graduate of Dartmouth College in 1844, and read law with his father. He was a partner with Rufus Choate whose daughter he married. During the Rebellion he served on the staff of Gen. Butler at New Orleans, and was afterwards appointed judge of the Recorder's Court in that city. He is said to have been a man of fine ability and large legal culture.

Mr. Bell came near losing his life from an attack of lock-jaw which was caused by stepping on a nail when the Academy building was burned, and he continued in feeble health for some years after. He received the highest honors of his Alma Mater, the degree of LL.D. in 1837. He died suddenly at Saratoga, in 1851, of heart disease which had pursued him for some years. Once whilst in Europe he suffered so severe an attack as greatly to alarm him. In physique Mr. Bell was rather large and strongly built, of commanding presence, with over-hanging eye-brows beneath a well formed and intellectual head.

SAMUEL CARTLAND

Was a lawyer in Haverhill from 1835 to 1838, and came to Haverhill from Lee, where he was born in 1797, and where he also received his earlier education. He graduated from Dartmouth College in 1816. He was prominent in political life, being a state senator in 1829–30–31 from the old Twelfth district, and was president of the senate the first and last year of his senatorial service. He was also acting governor in 1831 for two days, the governor having resigned, the president of senate became acting governor until a successor could be inaugurated, and Mr. Cartland being president of the senate for that year, the honor of the governorship fell to him for the short period named. He was also judge of probate. He stood high as a lawyer, and was a man of ability and character. Socially he was genial and attractive, of accomplished and gentlemanly manners, and most kindly feelings. His force and energy were not as conspicuous as his intellectual ability, but his ambition was large and was never fully satisfied. He is said to have aspired to a seat in Congress, and failing in that he went South for a time and afterwards to Maine, where he died at the age of forty-three. In physique he was of average build.

EDMUND CARLETON

Was the son of Dr. Edmund Carleton of Haverhill, a physician in his day of wide note, and was born in 1797. He received his early education at Haverhill Academy, and graduated from Dartmouth College in 1822. After graduating he taught in Virginia, and also read law with William Garnett of Tappahannock. Returning to Haverhill he finished his law studies with Joseph Bell, and was admitted to the bar in 1828. He began the practice of his profession at

Haverhill, and later settled in Littleton. As a lawyer he was averse to controversy, and preferred peaceful settlements of difficulties. He was well equipped for his profession, but ill health compelled him to abandon the law, and he engaged in active business. He was noted for his strong abolition sentiments, and was a man of strict conscientiousness. He married in 1836 Mary Kilburn Coffin, and their son Edmund is now living in Littleton.

HALE A. JOHNSTON

Was a grandson of Col. Charles Johnston, and was born in Haverhill in 1801. His parents were Capt. Michael and Sarah (Atkinson) Johnston. He was educated at Haverhill Academy and at Dartmouth College, graduating from the latter institution in 1825. After leaving college he taught for a while in an academy at Northumberland, Pa., and then read law for a time with Joseph McKeen of New York, and finished with Joseph Bell. He was admitted to the bar in 1829 at Haverhill, and began the practice of his profession there, but his career as a lawyer was brief, and he died of consumption in 1831. He is said to have been a man of hopeful professional prospects, and of a trained intellect.

EDWARD R. OLCOTT.

Edward R. Olcott was the son of Mills Olcott of Hanover, and was born in 1805. He was a graduate of Dartmouth College in 1825, and pursued his professional studies with Joseph Bell. After his admission to the bar he began the practice of the law in Hanover in 1828, continuing there for a few years, and then moved to Haverhill in 1830. Subsequently he went South to Louisiana, and attained, it is said, to the position of a judge of that state. He died in 1869.

DANIEL BLAISDELL.

Daniel Blaisdell was born in Pittsfield in 1806, and was

the son of Hon. Elijah B. and Nancy (Fogg) Blaisdell. His academic education was pursued at Kimball Union Academy and at Dartmouth College, and he was graduated from the latter institution in 1827. His law studies were pursued in the office of Joseph Bell, and he was admitted to the bar in 1830. For a few years he practiced his profession with John Nelson of Haverhill, but afterwards, in 1832, he moved to Lebanon. He became treasurer of Dartmouth College in 1835, and held that position till the time of his death. Meantime he continued in the practice of his profession, and was a constant attendant at court till near the close of his life.

Mr. Blaisdell was frequently called to places of trust and honor. He represented the town of Hanover in the legislature in 1839–40–41, and again in 1865–6, and was a state senator in 1863–4. He was also a presidential elector in 1860 on the Republican ticket. In religious sentiment he was a disciple of Dr. Channing and a man of exemplary habits and high character. He was conservative and cautious in action, and deliberate and exact in speech. His manners were courteous and refined, and he was a gentleman of the old school. As a lawyer he was painstaking and well read, and judicious as a counsellor. In personal appearance he was dignified and attractive, of full medium mould, neat in his dress, with heavy eye-brows and firm mouth, and his general look was that of a scholarly and cultured man. He married Charlotte Osgood of Haverhill, and died in 1875. A son of Mr. Blaisdell is constructing engineer in the navy yard at Brooklyn, and a daughter married Prof. Ruggles of Dartmouth College.

JONATHAN BLISS.

Jonathan Bliss was born in Randolph, Vt., in 1799. His parents were Jonathan and Maria (Martin) Bliss, and he graduated from Dartmouth College in 1824. His law studies were pursued in the office of Joseph Bell, W. C. Thompson of Plymouth, and at Northampton, Mass., and he began the practice of his profession at Plymouth in 1828. In 1832 he moved to Haverhill, and continued his profession there till 1836, when he went to Gainsville, Ala., where he practiced law to the close of his life in 1879. Mr. Bliss was successful as a lawyer, and at one time had accumulated a large property, much of which was swept away by the Rebellion. He was a man of business affairs, and a successful advocate. At the beginning of the war he was a Union man, but yielded to the sentiment around him. In physique he was large and well-built, somewhat striking in looks and of commanding presence. He married for his first wife Lucretia, daughter of William Leverett of Windsor, Vt., for his second, Mary, daughter of Dr. Samuel Kidder of Charlestown, Mass., and for his third, Maria Kidder of Medfield, Mass.

WILLIAM H. DUNCAN.

This gifted person was born in Candia, then a part of Londonderry, in 1807, and was an only child. His father, William D., and his mother whose maiden name was Mary McMurphy, were both Scotch Irish. His early years were passed in his father's store, for which, however, he had little taste and soon after he entered Pinkerton Academy, Derry, to fit for college. He graduated from Dartmouth in 1830, being amongst the more mature members of his class, and having for his commencement part the valedictory. Three years later he gave the master's oration.

Mr. Duncan's fascinating manners and brilliant talents made him a favorite with the young ladies of Hanover, one of whose most beautiful and accomplished belles, Sarah Olcott, daughter of Mills Olcott, a distinguished citizen and lawyer of that place, he afterwards married. Two of Mr. Olcott's daughters were already married, one to Rufus Choate and another to Joseph Bell, and he was thus brought into intimate acquaintanceship with some of the leading men of the times. When he was a senior in college he visited Mr. Choate in Salem, Mass., and heard Mr. Webster's argument in the famous Knapp murder case.

After leaving college Mr. Duncan went South and engaged in teaching school for some years. Meantime he studied law, and was admitted to the bar in Charleston, S. C. He returned to New Hampshire in 1834 and was married to Sarah Olcott, and began the practice of the law at Haverhill, but in a few years, on account of Mr. Olcott's failing health, he returned to Hanover to assist his father-in-law in his multiplied business. The large practice which he soon acquired was interrupted by the health of his wife, which made it necessary for him to pass the winters in the South, and this professional interruption was greatly aggravated by the settlement of Mr. Olcott's large estate as well as that of Mrs. Olcott, the former dying in 1845, the latter in 1848. Mrs. Duncan died in 1850, which greatly broke him up, and in a measure he withdrew from very active participation either in professional business or in general matters. He led meantime a quiet and lonely life in Hanover for thirty years, having rooms and an office in a business block and boarding at the hotel.

But he was a landmark after all. Commencement day at Dartmouth College saw him in lively and pleasant chat with the returning graduates who knew him in years gone by. His life may be said to have been a failure for two reasons. First, he was too sensative and retiring for the rough-and-tumble work and competition of the world, and second, the circumstances of his life diverted him from the earnest and unflinching pursuit of his profession, in which without doubt his unquestioned ability would have placed him amongst the foremost lawyers of the state, especially as an accomplished and masterful advocate. He was a natural-born orator. Had he entered the walks of politics, which however were distasteful to his refined and sensitive nature, he would doubtless have risen to the highest positions of honor and trust. At one time he was prominently thought of as a candidate for governor, but the matter received no encouragement from him.

At another time he was put forward as a tentative candidate for the United States senatorship, and it was arranged for him to speak at some of the more important points in the state on public issues. This was in incipient "Know-Nothing" time, and his political opponents were very anxious to get hold of his first speech, so as to anticipate his appearance in other parts of the state. The opening speech was at Hanover, his home, and a young man, a member of Dartmouth College, was engaged to take down the speech in short-hand. So when the time came, the short-hand writer was promptly in his place near the platform, but Mr. Duncan having been apprised of what his political opponents were attempting, in order to thwart their designs, spoke against time in a rambling way upon all sorts of subjects, interlarding his remarks with numerous anecdotes and laughable incidents, in the hope of wearing out the reporter. That gentleman, however, was instructed to take down the speech verbatim et literatim, and whatever dropped from the lips of the speaker was regarded as "grist" for the reporter's "hopper," and so down went incident and anecdote, sense and nonsense, sober and light, and page after page were thrown off, till at last, after telling a very absurd and most ludicrous story which of course the short-hand man took down, Mr. Duncan turned to him and with indescribable dramatic expression and painfulness of countenance, showing his fine sense of the fitness of things,—"For God's sake, Mr. Reporter, don't put *that* down!"

Mr. Duncan was a gentleman of the old school, graceful and elegant in manners, true in his friendships, of a gentle and winning spirit, one of the most charming social persons to be met with, and as a conversationalist could grace any presence. In politics a conservative Democrat, in religion a most devout Episcopalian. He died in 1883 and was buried at Hanover.

SAMUEL C. WEBSTER.

Samuel C. Webster was the son of David Webster of Plymouth, and was born there about 1787. He graduated from Dartmouth College in 1808, and read law with George Woodward. After his admission to the bar he began the practice of his profession in 1812 at Plymouth, where he spent the chief part of his professional life, except the short time he lived in Haverhill, when he was high sheriff. There is some doubt in regard to his practicing law at Haverhill. He was speaker of the house of representatives of New Hampshire in 1830, and was a man of ability and influence. He married Catharine, daughter of Moor Russell, and died in Haverhill in 1835.

NATHAN B. FELTON.

Nathan B. Felton was born in Pelham, Mass., now Prescott, in 1798. Of his early years nothing is known until he began to fit for college at Chester, Vt., where he remained about a year and a half, and then entered the junior year at Middlebury College, Vt. After graduation he immediately entered the office of Gen. Charles W. Field of Newfane, Vt., and was admitted to the bar at that place in 1824. In the same year he began the practice of his profession at Lebanon, where he remained about ten years, holding in the meantime the position of postmaster under President Jackson. Mr. Felton came to Haverhill in 1834, and continued to live here till the time of his death in 1876, the greater part of the time in the full practice of the law. He was clerk of the court for ten years, and also held the office of register of probate. He served the Town for some time as town clerk, and was also a representative to the legislature for several years.

Mr. Felton was slightly below medium stature and of slender frame, with bushy head and shaggy eye-brows, firm mouth and thoughtful face. Intellectually he was amply endowed, with large capacity of acquisition. He fitted for the junior class in college in eighteen months from the time he began to study Latin and Greek, an extraordinary feat even in those days when the requirements were not so exacting as they are now for entering college. He was fond of his books, and took great pleasure in following out investigations to the end, as far as his means of knowledge would allow. This habit made him a thorough lawyer, whose opinion was desirable and trustworthy for such as wished to know the law in a given matter. One who knew him well, and is eminently qualified to judge in the matter, pays this high tribute to his legal standing and acquirements, "Mr. Felton was a careful, painstaking and learned lawyer." The late William H. Duncan once remarked to me that Chief Justice Perley said to him that in knowledge of court procedure, Mr. Felton had no superior in the state, and that he himself on several occasions while holding court, had called in Mr. Felton's aid in reference to such matters. His mind was eminently judicial.

Mr. Felton was a man of marked integrity, in whose trustworthiness the entire community had the fullest confidence, and his death was sincerely mourned by all who knew him. He was a man of few words, but always weighed well what he said, quiet in his manners and of a subtle humor, and is said rarely to have carried to his home the cares and perplexities of his professional work. He was a man of great kindness of heart, and was a genuine friend of the poor and dependent, and the services which he rendered this class of the community was no inconsiderable item in his long professional career. He was far above the average of even educated persons in intelligence, and had always within reach both at his office and at his home a standard encyclopedia. He lived a plain and unostentatious life, and was one of the most esteemed members of the bar and of the community. Mr. Felton married Ann M. Reding, sister of Hon. John R. Reding and of the late Silvester Reding.

DAVID DICKY.

David Dicky came to Haverhill from Epsom about 1838-9, but he did not remain there many years. He was born in 1806, and graduated from Dartmouth College in 1835, rather late in life. He is said to have been a man of good ability, but lacked ambition and purpose in his profession, and was rather given to money-making. He married a daughter of John Nelson of Haverhill.

DAVID H. COLLINS.

David H. Collins was a lawyer in Haverhill from 1839 to 1843. He was born in Deerfield in 1812, and received his collegiate education at Dartmouth College, graduating from that institution in 1835. He held the office of register of probate for several years, and whilst in that position did excellent service in arranging the papers and making an index, so that the Grafton county office was one of the best ordered in the state. He was a man of much literary taste, and possessed a fund of wit and humor. He stood high in college as a scholar, and gave considerable attention to the study of literature and political science in his short life. His letters, it is said, show a fresh, keen and observing mind, and his style is pure and polished. He was esteemed by those who knew him best as a man of fine intellectual ability, even brilliant, and was considered one of the most promising young men in the state. In manners he was gentlemanly and refined, tending to a trifle of singularity, and was regarded as a little reserved by casual acquaintances, but with his intimate friends he was always the center of interest and sociability. In person he was tall and slender, with strong features, and withal a man of most worthy character. Owing to poor health he went from Haverhill to his native place, and died there of consumption at the age of thirty-one. He was an Episcopalian in religion, and left the larger part of his property to religious purposes. The last winter of his life he spent in the South.

JONAS DARIUS SLEEPER.

Jonas Darius Sleeper, son of Jonas and Sally (Bean) Sleeper, was born in Gilford in 1814, and came to Haverhill in 1848. In that year he was appointed clerk of the court for Grafton county, and held that position till 1860, when he accepted the cashiership of the State Capital Bank of Concord. This last trust he held only one year, and was then appointed clerk of the court for Merrimack county, the duties of which he continued to perform to the close of his life. He was a director in the State Capital Bank from 1861 to 1865, and continued such after the bank was changed to the National State Capital Bank.

Mr. Sleeper was a thoroughly trained man, and received his academic education at Gilmanton Academy and at New Hampton, and afterwards graduated from Brown's Univesity, R. I., in 1836. After leaving college he entered the office of Hon Josiah Quincy of Rumney, where he remained three years pursuing his professional studies, and was admitted to the bar in 1843. Soon after he began the practice of his profession at Hill, and remained there about six years.

Mr. Sleeper was elected a state senator for Grafton county for two terms, and was a man of utmost integrity and unimpeachable character. His abilities by nature and by training were of a high order, and in the discharge of the various duties, which important positions placed upon him, he was scrupulously faithful and trustworthy. He is described by one who knew him well, "as a gentleman in his deportment at all times, an honest man, one of the best of citizens, a very able, faithful and popular clerk of the court, and a friend to everybody and everybody a friend to him."

Mr. Sleeper was a singularly social man and a very genial companion. His life was most exemplary, and his habits were always correct. He was a man of generous impulses and actions, and was cordially helpful in a quiet and unobtrusive way in all deserving endeavors. In 1845 he married Martha Grace, daughter of Hon. Josiah Quincy, and died in Plymouth whilst engaged in a referee case in 1858.

JOHN S. BRYANT.

Mr. Bryant was born in Meredith in 1800, and after leaving his native place he lived in Bristol till 1839, and then moved to Haverhill. He was deputy sheriff for Grafton county for a number of years, and pursued also the business of a surveyor of lands. During these years he devoted his leisure hours to the study of Latin and the law, and was admitted to the bar at Haverhill in 1846, where he practiced till his death in 1873. Mr. Bryant was a self-made man, and from the time he was thirteen years old he took care of himself. He was full of energy, industry and perseverance, and enjoyed a good practice. In his early life he was interested in military matters, and was a captain of volunteers. He was a man of agreeable and cheerful manners, and was fond of conversation. Knowing the thorny path of those who rely upon themselves for an education, he was kind and helpful in aiding many during his lifetime in this direction. He was a constant attendant at church.

Mr. Bryant married Hannah P. Edwards, and had a family of three children. The son, George Franklin, died whilst a member of Dartmouth College. Ann became Mrs. Gardiner Elliott, and lived for many years in the South, and Louisa married Hon. George W. Burleigh of Great Falls. Mrs. Elliott has a son, George Frank, an officer in the

United States navy, who was in the expedition in search of the Long exploration party which was lost some years ago in the Arctic regions.

DAVID PAGE.

Mr. Page was born in Haverhill, Mass. in 1809, and came to Haverhill in early life. He was educated at the common schools and at the Academy, and read law with James W. Wood of Burlington, Iowa. He was admitted to the bar at Haverhill in 1844, and began the practice of law there. Previous to his study of the law he was engaged in teaching in Groton, Orford and Haverhill. At one time he was clerk in a store at Groton, and also engaged in business in Haverhill, aside from his profession. He was a justice of the peace, moderator of a town meeting in Groton, selectman of Benton, auditor for Haverhill a number of years and was captain of militia. In all these places he was faithful and competent. He was a member of the Congregational church.

He married Margaret Taylor of Derry, and they had four children. The oldest son died in infancy, Samuel T. (see infra), one of the daughters married Hon. Alvin Burleigh, a prominent member of the Grafton county bar and speaker of the house of representatives in 1887, and the youngest daughter, Martha, died soon after her marriage to Mr. Whitney of Keene.

Mr. Page was a kind hearted and peaceful citizen, unambitiously pursuing his profession, of gentle manners and slender in person.

CHARLES E. THOMPSON.

Mr. Thompson was born in 1802, was a graduate of Dartmouth College in the class of 1828. He practised law in Haverhill till 1855, and then went to Chicago. He married Mary Olcott of Hanover. He was a man of ability, suave in manners, and a favorite in society. Nothing stood between him and professional success except enslavement to appetite. He died in New Jersey in 1882, at the home of a daughter. Mrs. Thompson is still living, a charming old lady in Washington.

GEORGE W. CHAPMAN

Came to Haverhill in 1853 from Hill, where he had been engaged in the practice of his profession for several years. His academic education was pursued in Cleveland, Ohio, and at Northfield and Hill Academy, and he read law for a time with J. D. Sleeper of Hill, and also with Nesmith and Pike of Franklin, and was admitted to the bar at Plymouth in 1849. A large practice has rewarded his professional life, and he is one of the older and more prominent lawyers at the Grafton county bar. He has been Town superintendent of school, a member of the board of trustees of Haverhill Academy, and is now president of the board. He is also president of the Bradford Savings Bank, Vt. He is a man of generous impulses, and of most cordial and hospitable disposition, is fond of social life, and abounds in story and anecdote, especially of the bar and court. Mr. Chapman has been successful in the accumulation of an ample fortune, and now lives in ease and somewhat retired from hard professional duty. He married Eleanor Towle of Haverhill.

CHARLES R. MORRISON.

Judge Morrison was of Scotch origin, and his ancestors were persons of prominence. He was born in 1819 in Bath, the son of William and Stiva (Young) Morrison. His mother was the daughter of Joshua and Abiah (Ladd) Young, and a granddaughter of Judge Ezekiel Ladd of Haverhill. He received his academic education at Newbury, Vt., and pursued the study of the law with Goodall & Woods of Bath. He was admitted to the bar in 1842, and for a few years practiced his profession in partnership with Mr. Goodall. In 1845 he moved to Haverhill and continued

to practice there till 1851, when he was appointed judge of the court of common pleas, which position he held for four years, when the courts were reorganized. From 1856 to 1862 he practised his profession in Nashua, and in Manchester from 1864 till he moved to Concord a few years ago. In 1862 he was appointed adjutant of the 11th Regiment, N. H. Vol., and served gallantly in the War of the Rebellion till near its close, when he was compelled to leave his post on account of a dangerous wound which he received at Spottsylvania in the campaign against Richmond. He was also in the battles of Fredericksburg, Vicksburg, Jackson and Knoxville.

Judge Morrison is one of the most learned lawyers in the state, with an acute and critical legal mind. He is the author of several well-known law books, "Digest of the New Hampshire Reports," "New Hampshire Town Officers." He has also given much attention to literature, especially to theological studies, and wrote a book "Proofs of Christ's Resurrection from a Lawyer's Standpoint," a work which has been very highly spoken of by students in that line of thought and favorably received by the theological mind. He is a man of high character and a most excellent citizen. In his religious views he is a Congregationalist. He married Susan F. Fitch of Littleton.

NATHANIEL W. WESTGATE.

Judge Westgate was born in Plainfield in 1801, the son of a farmer. His early education he received in the common schools, and later he attended Kimball's Union Academy, from which he graduated in 1820. After graduation he taught school during the winter, and his health not admitting of his going to college, he entered the office of Hon. Charles Flanders of Plainfield, and was admitted to the bar at Newport in 1827. He began his professional career at Enfield, and remained there till 1856. Whilst at Enfield he held the office of school superintendent, was town clerk, and also post-master a term of years. On several occasions he was the Republican candidate for state senator, but owing to the strong majority against his party he failed of an election. In 1856 he was appointed register of probate, and since that time he has lived in Haverhill. He held this office for five years, and was then appointed judge of probate, a position which he filled till he was disqualified by constitutional limitation. He was also representative from Haverhill in 1861. In all these positions of trust and honor Judge Westgate was a faithful and trustworthy officer, bringing to his public duties a patience, fidelity and integrity that made him justly esteemed in the community in which he more immediately lived, as well as by the larger public which he so long and honorably served. Before his appointment to the office of register of probate he had built up a successful professional business at Enfield, and after coming to Haverhill he continued the practice of his profession as far as his official duties would admit, till within a few years. He has always felt a deep interest in all public matters, and shared with his fellow citizens in all burdens for the advancement of society. He is a man of much kindness of heart, an excellent neighbor, a good citizen and enjoys the society of his friends.

Judge Westgate married for his first wife Lydia J., daughter of Dr. Prentiss of Springfield. His second wife Louise was the daughter of Hon. Austin Tyler of Claremont. Of their children, Tyler was educated at Kimball's Union Academy, and has been clerk of the state senate, register of probate, postmaster, and is now engaged in mercantile life; William F. (see infra); two of the children, Jennie and George, are at home, and a son, Nathaniel, was a soldier in the War of the Rebellion, and died in prison at Danville, Va.

GEORGE F. PUTNAM.

George F. Putnam was born in Croydon in 1841. His

father's name was John Putnam and his mother's Almira (French) Putnam. He was educated at Thetford Academy, and at Norwich University, Vt., and studied law in the office of the late N. B. Felton and with Judge C. R. Morrison of Manchester. He was admitted to the bar at the latter place in 1867, and began the practice of his profession at Haverhill, but subsequently he moved to Warren and remained there seven years. During this time he was solicitor for Grafton county in 1874-6, represented the town in the legislature for two years, was a member of the constitutional convention in 1876, and was also school committee. When Mr. Putnam represented Warren he was the Democratic candidate for speaker of the House. He also represented Haverhill in the legislature in 1868-9, and was school committee of the Town. For several years he served as chairman of the Democratic state committee, and was a delegate to the Democratic national convention at St. Louis which nominated Gov. Tilden for the presidency.

In 1877 Mr. Putnam returned to Haverhill and took the office of the late Mr. Felton, where he continued the practice of the law with much success till 1882, when he moved to Kansas City, Mo. He at once took a prominent position at the bar of that city, and one of his earliest cases there was the defence of a man indicted for murder, whose acquital he secured. He has withdrawn from general practice before the courts, and now confines himself chiefly to the management of the National Loan and Trust Association of Kansas City. His election to this large moneyed institution shows how deeply he had won the confidence of business men in his ability and integrity.

Mr. Putnam is of medium height, somewhat stoutly built, quick and energetic in his gait, of a healthful and florid complexion, of superior abilities and well-trained. As an advocate he argued causes with fluency and ease, was forceful rather than elegant, always courteous to his brother lawyers and deferential to the court, a genial companion, though hardly a society man, as that term goes. He is regarded as an able lawyer, of great force of character, full of energy and capacity for work, public-spirited, of exemplary deportment and of generous impulses. He is a man of strong convictions, sometimes these border on the confines of prejudice, of a keen sense of justice which is apt to find expression in unornamented English, enjoys a good story and is quick to see the wit of things. Dartmouth College conferred upon him the honorary degree of master of arts in 1870. He married Mary, daughter of the late Silvester Reding.

LUTHER C. MORSE

Was born in Haverhill in 1834, the son of Daniel and L. (Colby) Morse. He was educated at Newbury, Vt., and at New Hampton, and graduated from Dartmouth College in 1860. His professional studies were pursued with Oliver A. Lull and with Hon. Nathaniel W. Westgate, and he was admitted to the bar in 1863. He began the practice of the law at Haverhill, and was in partnership with Judge Westgate. He was register of probate from 1860 to 1870. Public service and a careless life barred his professional advance, and in later years he has lived in the West. In his account of himself he mentioned as the most important event of his life that he " put in a substitute during the war." He is a man of humorous and genial nature.

SAMUEL T. PAGE

Is the son of David and Margaret (Taylor) Page, and was born in Haverhill in 1849. He was educated at Kimball's Union Academy, and is a graduate of Dartmouth College in the class of 1871. He studied law with his father, and with Cross & Burnham of Manchester, and was admitted to the bar at Amherst. Since that time he has practised his profession at Haverhill. His professional life has been much interrupted by official duty. He was private secretary to Gov. Weston in 1874, and has held the office of register of probate for eight years. In 1877–8 he represented the Town in the legislature, and again in the prolonged session in 1887. He spent some months in California as attorney in the interests of legatees to a large estate. He was also for several years superintendent of schools. He married Frances Maria Eaton of Manchester, and they have two children.

Mr. Page is a gentleman of affable and genial manners, and of quick mind.

SAMUEL B. PAGE.

Mr. Page was born in Littleton in 1838, and received his education at Kingston and Exeter, at McIndoes Falls, and Lyndon, Vt., and at Union College, N. Y. He read law with Woods and Bingham of Bath and at the Albany Law School, N. Y., and was admitted to the bar in 1861 in Vermont. He was also admitted to practice in the United States district and circuit courts in 1869. He began the practice of his profession at Wells River, Vt., and afterwards for a number of years he continued his practice at Warren and Concord. He is now at Woodsville. Whilst at Warren he represented the Town in the legislature from 1863 to 1869, and also was a representative from Concord in 1874. He was a member of the constitutional convention in 1876 from Haverhill, and represented the Town in the legislature in 1887. This was the session of the great railroad contest. Mr. Page was the parliamentary leader on one side during that controversy, and conducted the fight with marked skill and ability. He has also been a trustee of the State Normal School, and school superintendent for Haverhill. He is a man of talents and an able lawyer, affable in manners and of good presence. He married Martha C. Lang of Bath, who died recently, and they had four children. In 1868 Dartmouth College conferred upon him the honorary degree of master of arts.

WILLIAM F. WESTGATE

Is the son of Hon. Nathaniel W. and Louisa (Tyler) Westgate, and was born in Enfield in 1852. He was educated at Haverhill, Meriden and New London Academies, and at the Chandler Scientific School of Dartmouth College. He read law with his father and with Hon. Geo. F. Putnam, and was admitted to the bar in 1880. Since his admission he has practised his profession in Haverhill. He has been superintendent of schools and was a representative in 1883. In 1884 he was elected register of probate, and re-elected in 1886, which position he now holds. He is also a surveyor of lands and is engaged in insurance business. Mr. Westgate has taken an active interest in politics, and is a leader in the counsels and actions of his party.

CHAPTER XVIII.

DOCTORS.

Samuel White — John Porter — Samuel Hale — Martin Phelps — Isaac Moore — Amasa Scott — Edmund Carleton — Ezra Bartlett — Ezra Bartlett, Jr. — John Angier — Joel Angier — Anson Brackett — Simon B. Heath — Hiram Morgan — Henry Hayes — Edward Mattocks — Phineas Spalding — Henry B. Leonard — Thomas Tenny — Samuel P. Carbee — Haven Palmer — Moses D. Carbee — Clarence H. Clark — Edward J. Brown — Henry P. Watson — Charles R. Gibson — Oliver D. Eastman — Charles Newcomb — Myron S. Wetherbee — James B. Clark, Dentist — Moses N. Howland, Dentist.

Doctors like lawyers exert a large influence in the community in which they live. They are generally men of trained minds, often of the largest mental endowment, and rank favorably with any class of educated persons. Their relation to the community under peculiar circumstances gives them a strong hold on the affections and confidence of individuals and families. The doctors of Haverhill from the first will compare favorably with those of other country towns, whilst there are names in the list which for high character, professional skill and large ability, have more than a local renown. Of some of the earlier physicians not much has come down to our time, but through the care of the late Dr. W. H. Carter of Bradford, who knew him well, a minute account of probably the first physician that practised medicine in Haverhill is perserved.

SAMUEL WHITE

Was this first physician, and began the practice of medicine in this region in 1773. He was born in Plaistow in 1750, and studied medicine with a prominent physician in Haverhill, Mass., Dr. Brackett. After completing his studies he practised his profession in his native town for one or two years, and then came to Cohos, where a brother and sister, Mrs. Jacob Kent, were living, and concluded to try his fortunes in the infant settlement. He was well qualified by sound knowledge and self-reliance for the duties of his profession, notwithstanding his early advantages of education were somewhat limited. Although living in Newbury, he was in reality the physician of Newbury and Haverhill, since both settlements were as one community at that time. Indeed, he was for a while the only physician in all this region, and often was called long distances to see patients, going on foot or on snow-shoes over untrodden ways. There was no physician north of him, and he went as far as Lancaster on professional duty. During the Revolution he acted as surgeon to the soldiers stationed in this section, and on one occasion he accompanied troops to western Vermont. He had the confidence of the people, and was successful in treatment of diseases. He was fond of story, and abounded in wit and humor, remarking on one occasion that he had "poor luck with his patients in their last illness." Two of his book accounts,—1773 to 1790,—were in existence a few years since, and give an insight into the medical practice of that day. For an ordinary visit the charge was a shilling, about twenty-five cents; to Haverhill, from two to six shillings. Medicine was always charged extra. Dr. White used few remedies as a rule, although he mentions one hundred and fifty remedial agents in the two book accounts mentioned above. Some sort of physic stands first, being used one thousand six hundred and thirty times. Bleeding was common, five hundred and four times. Surgical operations were few and confined mostly to minor cases; ten arms and three legs were set during the period covered by the two book accounts. He mentions during the same period only seven confinements, due probably to the greater employment of mid-wives in those days. Alcohol took the place of opiates. Dr. White had a large family of children, consisting of several pairs of twins.

JOHN PORTER

Is spoken of as Dr. Porter as early as 1776 in connection

with the preliminary evidence in regard to Col. Asa Porter's connection with the conspiracy to hand the Cohos country over to the British. But whether he was a practising physician of Haverhill is not certain. Nothing is known of him except that he was probably a brother of Col. Asa Porter.

THADDEUS BUTLER.

Dr. Butler was one of the earlier physicians of Haverhill, but of whom little is learned. He probably came to the Cohos Settlement in the closing years of the Revolution, as he was married before 1783, and he died within a few years, as his widow, who was a daughter of Col. Timothy Bedel, married Samuel Brooks in 1787 or 1788.

SAMUEL HALE.

Samuel Hale's name is mentioned in the Proprietors' record as a physician, and in 1778 he is voted eighteen shillings for doctoring Ezekiel Chapman's family, but whether he was a settled physician in Haverhill is not certainly known.

MARTIN PHELPS.

It is not certain when Dr. Phelps came to Haverhill, but it was as early as 1782, since in that year he acted as attending surgeon to the soldiers at Haverhill under Col. Charles Johnston. His name appears as one of the original members when the First Congregational church was organized in 1790, and he was chosen a deacon in the church. Nothing can be learned of his early days, and little is perserved concerning his life in Haverhill, except that tradition comes down that he was a man of great excellence of character, and was regarded as a competent physician in those days when medical science was crude as compared with its present advanced position. He lived on Ladd street where Mrs. Osgood Morse now lives. He married a daughter of Samuel Ladd. Dr. Phelps moved from Haverhill in 1792, and according to tradition went to Keene.

ISAAC MOORE

Was a practising physician in Haverhill as early as 1787. He was of Scotch origin, and was born in Worcester, Mass., in 1765 and came to this region in early life. He was trained in a rugged atmosphere, and saw when only fifteen years of age the sacking of Royalton, Vt., by the Indians and British. He remained in Haverhill only a few years, and then, 1790, moved to Bath. By a vote of Bath in 1789 Dr. Morse was directed to " set up a house of inoculation " in that town, but the prejudice against the project was so strong that the building was torn down before it was finished. The next year, however, he renewed the project and completed a small-pox hospital, and advertised the same in a paper in Windsor, Vt., for the accommodation of " those who wished to take the small-pox by the easy and safe method of inoculation." During his residence in Bath he also was the attending physician to many people in Littleton, and finally moved to the north part of the town in 1806, but remained only a few years and returned to Bath. He was somewhat prominent in town matters, and kept a public house in his closing years, which it is thought had some relation to his early death in 1818. His wife was a daughter of Col. Timothy Bedel, and was quite young at the time of her marriage. They had a family of thirteen children. Dr. Moore is reported as a man of much natural talent, and as having a genius for medicine and the treatment of diseases, though his knowledge of books was not large. He was noted for his humor, and is said to have been somewhat rough in manners and speech which shocked those of refined tastes.

AMASA SCOTT.

Dr. Scott came to Haverhill as the successor of Dr. Phelps and lived in the Phelps house on Ladd street, which he kept as a sort of hospital tavern for invalids. Of him even less is known than of Dr. Phelps. He moved from Haverhill at the beginning of the present century, probably went to Hanover; at least he lived in Hanover in 1815, for in that year he went to Warren to attend spotted fever patients, which disease raged with such fury and destructiveness in that town, and is said to have had excellent success in treating such cases, when other physicians seemed entirely to have failed. During Dr. Scott's residence in Haverhill he served as moderator in 1800–1–2.

EDMUND CARLETON.

Dr. Carleton was born in Haverhill, Mass., in 1771, and studied medicine in Dover. He came to Haverhill in 1796, and pursued the practice of his profession for over forty years, dying in 1838. He was a prominent man in the community, and especially took an active part in the work of the church, in the history of which he was a large and influential factor, and held the office of deacon for nearly a quarter of a century.

In his profession he stood high, being perhaps the leading physician in this region, and he enjoyed a large and lucrative practice. He was much in demand for consultation with neighboring doctors. He was regarded as a progressive physician in his day. Even as long ago as in his earlier practice, it is said, he used the more diminutive doses in the administration of medicine, and maintained that he found better results than could be secured by the customary method then in vogue. In this he simply anticipated a change that has now become the rule, and the fact distinguishes him as a man of an inquiring and scientific turn of mind.

Dr. Carleton lived at first in a small house which stood a little south of the large house he afterwards built and which for many years was the residence of his son Arthur. Dr. Carleton had a family of seven children. Edmund, the oldest son, (see Chap. XVII); two sons moved to Indiana, and Arthur remained on the old homestead. He married

Sarah A. Atherton, a woman of much intelligence and of noble character. One of Dr. Carleton's daughters, Joanna, became Mrs. Wilder, now living in St. Johnsbury, Vt., and is the only survivor of Dr. Carleton's family. Mrs. Charles Adams of Windsor, Vt., is a granddaughter of Dr. Carleton.

Dr. Carleton died of cancer, and for several years before his death he had retired from practice. He was a quiet but genial man, with a spicing of quaint and subtle humor. Though undemonstrative in manner and conversation, he was full of animation when he got interested in a subject, and had a habit of enforcing his argument with the phrase, "fact is." He had a shrewd mind and a keen insight into men and things, and was a man of great good nature, whom everybody esteemed and loved, and he combined with this, kind words and acts with dignity of deportment. He was pre-eminently a good man, and was the friend of the church and of the minister. His life illustrates the words, " the good we do lives after us."

EZRA BARTLETT.

Dr. Bartlett was a very prominent person both as a physician and as a public man in Grafton county. He was born in Kingston in 1770. His father was Josiah Bartlett, governor of the state in 1790, and also one of the signers of the Declaration of Independence. Dr. Bartlett before moving to Haverhill in 1812 was a practicing physician for some years in Warren, where he had gained a wide reputation as a skilful physician and surgeon. He was in active practice in Haverhill for thirty-six years, and was during that time a leading physician in this region, sharing the field part of the time with Dr. Carleton. He was frequently called for consultation in neighboring towns. Dartmouth College conferred upon him the honorary degree of Master of Arts in 1829.

In addition to his duties as a physician he held many positions of public trust and honor. During his residence in Warren he represented that town in the legislature. In 1822 he was a member of the governor's council, and was at one time a presidential elector and a state senator. He also held judicial positions, though not a professional lawyer, as in early times persons were elevated to such places, whose knowledge of the law was not a prime qualification. Clergymen, physicians and merchants wore the ermine, and it is said they made better judges than professional lawyers did. Dr. Bartlett was an associate judge of the court of Common Pleas, judge of the Circuit court, and chief justice of the Court of Sessions, and all these places he filled with credit to himself and with fidelity to the public.

Dr. Bartlett had a large family of children, and of the seven sons, five adopted the profession of their father, some becoming quite eminent as physicians. One of the sons, Josiah, was a skillful practitioner in Strafford, and lost his life in the great draw-bridge disaster at Newalk, Conn.; another son, Levi, was a physician in Syracuse, N. Y.; Ezra, (see infra.)

Dr. Bartlett was a man of character and high standing, and exerted a strong influence, not only as a professional man, but also in a general way on the community. He died in 1848.

EZRA BARTLETT, JR.

Dr. Ezra Bartlett, Jr., son of the above, was born in Warren in 1811, and came when a year old with his parents to Haverhill. His early education was received in the common schools and at Haverhill Academy, where he fitted for college, but did not enter. After studying medicine with his uncle, Dr. John French of Bath, and with his father, he attended lectures at the medical department of Dartmouth College, and graduated in 1832.

He went to Virginia and began the practice of medicine

in Warminster, but remained only one year. Being called to Haverhill on account of his father's illness, he entered into partnership with him. He practised his profession, however, only a few years in Haverhill, and then went to South Berwick, Me., where he continued fifteen years. After this he was a physician in East Boston for four years and then moved to Exeter, where he has continued to live and to practice medicine till within a few years, when he retired from active professional duties.

During the last two years of the War of the Rebellion he was a "contract surgeon," and was assigned wherever his services were most needed. He was for the greater part of the time on duty with the armies operating in Tennessee and in Georgia. After Gen. Sherman's march to the sea, he went to Hilton Head, S. C., and soon after returned home.

Dr. Bartlett married twice: first, Sarah Calef of Saco, Me., and second, Mrs. Eleanor Augusta Tucker, widow of John Hubbard, a lawyer of South Berwick, Me. By the first marriage there is one surviving child, Josiah Calef Bartlett.

Dr. Bartlett has been a very successful and skillful physician, and has always enjoyed a large and lucrative practice. He is fond of social life and enjoys the society of his friends.

JOHN ANGIER.

Dr. Angier was born in Fitzwilliam in 1784. Of his early education nothing is known. He first began the practice of medicine in Alstead, but very soon after that he went to Maine for a short time, and then returned to Alstead. In 1827 he came to North Haverhill, and was, it is said, the first physician that lived in that part of the Town. He is reported to have been a good physician with quite an extensive practice. He died in 1836, losing his life by being thrown from a buggy whilst on a visit to Weathersfield, Vt. He was a large man, over six feet high, well built. He took an active part in public matters, and was a man of energy and ability. In looks he resembled, it is said, Gen. Jackson, so much so, that when the hero of New Orleans came to Concord during his presidency, Dr. Angier who was a member of the legislature and one of the marshals when Gen. Jackson was escorted to the State House, was taken for the old hero by the throng which was present on that occasion.

Mrs. Nathaniel M. Swasey is a daughter of Dr. Angier, and two sons, J. Dorsey and George W., (see Chap. XIX.)

JOEL ANGIER.

Dr. Joel Angier was a nephew of Dr. John Angier, and came to Haverhill in 1840 from Acworth. He was a physician at North Haverhill for five or six years, and then moved to Swiftwater and later to Bath, practising his profession in both places. He is said to have been a good physician. From Bath he went into the western country.

ANSON BRACKETT.

Dr. Anson Brackett was born in Wheelock, Vt., and pursued the study of medicine with Dr. Alexander of Danville, Vt., and took his degree of M. D. from the Medical College of Burlington, Vt. He began the practice of medicine in North Danville, Vt., but in a few years he moved to Lyons, N. Y., where he gained much success in his profession. Afterwards he came to Haverhill and remained here about six years, and then moved to Gainsville, Fla., where he lived till his death. Dr. Brackett married twice: first, Mary Chamberlain of Lyndon, Vt., and second, a lady in Massachusetts. He had no children.

Dr. Brackett was a man of more than ordinary ability, and with his natural talents he combined great energy and decision of character, which made him a leader in his profession. Though not a liberally educated man in academic studies, he was well-read in the science of medicine, and was not only one of the leading physician of the vicinity whilst he lived in Haverhill, but after going to Gainsville, Fla., he rose to be one of the first physicians and surgeons in that State. He displayed in early practice an aptitude and skill in surgery, and performed whilst in Haverhill some very important operations. He amputated the leg of Frank B. Palmer, who afterwards became famous as the inventor of a world-renowned artificial limb. The case was a very critical one, the leg being torn in a bark mill in Bradford, Vt., and the patient was much exhausted before the operation was performed. Dr. Brackett was an uncompromising temperance man, and would allow no stimulants to be administered to the young man, but after the limb was taken off, and being appealed to by his assistant physician, he consented to a strong cup of tea being given the patient. Those who knew Dr. Brackett and had an opportunity to estimate his abilities and learning, give it as their opinion that had he passed his professional career in one of our larger cities, he could have gained a foremost rank as a skilled physician and surgeon. He was a man of high character, devoted as a husband, true as a friend, and faithful to all his public duties.

SIMON B. HEATH.

The record of this person is brief and his life may be said to have been a failure. He was a man of considerable natural ability, but as is so often the case, it was sadly misused. Dr. Heath studied medicine with Dr. Brackett, and when the latter moved to Florida, he took his place as a practitioner in Haverhill. In a year or two he associated with himself Dr. Hiram Morgan, but the partnership did not prove happy, and was soon dissolved. In 1842 Dr. Heath left Haverhill and moved to Groton, Vt. His besetting infirmity was intemperance.

HIRAM MORGAN.

Dr. Morgan was born in Rochester, Vt., in 1804, and received his early education in the common schools of his native place. He was a bright-minded boy, and gave early promise of future usefulness and success. He began the study of medicine with Dr. Page of Bethel, Vt., and graduated from the medical school of Woodstock, Vt., in 1833. He first practised his profession in Hancock, and afterwards in Corinth, Vt., and then came to Haverhill and was for a short time in partnership with Dr. Heath. After a professional career in Haverhill for ten or twelve years, he went to New York and attended a course of lectures in that city, in order to prosecute his work more successfully, but soon after his return he was stricken with a severe disease and was so broken in health that he relinquished the practice of medicine during the remainder of his life. Dr. Morgan was a man of natural ability, and but for his health he would undoubtedly have risen to a very high position in his profession. Soon after coming to Haverhill he married Elizabeth, daughter of Col. Edward Towle, a woman of most gentle spirit and of refined tastes and culture, of whom the late William H. Duncan said, "The death of Mrs. Elizabeth Towle Morgan has taken away from the refined and intelligent society of Haverhill one of its most valued members."

HENRY HAYES.

Dr. Hayes was a Scotchman, and came to Haverhill from Stanstead, Canada. He pursued his professional studies with Dr. Colby of that place and was highly commended to the people of Haverhill by his preceptor. When he began the practice of medicine in Haverhill his prospects were good, and he was employed by many of the best families who became warm friends of his. But at that time there was a super-abundance of physicians in Haverhill, and the competition was so sharp, that Dr. Hayes moved to Bradford, Vt., and practised his profession there for a time. He afterwards went to Irisburg, Vt., and remained several years, and then settled as a physician in Hartland. Vt., and later in Massachusetts where he died. Dr. Hayes was a well-read physician, but he did not seem to stay long in any one place, or take deep root.

EDWARD MATTOCKS.

Dr. Mattocks was a son of Governor Mattocks of Vermont, and came to Haverhill about the same time that Dr. Hayes did, but he failed in securing business, and soon left for Lyndon, Vt. He died young and was unsuccessful in his profession.

PHINEAS SPALDING.

Dr. Spalding easily ranks amongst the ablest of the physicians who practised medicine in Haverhill. He also is amongst those who practised their profession here for a long term of years. He was born in Sharon, Vt., in 1799, and is the son of Reuben and Joshua (Carpenter) Spalding. He is the seventh in descent from the first American ancestors of that name. His father at the age of fourteen, with an older brother, came from Connecticut to Vermont before the Revolution, and settled in Sharon. He was a man of strong character and sterling worth, prominent in civil and religious matters, a deacon in the church for fifty years, and a soldier in the Revolution. He lived to be ninety-three years old. His wife was a woman of excellent character, and was devoted to the interests of the family.

The early years of Dr. Spalding were passed on the farm, and his educational advantages were somewhat scanty, but by diligent application to study at night, after the work of the day was over, and with a strong desire to enlarge the range of his knowledge, he managed to lay the foundations of a good education and was enabled to teach school, both in his native town and also in Montpelier, where he taught

for four years. He was very successful as a teacher, and threw into his work the full force of his natural energy and enthusiasm. Meantime he read medicine and pursued the study of Latin with his brother James. Afterwards he attended two courses of lectures at the medical school of Dartmouth College, and graduated from that institution in 1823. He began the practice of medicine at Lyndon, Vt., where for fifteen years he enjoyed a successful and prosperous professional career, and was one of the leading citizens of that town. In 1835 he received the honorary degree Master of Arts from the University of Vermont. Dr. Spalding moved to Haverhill in 1839, but the year before he settled there he took a course of lectures at the Harvard Medical College and then went to Brooklyn, N. Y., with the intention of practising his profession in that city, but owing to the delicate health of his wife he abandoned his plan and returned to Lyndon and soon after moved to Haverhill, where he has since lived, in the enjoyment of an honored position in his profession and of a large and successful practice, till advancing age admonished him to lay down a calling which he loved and adorned.

Dr. Spalding has always taken a deep interest in his profession, not only as a practitioner, but also in the advancement of medical science. He attended regularly the various medical associations of which he was a member, and contributed both to the papers which came before these bodies and also to their discussions. He has been a member of the Washington county and the Caledonia county Medical Societies of Vermont, and was the originator of the Moosilauk Medical Society of New Hampshire and its president for many years. He was a delegate on several occasions to the American Medical Society and a frequent contributor of articles and reporter of numerous cases to medical journals. One of these was of special interest, a case of "inter-capsular fracture of the thigh-bone." This case he had successfully treated, though at that time a cure of such had been denied by the highest authority. The case was first reported in the New England Medical Journal for 1827, and afterwards an autopsy verified the cure. This verification was reported in the Boston Medical Journal. He also was a lecturer in 1841 on surgery in the Woodstock (Vt.) Medical College, and had as associates in the faculty such well-known men as Drs. H. H. Childs, Alonzo W. Clark, B. B. Palmer and S. W. Thayer. He has been a positive factor in the advancement and achievement of his profession, both where he lived and through his contributions. His mind is both practical and scientific, and he is instinctively thorough.

In addition to his medical acquirements he has been a well-read man in general subjects of history, religion and philosophy, and has been by no means a mere technical student. He has also written much for the secular and religious press, and within a year or two — he is now in his 90th year — he has written for the interest and pleasure and instruction of his family and intimate friends. "Spalding Memorial," a volume of three hundred and fifty pages, which discloses a wonderful tenacity of memory and use of his mental powers.

Dr. Spalding has always taken a deep interest in public matters, and whatever concerns the well-being of society. He was an early advocate of temperance, and organized in 1828, it is supposed, the first temperance society of Vermont, and was president of the Caledonia County Young Men's Temperance Society when he moved from that state. He has always discarded the use of alcohol as a beverage, and also the use of tobacco. He has taken a prominent leading part in church matters, being a deacon in the Congregational church in Lyndon, Vt., also chosen to the same office in the church at Haverhill, which however, he declined, and has been one of the most active, valuable and liberal members of the church. In all matters of public interest, whether of town, church or state, he has been an energetic and public-spirited leader. The first meeting in this region in reference to the B. C. & M. railroad was held in Haverhill, and was called by him and Harry Stevens of Barnet, Vt. He has also been a warm friend of education: was the prime mover in securing Lyndon Academy, took an active interest in Haverhill Academy, was one of its trustees for many years, gave to it time and money, and served for two years as superintendent of schools in Town.

Dr. Spalding would have been a remarkable man in any community. His intellectual endowment is large, and his common sense is a conspicuous trait of his make-up. His sense of humor is the least prominent feature of his mental character. His reasoning is direct and mathematical, and he always sees things in the concrete, and not as an abstraction, though he is not wanting in a certain poetical turn of imagination. Morally, his ideal is high, and his sense of right and wrong is keen. His religious nature is developed more through his intellect than through the emotions, though his kindness and sympathy are tender and deep. He takes large views of things, though a strong partisan in church and politics, and is never trivial in the treatment of questions of duty and action. What he does he does intelligently and from a conviction of what he sees is right. He is social, hospitable, fond of company, loves argument, and is entirely free from demagogism. He is a staunch friend of all that is good, and steadfast in purpose—full of hope, courage, energy.

Dr. Spalding married twice: first, Caroline B. Lathrop, and they had two children, Caroline A., Mary G., Mrs. Jas. H. Towle. Mrs. Spalding died within three years after coming to Haverhill, and was a woman of superior worth. For his second wife he married Charlotte Merrill, and their children are Frank M., living in Kansas, and Ada L. who married Henry D. Janes of New York. Mrs. Spalding died recently and was a woman of marked excellence of character and of womanly grace and refinement. Miss Caroline A. Spalding lived at home all her life and died a few years ago. She was a woman of superior ability and highly cultivated, and had gained an honorable position in literature, especially in poetry, a collection of which is published in the "Spalding Memorial" volume. She was Haverhill's literary woman.

HENRY B. LEONARD.

Dr. Leonard was the son of Gains and Eunice (Spalding) Leonard, and was born in Sharon, Vt. His early days were passed on a farm, but by perseverance he acquired a fair academic education, and commenced the study of medicine with his uncle, Dr. James Spalding of Montpelier, Vt., and graduated from the Medical College at Woodstock, Vt. He began the practice of his profession at North Haverhill in 1842, and continued to do so till his death. He married Nancy Swasey of North Haverhill. They had no children. Dr. Leonard acquired a good reputation as a physician, and had quite an extensive and successful practice. He was a man much respected by his fellow citizens, and represented the Town in the legislature for several years.

HOMER H. TENNY.

Dr. Tenny became a practising physician in Haverhill in 1858, but on account of ill health he did not remain long in Town. He moved to Kansas where he practised his profession for a number of years till his death. He was a man of excellent character, and gained an honorable position in his profession. He married Sarah Johnston of Haverhill. They had no children.

SAMUEL P. CARBEE.

Dr. Carbee is the youngest son of John H. Carbee, and was born in Bath in 1836. In his youth he attended the common schools in his native town and afterwards pursued

his studies at Newbury Seminary, where he fitted himself to become a teacher in the public schools and followed that occupation for a time. In 1850 he began the study of medicine with Dr. Albert H. Crosby of Wells River, and continued his studies with Drs. Dixi and A. B. Crosby of Hanover, but these were interrupted in 1892, when he enlisted as a private in the 12th Regiment N. H. Vol. He was subsequently commissioned an assistant surgeon, and served in that capacity till the close of the war. He was with his regiment at the battles of Fredericksburg, Chancellorsville, Gettysburg, and was with the Army of the Potomac from the Wilderness to the capture of Richmond.

After his discharge at the close of the war he at once resumed his medical studies at Dartmouth College, from which institution he graduated in 1866. He began the practice of medicine at Haverhill as the successor of Dr. Tenny.

Dr. Carbee has pursued his profession with enthusiasm and success, and has built up a large and lucrative practice. He is a man of energy and force, and wields a large influence. On a visit to the West several years ago he was prostrated with illness, and since his return he has somewhat withdrawn from the extensive practice of former years. In the sick room he is a general favorite, has a large circle of warm friends, and is a man of generous impulses and cheerful disposition. He is a member of the White Mountain and New Hampshire Medical Societies, and for many years he has been medical examiner of leading life insurance companies. He also served for twelve years on the examining board for pensions with Dr. Watkins of Newbury and Dr. Nelson of Wells River.

Dr. Carbee has always been interested in public matters. He has been a delegate a number of times to county and state political conventions. In 1884 he was elected county commissioner on the Republican ticket and re-elected in 1886. He is public-spirited and gives cheerful aid in all matters for the progress of society. He is a member of the the board of education under the town-system. Dr. Carbee married N. Della Buck, daughter of the late Lyman Buck.

HAVEN PALMER.

Dr. Haven Palmer, son of Lewis and Susan H. Palmer, was born in Jefferson in 1843. His early education was acquired in the public schools and at Lancaster Academy. He began the study of medicine with Dr. Barney of Lancaster, and attended lectures at Bowdoin Medical College, from which institution he graduated in his profession. He first practised medicine at Wentworth, remaining a little over a year, and then went to Haverhill in 1872 and was in partnership with Dr. Samuel P. Carbee for a year or two. Afterwards he settled in Meredith where he continued till 1883. He is now a practising physician in Plymouth. Dr. Palmer is a successful practitioner and stands high in the profession, and is a man of high character. Being asked on occasion of a critical consultation to "take something," he declined, whereupon his brother physician said, "You are one in a thousand." "So be it," was the firm temperance answer. Dr. Palmer married Lucy J. Ellis of Lancaster.

MOSES D. CARBEE.

Dr. Moses D. Carbee was born in Newbury, Vt., in 1847, the son of Thomas H. and Olive L. Carbee. He pursued his academic studies in the Academy at Lancaster, and studied medicine with Dr. Frank Bugbee of that Town. He attended lectures at the medical department of the University of Vermont, and graduated from that school in 1873. His first practice was at Lunenburg, Vt., but he remained there only a short time, and then coming to Haverhill in 1874 he entered into partnership with Dr. Samuel P. Carbee, which continued till 1882. Since then he has been in practice by himself. He was post-master under President Hayes' administration. Dr. Carbee also at one time was engaged in teaching. He married Mary F. Dexter of New York. The winter of 1886-7 he spent in California, on account of his health. He is sympathetic and faithful in his professional duties.

CLARENCE H. CLARK.

Dr. Clark's professional career was short. He came to Haverhill in 1879, and began the practice of medicine. He was born in Newbury, Vt., and studied with Dr. Watkins of that place. His early school advantages were limited. He graduated from Dartmouth Medical College in 1878, and then went to Montreal as a subordinate officer in the hospital of that city, meantime attending lectures in his profession. He was well equipped for his duties as a physician, and was enthusiastically and studiously devoted to his profession. He remained in Haverhill only a few years, when on account of his health he was compelled to seek a warmer climate, spending one winter in Colorado, but the disease under which he labored had gone too far in its fatal work, and he returned only to die in early manhood. During his short professional career in Haverhill, he won the esteem of a large circle, on account of his amiability and noble traits of character. He entered his professional life with bright prospects of the future. Dr. Clark died of consumption.

EDWARD J. BROWN.

Dr. Brown was born in Burke, Vt., in 1851, the son of Dr. Ira and Emily (Clark) Brown. His early schooling was received in his native place and at Wells River. He fitted for college at Kimball Union Academy, Meriden, and graduated from Dartmouth College in 1874. After leaving college he taught for several years in the West, and then began the study of medicine with his father, and graduated from the medical department of Dartmouth College in 1878. He then continued his studies in New York, and settled first in Littleton, remaining only one year, and then came to

Haverhill in 1880. Dr. Brown went to Minneapolis in
1882, where he has since lived. He has been largely engaged for the state and city boards of health in quarantine
duty as physician and inspector. He is a member of the
state medical society, and also of that of the city of Minneapolis, and is professor of chemistry, toxicology and preven-
tative medicine in the Minneapolis College of physicians and
surgeons. He is the founder of the society for the preven-
tion of vice in Minneapolis.

Dr. Brown is well-equipped in his professional studies,
and to a mind naturally acute and fond of investigation, he
adds the advantage of thorough training. He is self-reliant
and independent, and is fond of literary pursuits. He is a
man of high character and honor.

HENRY P. WATSON.

Dr. Watson's American ancestry settled early in the historic town of Salisbury, and belonged to the Society of
Friends. He is the son of Hon. Henry L. Watson, M. D.,
and was born in Guildhall, Vt., in 1845. His early education was pursued in the common schools of his native town
and the Essex county grammar school, and he fitted for college at Newbury Seminary, Vt. He began the study of
medicine with his father, continuing under the instruction of
Drs. Dixi and A. B. Crosby of Hanover, and attended lectures at the Dartmouth Medical College from which he graduated in 1866. He first practised his profession in
Groveton, but in a year or two he moved to North Haverhill
and continued there in the practice of medicine for about fifteen years, when he came to Haverhill Corner.

Dr. Watson came by a genius for medicine from his father
who was a prominent practitioner in Vermont, as well as a
citizen of public position, having been a state senator in
Vermont for two terms, and then candidate of his party for
speaker in 1756 and '57, when a representative, besides hold-

ing other places of public responsibility and trust. The son has devoted himself almost exclusively to his profession, in which he is a close and thorough student, and is in the enjoyment of a large and successful practice. He is also widely known as a skillful and successful surgeon. He is now a member of the examining board for pensions at St. Johnsbury, Vt.

Dr. Watson is a man of undoubted ability, and is closely devoted to his calling, and stands high with his brethren in the profession. He is social and genial, and takes a deep interest in all matters of public concernment. He has been school superintendent and health officer and is also a justice of the peace.

He married Evelyn Marshall of Northumberland, and they have three children; the oldest son is a member of the Freshman class in Dartmouth College.

CHARLES R. GIBSON.

Dr. Gibson was born in Alstead in 1852, the son of Reuel and Emily (Barnard) Gibson. His father was a farmer, and his early education was acquired at the common schools. Fitting for college at Appleton Academy, New Ipswich, he graduated from Bowdoin College in 1872. He read medicine with Dr. S. T. Smith, and attended lectures at Bowdoin Medical College. After graduation he was a subordinate officer for a year and a half in Maine General Hospital, Portland, Me. He began his professional life at Woodsville in 1877, and is a skillful and successful practitioner, and a man of standing. He married Jennie Park of Plymouth in 1880. They have no children. Dr. Gibson is a member of the local board of health, and a member of the Woodsville high school board of education. He is also secretary of the White Mountain Medical Society.

OLIVER D. EASTMAN

Was born in Sonora, California, and his father dying, he

went to live with grand-parents in Vermont. His early education was received at the common schools, and he fitted for college at Newbury Academy, Vt., and graduated from Dartmouth College in 1882. He read with Dr. H. P. Watson and in Dartmouth private course, attending lectures at Burlington, Vt., and Dartmouth Medical Colleges. He began the practice of medicine at Piermont, N. H., and came to Woodsville in 1884. He married Addie D. Davis of Pike Station in 1882, and they have three children. Dr. Eastman is a careful and painstaking physician, and enjoys a large practice.

CHARLES NEWCOMB.

Dr. Newcomb was born in Montpelier, Vt., in 1858, the oldest son of Luther Newcomb, who for over twenty years was clerk of the court for Washington County, Vt. His mother's name before her marriage was Amanda Thomas, daughter of Gen. Stephen Thomas of West Fairlee, Vt. His grandfather Newcomb was one of the pioneer physicians of northern Vermont, and settled at Derby in that state. Dr. Newcomb was educated at Montpelier and is a graduate of the Washington County grammar school of that place. He read medicine with Dr. C. M. Chandler of Montpelier, and attended lectures at Dartmouth Medical College and at the medical school in the University of Vermont. He took seven courses in both institutions, and graduated from the latter school in 1880. He began the practice of his profession at West Fairlee, and was one of the physicians to the miners at Ely mines. In 1883 he moved to Washington, Vt., and in 1887 he came to North Haverhill. Dr. Newcomb is well equipped for his profession, and has won a good share of success in the short time of his practice in Town. He married Elmira J. Hunt of Washington, Vt. They have one child.

MYRON S. WETHERBEE.

Dr. Wetherbee was born in East Haverhill, and his parents were Charles and Abigal (Woodward) Wetherbee. He received his education at the common schools, and has practised medicine at North Haverhill for twenty-five years. He is an eclectic physician, a school of doctors that take what they consider the best in other systems of practice. Dr. Wetherbee is also engaged in farming. He married Eliza A. George and they have two children.

DENTISTRY.

Haverhill has little history that belongs to this profession. Some of her physicians may have combined dentistry with their other professional duties, but the fact is not mentioned in our memoranda of that profession.

JAMES B. CLARK.

Dr. Clark was born in Bath in 1825, and came to Haverhill when a boy about twelve years of age. He has been a dentist in Town for nearly twenty years, and resides at Haverhill Center. Dr. Clark has lived away from Haverhill a part of the time. He combines farming with his profession. He married Drusilla M. Bisbee of Haverhill.

MOSES N. HOWLAND.

Dr. Howland is a settled dentist in Lisbon, but for about ten years he has had a branch office in Haverhill. At first he was in his office at Haverhill each week, but at present he comes once a month. Dr. Howland married a daughter of the late Elder Shipman of Lisbon.

CHAPTER XIX.

HAVERHILL ABROAD.

Haverhill's honorable career Abroad — Charles J. Adams — J. Dorsey and George Angier — Louisa Page Babcock — Bacon Brothers — Barstow Brothers: Alfred, Anson, Gardner — George Barstow — John Barstow — Mary Barstow — Hazen Bedel — John Bedel — James W. Bell — John Bell — James P. Brewer — Samuel Brooks — Edwin Brooks — Edward C. and George Burbeck — James A. Cutting — Frederick Crocker — Noah Davis — Moses Elkins — D. L. Farnsworth — Charles N. Flanders — Lucien H. Frary — Warren Gookin — Michael Gray — Hunts: Caleb S., Horace, Prescott, Helen — Johnstons: Charles, Hannah — John Kimball — William H. Leith — Merrill Brothers: John L., Benjamin, Charles H. — William Merrill — Arthur Mitchell — Morse Brothers: Peabody A., George W., Isaac S. — Robert Morse — Joseph B. Morse — Thomas L. Nelson — Niles Brothers: Alonzo F., Horace L. — George B., Nellie and Clara Nichols — Person Noyes — John A. Page — Moses S. Page — James H. Pearson — Samuel P. Pike — Elizabeth Abbott, Mary Webster, Henrietta Mumford and George Carrington Powers — John Reding — Rodgers Brothers: Levi and M. Carleton — Jonathan H. and Chester Rowell — Frank A. Smith — Lyman D. Stevens — Smiths: Lyndon, Arnold, Stephen, Sanford, Carlos — William P. Stowe — The Tarletons — Towles: Frederick and James — Nathaniel Wilson — Edward B. Wilson — William F. Whitcher — Harvey B. Wilmont — John L. Woods — Franklin P. Wood.

A community or family shows the vigor and activity of its life in the fact of its perpetuation and progressive tendency. When the tide is full it overflows and spreads out into new limits. This tendency to spread abroad has been a marked characteristic of New England, from whose populations a constant stream has flown out into other parts of the country. Haverhill has been no exception to the general fact, but has contributed her full share of sons and daughters who have gone out from the old hive, making their mark and contributing an active factor in the growth and progress of other communities. It will, therefore, be the aim of this chapter to chronicle the life of this overflow as being a legitimate part of the history of the parent community. This record of the Town in this respect may not be as brilliant as that of some other towns. A numerous host of great names may not be found in the sketches given in this chapter, still the record is such as to reflect honor upon the Town and to show that in usefulness, success, influence and worthy endeavor, the Town has no cause to blush for her sons and daughters abroad, many of whom if not great, as the world goes, are amongst the noblest spirits of the age. Doubtless there are names that rightly deserve a place in this chapter, but which have escaped attention or fallen from memory in the dimming years of the past. The sketches cover the lives of such as have gone forth, and who by their energy, push, enterprise and devotion to duty, have been a positive factor in advancing the interests of society and have given strength and usefulness to human life.

CHARLES J. ADAMS

Was born in Haverhill, and is the oldest son of Stephen Adams. With his three brothers, Michael, Horace and Ezra, he went to Lowell, Mass., where they became extensively engaged in the furniture business, the firm name now being Adams & Co., and is the largest in that city. Charles J., whilst he lived in Lowell was city marshal for a number of years, and he was also for a time deputy sheriff of Middlesex county. He afterwards moved to Cambridge, Mass., and had charge of the jail and house of correction for thirty-three years. He is still living in that city, at the age of seventy-seven.

J. DORSEY AND GEORGE W. ANGIER.

Sons of Dr. John and Nancy (Mann) Angier, were born in North Haverhill. Very early in life they went to northern Pennsylvania and carried on the lumber business with much success. Whilst thus engaged they observed on a mill-pond or pond of water oil floating, and Mr. Dorsey Angier after thinking the matter over, made up his mind that the oil could be turned to use if it were gathered, and suggested the digging of pits three or four feet square, into which the water was allowed to flow, and then the oil was caught by woolen blankets and wrung out. The process was slow, but as oil at first commanded a high price, it proved sufficiently remunerative. Meantime, he insisted that the oil could be procured by sinking wells, maintaining that as the oil comes with the water from the earth, there must be pools of oil in the earth. This idea was put into execution, and a well was sunk near the mill-dam or pond above mentioned, and at the depth of sixty-nine feet, oil was reached. This gave immense impulse to the oil search, and one hundred wells were sunk in that section of the country. The Angiers made handsome fortunes, and are now living in Titusville, Pa.

MRS. LOUISA PAGE BABCOCK

Is the oldest daughter of Samuel and Louisa (Merrill) Page, and was born in Haverhill in 1820. She attended the Academy in Haverhill in her girlhood years and with her husband was amongst the earliest emigrants who went to California after the gold fever broke out in '49. With a strong and energetic spirit she took hold of the pioneer life of those days, and by industry, first in making rough clothing for the gold diggers, and then in taking boarders, she laid the foundation not only of enlarged usefulness in later life, but of financial success to an unusual degree. With excellent business judgment she wisely invested her careful earnings in real estate in San Francisco, where she now resides surrounded with the easy comforts of her industry, energy and forethought. Mrs. B. is a person of strong mind and womanly character and has made herself felt in christian and philanthropic work. In religious sentiment she is an Episcopalian, and has taken an active part in supporting the church of which she is a member. Her first marriage name was Evans and then Nason, before she became Mrs. Babcock.

BACON BROTHERS — ELMER C. AND SUMNER P.

The former lives in Cleveland, Ohio, and is a wholesale dealer in lightening rods. The latter is engaged in the iron business in the same city.

ALFRED BARSTOW

Is the son of Dea. Henry and Frances (Pierce) Barstow, and was born in Haverhill in 1829. He lived there till he was eleven years of age, when his father moved to Claremont. Whilst in Haverhill he attended the district school in his earlier years, and afterwards the academy of which he was the young janitor, taking care of the rooms and building the fires for his tuition. At Claremont he continued his studies till his father moved to Lowell, Mass., in 1844, where for four years he worked part of the time in the mills, and part of the time he was a student at the grammar and high school. At the age of nineteen he entered the law office of his cousin, George Barstow of Manchester, remaining there for about a year, and when the California gold fever swept over the country he joined the Argonauts in 1849. He afterwards finished his law studies with the famous firm of Halleck, Billings & Park of San Francisco, and was admitted to the bar in 1858 in that city. In 1868 he was admitted to the practice of law in the United States Supreme Court. From 1859 to 1865 he was connected with the post office department as special agent and as assistant superintendent of railway mail service. Mr. Barstow was also a justice of the peace of San Francisco for two years, an office there of great responsibility and honor,—there being only six justices in the whole city,—with a salary of $2,400 per annum. Meantime, he was interested in growing grapes in Santa Clara Valley, having now over one hundred acres under successful cultivation. He married in 1868 the daughter of his law partner, ex-Judge A. L. Rhodes of the supreme court of California. His home is in Oakland, Cal., and his office in San Francisco. The firm of Rhodes & Barstow is prominent and successful.

Mr. Barstow is a man of ability and force of character, a genial companion, of an inquiring mind, somewhat speculative and untraditional.

ANSON BARSTOW,

Brother of the above is a grain merchant in Oakland, Cal.

GARDNER BARSTOW,

Also a brother, is engaged in grain business in Chicago.

GEORGE BARSTOW

Was the son of William Barstow of Haverhill. He was educated at the Academy and at Dartmouth College, but did not graduate from the latter institution. He read law with the distinguished Robert Rantoul of Boston, and began the practice of his profession in that city. He afterwards moved to Hillsboro, and later to Manchester, and then to San Francisco, Cal., where he died. Mr. Barstow was a man of ability and character, and gained success in his professional career. He became interested in politics, and was a member of the California legislature, being honored with the speakership of the house of representatives of that body. He also wrote a history of New Hampshire before leaving the state, and was a man of literary tastes and culture. He married Emily Shepley of Saco, Me.

CHARLES W. BARSTOW,

Brother of the above, was educated at the Haverhill Academy and was a devoted and successful Moravian minister. He now lives at Ames, Iowa.

JOHN BARSTOW

Is the son of the late Ezekiel H. and Eunice (Clark) Barstow, and was born in 1858. He fitted for college at St. Johnsbury, Vt., and graduated from Dartmouth College in 1883. He afterwards studied theology in Hartford, Conn., and completed his theological studies at Andover, Mass., and is now settled at Groton, Mass. During his theological course he spent one year in Europe and the East in travel. He has the promise of success.

MARY BARSTOW,

Sister of the above, was born in 1850, and was educated at Bradford Academy, Mass. After graduating, she was appointed teacher of music in her alma mater, and has held that position with eminent success for over eighteen years.

HAZEN BEDEL

Was born in Haverhill in 1818, and received his education at the common schools and at Haverhill Academy, quitting school at the age of twelve years. It was in his early childhood that his father, Gen. Moody Bedel, became financially embarrassed and was reduced to poverty. During this time he lived for five years in a family by the name of Jacob Williams, on the corner opposite the " Bliss Tavern," who kindly cared for him and sent him to the Academy for four years. This sunny episode in his childhood experience has always given Haverhill a warm place in his heart. " The good we do lives after us."

Mr. Hazen learned the shoemakers trade, but quit that for a clerkship in a store at Lancaster and at Colebrook, which he held till he was of age. He has often been called to public positions, being early commissioned a justice of peace, and at the age of twenty-six he was appointed colonel of the 24th Regiment, N. H. militia, serving in that position four years. He was a member of the constitutional convention of 1850 and also of that of 1876, has represented the town of Colebrook in legislature, was a councillor for two years, when Walter Harriman was governor, judge of probate for Coos county, county commissioner, a state commissoner for laying out appropriations for highways and postmaster for sixteen years. In addition to these he has been repeatedly entrusted with the management of town affairs, and has been many times appointed a referee in the adjustment of causes. He has also been in much request in settling estates.

Mr. Hazen began mercantile life in Colebrook in 1844

and continued in that business for about thirty years, when he retired from it for the purpose of engaging in the manufacture of lumber and starch. He also has interests in starch mills in Aroostook county, Maine. He has lived in Colebrook since he began business there, and has been a successful, enterprising, influential and highly esteemed citizen of the Town and county. He married Ann S. daughter of Dr. Lyman Lombard of Colebrook, and of their six children three are living, a son and daughter in Colebrook, and a daughter is studying medicine in Washington, D. C. Mr. Hazen belongs to the order of Masons, and has held high degrees in that fraternity.

JOHN BEDEL,

A younger brother of the above, was at the time of his death one of the most honored and esteemed citizens of Bath. He was born in 1823, whilst his father for a time was living in Indian Stream, in Coos county. He received his education in the common schools in Bath and at Newbury Seminary, Vt., and had the honorary degree of A. M. conferred upon him by Dartmouth College in 1869. He pursued his law studies with Hon. Harry Hibbard of Bath, but before he was admitted to the bar he volunteered in the Mexican war, and was a lieutenant under Gen. Pierce. After the close of that war he finished his law studies, and was admitted to the bar in 1850, and at once began the practice of his profession in Bath. In a few years he was appointed to a special service in the treasury department in adjusting the claims of government agents who had made *ex parte* settlements with "Uncle Sam." When the civil war broke out he resigned his duties at Washington, and offered his services to his country. He was appointed major of the 3d Reg. N. H. Vol. and soon after he was promoted to be lieutenant colonel, and whilst in prison at Columbia, S. C., he was made a colonel. He was taken prisoner in one of the assaults on Fort Wagner,

Charleston Harbor, and remained such for over a year, enduring much suffering and privation. After he was paroled he at once went to Washington, and laid before the authorities the sufferings of our soldiers in Rebel prisons. There can be no doubt that his earnest presentation of the necessity of an exchange of prisoners brought about that result. Soon after his return to his regiment he was promoted to be a brigadier general of volunteers. When the war ended he returned to Bath, and engaged extensively in the manufacture of starch. He represented Bath in the legislature for two years, and was the Democratic candidate for governor in 1869 and again in 1870. On both occasions, notwithstanding his splendid service in the war, he failed of an election. Gen. Bedel married Mary Augusta, daughter of Hon. Jesse Bourns of Nashua. Only three of their seven children are living. Gen. Bedel died in 1875.

JAMES W. BELL,

Son of the late James Bell of Bolton, was born in Haverhill. He received his early training at Haverhill Academy. He followed the business of a decorator in Boston, and was associated with his brothers-in-law, McPhersons, in that profession. He gained large success in his business, and during the administration of President Grant he was decorator of the White House, and was widely and prominently known. He is now retired on an ample fortune.

JOHN BELL,

Brother of the above, was born in Haverhill, and received his education at the Academy and at Bolton, Mass. He is a prominent and successful dentist in Boston, and pursued his professional studies in that city. He lives at Chelsea, Mass.

JAMES P. BREWER

Was born in Claremont in 1818, and came to Haverhill with his parents when only a few months old, and may, therefore, be properly claimed as a Haverhill boy. He lived in Haverhill till nearly eighteen years of age, and then went to Claremont, where he carried on the business of a merchant for over a quarter of a century. The trade of the store was very large. On one occasion, before the times of railroads, he bought 40,000 bushels of wheat in Michigan, which he had ground into flour, and then shipped to Whitehall, N. Y. by water, from whence it was carried across the Green mountains by teams, to Claremont, and sold for $4.00 and $4.50 a barrel. Subsequently he moved to Pittsburg, Pa., and was engaged very extensively in the lumber business for a number of years. For the last ten years he has lived in Cleveland, Ohio, and has in a great measure retired from active business life. Whilst in Pittsburg he was chiefly engaged in the cutting of box-boards for the manufacture of glass boxes. The mill was a very extensive one, running day and night with fifty-three circular saws, and two uprights for sawing logs of immense thickness. The sale of saw-dust more than defrayed the cost of coal for steam-power, whilst the coarse dust from the upright saws was consumed with the coal.

Mr. Brewer has been eminently successful in all avenues of enterprise in which he has engaged. He is a man of great energy and force of character, of superior business ability, and has justly amassed a large fortune in the forty years of his active business life. In his earlier days he had to struggle with poverty, and received only a common school education, with the exception of a single term in Haverhill Academy, the tuition for which he paid out of his earnings after he left the school. At the age of about sixteen he made every mortice and tenon in the old part of the little house his parents lived in next north of the Methodist church. He is entirely self-made and owes little to circumstances, and is a man of large intelligence and careful observation, whose conversation on the many practical questions of business and finance is instructive and entertaining. He has been in every part of our country. In manners he is agreeable and dignified, with a frank and kindly nature, and is a good example of the best type of American character. In physique he is tall and well built with a strong and winning face.

Mr. Brewer married Mary C. Bingham of Claremont, whose father was a college class-mate and the room-mate of Daniel Webster. Paran Stevens, the great hotel man, was an uncle of hers. Her mother's maiden name was Poole, from which Mr. Brewer gets his middle name, and was the daughter of Gen. Poole of Hanover. They have no children. The immediate occasion of their moving to Pittsburg was Mrs. Brewer's health, who was a great sufferer from catarrh and bleeding of the nose, and the change proved a perfect cure.

SAMUEL BROOKS

Was born in Haverhill in 1793 and was the oldest child of Samuel and Anna (Bedel-Butler) Brooks. He married Eliza Towle of Haverhill, and for a short time lived in Newbury, Vt. Afterwards he moved to Canada and became prominent as a merchant in Stanstead. Later he lived in Lennoxville where he was extensively interested in trade and agriculture. In 1837 he was sent as a delegate by leading citizens of the eastern townships to London, for the purpose of enlisting capitalists in the development of the resources of that region. Being successful in his mission the British Land Company of London was formed in the following year, and he was appointed agent of the company. He changed his home to Sherbrooke which was the central point of the companys' operations. He was also manager of a branch of the city bank of Montreal. During all these years he took an active and prominent part in every enterprise, and represented his county most of the time till his death in the provincial legislature. He was an active promoter of the Grand Trunk railroad from Montreal to Portland, and was a man of large liberality and warmly devoted to all endeavors for the upbuilding of society in every good and worthy way, and the church found in him a staunch and true friend.

Two of Mr. Brooks' sons, William and Charles have been successful in business, and now reside in Chicago. For many years they lived in Lennoxville and Sherbrooke, Canada. Samuel Towle is a graduate of Dartmouth College in the class of 1874, and of McGill University in medicine and practised his profession for a number of years at Sherbrooke, Canada. Afterwards he moved to St. Johnsbury, Vt., where he has since lived in the successful pursuit of his profession, and is a well-known physician and a man of high character. Edward Towle is also a graduate of Dartmouth College, and became prominent as a lawyer. He was for several years a senator in the Dominion Government at Ottawa, and is now one of the judges in the Canadian courts. The only daughter became the wife of Justice John Sewell Sanborn, a prominent man in Canadian politics and government, and a brother of the late Prof. Sanborn of Dartmouth College.

EDWIN BROOKS

Is the youngest son of Samuel and Hannah (Bedel-Butler) Brooks. He was liberally educated and practised law in New York with success for many years. Afterwards he went to California and continued the practice of his profession in San Francisco. He is distinguished as a linguist as well as a lawyer, and bears the multitudinous name of Edwin Luke Brown Brooks. He is still living.

BURBECK BROTHERS—EDWARD C. AND GEORGE,

Sons of William H. and Sally Putnam (Carleton) Burbeck. The former was born in Hanover in 1846, fitted for college at Meriden, and graduated from Dartmouth College in 1871.

After leaving college he was principal of the high schools at East Abington and at Winchendon, Mass., and of Mt. Pleasant grammer school, Nashua, where he remained fourteen years, and is now principal of the Danvers (Mass.) grammer school. He married Luella Carleton of West Newbury, Vt.

GEORGE BURBECK

Was born in Haverhill in 1850, fitted for college under Rev. E. H. Greeley and at New London, and is a graduate of Dartmouth College in the class of 1875. Immediately after leaving college he went to California, and was a clerk in the post office at Oakland for several years, and is now teller in the first national bank of that city. He married Ella B. Gifford, and is deacon in the First Congregational church of Oakland.

JAMES A. CUTTING

Was the son of Abijah Cutting, and was born in Haverhill. He was noted for his inventive genius, but was not always successful in his plans. At one time he was a pension agent in Boston, and accumulated a handsome property. He devised the Aquarial Garden in Boston, and invented a locomotive spark extinguisher. He was also the inventor of the ambrotype. He was a man of undoubted genius in his line of work, and had a name for integrity. He died in Boston many years ago.

FREDERICK CROCKER

Is the youngest son of Edward Bass and Elizabeth (Gibson) Crocker, and was born in 1811 on the Isle of Orleans about five miles below Quebec, where his father lived in the earlier years of this century, but at the breaking out of the war of 1812 he returned to North Haverhill, his native place. Frederick lived in Haverhill and in Bath till 1842, when he went South and engaged in business with much success. In

1840 he returned North, and soon after married Hannah B. Dodge of Bath. Of their family of twelve children only two sons are living. Mr. Crocker and others from this section went to north-western Pennsylvania and engaged in the lumber business, which however did not prove a fortunate venture, and the accumulations of former years in the South were swept away. Afterwards he moved to Olean, N. Y., and entered into business again, this time with better success. Whilst on a trip to Pittsburg with lumber in 1859, he heard of the discovery of petroleum on Oil Creek, and at once hastened to the fields of discovery and engaged in the oil business. Whilst studying the surface-indications of petroleum in that section he remembered that he had seen similar indications in northern Alabama and near the mouth of the St. Lawrence river, and formed the theory that the oil lay in a belt running from the mouth of the St. Lawrence river to the western side of the Gulf of Mexico, a theory which is now accepted as the correct one in regard to the trend and locality of the oil belt.

Mr. Crocker has made and spent hundreds of thousands of dollars in search of oil-deposits. A few years ago he with others organized a company to operate in Washington county, Penn., in the search of oil on the theory which he had previously formed. Numerous wells were drilled in that region, and although little oil was found these wells furnished an unlimited quantity of gas of very great value, which was conveyed to Pittsburg in pipes many miles away, and so generally has this gas come into use for fuel in manufacturing, that the use of coal is now almost entirely done away with, and the once smoky and sooty city of Pittsburg is, in the words of Mr. Crocker, "a clean city." The company to which he belongs owns wide tracts of leased oil-lands in that section of the country, and petroleum is found in large quantities in all directions. Mr. Crocker is still an active, enterprising man at the advanced age of 79 years.

NOAH DAVIS

Is the son of Noah and Freelove (Arnold) Davis, and was born in Haverhill in 1818. He was seven years old when his father moved to Albion, N. Y., and received his education in the common schools of that state, with the exception of a single term at the Weslyan Seminary, Lima, N. Y. After pursuing his law studies the requisite time, he was admitted to the bar in 1841, and began the practice of his profession at Buffalo, where he remained only a short period, and then moved to Albion and formed a partnership with the late Sanford E. Church, who afterwards was chief justice of the court of appeals of New York. This partnership continued until 1857, when Judge Davis was appointed to the supreme court bench of New York to fill a vacancy, and in the following fall of that year he was elected for the fall term of eight years, serving the last of the eight years as a judge of the court of appeals. He was elected for a second term, but before the expiration of the time he was compelled to resign on account of failing health. In 1869 he was elected to congress from the Rochester District, but only remained in that position till the close of the long term, when he was appointed United States district attorney for the southern district of New York, which office he held for about three years, and then took his seat on the supreme court bench in the city of New York, to which he was elected for a term of fourteen years.

Judge Davis is a man of the highest character and of great ability, and is esteemed one of the ablest jurists in the country. He is one of the foremost citizens of New York, and sat in the famous trial of William M. Tweed, the archplunderer of that city.

JOSEPH B. MORSE

Is the son of John and Eunice (Willoughby) Morse, and was born in Haverhill in 1814. He fitted for college at

Haverhill Academy, and graduated from Dartmouth College in 1848, at the age of thirty-four. He taught successfully for eighteen years as principal in the Harvard grammar school, Cambridge, Mass. Mr. Morse is a Universalist clergyman, and now resides at Hanover on a farm on account of impaired health.

MOSES ELKIN

Was born in 1802, received his education at Hampton Academy, was very successful as a teacher in New York and Wisconsin, and also preached as a Methodist minister.

D. L. FARNSWORTH

Is the son of Stephen and Mary Ann (Locke) Farnsworth, and was born in Haverhill in 1838. His education was received at East Haverhill. He was always full of energy, and went to California in 1858 to seek his fortune in that state, a young man of only twenty summers. At first he worked on a farm, and then drove a team at the mines. Afterwards he went to San Francisco and engaged in the milk business, at first with twenty cows and at last with one hundred. Changing from this to draying he has become the largest drayman in San Francisco, employing over one hundred horses and sixty men. In 1884 he was elected supervisor, and was chairman of the street committee. He married Fannie P. Locke, and they have two children, Silas B. and Lottie P.

CHARLES NELSON FLANDERS,

Son of Peter and Mary E. Flanders, was born in 1845. He is a graduate from Dartmouth College, 1871. Andover Seminary, 1874, was ordained and settled at Westmoreland the same year, afterwards acting pastor at Wapping, Conn., and is now installed pastor at Newport. He married Emily Page of Haverhill, and they have three children. At Westmoreland and Wapping he was school committee, and is now a trustee of Kimball Union Academy. Mr. Flanders has been an efficient minister, of thoroughly manly character and ability, and has always been most highly esteemed.

LUCIEN HASKELL FRARY

Was born in Haverhill in 1839, and is the son of Charles S. and Abigail (Haskell) Frary. His early education was pursued at Haverhill Academy, and at the age of fourteen he entered the *Democratic Republican* office in Haverhill, where he remained till he was of age. Fitting for college under private tutors he entered Dartmouth College in 1862, and graduated in course. He worked his way through college without aid from any source, except his own industry and energy. After graduating he studied for the ministry at Andover Theological Seminary, and graduated from that institution in 1869, when he was ordained and settled as pastor of the First Congregationalist church, Middleton, Mass., where he remained five years, and then became pastor of the Congregationalist church, Waymouth, Mass., continuing there over eleven years, when on account of the health of his only child, he was compelled to resign, and is now pastor of the Congregational church, Sierra Madre, California. Mr. Frary has been singularly successful as a minister, gaining not only a deep hold upon the churches which he served, but also upon the communities in which he lived. On leaving Weymouth the church made a most complimentary record of their feelings toward him, and also gave expression to their deep regard in a handsome pecuniary token. During his ministry at Weymouth he received several very flattering calls to other churches,—First Church, Minneapolis, Minn., and College Street church, Burlington, Vt. He has devoted himself entirely to the duties of the church, giving his best time and brain, and is a most interesting and effective preacher, and a man of talent. Some years ago he made an extensive tour of southern Europe, going as far east as Palestine and Egypt, and wrote his impressions for a local paper. He also allowed by request several sermons to be published. He has a hopeful and sunny heart, is thoroughly true in his friendships, and catholic in opinion. He married first, Susan E. True of Meriden, who lived only a few years, and then Louise Parker of Dunbarton. They have an only child, a daughter in frail health.

WARREN D. GOOKIN

Born in 1810, was the son of Richard and Rebecca (Denman) Gookin. He was educated at Haverhill Academy and Dartmouth College, graduating from the latter institution in 1830. The early part of his life was passed in Cuba, where he was interested in a sugar plantation. He also devoted some time in travel. Finally, he came to New York and was extensively engaged as a shipping merchant, in which business he gained large success. He died in Brooklyn in 1874. A scholarship in Dartmouth College, known as the "Gookin Scholarship," was founded by him. A daughter of Mr. Gookin married Edwin S. Waterman, and lives in Brooklyn.

MICHAEL GRAY

Was the son of Ebenezer and Ruth (Johnston) Gray. He was born in 1789, and received his early education at Haverhill Academy. He then went to Scotland and graduated at Ruthersham Seminary. After graduation he returned for a short period to his native place, and then went to England, and was settled over a Congregational church in London in 1813. Of his subsequent history little is known, except that he is reputed to have been a very eloquent preacher and a man of large influence.

CALEB S. HUNT

Was the oldest son of Caleb Hunt. He graduated from Dartmouth College in 1832, and read law in the office of

Lieut.-Gov. Read of Massachusetts, whose daughter he married. For a number of years he lived in New Orleans engaged in the cotton-gin business, and then coming to Brooklin he carried on the manufacture of cotton-gins.

HORACE HUNT

Graduated from Dartmouth College in 1847, and afterwards studied law in Detroit. Soon after his admission to the bar he relinquished his professional aims and returned to Haverhill and bought the Towle farm. After a short residence in Haverhill he went to Boston and engaged in business. He organized the Boston Machine Company, and was also its treasurer. He was successful in business and amassed a large property, but a few years ago he met with some financial reverse on account of endorsements. He married Annette Towle of Haverhill.

PRESCOTT HUNT

Was educated at Haverhill Academy, and then went to Boston in the employ of the Boston Iron Company as a clerk at first, and afterwards he became a partner. These works were largely engaged during the war in casting immense guns and in the manufacture of plates for the iron-clads. He was also president of one of the national banks in Boston. Like his brother, he endorsed heavily for others, and through the financial embarrassment of some of these, he met with heavy losses. He has two sons in business in Boston.

HELEN HUNT.

The youngest daughter of Caleb Hunt, and sister of the above, married Hon. Stoddard Colby, a prominent lawyer of Montpelier, Vt., who died some years ago, and at one time was register of the United States treasury. Mrs. Colby was a leader in Washington society, and is a very accomplished lady. She now lives in New York. They had two children.

CHARLES JOHNSTON,

Son of Capt. Michael Johnston, born 1789, graduated from Dartmouth College 1813, studied theology with Rev. Grant Powers and Dr. Lyman Beecher, labored as an evangelist in Connecticut and New York with Dr. Nettleton, and was pastor of a Presbyterian church, Otisco, N. Y. He was a man of much force of character.

HANNAH JOHNSTON,

Sister of the above, was born in 1793, and received her education at Haverhill Academy. She was married to Rev. Silas McKeen, D. D., in 1821, and of their four children, Philena, the oldest, was carefully trained in scholastic studies, and also in the fine arts, especially music, and has been successfully engaged in teaching in the Ohio Female College, and in the Western Female Seminary, Oxford, O. For many years she has been the accomplished principal of Abbott Academy for ladies, Andover, Mass. Her sister Catherine, was at one time a teacher in Mount Holyoke Ladies Seminary, Mass., and died in West Virginia. A son, George W., was a graduate of Dartmouth College and died in early manhood, and is said to have been a young man of much promise. The youngest daughter, Phebe Fuller, was associated in teaching with her eldest sister both in Ohio and at Andover, and died a few years ago in Baltimore.

The mother of these children was a woman of rare christian character and graces, whose "price is far above rubies," a devoted wife and mother, wise in speech and discreet in action, and a friend of the poor and needy. She was superintendent of the first Sabbath school organized in Haverhill about 1818.

JOHN KIMBALL

Was the eldest son of John and Mehitabel (Carleton) Kimball of Haverhill. He pursued his early education at Haverhill Academy, and graduated from Dartmouth College in

1822. He read law and successfully practiced his profession, first in Claremont, and then in Putney, Vt., where he lived till his death. For several years he represented the latter town in the legislature, and was also a state senator from Windham county. During his senatorial service he was chosen president of the senate. He was a man of high character and influential in the state.

WILLIAM H. LEITH

Was born in Haverhill in 1859, and is a son of George W. and Evelina (Frary) Leith. His early education was pursued at Haverhill and Plymouth, and was completed at Braintree, Mass. He began the study of medicine under Dr. Samuel P. Carbee of Haverhill, and in 1883 he graduated from the medical department of the University of Vermont amongst the first in his class. After a competitive examination for the place of home surgeon to the Mary Fletcher Hospital at Burlington, Vt., he was appointed to that position which he held for one year, and on leaving he was presented with the special thanks of the trustees for "professional and faithful service." He began the practice of medicine at Guildhall, Vt., remaining there two years, and then moved to Lancaster, where he has met with flattering success. Dr. Leith is a young man of ability, a careful student in his profession, of pleasing manners and has a large share of professional enthusiasm. If his life is spared he can hardly fail of an honorable name in his profession.

MERRILL BROTHERS—JOHN L., BENJAMIN AND CHARLES H. Children of Dea. Abel K. Merrill. John L. was born in 1833, and received his early education at Haverhill Academy and fitted for college at Kimball Union Academy. He graduated from Dartmouth College in 1856, and studied for the ministry at Princeton Theological Seminary. His first pastorate was over the Presbyterian church in Chanceford, York county, Pa. Afterwards he settled at Acworth and Marlborough, remaining in the latter place about eighteen years, and is now the pastor of the Congregational church at Rindge. He was for a time principal of the high school, Lancaster, Pa., after leaving Chanceford. During his ministry at Acworth he wrote the history of that town. Mr. Merrill is a man of high character, and a safe and judicious counsellor, and has been eminently successful in his profession. He married Mary L. Murphy of Chanceford, Pa., and of their three children two are living.

Benjamin, born in 1835, received his early education at Haverhill and at Kimball Union Academy, and afterwards graduated from the scientific department of Dartmouth College in 1858. He studied theology at Princeton Seminary, and began his ministry as a missionary amongst the miners of Barton, and also preached at Piedmont, W. Va. After a few years he became pastor of the Congregational church at Pembroke. Later, he was settled over the Presbyterian church at Ausable Forks, N. Y., and at the present time he is ministering to the Congregational church in Swanzey. He married Joanna Walker Gildersleeve, and of their three children only one is living. Mr. Merrill has published several sermons.

Charles H., born 1845, fitted for college at Kimball Union Academy, and is a graduate of Dartmouth College in the class of 1867. He pursued his theological studies at Andover Theological Seminary, and was first a pastor at Mankato, Minn., where he was ordained, and then at West Brattleboro, Vt., remaining in the latter place for over fourteen years, when he was appointed field secretary of the Vermont Domestic Missionary Society, and is now living in St. Johnsbury, Vt. He has published several sermons and addresses, is a very scholarly man, and has been a successful and esteemed pastor. He married Laura B. Merrill, daughter of Daniel Merrill of Washington, D. C., and they have four children.

WILLIAM MERRILL,

Is the youngest son of Capt. Benjamin and Sarah (Haynes) Merrill, and was born in Haverhill in 1827. He was educated at Haverhill Academy, and also attended school at Plymouth. After teaching for a short time he went to Boston as a clerk in a dry goods mercantile house, and a few years later he engaged in the cloth and woolen jobbing business in New York, at first as a clerk and afterwards as a partner, and was for some years the foreign buyer of the house.

Mr. Merrill withdrew from mercantile life and engaged in banking and brokage, from which, however, he was compelled to retire on account of his health. He has lived in Brooklyn since 1850, and has taken an active interest in city and church matters. He is a member of Rev. Dr. Storr's church. His wife was Julia Wright before her marriage, daughter of John Wright of Brooklyn, at one time collector of the port of Buffalo.

Mr. Merrill is a gentleman of refined manners and tastes, of high character and intelligence, and greatly esteemed by all who knew him. He is the generous giver of the Dea. Merrill Memorial Chapel, Haverhill.

ARTHUR MITCHELL,

Son of David and Salome (Davis) Mitchell, was born in 1864. His education was pursued at Haverhill Academy, and he entered Dartmouth College in 1882, but remained only one year, when he was compelled to leave on account of his eyes. Subsequently he studied medicine in Boston, graduating from the medical department of Boston University in 1886, and is now practicing his profession in Medfield, Mass. He is enthusiastic in his work, and has a promising future.

PEABODY A. MORSE,

Son of Bryan and Susanna (Stevens) Morse, was born in 1805, and graduated from Dartmouth College in 1830. After leaving college he went to Fredericksburg, Va., and acted as tutor in the family of Judge Brooks of the supreme court of Virginia. Meantime, he pursued his legal studies under that gentleman's direction until he was admitted to the bar. In 1833 he went to Louisiana, and settled in Natchitoches, where he engaged in the practice of the law for many years. For a long period from 1838 he was a member of the Louisiana Legislature, and served with great usefulness, prominence and distinction in that body. In 1843 Gen. Morse moved to California, and at once took high and responsible position, filling many offices of importance, honor and trust, amongst others that of judge of the court of San Francisco, and commissioner of the funded debt. In 1854 he returned to Lousiana with his family and resided there till his death in 1878. At the time of his decease the bar of Natchitoches took special notice of the event, passing very complimentary resolutions, and appointed a delegation to attend the funeral. Judge Morse married Miss Sampayrac. When in college being asked what his father's business was, he returned this characteristic answer,—"Now, my friend, you've got me. If you had inquired what it was not, I could very easily have answered."

GEORGE W. MORSE.

Brother of the above, was born in 1812, and at the time of his death was a resident of Washington, D. C., though for many years previous he lived in Lousiana. He was educated at Haverhill Academy, developing at an early period of life wonderful mechanical and inventive skill. At the age of eighteen he invented a gun with a "magazine lock," by which the gun could be fired sixty times without priming. He is the real inventor of the "metallic cartridge case" which alone has made breech-loading small arms a success, but unfortunately on account of the imperfect manner in which his lawyer drew his patent, he lost his claim to being the first inventor of the "metallic cartridge." Mr. Morse, however, conscious of the great wrong which had been done him in being denied priority of invention by which others have probably amassed fortunes, brought his claim before Congress and petitioned that body that some compensation might be granted him for the use of his invention in the arms of the government service. The matter was considered in 1884, and the committee to whom Mr. Morse's claim was referred, after giving the matter the most careful consideration, aided by an expert from the Patent Office and by officers in the Ordnance Department, closed the report on the matter with the recommendation that the claim be allowed. Accordingly, a bill was introduced appropriating $25,000. Brig.-Gen. Benet, chief of ordnance to whom the report of the committee was referred, uses this language. "In my opinion Mr. Morse fairly and justly deserves this much at the hands of Congress, and I strongly recommend the passage of the bill." And this recommendation of the chief of ordnance was concurred in by the Secretary of War, Hon. Robt. T. Lincoln. The "metallic cartridge" was invented in 1856.

The name of Morse is connected with two of the most important inventions that have been given to the world. One of these is the electric telegraph which has revolutionized the method of transmitting news rapidly from all parts of the world, so that in a few hours the nations of the earth can be put in communication with each other, and the state of commerce and industry and markets of one day may be read at our breakfast tables the next day. The other invention is the "metallic cartridge case" for breech-loading guns, which has created an equal revolution in the fire-arms of the world. The honor of this last invention belongs to a son of Haverhill, according to the judgment of those who have the best means of information, including not only ordnance officers in our own army and experts in the Patent Office, but also according to the highest army and naval opinion of Great Britain. "In conversation with officers of all nationalities," writes an English officer to Mr. Morse, "I have always said that you are the inventor of the 'metallic cartridge case.'" Tardy justice has been done Mr. Morse's name, and only a partial renumeration has been rendered him for his great invention in fire-arms.

Mr. Morse died in 1888 in Washington.

ISAAC S. MORSE,

The youngest son of Bryan and Susanna (Stevens) Morse, was born in 1817 and received his education at Haverhill Academy. When his father moved to Lowell, Mass., in 1833 to engage in mercantile business, the son entered his store as a clerk, but in 1837 he began the study of law in Lowell, attended afterwards the law school at Cambridge, and was admitted to the bar in 1840. He and Gen. B. F. Butler were admitted at the same time, and for many years fought the law-battles in Lowell. He was for a time city solicitor of Lowell. He married Eloise La Barte and they had a family of four children, two of whom, daughters, are living. Emma married B. F. Hosped, a paper manufacturer of Holyoke, Mass., George A. was a lawyer and a daughter is living with her father.

Mr. Morse moved to Cambridge in 1861, and has resided there ever since. He served in the board of aldermen of that city, and also represented it in the legislature. He has for many years been a prominent citizen of Massachusetts, and has gained a wide reputation as an able and accomplished lawyer. His success in his profession would easily satisfy any reasonable ambition. Soon after moving to Cambridge he was elected district attorney for Middlesex county, and continued in that office from 1855 to 1871, an unusually long period of service, and which is an honorable tribute to his capacity as a lawyer and his fidelity to the trust committed to his care. While serving in this office it fell to his lot to conduct the case of the government in the famous Kalloch trial. Mr. Morse was then in his prime, about forty years of age, and the trial created great interest not only in Massachusetts but in all New England and the country, on account of the heinousness of the crime and the prominence of the accused. Mr. Morse was at his best during the long contest. A journal of that date, speaking of his conduct of the case and his argument to the jury, said, "Every great occasion is apt to bring forth great men. Men never display all their energies and talents except upon great emergencies, and this truth was never more clearly shown than in the case of Mr. Morse, prosecuting attorney for the county of Middlesex. The trial of Mr. Kalloch has had the effect of bringing him before the public in a prominent position, and a permanency he never would have attained, had he dug for years into the ordinary criminal cases under his jurisdiction."

Mr. Morse declining a re-election retired from the office of district attorney in 1871, and the members of the Middlesex bar with other distinguished gentlemen gave him a complimentary dinner at Young's Hotel. Amongst those present were such prominent persons as Gen. Banks, Dr. George B. Loring, Col. Daniel Needham and many others. Gen. Banks in his remarks on this occasion said that "the district attorney was eminently a judicial officer, whose primary duty it was not to convict all who were brought before him, but to find out whether conviction was deserved. In this respect Mr. Morse had demonstrated in his own career the true district attorney." At the close of the dinner, greatly to the surprise of Mr. Morse, he was presented by his friends with an elegant service of silver plate. Since then he has devoted himself with industry and fidelity to a large and lucrative law practice.

The following anecdote is related in a Boston paper of recent date, and illustrates Mr. Morse's quick wit and keen mind. Robert Morris was a prominent colored lawyer at the Suffolk bar, and on one occasion was defending a colored dress-maker who was charged with stealing silk from her customers and substituting for it poorer material. A lady witness against the dress-maker testified that she could tell the value of silk within twenty-five cents per yard. Mr. Morris on cross-examining the witness, taking advantage of the common opinion that colored persons are hard to distinguish from white persons, asked the witness if she could recognize a colored man who had brought a bundle to her. "No; I think that colored folks all look pretty much alike to me." "Oh, they do, do they?" was lawyer Morris' quick reply. "We'll see." Then turning to the court room, where many interested colored spectators were seated, he requested several gentlemen of color to stand, and then asked the witness: "Now, look at me and these other gentlemen, and tell the court whether you could tell us apart."

"I don't see much difference," she replied. "Perhaps by studying you all I could, but your heads are all shaped alike and except that some are darker than others, I should find it difficult to distinguish."

"Now, madam," said Mr. Morris with an air of oppressed humanity, "do you mean to swear, after telling the jury that you can judge of the value of silk within twenty-five cents a yard, that you can't tell the difference between Mr. Johnson here and me?"

Without waiting for the witness to reply, Mr. Morse broke in: "She claimed to be a judge of silk, not a judge of wool."

Squire Morris took the retort in the best of humor, but nevertheless it broke the force of his cross-examination.

In 1857 Dartmouth College conferred upon Mr. Morse the honorary degree of Master of Arts.

ROBERT MORSE,

A son of Stephen and Sally (Kay) Morse, was born in

Haverhill in 1792, and afterwards lived in Rumney. He was the organizer in 1814 of the first permanent stage line between Concord and Haverhill, and in the spring of that year, he with a party of invited guests, came over the route in the first stage. Subsequently, he became noted as one of the great stage proprietors and mail carriers between Concord and Haverhill, and he was also interested in other lines. He was a man of great force and energy in pushing enterprises.

JOSEPH B. MORSE,

Son of John and Eunice (Willoughby) Morse, was born in Haverhill in 1814. He fitted for college at Haverhill Academy, and graduated from Dartmouth College in 1848, at the age of thirty-four. He was principal of Howard Grammer School in Charlestown, Mass., for eighteen years. Mr. Morse is a Universalist minister, but in later years, on account of impaired health, he has lived in Hanover on a farm. He married Sarah M. Ripley.

THOMAS LEVERETT NELSON,

The oldest son of John and Lois (Leverett) Nelson, was born in Haverhill. He entered Dartmouth College in 1842, and graduated from the University of Burlington in 1846. After his admission to the bar he began the practice of law in Worcester, Mass., and soon rose to be one of the leading members of the Worcester county bar. He is now United States Circuit Judge, and lives in Worcester, Mass. Judge Nelson is a man of ability and a learned jurist.

ALONZO F. NILES

Is the oldest son of Joseph B. Niles, and received his education at Haverhill Academy. His first start in life was as cook on a raft to Hartford, and then he went to Springfield, Mass., where he has been in business for nearly forty years. He is the founder of the well-known wholesale and retail house of that city, first for twenty years under the name of A. F. Niles, and afterwards A. F. Niles & Son. They are dealers in groceries, fish, provisions and fruit, and have also a meat market connected with their establishment which is one of the best equipped in the city, and their business is one of the largest in their line in Springfield. In a volume, "Massachusetts Industries," the firm is thus spoken of: "The founder of this wide-awake house, Mr. A. F. Niles, is a native of New Hampshire, and a gentleman possessing the most commendable business characteristics, being enterprising, energetic, industrious, liberal in methods and the soul of integrity. His son, Mr. O. W. Niles, was born in Springfield, and is now in his twenty-ninth year. He is a young man of exceptional business capacity, prompt and reliable, pushing, popular and praiseworthy, and commands hosts of friends. There is no business house here more popular or more deserving of its success, and the host of patrons who have entered into business relations with it is increasing."

Mr. Niles married a sister of Dr. Wetherbee of North Haverhill, and they have three children. He is a deacon in the Memorial church, Springfield, and a prominent citizen of of that city. He is intelligent, genial, and devoted to his family.

HORACE L. NILES,

Brother of the above, also lives in Springfield and was for many years in business with Alonzo F. He served in the war, and was taken prisoner at Ball's Bluff, being confined in Libby prison three months. For several years he lived in Nebraska, and carried on farming. He is now engaged in mercantile business in Springfield.

GEORGE B. NICHOLS,

The son of Jonathan S. and Myra (Montgomery) Nichols, was born in Haverhill. He was educated at Haverhill and

Kimball Union Academies, and graduated from Dartmouth College in 1864. Since leaving college he has been engaged in teaching at Webster, Nantucket and Somerville, Mass., in which profession he has gained praiseworthy success.

NELLIE P. NICHOLS,

Sister of the above, received her education in Haverhill Academy and at Mt. Holyoke Seminary. She has been a successful teacher since graduation.

CLARA I. NICHOLS,

Daughter of Jonathan S. and Elizabeth (Page) Nichols, was educated at Haverhill Academy and at State Normal School, Plymouth. She has devoted herself to music, and has gained much success in that profession. She has recently married John Donovan, a civil engineer of talent and enterprise.

PERSON NOYES

Was born in 1827. His father was the only son of Timothy Noyes. At the age of eighteen he went to Lowell, where he has since resided. For a while he worked in the mills, and then for fourteen years he was in the furniture business, and since then he has been the head of the Noyes Manufacturing Co., makers of mill and railroad specialties. He married Adelaide Closson of Lyme, and of three children, the daughter is a teacher in Hartford, Conn., two sons are at home, and one in Pennsylvania. Mr. Noyes modestly says he has been "fairly successful."

JOHN A. PAGE

Is the second son of Gov. John and Hannah (Merrill) Page, and was born in Haverhill in 1814. He received his education at Haverhill Academy, and served for a short time as a clerk in a store in Portland, Me. Returning to Haverhill, he engaged in mercantile business at the Brook, and continued to do so, until at the resignation of Mr. Bunce he was chosen cashier of Grafton County Bank. Afterwards he became cashier of the bank of Danville, Vt., and continued in that position for some years, when he was called to be superintendent of the Passumpsic railroad. Later he was chosen cashier of a bank in Montpelier, Vt., and has lived there to the present time. He is now largely retired from active business, but continues as president of the National Bank of Montpelier. Mr. Page was state treasurer of Vermont for sixteen years in succession, and proved an able and faithful public officer. He has addressed himself to business from the first with diligence, prudence and good judgment, and has accumulated a handsome fortune. He has been one of the leading and influential citizens of Vermont, and is held in high esteem by his fellow citizens. Mr. Page married Martha Ward of Haverhill, and their only child, a son, is engaged in stock-raising in the west.

MOSES S. PAGE

Was born in 1838, and is the youngest son of Samuel and Eliza (Swasey) Page of Haverhill. His education was acquired in the common schools until he was old enough to attend school away from home, when he was sent to St. Johnsbury Academy, Vt, and also to the seminary at Newbury, Vt. At the close of his school years he entered the jewelry store of Henry Towle of Haverhill, as an apprentice in that business, and remained there a little over two years. Afterwards he went to Boston and got a situation with a jewelry firm there, and though he began at the low wages of four dollars per week, he soon had his wages advanced on account of his industry and strict attention to business. Later he was offered a place in the management of a loan office, but was somewhat in doubt as to his ability to make an honest living. Being assured, however, that he was at liberty to manage the business to suit himself, he entered upon its duties. After a few years he in company with another person bought out his employer, and they continued the loan business for eleven years at the old stand on Salem street, when Mr. Page assumed the entire ownership and control of the concern, and has remained in the business at the same place till the present time. Near the close of the War of the Rebellion he served one hundred days in the 6th Reg. Mass. Vol.

Mr. Page has gained much success in business and has been a careful and wise financier. He is largely interested in real estate in Melrose, and also is a stockholder in the Farmers Trust and Loan Company of Anthony, Kansas, of which he is the vice-president. He is a man of intelligence and close observation, and has travelled extensively both at home and abroad. Where he resides he has always taken an active and praiseworthy interest in all matters pertaining to the public, and is a public-spirited and enterprising citizen. He is prominent in church and philanthropic matters, and is a deacon in the Congregational church of Melrose. Mr. Page married in 1869 Harriet E. Hibbard of Concord, Vt., and has a family of two children living, having lost a son a few years ago by a tragic death.

JAMES HENRY PEARSON

Was born in Haverhill in 1820, and is a son of Maj. Isaac and Charlotte (Atherton) Pearson. He received his education at Haverhill Academy, and afterwards was engaged with his father in the manufacture of lumber. In 1851 he moved to Chicago and cast in his life and fortunes with that young and growing city where he still resides. Mr. Pearson has been very successful as a lumber merchant, inheriting both his father's and grandfather's genius in that line of trade, and is one of the prominent business men of that city. Besides his large yards at Chicago, he has extensive mills and lumber tracts at Saginaw, Mich. He is also connected with banking institutions both in Chicago and in Saginaw. And though a very busy man, he has always taken a very deep interest in the moral and religious welfare of Chicago, giving freely of his time and means for the advancement of all that is good and worthy for society. He is a man of great excellence of character, full of kindness and good will, and of a genial spirit. He married Sarah Elizabeth Witherell, and they have a family of four children. His only daughter is married to Prof. Scott of the Chicago Theological Seminary and lives in that city. Two sons are in business with their father, one in Chicago, the other at Saginaw, and the remaining son is in Paris pursuing art-studies. Mr. Pearson is a worthy representative of the sturdy, energetic and noble New England stock.

SAMUEL P. PIKE

Was born in Haverhill, 1854, son of John D. and Jane (Poor) Pike. His early advantages were limited, and his education was obtained in the district school in winter, whilst in summer, from the age of ten to eighteen, he worked on a farm. At the latter period he went to Tilton on a milk farm for one year, and then at Lowell, Mass., where he drove a milk wagon. Later, he bought the route and ran it for one or two years, when he engaged in the provision business which he still continues. Mr. Pike has been a most successful man, and does a very extensive business, not only in Lowell, but also has a branch store in Manchester, selling in both places $250,000 worth of goods. He married Jeannette W. Hart and they have five children. His residence is on a fine farm four miles from Lowell, at Wamesit, Tewksbury. He is public-spirited, full of energy, and greatly esteemed where he lives.

POWERS — ELIZABETH ABBOTT, MARY WEBSTER, HENRIETTA MUMFORD, AND GEORGE CARRINGTON,

Were children of Rev. Grant and Eliza Howard (Hopkins) Powers. All are filling or have filled important positions. Elizabeth A. became the wife of Joseph D. Foot of Amboy,

N. J. Afterwards, she moved to Buffalo, N. Y., and was principal for twenty-four years of a ladies seminary. She now resides in Virginia. Mary W. married Tracy Robinson of Panama, and now resides there. Henrietta M. married Rev. John Kelley of Patterson, N. J., and now lives in Washington, D. C. George C. is a wholesale grocer in Boston, Mass.

JOHN REDING

Is the son of Silvester and Ellen D. (McClary) Reding. He received his earlier education at Haverhill Academy, after which he served as a clerk for one year in Wentworth and Bradford, Vt. He then entered the Commercial College at Poughkeepsie, N. Y., and pursued a commercial course of study. He commenced business life in Boston, and is now a member of the firm of Moore, Smith & Co., one of the oldest Boston houses. Mr. Reding is a courteous and agreeable gentleman. He married Laura C. Wolcott of Quechee, Vt.

RODGERS BROTHERS — LEVI AND M. CARLETON.

Both children of Levi and Mehitabel B. (Carleton) Rodgers. The former was born in Guildhall, Vt., in 1843, and at the age of nine came with his mother to live in Haverhill. He fitted for college at Haverhill and Kimball Union Academies, entered Dartmouth College in 1862, graduated in course, and for several years after was principal of a grammar school in Cleveland, O. He studied theology at Andover, graduating in 1871, and became pastor of the Congregational church, Claremont, where he remained nine years as a successful pastor. He was then settled in Georgetown, Mass., the successor of Rev. Charles Beecher, and is now there. He married Ellen S. Dimick of Quechee, Vt., a woman of superior worth and accomplishment. She died in 1883. Mr. Rodgers has been successful as teacher and pastor.

M. Carleton was born in 1847, fitted for college at Kimball Union Academy, and graduated from Dartmouth College in 1871. He taught in Tingloro, Walpole and New Bedford, Mass., remaining in the latter place nine years and then moved to Virginia and engaged in farming for several years. He is now in business in Bridgeport, Conn. He married Laura J. Chamberlain of McIndoes Falls, Vt.

JONATHAN H. ROWELL'S

Parents were Jonathan B. and Cynthia (Abbott) Rowell, and he was born in 1833, their second son. He left Haverhill with his father in 1846, at the age of thirteen, and has lived in McLean county, Ill. Losing their father a year after he moved west, the family having to care for itself, as Mr. Rowell had met with financial reverses before leaving Haverhill. Jonathan H. taught school and worked on the farm till he was twenty-one years old, when he entered Eureka (Ill.) College, of which he is a graduate. After graduation he was professor in mathematics in his Alma Mater till the War of the Rebellion broke out, when he enlisted in the 17th Ill. Infantry and served three years as lieutenant and captain, and took part in the principal battles fought by the "Army of the Tennessee," which was Gen. Grant's original command. At the close of the war Capt. Rowell entered the law school of the university of Chicago, and graduated from that institution in 1865. Since then he has practised his profession in Bloomington, Ill. He was first state's attorney of his district four years, and served six years on the board of education of Bloomington. Two years he was a master in chancery for that county. In 1882 he was chosen to Congress, and has held his seat since that time. He was a Garfield and Arthur elector in 1880, and has taken an active and prominent part in all the political campaigns since the close of the war, and is one of the leading men of the state in the councils of his party. In Congress he has actively engaged in all the more important measures of legislation before that body, and has served on the committee of war claims, District of Columbia, and elections. He represents the most wealthy district of the state outside of Cook county which includes the city of Chicago.

Capt. Rowell is an able and successful lawyer, well known not only in his own district, but throughout the state. His record both in civil and military life is most honorable and successful. His wife is a native of Illinois, but her parents were from New England, and of their children, a son and daughter are graduates of the university of Michigan.

CHESTER ROWELL,

Brother of the above, is a distinguished physician in Fresno, California, and has also taken an active and prominent part in politics.

HORACE O. SOPER

Was a graduate of Dartmouth College in 1825 and belonged to the Soper family of Haverhill. He lived in New York and was a lawyer. In 1847 he was appointed a county judge and continued in that position till 1851.

LYMAN D. STEVENS

Is the son of Caleb and Salley (Dewey) Stevens, and was born in Piermont in 1821, meeting with an accident in boyhood, which disabled him for manual labor, he was trained for a professional life. He received his early education at Haverhill Academy, and afterwards entered Dartmouth College, from which he graduated in the class of 1843. After leaving college he taught the academy at Stanstead, Canada, for two years, and in the meantime he pursued the study of law under the direction of E. C. Johnson, Esq., of Derby Line, Vt. In the fall of 1845 he went to Concord and continued his professional studies with the late Chief-Justice Perley, and was admitted to the Merrimac county bar in 1847. He at once opened an office in Concord and began the practice of his profession in that city, and continued to do so until 1880, when he retired from professional life and surrendered his business to his son.

Mr. Stevens has been married twice, first to Achsah Pollard French of Concord, and his second wife's maiden name was Frances Childs Brownell of New Bedford, Mass. There are two children by each marriage. Henry Webster, the oldest son, is a rising young lawyer in Concord.

Mr. Stevens at the time of his retirement, was one of the prominent members of the Merrimac county bar, and had gained large success, both in his profession and in other business, and retired with an ample fortune and an honorable career. During the years of his more active life he was frequently called to positions of honor and trust. He was appointed by Governor Gilmore to settle the war claims of New Hampshire against the general government arising previous to 1863, and represented with two others as commissioners the state at the dedication of the national cemetery at Gettysburg in 1863. For four years he was a representative in the legislature from the city of Concord, and twice he was elected mayor of that city. In 1872 he was a presidential elector when President Grant was re-elected. Afterwards, 1880-1 he served for two years as a member of the executive council, and was chosen a state senator in 1884.

Mr. Stevens has also been intimately connected with business and money interests, having been president of the Merrimac County Savings Bank from its organization, and a director in the National State Capitol Bank since 1865. In addition to these he has been called to other positions of trust and responsibility. He served many years as a trustee of Boscawen and Kimball Union Academies, and since 1881 he has also been a trustee of the New Hampshire College of Agriculture and Mechanic Arts. In religious and benevolent matters he has taken an active and prominent part. He has been vice president of the New Hampshire Home Missionary society, and since 1871 its careful and trustworthy treasurer.

He is also treasurer of the Ministers and Widows Charitable Fund. Mr. Stevens is connected with the South Congregational church and society, and is one of its most efficient useful members, and is a man of high character and integrity. He is a warm and steadfast friend, and a most cordial and courteous gentleman.

SMITH BROTHERS — LYNDON ARNOLD, STEPHEN SANFORD, AND CARLOS,

Were sons of Rev. Ethan and Bathsheba (Sanford) Smith, and were born in Haverhill near the close of the last century. Lyndon Arnold was fitted for college at Hanover Academy, and graduated from Dartmouth College in 1817. He married a daughter of President Griffin of Williams College, and gained a prominence in his profession as a skillful physician in Newark, N. J.

Stephen Sanford Smith was a minister of large usefulness, and was pastor of a church in Chicago during his last years.

Carlos Smith was a graduate of Union College, a successful minister, and was honored with the title of D. D.

FRANK A. SMITH

Was born in Haverhill in 1855, son of Henry and Sarah M. (Pike) Smith. At the age of sixteen he engaged as a clerk in a store in Biddeford, Me., where he remained five years; the last year a partner in the house. Afterwards, he was a merchant at Woodsville, in the firm of Cutting & Smith, but in a year or two he began a course of study at New Hampton, and at the close of his academic course, he read medicine with Dr. D. W. Hazeltine of Springfield, Vt. He attended one course of lectures at Burlington, Vt., and two courses at the College of Physicians and Surgeons, New York City, graduating from the latter place in 1884. He began the practice of his profession at Reading, Vt., where he still continues, and in the few years of his professional life he has met with much success and is in possession of a steadily growing business. Dr. Smith is a rising man. He married Martha Alice Warren, a native of Haverhill, and daughter of Charles P. Warren.

WILLIAM PAGE STOWE

Is the son of Joseph and Priscilla (Page) Stowe, and was born near Sugar Loaf, East Haverhill, in 1831. The Stowes are of Puritan stock. Dr. Stowe left Haverhill with his parents when quite young, and went to Wisconsin, then an almost unbroken wilderness. He pursued his academic education at Lawrence University, from which he graduated in 1858, and entered the ministry of the Methodist Episcopal church, filling several of the most important pulpits of the Conference, and was presiding elder for eight years of the Milwaukee district. He was chosen in 1880 by the general conference agent of the Western Methodist Book Concern, which position he now holds. He has been a member of the last three general conferences, and also of the Centennial Conference. In 1884 he received the honoary degree of D. D. During the Rebellion he was chaplain of 27th Reg. Wis. Vol. He married Grace H. Bond of Buffalo, N. Y., and they have three children, Hester P., a graduate of Buffalo Female College, and now connected with a German Kindergarten in Berlin, Germany; Bond, a student in Chicago Medical College and a graduate of Northwestern University, and Will C., a member now of the same university. Dr. Stowe is a man of ability and much force of character, and has won an honorable place.

TARLETONS.

The following are children and grand-children of Col. William Tarleton:

JOSIAH BRADLEY

Lived in Chillicothe, Ohio, was high sheriff of the county and an associate judge, and was successful in business.

GEORGE W.

Lived in Concord for a time after the death of his father, and then went to Mobile, Ala., and became very wealthy.

THOMAS J.

Also lived in Mobile, and was a man of very supreme ability and excellence.

ALBERT

Was engaged at one time in the iron business at Krysville, N. Y., and died in Alabama.

JAMES M.

Was a merchant in Alabama, a warm personal friend of the late Ex-President Pierce, by whom he was appointed consul to Australia.

HORACE,

A grandson of Col. Tarleton, and son of Amos, went South and was there during the early part of the war. He married a Miss Barstow of Piermont. He now lives in Brooklyn, New York, and is engaged in the business of compressing cotton.

AMOS TARLETON,

Brother of Horace, is the only son of the second generation, except Henry, that now lives in this section of country. He was educated at Haverhill Academy, and then went to Boston as clerk in a store. Health failing him, he was advised to spend some time at the sea-shore at Shirley Point. He remained there several years in a hotel, meantime getting an idea of that business, and soon after became the proprietor of the Ocean House, Chelsea Beach, which he kept for thirty-one years with very great success, enlarging the house to its present size. He retired from the business in 1880. He now resides in Haverhill in the Col. Johnston place, which he has fitted up in convenient and attractive style. Mr. Tarleton is a gentleman of intelligence and wide experience, and large acquaintanceship with men and things, of gentle manners and an agreeable companion. He has never married.

TOWLES — FREDERICK AND JAMES.

The former was the son of Col. Simon and Susan (Hall) Towle, and spent the larger part of his life in Tallahassee, Fla., where he carried on successfully the business of a jeweler. He died in New York in 1857.

James H. is the second son of Henry and Susan (Pierce) Towle. His father was a jeweler, and carried on that business in Haverhill for many years. James H. was a clerk in his father's store. Afterwards he went to New York, and engaged in the same business, and for a number of years he was a member of the firm of Fellows & Co,, Maiden Lane, N. Y. He retired from active business a few years ago. He married Mary G., daughter of Dr. Spalding of Haverhill, and they have one child, a daughter. Mr. Towle is a genial and social gentleman.

NATHANIEL WILSON

Was born in Haverhill in 1808, and is the youngest son of Nathaniel and Sarah (Pearson) Wilson. He fitted for college at Haverhill Academy, and graduated from Dartmouth College in 1829. After leaving college he taught the academy at Lancaster for two years, and was a popular and successful teacher. He was also at the head of the High school in Augusta, Me., for one year. After the close of his service as teacher he began the study of the law with Hon. George Evans of Gardiner, Me. He was also for a short time in Mr. Bell's office before he taught at Lancaster. In 1834 he was admitted to the bar in Kennebec county, Me., and immediately began the practice of his profession at Orono, Me., where he has continued to live till the present time. He married Sarah H. Boardman of Lancaster, a most accomplished and beautiful woman, who died two years after their marriage. Afterwards, he married Abbie Ann

Colburn of Orono, and of their children the oldest son served in the War of the Rebellion in the expedition against New Orleans. Two are graduates of Bowdoin College, one a successful lawyer at Orono, and the other a popular and talented Congregational minister in Mass. He has also a son who is a physician, and two who are enterprising business men. One of the daughters is the wife of Prof. Jordon of Orono, and another lives in Kansas, where her husband is a rising lawyer.

Mr. Wilson has been prominently identified with all the leading interests of his adopted home, taking a leading part in all matters for the moral and religious upbuilding of the community. For thirty years he served on the school board of Orono, and was largely instrumental in securing the location in that place of the State College of Agriculture and the Mechanic Arts, and was also for a time in its board of trustees. He has held at different times most of the various town offices, and whilst a member of the legislature, where he served with honor, he was a member of the judiciary committee, and made a very able speech in favor of a bill to increase the salaries of the supreme court judges, which placed him amongst the ablest and most influential members of that body. He has taken a deep interest in temperance, and at one time was Grand Worthy Patriarch of the order of Sons of Temperance. As a lawyer, he has been highly successful and trusted, and has done a large business, winning a full share of closely contested cases. In politics Mr. Wilson was originally a Henry Clay Whig, but when that party went to pieces he became a national Democrat, and was an earnest advocate of Gov. Tilden for the presidency. In religious sentiment he is a Congregationalist. He is now in his eightieth year, and with the exception of his hearing he enjoys excellent health, and still retains a lively interest in his native town. He feels a just pride in his children.

EDWARD B. WILSON

Is the youngest son of Isaac P. and Rhoda (Brainard) Wilson, and was born in Haverhill in 1840. His wife was Luella E. Woodward of Haverhill. He received his education at the common schools and Haverhill Academy. Previous to attending school at the Academy he was a clerk at North Haverhill for one year and also a clerk in the post-office at Haverhill for two years. After leaving the Academy he was for two years in the registry of deeds office under Mr. Augustus Whitney, and then at the age of nineteen he went to Boston, and for six years he was in the employ of Houghton, Sawyer & Co. When the house of Morse, Shepard & Co. started he entered their employ, and rose to be a partner in the firm of Morse & Shepard, and is now at the head of the firm of Wilson, Lanaler & Co., in the wholesale dry goods business. Mr. Wilson is an active, energetic man, and has won honorable success in life. He lives in Newbury, Mass.

WILLIAM FREDERICK WHITCHER

Is the son of Ira and Lucy (Roger) Whitcher, and was born in Benton in 1845. He received his early academic education at Tilton Seminary, and graduated from Middletown, Conn. He at first entered the ministry, but afterwards devoted himself to journalism, and is now editor-in-chief of the Boston Evening Traveller.

HARVEY B. WILMOT'S

Father came to Haverhill in the early part of the present century. Haran Wilmot is a brother and Frank L. a nephew. Harvey has been a very successful business man in the clothing trade in Boston.

JOHN L. WOODS,

The only son of John L. and Mary Ann (Swasey) Woods, was born at Woodsville. He went West quite early in life, and when the War of the Rebellion broke out, he became Quarter-Master in the army. At the close of the war he was put in charge of government property, to dispose of it. Before the war he was in the railroad business at St. Louis. He is now in the service of the Pullman Car Company, and resides at Pullman, Ill.

FRANKLIN P. WOOD

Was born in Enfield, 1844, but came early to Haverhill. He fitted for college at Kimball Union Academy, and graduated from Dartmouth College in 1868. For a time after graduation he was a teacher in Kimball Union Academy, and then spent two years in Union Seminary, New York, and finished his theological studies at Andover, Mass. He married Abby O. Drew of Waterbury, Vt., and they have four children. He was pastor of the Congregational church, Acton, Mass., from 1871–84, and now resides there. He has been a successful pastor.

CHAPTER XX.

DOMESTIC AND SOCIAL LIFE.

Time-Changes — Life Simple — Two Classes come to Haverhill, the Well-to-do and Enterprising, and the Dependent — The first House — Frame Houses, two sizes — The great Fire-place and Chimney — The Children and "Popped Corn" — "Lug Pole" — "Trammels" — Crane — Frying-pan — Dutch Oven — Spit — "The Goose Hangs High" — Furniture — Pots and Kettles — The Dresser — Pewter Dishes — Wooden Dishes — Two-tined Forks — Hemlock Brooms — Sanded Floors — Carpets Rare — Domestic Duties — Wants Few — Life Happy and Virtuous — Diet — Tea and Coffee — Drinks — Flip and Punch — Wine — Drinking Social — Sugar Making — Paring-bee — Games — Huskings — Muster-day — Social Character of Church-going — Society People — Official Position and Moral Worth — The Commencement of New Order — Rebellion against forced payment of Ministers' Taxes — Church-Going less Universal — The Stage-coach — Blinds, Pictures and Ornaments — Wooden Plates, Sanded Floors, and Hemlock Brooms Yield — First Four-wheeled Carriage — First Piano — Chaises — Wagons — Clocks.

A century and a quarter makes great changes in the domestic and social habits of a people. In intervals of a few years we hardly notice such changes, but after a considerable lapse of time the difference between the Now and the Then is very marked. Our fore-fathers would be surprised indeed, were they to come back and see things as they are, in comparison with things as they were, and we were to be transferred to their modes of living, would be equally surprised. Life in those earlier days was simple. The range of experience was much narrower than it is now, and the means and facilities of life were far fewer and less varied. What was luxury then, is only comfort now, and the luxuries of to-day was not even a dream to our hardy ancestors, whilst the poverty and denials of those times would be considered unendurable now.

Two classes of people came to Haverhill, as they came to all other frontier abodes, those of means and enterprise, and those who had little of these. The former were men and women of large ability and force of character, who were leaders where they came from, and were willing to found new homes and enlarge their opportunities and fortunes. Of this class, Haverhill had more than her full share, as here was the garden of the Northern Connecticut valley, with its hopefulness and prosperity inviting to enterprise. The other class was much the more numerous, and being without means and without much energy and thrift, they were dependent and with little influence in the new settlement. They were the "hewers of wood and the drawers of water." When the Revolutionary struggle came on, they were the first to take alarm and to desire safety and shelter away from danger. They had no great interests to fight for here, and consequently they were easily tempted to hasten back to their original homes. Some did go back, and others were prevented from going by the commanding influence of the leaders of the settlement and the prompt measures which they took in furnishing arms to the dependent class.

The earliest settlers, even those that possessed property and had the enjoyments of refined life in their former homes, built and lived in log houses the first years of their Cohos life. These of course were small, with conveniences and comforts the most primitive, but in the case of the well-to-do they were only temporary, to be displaced by the earlier farm houses which began to be built about 1773. These were of two sizes, the half house about twenty-five feet square, small and low, some of which are still standing, and the double house, twenty-five feet one way and forty feet the other. The former satisfied the aims of the unambitious, whilst the latter were an indication of thrift and progress in worldly attainments. This latter house is still to be met with, either in its original form, or somewhat modified in the course of improvement, with two rooms front and a large room back of these, used chiefly as the living-room, and a small bed-room off from this main room. The old Col. Johnston house is of this style. Shutters or blinds were unknown in the earlier days, and the windows and window-glass of a greenish shade were small.

From the family room was built an immense chimney with fire-place large enough to receive huge logs, and sufficiently roomy to accommodate the whole family of children, who in the long winter evenings were seated on wood blocks at either end of the fire-place. The large stick back was called the "back-log," from three to six feet long sometimes, and would last several days. On this was placed a "top-stick," and in front the "fore-stick." Between these were the bed of coals and the fire wood. Much of the heat went up the immense chimney, but the mass of burning wood and coals and the heated bricks furnished generous warmth for the inmates. The ample flue carried off the dense volume of smoke that arose from the blazing fire, whilst the stars on clear nights could be seen by the prattling children in the chimney corner. Many were the good times they had in the olden fire-place, roasting green corn in the husk on chill and lowry days, crunching apples in the long fall and winter evenings, and popping corn in the ashes.* Back of the fire-place was the old brick oven, and in one corner of the chimney hung the dim Roman oil lamp with its bird-like beak.

The chimney place served another purpose as well as for warming and amusement. Here the meals were prepared. Over head was the "lug-pole," as it was called, made of a green stick of wood, and placed far enough above the fire so as not to become ignited by the heat and flames. From this pole hung the "trammels." These were long straight pieces of iron punched with holes into which the "pot-hooks" were set, so that the pot or kettle could be lowered or raised at pleasure. The "crane" was a later contrivance and served the same purpose as the "trammels" and "pot-hooks." The

---

* The hot ashes were drawn out and little wells or trenches made, and then a handful of corn was thrown into these and quickly covered up. In a few moments the corn would pop out into the fire-place or room.

frying-pan was set directly on the coals which the good house-wife drew out from the back-log, or it had long legs which straddled the embers, and was easily shifted by the long handle. There were also in use the "Dutch oven" and the "spit" for roasting meats. The "Dutch oven" was made of iron, shaped something like a deep covered dish, and had short legs. The cover with guard around the rim was filled with live coals, so as to aid the cooking by heating from above. The "spit" was a tin oven with dripping-pan, on which the meat or food was placed, shaped like a fire-blower, and was open on the fire side. On the side from the fire it had a door, through which the meat was turned on the "spit." Another way of roasting was by suspending the fowl from a point in the chimney by a string, and giving the fowl a rotary motion so as to bring each part to the heat. This is said to have been an epicurian mode of cooking the goose.

Fire was kept over night by covering up the embers with ashes. Sometimes when it went out a few coals or a brand were borrowed from a near neighbor. But our fore-fathers could always "strike fire" with the steel-ring, flint and tinder. *

The houses were fitted up with furniture made of wood from the neighboring forests. Pots and kettles were of iron, copper and tin. In the kitchen was the "dresser," a sort of open cupboard, containing the pewter dishes, which in all well-regulated families were highly polished, and the mugs and knives and forks. In the houses of the poor, wooden dishes were found instead of the pewter. Three-pronged forks were unknown. Hemlock brooms were in common use, and the floors were sprinkled with clean white sand.

---

* The tinder was a soft, dry, spongy substance called "punk," found in wood. It was shaved in thin slices and laid on the flint, and then when the latter was struck with the steel the sparks would ignite the tinder. Every family had this fire outfit.

Carpets had not yet come into use, except in rare cases, till the early part of the present century. Every thing was home-made. House-wives spun and wove, and also did the knitting, and sewing and mending. The walls were bare of pictures and ornaments, and the era of pianos, and laces, and Venetian blinds were a generation in the future. If the work of our great-grandmothers was hard with their few conveniences as compared with our ample facilities and larger means, their necessities were far less exacting, and they were satisfied with a simple mode of life, out of which they managed to extract many a sweet, and gave to the world an example of contentment, industry, and moral purity.

The better class were good livers, though the luxuries of life were few and sparingly used. Meat was eaten in large quantities, both that which was obtained from domestic animals and that which was secured by hunting and fishing. Wild animals abounded in these times, and the forests were hunted for bear, moose, deer, and smaller game, whilst the waters swarmed with fish, which were caught in large quantities and used as food. Wheat was not much in use at first, but in families of easy circumstances when company was entertained, the table was usually served with white or wheaten bread. Barley-cake was a common article of food, but buck-wheat was not much in favor. The most general kind of bread was that which was made of rye and Indian meal, and this appeared on the table at each meal. The Indian pudding was a great favorite if we may judge from the frequency with which it made its appearance at meal time. Potatoes were not much in vogue in the earlier days, but turnips and parsnips were common vegetables for the table. Common yellow corn was used in the green state. Sweet corn was not then known. Pumpkins also were a common article of food, and were prepared by cutting a hole in one end and removing all the seeds and soft parts, and being filled with milk, they were baked in a hot oven for six or eight hours. This was a favorite dish. Squash was not much in use amongst the early settlers.

Tea was a rarity in these times, and coffee was made from corn, rye, beans and wheat, roasted. There were other drinks. Punch was one of the most common, and was made in large bowls and passed around to the company, each person drinking from the bowl in which the beverage was prepared. Flip was another popular drink, made in mugs of beer and later of cider, and heated by the "flip-iron" or "logger-head," or even by the fire-poker. After orchards began to bear, and when cider was plenty, the "juice of the forbidden fruit" was taken "straight" and freely. Wine was seldom used and was confined entirely to those who formed the aristocracy or the society of the settlement. All drinking was of a social character, and generally the same mug or bowl was passed from mouth to mouth.

Sugar-making was a social event. Everything was primitive, no large pans or evaporators, but old fashioned iron kettles hung on green poles over cracking fires, to reduce the sap to syrup, and then a kettle hung on a pole to sugar off by. The boys and girls had jolly times over their syrup and snow and birch paddles made sweeter by ruby lips, and the gallant beaux would blister their tongues to see if the syrup was cool enough for their sweethearts. And so with song and many a silver laugh, the sugar party went on into the late evening.

Quite an incident was the paring-bee in bringing the young folks together. The large boys and young men mounted the paring machines and peeled the apples, whilst the larger girls and young ladies quartered and cored them, and the watchful mothers with the smaller boys and girls, did the "stringing," and hung them in graceful festoons over the kitchen poles. Then came the supper, bountiful and appetizing, and further on in the evening "blind-man's buff" and "turn the plate," with forfeits willingly given and quickly taken, and so "chasing the squirrel," and "passing the handkerchief," and "Simon says hands up," the midnight hour drew on, and the boys went home with the girls in the wee hours of the night.

Then, also, the huskings in the bright October evenings, when the air was crisp and the stars over head jeweled the sky. These were common in early times, and the company was often large. The unhusked corn was piled in a heap in the centre of the great kitchen, and the huskers,—men, women, boys and girls,—sat around the fire on the floor. From the immense fire-place supplied with pitch knots and wood, came abundant light, casting a spectral hue over the room and its occupants. The hours were varied with song and story, and the red ear, the eager search of all, was awaited with many a laugh and joke and guess. When the pile was husked, cider was passed around, and the young people indulged in a little dancing. Later, came the supper of baked beans and Indian pudding, pumpkin pies, doughnuts, cake and cheese, and afterwards a renewal of the dance, the gay company singing, "We won't go home till morning," and generally they didn't.

Muster-day also had its social feature, and was a great event in early times. Every body saw every body far and near on that occasion.

The social character of church-going was stronger then than now. The people generally went to church. Meetings were held morning and evening, with an hour's intermission between the services. Those from a distance took a bite of cheese and bread. Sabbath schools there were none, and the hour was spent by the women in social chat about domestic matters, and the latest neighborhood news was served up for the week. The men talked over the news and events of the outer world, if any thing more than ordinary came to hand, as well as the home news. To many this was the only time when they learned what was going on in the outer world.

Papers were a rarity, and the leaders of society would be surrounded by groups of men and boys, listening to what was said. Sometimes a little business was initiated, incipient steps taken toward purchases and trades, or what could be had or done that was needed. The hour was a sort of exchange time, when seller and buyer, like the good deacon, would talk, saying, "If it was to-morrow, what and so." This was generally done in a quiet way, and was known as "horse-shedding." Our fore-fathers were not especially wicked in this. It was not greed that made them use "holy time" for the initiation of such matters, but they were governed by circumstances, sometimes well-nigh by necessity, and it may be doubted if their "walk and conversation" was not fully as exemplary as that of people to-day who go to church.

Such was the general domestic and social life in Haverhill to the early quarter of the present century. The rich and society people of that day had of course their little gatherings, and were a class by themselves distinct from the great mass of the people. It is said, and it is quite true, I think, that the society people of early Haverhill were generally in better circumstances of property and education than the same class in the surrounding towns. There was a genuine aristocracy which gave character and influence to the Town, and this class was composed of men and women of superior endowment. Official position in those days represented moral worth and capacity.

But the ways and customs of old have changed. The first quarter of nineteenth century marks the commencement of a new order of things. Rebellion against forced payment of taxes for support of the gospel begins to show itself. Church-going, though still regarded as an item of respectability, is less universal. The advance line of modern social and domestic civilization is coming apace. The stage coach is heard in the near future, and horse-back riding begins to decrease. Blinds, pictures and ornaments appear here and there. Wooden plates give way about 1815, as do also sanded floors and hemlock brooms. I am told that the first four-wheel carriage was brought to the Cohos Country in 1814 and belonged to Benjamin Sweat of Piermont, and much later the first piano appeared in Haverhill. Chaises were introduced in 1805 and wagons a little later. Stoves were not known at the close of the last century. Cook stoves came into use about 1815 and clocks a little earlier. The large fire-place gave way to the iron frame, and the Franklin stove succeeded this. Paring-bees and huskings are still features of secluded country life, but not as of yore, and many of the customs and ways of the olden times are dim shadows of the past, or so changed that they are hardly recognized. No longer the "curfew tolls the evening bell," and the olden lights glimmer only in memory.

CHAPTER XXI.

MISCELLANEOUS.

INDIAN NAMES.

The Indian names which were given to the territory of Haverhill and its rivers have been retained in part. The country was known in earliest times as Cowass, Kohass and Cohas or Cohos, all different spellings of the same name. "Cowass" appears only once in the Town records. But soon after the country began to be settled it was almost always called Cohos. In later years, however, the *h* has been dropped, and it is now almost invariably written Coos. This is unfortunate, as it is misleading as regards to the proper pronunciation of the name, sometimes pronounced as if *oo* were one long *o*. In this volume the spelling has been uniformly Cohos, as probably the most correct. *Cohos* it is said means *crooked*, and was borrowed from the Cohasaukes, a part of the St. Francis tribe, *uck* or *auke* meaning *river or place*, and was applied to the territory of Haverhill, on account of the crooked course of the river and the consequent large bends of the land, the immense bows, the most striking of which are the "Little Ox-Bow" in Haverhill, and the "Big Ox-Bow" in Newbury, Vt. A similar geographical condition of the territory presents itself at and above Lancaster, and hence that territory in early times was known as "Upper Cohos," whilst the territory of Haverhill and Newbury, Vt., was known as "Lower Cohos."

Ammonoosuc means the *fish place* or *river*. The Indian way of spelling or pronouncing the word was *Namaos Auke*, in which can easily be detected the word Ammonoosuc. This word by many of the best authorities is written with only one *m* and a *k* at the end.

Connecticut means the *long-deer-place* or *river*, and the

Indian spelling or pronunciation of the word was *Quinne-Attuck-Auke*. Here also may be readily traced the word Connecticut. The word "long" in the Indian name most likely refers to the large range of territory in which the deer were found.

In a map of the Cohos Country published in London in 1768 for his Majesty, the Indian name for the Oliverian is given as *Umpammonoosuck*, composed of the two Indian words in Ammonoosuc (Namaos Auke), and following the analogy of that word, the former would mean *some-sort of-a-fish-place* or *river*.

INDIANS.

When the Power's expedition passed through the Cohos Country as far north as Lancaster, there were no Indians then occupying the territory, although as he reports in his Journal of that expedition, there were "cleared intervals" at what is now Ox-Bow, and when Page and Pattie came to Ox-Bow in 1761, the hills of corn though grown over with grass, were still visible, showing that the Indians had been in some kind of occupancy of the territory till within a few years.

The Indians who occupied the Cohos Country were a part or branch of the St. Francis tribe, whose head-quarters were on the St. Francis river, where they had an extensive settlement. Whether they occupied the country permanently may perhaps be a question of some doubt, especially the New Hampshire side, though there are reasons for believing that at least for a time they had a permanent settlement in the Cohos Country, and cultivated the "cleared intervals" in raising corn, the hills of which could still be seen in 1761 by the first white settlers.

There are marks of a permanent Indian settlement on the Vermont side of the river, which were still visible when the country was first settled by the white man. Traces of an old Indian fort were to be seen, and various kinds of Indian implements were found, such as stone mortar and pestle, arrow heads, flints, etc. Also ash-heaps and human bones were torn up by the plow.

It is however quite probable that in the later years before the country was discovered and occupied by the white man, Indians did not abide in this region as their permanent settlement, but only occupied the country temporarily for purposes of hunting and raising corn. This seems to be probable from the fact that when Powers passed through the Cohos Country in 1754, no Indians were there in occupancy of the territory, nor were there any fresh traces of such occupancy. There were also no fresh traces of Indians being in permanent possession of the country when the first white settlers came in. Grant Powers in his History of the Cohos Country makes the statement that Page and Pattie were surrounded by Indians in the winter of 1761, which they spent at Cohos, but this is not conclusive that a permanent settlement of Indians was at that date there. The old fort spoken of had trees growing within it as thick as a man's thigh, and this would indicate an abandonment of the territory as a permanent home of the Indians.

Indians, however, continued to abide at Cohos after the country was settled by the white man, and their presence at that time and in previous years may be explained in this way. This country abounded in game, and if ever permanently occupied by the St. Francis tribe, which is quite probable, such occupancy may have ceased on account of the Indian wars. Indeed, there is a tradition that after the fight with Lovewell the Indians said they would have to abandon Cohos.* But though it may have been abandoned

---

* This can hardly be called a fight. Capt. Lovewell surprised a camp of Indians in the night and killed them all in their sleep; but it struck terror to the hearts of the savages, and may have caused the Cohos branch to abandon this region. The scene of Capt. Lovewell's

by the Indians as a permanent home, they still held it as an out-post, a hunting-ground, and as especially well-fitted for raising corn. And marks of the latter, as above stated, were found both by Powers and the first settlers.

An interesting fact in my possession may throw light on this matter. The late Mr. Hayes of Windsor, Vt., who was mail agent between Springfield, Mass., and Newport, Vt., once told me that the first ripe corn between Springfield and Newport, was usually found on the meadows at Newbury, this being the earliest ground between the two points. This may explain the relation of the St. Francis' tribe of Indians to the Cohos Country. Years after it may have been abandoned as a permanent abode, it was occupied as a hunting ground and sure spot to ripen corn, and in this way it continued to be a feeder to the large and permanent settlement of the tribe on the St. Francis river.

FAIRS AND MARKETS.

In the charter of Haverhill as in the charters of all other towns, certain provisions were made which in these days were rather deemed as privileges. One of those provisions was for the establishment of a fair twice a year as soon as there were "fifty families resident and settled in the town." This idea of a fair was brought from England and Ireland, and fairs still continue in some places in the old country. Russia and the East have their great annual fair on the Volga at Nijni Novgorod, lasting several months. These town fairs were seasons for trafficking. It is however not known whether a fair was ever inaugurated in the Town; indeed, so good authority as Hon. A. S. Batchellor, gives it as his opinion that only one town in the state ever begun, and con-

---

exploit was in the town of Wakefield, and the pond near by is now called Lovewell's pond.

tinued the custom of a fair, and that was the Scotch-Irish settled town of Londonderry, where a fair in olden times was held for a week in October.

The other provision was that for a weekly market day. This idea also came from the mother country, and the market was held one or more days in each week. It may also be doubted whether the observance of this privilege was ever in vogue, at least more than nominally.

WILD ANIMALS, GAME AND FISH.

When the early settlers came into the Cohos Country, and even long after, the region abounded in wild animals and in great variety of game and fish. The Connecticut was plentifully stocked with the finest of salmon, and the brooks furnished abundance of trout. Otter, mink and beaver inhabited the banks of the rivers and streams in large numbers, whilst bear, wolves, moose and deer filled the forests. Capt. Powers' party shot a moose on Baker's river on their way to the Cohos Country. Even as late as 1769 moose yarded in the winter on the meadows, and bears came into barn-yards and destroyed sheep and small cattle. Grant Powers tells how Mrs. Col. Kent of Newbury was surprised one Sabbath morning, whilst her husband had gone to church, by three monster bears that came and looked into the open door of the room where she was sitting. An article in the warrant for town meeting in 1769, to see if the Town would provide a " stock of ammunition," indicates the exposed condition of the settlement to the attacks of ferocious animals. At the same meeting " 20 shillings" were voted for each wolf caught or killed, and votes of bounties for the destruction of wolves, were frequent in subsequent years.

But although wild animals were numerous in this region in early times, tradition hands down no striking adventure or death struggle with bears or wolves, such as are recorded of other towns in their early settlement. Doubtless Haverhill had her numerous exciting hunts of various sorts. Deer were pursued for the food they furnished, and bears were slain for a like purpose and for their skins, and no doubt the moose that yarded on the meadows as late as 1769 were not left in absolute possession of their camping ground, but none of these that are worth recording, have come floating down the tide of tradition, so that Grant Powers was compelled to go out of Town for the bear story that garlands his history.

AN EGYPTIAN PLAGUE.

In 1770 the Connecticut valley from Lancaster to Northfield, Mass., was invaded by an army of worms. They crossed the country from west to east, making their appearance in the latter part of July and literally covered the land. In general color they were brown with a black stripe on either side running lengthwise, and in size they were from one to three inches in length, and moved rapidly, only pausing when they took food. They filled the houses and invaded the dough-troughs of the people. In solid masses they crawled up the sides and over houses, so that the boards and shingles were hid from view. Entire fields of wheat and corn were drowned by them, but pumpkin-vines, peas, potatoes and flax were left untouched. They climbed the wheat-stalks and cut off the head which was quickly eaten. Corn almost man high and standing thick in fields, was so thoroughly consumed that only the bare stalks were left, after the army of worms passed through the fields. Suddenly about the first of September they disappeared, and not a trace of their dead bodies could be found. Where they went or what became of them no one ever knew. They appeared again in 1781, but in small numbers, and did very little injury. But in their first invasion they left the country by their havoc in a destitute condition, and had it not been for the immense crop of pumpkins whose vines the worms did not touch, and the abundance of pigeons that filled the forests that season, great distress, if not actual starvation, must have come to multitudes of families in the neighboring towns that were not so well provided with a surplus of provisions as the people of Haverhill were. Col. Tyler of Piermont said his father drew hay from Newbury in a hand-sled on the ice, to feed his cattle the winter after the worm-invasion, and the people of Piermont at the request of Haverhill and Newbury, floated down the river in cribs made of logs, immense numbers of pumpkins, that town being left especially destitute by the destroyer.

THE PIGEONS.

In the autumn of the same year of the worm-invasion, there was an unparalled flight of pigeons into the Cohos Country. The forests and fields were black with these feathery advents. They came immediately after the worms so suddenly disappeared, and their coming was a timely aid to the people in the new settlements. They were especially numerous on the meadows of Haverhill, and were captured in immense quantities. It is related that Col. Jonathan Tyler and two of his brothers took in the course of ten days over four hundred dozen of these birds. The people picked and dried them in large quantities for their winter meat, as a substitute for other meats of which they were deprived by the ravages of the worms in the destruction of crops on which hogs and cattle could be fed. The feathers, too, served as useful material for beds and pillows.

THE GREAT FLOOD.

The early settlers "pitched," as they termed it, their homes on the meadows. In those days floods were not so sudden and precipitous as they have since become. Forests were then dense and the ground was covered with thick undergrowth, so that the water was held in reserve and more gradually declined to the river channel. But the river had its high waters then as now. Probably the greatest flood in the history of this region since its settlement, occurred in 1771. In that year the inhabitants were driven from their homes on the meadows, and afterwards built new houses on the high ground. The river rose to such a height that the ground in many places was covered with sand to the depth of two and three feet, and the inhabitants not only lost their crops for the season, but in some places the soil was torn up by the powerful current and carried away. A horse it is said, happened to be tied to a log in a stock-yard at Great Ox-Bow, and was carried down the river as far as Hanover, where he was taken out alive, his head being supported above the water by the log. Other animals were swept away by the flood, and much damage was done to property. It does not appear that any lives were lost, though there were some narrow escapes.

HOUSES OF REFUGE.

In the earliest days of the settlement when only a blazed road led into and from the Cohos Country, transportation in summer was by pack-horses and in winter on sleds drawn by men. In this way the first mill-crank was brought into this region. The party had hard work in the long journey from Concord to Cohos, a distance of nearly seventy miles. Judge Woodward and John Page were of the party, and they came near perishing in crossing Newfound lake, but finding themselves growing drowsy from exhaustion and cold, they made one strenuous effort to reach a camp in the woods. Now this camp or retreat was one of a series which the earliest settlers had built through the blazed forests from Haverhill to Salisbury, ten or twelve miles apart, and they were furnished with fuel and means of kindling a fire, so that if parties or individuals were overtaken by fierce storms and pitiless cold whilst on their way to or from Cohos, they could at least find temporary shelter from the cold and a protected place to lodge in.

A NOTED CHARACTER.

I am indebted to the kindness of my friend, Rev. Henry A. Hazen, who has done most valuable service in antiquarian research, for the following sketch of a noted person who came to Haverhill, it is said, before the Revolution, and who always seemed to be something of a mysterious character. What follows may throw some light upon the man and the mystery. The account is taken from the Introduction, pp. 125-28, of a book published in Boston in 1884, entitled "Tea Leaves," by Francis S. Drake.

"CAPTAIN MACKINTOSH was a tradesman of Boston, who acquired great prominence in the local disturbances of the town, prior to the outbreak of the Revolution, but who disappears from her history after that period. He first came into notice as the leader of the South End party in the celebration of Pope Day which took place on the 5th of November in commemoration of the discovery of the Gunpowder plot. In 1765 the two factions of the North and South Ends harmonized, and after a friendly meeting in King, now State Street, marched together to Liberty Tree. The leaders, Mackintosh of the South, and Swift of the North End, appeared in military habits, with small canes resting on their left arms, having music in front and flank. All the property used on such occasions was afterwards burnt on Copps Hill. Mackintosh was a ring-leader in the riot of Aug. 26, 1765, when Lieut-Gov. Hutchinson's house was destroyed, and was arrested in King Street next day, but was immediately released by the sheriff, on the demand of a number of merchants and other persons of character and property.

"From the diary and letters of Thomas Hutchinson, we take the following passage:

'The Governor had even moved a council, the day after the riot. The sheriff attended, and upon inquiry, it appeared that one Mackintosh, a shoemaker, was among the most active in destroying the Lieut.-Governor's house and furniture. A warrant was given to the sheriff to apprehend him by name, with divers others. Mackintosh appeared in King Street, and the sheriff took him, but soon discharged him and returned to the council-chamber, where he gave an account of his taking him, and that Mr. Nathaniel Coffin and several other gentlemen came to him and told him that it had been agreed that the Cadets and many other persons should appear in arms the next evening as a guard to security against a fish riot, which was feared and said to have been threatened, but not a man would appear, unless Mackintosh was discharged. The Lieut.-Governor asked, 'but did you discharge him?' 'Yes.' 'Then you have not done your duty.' And this was all the notice taken of the discharge. The true reason of this distinguishing Mackintosh, was that he could discover who employed him, where as the other persons apprehended were such as had collected together without knowing of any previous plan.'

"Mackintosh was styled the First Captain-General of Liberty Tree and had charge of the illuminations, hanging at effigies, etc. Long afterward, on speaking of the tea party, he said, 'It was my chickens that did the job.' My informant, Mr. Schulyer Merrill, then a boy of ten, remarks that it was a mystery to him, at that time, how chickens could have any thing to do with a tea party! Mackintosh is described by Merrill as of slight build, sandy complexion, and nervous temperament. He died in extreme poverty at North Haverhill, N. H., about the year 1812, at the age of seventy. His unmarked grave can be pointed out by Mr.

Merrill, who still resides in North Haverhill at the age of eighty-two."

Such is the account given of the person who came to Haverhill at an early date by the author of "The Leaves." Tradition has handed down the fact that he claimed to have been the leader of the Tea-party that threw overboard the tea in Boston harbor, and being a bold leader who may have got himself into trouble in the "local disturbances of the town" [Boston], he left his old abode and came into the Cohos Country.

HORSE MEADOW.

Grant Powers gives the origin of the name. In 1763 some soldiers who had enlisted in Pennsylvania in the British army at the beginning of the French war, and who were detained after peace was declared, deserted and made their way through the woods to the head waters of the Connecticut, and then down the river. Coming to Haverhill much famished and finding a horse loose on the interval now known as "Horse meadow," they killed the animal and satisfied their hunger, not knowing that there were English settlements near by. And this incident, it is said, gave origin to the name of Horse meadow. Nearly a century afterwards a lad, * working on the farm now owned by the county, was passing along the road, when a gentleman and a lady in a fine carriage drove up and stopping, asked what place it was. The name being given, the gentleman asked the origin of it, and was told the story as related by Mr. Powers. "Why!" exclaimed the gentleman, "I shall have something to tell my old mother when I get home. My grandfather was one of that party and ate of that horse. Many a time I heard the story, but I never supposed I should see the place."

---

* Rev. Levi Rodgers.

THE POOR.

In early times before town poor-houses were appointed, the poor were taken care of by individuals. They were put up at auction and struck off to the lowest bidder. Thus in 1798 the sum of 22£, 6s, 2d, was allowed Ezekiel Ladd for the care of the poor for the fiscal years 1797–8. A poor-farm was bought in 1838.

HOG-REEVE.

This in the early years of the settlement of the Town was an office of much usefulness, and the most respectable citizens were called to fill it. It was known under several names, as "hay-wards," "field-drivers." In those days the fields were exposed to stray hogs, and it was the duty of the "hay-wards" or "field-drivers" to take care of these intruders. The method of treatment was to insert a piece of wire in the hog's nose and twist the ends together. In this way rooting would be prevented. In later times the office fell into disrepute, and was often voted as the humor happened to take the town-meeting, to some one as a joke, more generally to some young man who had married during the year. The office seems to have dropped out entirely.

TYTHING-MAN.

The office of the tything-man has also come and gone. It was peculiar to the times of the early settlement of the Town, and was an affair of great importance as our forefathers viewed things. The duty of the tything-man was at first to inspect licensed houses and to give information of all disorders to a justice of the peace. That duty afterwards passed to the constable, and the tything-man's functions were restricted to keeping order on the Sabbath, and was more of a religious office. Taverns were prohibited on the Sabbath from entertaining inhabitants of the town; likewise all labor, recreation, travelling and rudeness at places of public worship were forbidden on that day, and the tything-man was to see to the enforcement of these requirements. He also attended to the duty of observing order in church and enforcing a proper regard to the services of the sanctuary. The tything-man sat near the minister, and sometimes among the audience, with his pole in hand to see that everybody behaved and kept awake. It is said he would often stand up and with his long wand punch some one in the side or back, who chanced to be overcome with drowsiness, whilst the boys who happened to drop into any misdemeanors were admonished in the same way.

COURT AND COURT HOUSES.

Soon after the organization of Grafton county, which was in 1771, some of the more energetic citizens of Haverhill, chief of whom was Col. John Hurd, took steps to make Haverhill the western county seat, and accordingly in 1773 the courts were brought to Haverhill, a superior and an inferior court. The former was called the Court of Common Pleas, the latter the Court of Sessions. Col. John Hurd was chief justice of the Common Pleas, with Col. Asa Porter of Haverhill, Daniel Hobart of Plymouth, and Bezaleel Woodward of Hanover as associate justice. Col. John Fenton of Plymouth was clerk. These were all men of mark. The Court of Sessions was composed of the justice of the peace. The Common Pleas does not seem to have organized till the close of the Rebellion, and the stirring events of those times in the Cohos Country seem to have closed the courts of justice, and law was administered either by local committees or by the military.

The Court of General Sessions of the Peace met the first

time in Haverhill in 1774, and the records of its first session are as follows: "At His Majesty's Court of General Sessions of the Peace begun in and held at Haverhill in and for the county of Grafton, on the 3d Tuesday in April, being the 19th of the same month, in the 14th year of the reign of George the Third, by the grace of God, of Great Brittain, France and Ireland, Defender of the Faith, etc., Annoque Domini, 1777." At this first meeting the justices present were John Fenton, Bezaleel Woodward, Israel Morey and John Whealley. Subsequently, the number of justices was much greater, on one occasion the records note the presence of twenty-two. The Court of Sessions continued till 1794, when by act of legislation it was changed or merged into the Court of Common Pleas with four judges. Afterwards, 1805, as the records show, the court consisted of three judges, a chief justice and the associates.

It was in 1772 that the Proprietors first moved in the matter of bringing the courts to Haverhill. Col. John Hurd was chosen agent of the Town to petition the General Assembly in regard to the matter, and for this service he was voted " 1,000 acres of land in the undivided land in the town-ship of Haverhill," with " liberty to pitch it in a square form," upon condition that he should succeed in securing the holding of one half the inferior courts and one superior court in Haverhill. A copy of this vote was to be sent by Col. Asa Porter to Portsmouth by the "easiest method." What this "easiest method" was we are not informed, but it was not by mail, as no post-route was established at that early day. Quite likely the said Col. Porter was to watch his chance to send the vote by some one who might be journeying that way. But although Col. Hurd was fortunate enough to persuade the Provincial Authorities to accede to the wishes of the Proprietors, he was not so successful in coming into his " pitch" of 1,000 acres of land. The Proprietors refused to share with Asa Porter,

John Hazen, and others, their proportion of the 1,000 acres which were voted. And still later, 1779, the Proprietors voted to "lay out the land said to be claimed by Col. John Hurd into lots, and to be drawed as other lots." What the difficulty was, is not known, but this may be a hint to account for the fact that between Col. Hurd and the citizens of Haverhill, there had sprung up "mutual disaffection."

After the courts were appointed to be at Haverhill, the Proprietors immediately made provision for the location of the building, and a piece of land "200 rods square, and a road 2 rods wide and 200 rods long," were voted "opposite Great Ox-Bow to accommodate the court house and jail." The location was a little north of North Haverhill village on the west side of the road. The court house and jail were built of wood, and Asa Porter acted as agent. Some extravagance seems to have been indulged in, and the court ordered a committee to investigate Porter's account, and this committee reported that the account was a "very extravagant" one. Col. Charles Johnston and Jonathan Haley were added to the committee to complete the buildings, and they recommended that they be finished in the "plainest and most frugal manner." The court also directed that "stocks and a whipping-post" be erected.

The building of the court house and jail was quite an event in the new settlement, and was achieved, besides the expenditure of labor and material, with considerable "spirit," since the amount of rum used on that occasion was over sixty gallons. Col. Porter's account for building the court house and jail was £386, 5s, 2d, or about $1,931, which in those times was, in the language of the investigating committee, a "very extravagant" sum. The shingles used were some of them sixteen inches wide, and were, it is said, perfectly sound when the building was taken down over a half century after it was built. It was a large structure, about 80x50 feet, and two stories high. The upper story was used as the court-room. At the west end was the jail, and at the east end were rooms for the sheriff and jailer. After it was abandoned as a Court House it was used as a dwelling. The building had a lonely and desolate look, and the children on their way to school did not dare to enter it. The windows were glazed with small green glass, at which the boys would throw stones or clubs as they passed. They finally succeeded in breaking them all in, though as one of these boys remarks, "it took a pretty stoutly-thrown club to demolish them as the panes were made of thick glass."

Early there was a movement to make the south end of the Town the important point. Here was ample water-power, besides enterprise and public spirit which were prompt in utilizing advantages. In 1783 the removal of the Court House to the Corner was agitated, and a committee consisting of Moses Dow, Ezekiel Ladd, and James Woodward, recommended the building of a court house and jail on an "eminence a little south of the Brook on land of John Ladd." A year later another committee was chosen for the same purpose, and the composition of the committee, — Charles Johnston, Moses Dow, Timothy Bedel, James Woodward, — shows the fine hand at work in shaping things for the pre-eminence of the Corner. Afterwards, 1793, certain citizens of Haverhill, at the head of whom was Charles Johnston, erected a building near the site of the present Academy building, and offered the same to the county for the use of the courts. The court-room was in the second story, and the courts were held there and in its successor after the original building was built till about 1843, when the present Court House on Court Street was built.

In earlier days eminent lawyers rode the circuit, as it was called, and conducted the trial of causes in the courts all over the state. Grafton county courts had the full share of these visiting attorneys, amongst whom were such well-known persons as Jeremiah Smith, Ezekiel Webster, George

Sullivan, Richard Fletcher, Parker Noyes, Levi Woodbury, Ichabod Bartlett, and Joel Parker, men eminent in the profession and known far and near, not only for their learning and ability, but some of them as eloquent advocates; and the mute walls of the Academy building were they to speak, could tell of many a battle of these legal giants, of the fire of intellect and the flash of wit. People gathered in crowds to listen to the great leaders of forensic eloquence. And in this old court-room, too, Haverhill's greatest lawyer, Joseph Bell, maintained the honor of the Grafton county bar in conflict with some of these noted lawyers.

In earlier days, too, the court terms were longer than they are now, and the lawyers, their clients, sheriff and deputies, jurors and witnesses, came to stay till the business that called them here was finished. They came in their own teams largely. The great lawyers and judges travelled in their "one horse shay," and as Mr. Duncan relates in his reminiscence of the late Mrs. Morgan whose acquaintanceship with the olden bar was so extensive, and the taverns were crowded for weeks with the legal fraternity and their clients. The court and the bar had a room and table set apart for themselves, and to this elect company no layman was admitted, however high in influence and social standing. And on the Sabbath, it is said, the judges and the great lawyers were accustomed to go down to Piermont in the old meeting house with its high-back pews, on the top of the hill just south of Mr. Brainard's house, to hear the Rev. Robert Blake, a Scotchman of eloquence and power. A pew was set apart as the judges pew. Haverhill was a noted point in those days, and the influence of the court and bar upon the place was a considerable factor in her history.

TWO HISTORIC FARMS.

THE HAZEN FARM. John Hazen, the founder of the

Town, was accorded the privilege of choosing his "pitch" before the other grantees were allowed to draw their shares. He accordingly selected his five shares in Ox-Bow meadow all in one plot, and the farm was always known as the "Hazen Farm." It was about one mile square, and is now in possession of Nathaniel M. Swasey of North Haverhill. The old buildings on the farm are supposed to be the original buildings which were erected after the temporary huts were put up, and if that is the fact they are over a hundred years old. The farm has been in the Swasey family for about three-fourths of a century. High Sheriff Edson owned it before it came into the possession of Gookin and Swasey.

THE FISHER FARM. The "Fisher Farm" several times mentioned in these pages was a famous tract of land extending from the Ox-Bow to the eastern part of the Town. It was a mile wide and between five and six miles long and contained over 2,400 acres. The "Hazen Farm" bounded it on the west. This tract was covered with the finest of pine, and was an unbroken wilderness till the beginning of present century, when it passed into the hands of Gookin and Swasey, who manufactured vast quantities of lumber from it.

How this tract came into the possession of Mr. Fisher is not known, except that as was common in the chartering of towns at that time, certain persons who stood near the "throne of power," were given the privilege of reserved land, perhaps as compensation for their services in securing these charters.

John Fisher was an Englishman who was royal naval officer at Portsmouth, and afterwards assistant secretary of state in England. He was connected by marriage with Gov. Wentworth, and at the breaking out of the Revolution, his sympathies being with the royal party, he was compelled to leave the country. His lands in Haverhill were confiscated during the Revolution and the tillable portion was farmed for the benefit of the troops who were stationed at Cohos at that time. Afterwards an act was passed by the legislature by which these lands were restored, and he and his agents were granted the right of selling and of giving a legal title. He died in England about 1805. All his children except a daughter, Mrs. Shafter of Portsmouth, also went to England. To Mr. Fisher was granted in 1772 a township which was called Danzick for some time, and afterwards Fishersfield until it was changed to Newbury in 1837. A plan of the "Fisher Farm" is found in the Proprietors' records drawn by John McDuffee.

THE GREAT PINES.

The territory constituting the Town of Haverhill was famous for its immense pines, especially the plain at North Haverhill, where may still be seen the marks of these giants of the primitive forests, whose half-decayed trunks blackened by fire are lying on the ground here and there east of the village, and in the huge stump fences which are found in that part of the Town. Many of these pines grew to an extraordinary size, towering into the sky, from which was manufactured the finest lumber. One who remembers well these tall trees along the brook above the Swasey mills, tells of one cut near Briar hill, seventy feet of which was hauled to Swasey's mill, the butt-end measuring four feet and the smaller end over two feet, and which cut 4,000 feet of lumber, 2,500 of which was "clear stuff." "I remember," says this same person, "seeing and pacing off the length of a pine that grew near the head of the Swasey mill-pond, which had long been felled by the axe, and had gone to decay, especially the top, but it measured then ten rods in length upon the ground. How much of the top had rotted, so as not to be visible, I could not say, but fifty or sixty feet must have disappeared." This pine with others, it was said

by old men, was cut for the "King's masts" before the
Revolution. However, whether any masts were ever cut in
Haverhill for His Majesty's Royal Navy may be a question,
but the charter provided that "all white pine and other pine
trees within the said township fit for masting our [the King's]
royal navy may be carefully preserved for that use, and not
to be felled without our [the King's] special license for so-
doing." Later, masts in large quantities were floated down
the Connecticut from the pineries of Haverhill, and found a
market on Long Island Sound.

DRINKING HABITS.

In earlier times the habits and usages of the people were
in some respects different from what they are now. The use
of spirituous liquors as a beverage was universal. It was
not then regarded either as contrary to health or inconsistent
with morals or respectability to drink liquor. Drunkenness,
however, for various causes, such as the greater vigor of our
fore-fathers, their simpler ways of living, their greater freedom from the excitement of business and enterprise, and the
purer quality of the liquor, was not as prevalent then as it
became in later years. When the Sinclair tavern was built
and the sign-pole raised, the whole crowd, it is said, was
drunk, and one of the prominent citizens on Ladd street,
who aided in raising the sign-pole, went home so far to
"windward" that he tied his horse up by the tail. Neither
was drunkenness considered as specially disgraceful. The
most reputable citizens took their daily drink, and even
clergymen were patrons of the social glass. I well remember when a lad forty-five years ago, that the superintendent
of the Sabbath school in my native place, a man who was
universally esteemed as one of the most devout and exemplary citizens of the community, was the proprietor of a
large brewery, to which multitudes flocked daily for their

mug of ale. In such a condition of society it is not strange that the foremost citizens were inn-holders and venders of intoxicating liquors. The records give scores of names of persons who had applied for the privilege of selling liquor. Such well-known persons as Luther Richardson, the Ladds, Joseph Bliss, Joshua Howard, James Woodward, Joseph Hutchins, John Page, Moody Bedel, A. J. Crocker, Samuel Brooks, Nathaniel Merrill, John Montgomery, Asa Boynton, and many others took out licenses as "taverners and venders of spirituous liquors." From 1793 to 1797, a period of four years, the records show that thirty persons were granted this privilege.

In the Proprietors' records are numerous entries of votes to pay liquor bills contracted for their use, or for the use of persons in their employ. In 1774 money was voted to pay for "four and one-half gallons of rum expended in laying out the 100 acre lots." At another time it was ordered to "pay Charles Johnston for one gallon rum," and Asa Porter for "two gallons rum expended for the use of the Proprietors." This last looks as if these fathers were in the habit of "taking something," when they met for consultation for the advancement and prosperity of the new settlement. Various other entries of the payment of rum-bills are found, and on occasion of the building of the first court house it took sixty gallons of the "ardent" to complete the temple of justice.

PIERMONT BOUNDARY DISPUTE.

Early in the settlement of the Town a dispute arose in regard to the boundary between Haverhill and Piermont. The lines of Haverhill as described in the charter are unbroken, and the southern boundary of the Town ran in a straight course from the Connecticut river in a south-easterly direction parallel with north line. A reference to the present map of the Town shows that this south line is broken at a point about two and a half miles from the river. The jog in the Town occurs at Porter's Hill, and was occasioned by the settlement of a long controversy between the two towns. A map of the Town drawn on the Proprietors' record book does not contain the "jog" as it now appears on the Town map.

The dispute arose in this way. In 1760 the government of New Hampshire ordered a survey of the Connecticut river from No. 4 northward, and at the end of every six miles on a straight line, to mark a tree or set a boundary on each side of the river for a township. This survey was made on the ice in March, and extended northward to the north-west corner of Haverhill. When Capt. Hazen took out the charter for the Town a new survey was made, beginning at the north-west corner of the Town, and the first boundary, that of 1760, was found to be distant a little over seven miles from the northern starting-point, about a rod south of where Bedel's bridge stands. The surveying party, however, did not stop here, but went a mile and some rods further, and set the stake at this last point. In 1808 Blanchard and Chamberlain who made the first survey, were brought on the ground to determine the original bound, and they testified under oath that the boundary was at the point near Bedel's bridge. It has been suggested that the fraud was instigated by the Proprietors of Haverhill and Newbury, and that the second surveying party acted under their direction. But of this there is nothing at all reliable. Two things are doubtless true: the original survey was not very accurate, and the second surveying party, for some reasons saw fit to carry the south stake of Haverhill and Newbury down something over a mile, and as a consequence both Piermont and Bradford are short towns.*

---

* The survey of 1760 it is said was made under the direction of Gen. Jacob Bailey. If this is the fact, we may have a clue to the enlargement of the Haverhill and Newbury boundaries.

The first mention of this dispute is in the Proprietors' records of 1770, at which time a committee was appointed to "wait on the governor [and] council, to petition them to settle and determine the bounds between the towns of Haverhill and Piermont." Col. James Bailey was appointed to that service, and three others were chosen, John Hazen, Jonathan Sanders and Maxi Hazeltine, whose duty it was to instruct Col. James Bailey as they "shall think proper" in relation to the matter intrusted to his care.

This controversy which was irritating and expensive to both parties, extended over a period of about twelve years before it was finally settled. Jonathan Sanders and William Eastman were especially afflicted by the dispute, and against them the Town of Piermont entered suits of ejectment for occupying lands which were claimed under the charter of that town. But the Proprietors of Haverhill had a common interest with Sanders and Eastman, as the loss of these lands would entail upon them a redistribution of shares in compensation to Sanders and Eastman. Accordingly, at an early date, 1770, they came to the aid of the distressed occupants of the disputed territory, and voted to "pay Messrs. Sanders and Eastman for any charge or costs which hath [arisen] or may arise to said Sanders and Eastman in defending themselves against any action or actions which the Proprietors of Piermont have commenced against them or either of them." The year following a proposition was made at a Proprietors' meeting to submit the disputed boundary to referees, but the proposition was promptly voted down, and John Hazen, Asa Porter and Charles Johnston were appointed agents to assist Sanders and Eastman in carrying on the suits which were commenced against them by the town of Piermont.

Four years later the boundary question again came up at a Proprietors' meeting, and a committee was appointed with full powers to act with a committee of Piermont to settle the disputed boundary "either by themselves or by leaving it out to men." No definite progress seems to have been made, since at a Proprietors' meeting in 1779 a committee of five was appointed to "meet Col. Moulton and others of the Proprietors of Piermont, agreeable to a letter received from Jonathan Moulton and others, at Col. Webster's at Plymouth on the 15th day of September, 1779, in order to come into some agreement to settle the boundary line between Haverhill and Piermont." From which it may be ininferred that between the years 1775 and 1779 some correspondence had been carried on in reference to the matter in controversy. However, nothing conclusive was achieved at the Plymouth conference, and another committee was chosen soon after, 1781, which was more successful in its work, and a final settlement was reached on the 18th of September, 1781.

On the 11th of October following, at a Proprietors' meeting, it was voted to "confirm and make valid in law the agreement made and entered into the 18th day of September last by and between Jonathan Moulton of Hampton and Richard Jenness of Rye, Esqs," who represented the Proprietors of Piermont, and Asa Porter, Charles Johnston, Moses Dow, James Woodward, John Page, Amos Fisk, John Rich," who acted for the Proprietors of Haverhill. The conditions of the agreement are in these words:—"All the meadow-lots, all the house lots, and all the first division of 100 acre lots as laid out and bounded by the said Proprietors of Haverhill, shall be and remain unto the said township and Proprietors of Haverhill, and that all suits at law already commenced relative to the premises, and now pending, shall cease and be no further prosecuted than is necessary to carry this argument into execution." The eastern line of the 100 acre lots is near the Union school house on Porter Hill.

Thus ended this long and perplexing controversy between the two towns. At one time it was suggested by some of the proprietors that they apply for a new charter, as the easiest way of a solution of the difficulties, but a majority firm in the conviction of their rights and resolute in their purpose to maintain the southern line as they understood it, rejected the suggestion. The river lands were a great prize and by far the most valuable part of the grant of Haverhill; and at no point on the river were the intervals wider or more fertile than on a part of disputed territory, and the fathers of Haverhill stuck to their treasures with a tenacity worthy of human nature.

There is a vague tradition come floating down to the present time that the commissioners from Haverhill in settling the dispute, were more than a match for the commissioners who acted for the town of Piermont. However, the immense whet-stone ledges which have since been developed in this disputed territory, and out of which greater dividends have been made than from the rich meadows on the river, may be a compensation for the disadvantages which Piermont is supposed to have suffered in the settlement of the boundary question.

In this settlement certain persons in Haverhill were divested of their 80 acre lots which were in the 3d Division, but they were re-embursed by lots given them in the 4th Division. In order to do so, the 100 acre lots of the 4th Division were reduced to 70 acre lots, so as to make up to each share-holder who lost by the settlement, an equal portion of land with the rest.

THE VERMONT UNION.

At one time the territory now constituting the state of Vermont was claimed both by New Hampshire and by New York. The governor of the Province of New Hampshire, under a royal commission, was given power to make grants of unoccupied lands within his government, and claiming the territory west of the Connecticut river, he granted a charter of the town-ship of Bennington, [Vt.,] to sundry individuals. This was in 1749. Although the governor of New York protested against the action of Gov. Wentworth, the latter continued to grant charters as late as 1764, and the number of these charters up to that year was 138. The matter of jurisdiction between the two Provinces being submitted for decision to the crown, resulted in favor of New York. New Hampshire withdrew her claim after this verdict, but the attempt of New York to deny the rights of those to whom grants had been given by New Hampshire, aroused great opposition and finally resulted in the organization of Vermont into an independent state. A constitution having been formed and adopted in 1778 by the townships which received their charters from the governor of New Hampshire, their representatives assembled in the same year at Windsor, Vt., for the enactment of laws for the government of the new state. The legislature was immediately waited upon by a committee from sixteen towns in New Hampshire, representing "that their towns were not connected with any state with respect to their internal police," and asking that they might be admitted to become part of the new state. These towns extending along the river from Cornish to Dalton and including several towns back from the river, were as follows: Cornish, Lebanon, Dresden [Hanover], Lyme, Orford, Piermont, Haverhill, Bath, Lyman, Apthorp [Littleton], Enfield, Canaan, Cardigan [Orange], Landaff, Gunthwaite [Lisbon], Morristown [Franconia]. A union was formed and the delegates from the sixteen New Hampshire towns took their seats with the delegates from Vermont. James Bailey was the representative from Haverhill.

The reason for the application of these towns for admission to the Vermont assembly at Windsor, was disaffection with the Provincial Government of New Hampshire, so that for the years 1777-8, Grafton county refused to send a representative to the Council or General Committee of Safety. But an event occurred soon after the Union was formed which led to its speedy dissolution. The sixteen towns east of the river requested that those towns be erected into a separate county. This the assembly refused, and as a consequence the towns east of the river withdrew.

At this junction a new plan was developed. This was the formation of another union which should also include the towns on both sides of the Connecticut river. This project was favored by what was known as the Dartmouth College party which was ambitious, it is said, to make Hanover the capital of a new state which was to include the Connecticut valley. A committee of representatives from towns on both sides of the river met at Cornish. Thirty-four towns on the east side were in this new movement. Matters looked serious and there was danger of violent collision between New Hampshire and Vermont in regard to the river towns. Congress at last intervened and laid down the boundaries of Vermont: Connecticut river on the east and on the west a "line drawn twenty miles eastward of Hudson river to Lake Champlain." Vermont finally accepted the boundary of the state as thus laid down, and the representatives from the east side of the Connecticut river withdrew from the Vermont Assembly with indignation. Gen. Washington also threw his influence into the scales against the formation of a state in the Connecticut valley. This last Union ended in 1783. Col. Timothy Bedel and Joshua Howard were the delegates from Haverhill in the second Union.

During all this time of conflict in regard to the disputed territory. Cols. Charles Johnston and John Hurd stood loyally by the New Hampshire authorities, and exerted themselves, after the unions were broken up, in bringing back the revolted towns of Grafton county into harmony with and allegiance to the New Hampshire authorities.

LIBRARIES.

The history of Haverhill libraries is neither brilliant nor long, though the endeavor of individuals to secure these needful means of an intelligent community are deserving of mention. The earliest attempt in this direction was in 1801, when a charter was secured for the incorporation of a library. It was called the "Social Library," and Charles Johnston was the chief mover in the matter. With him were associated John Osgood, Israel Swan and John Page. Of the subsequent history of this library nothing is definitely known, but it would seem that it was afterwards, 1812, changed to "Aurelian Social Library." Again, 1829, there were two libraries chartered, one called the "North Social Library," the other the "South Social Library," and these it is quite likely were continuations of the original "Social Library."

There was again a library which came into existence about 1845, which also was called the "Social Library," but inquiry fails to show that this last was a re-organization of that of 1829, though it is more than probable that it was, as the name would seem to indicate, and possibly some books belonging to the earlier librarians, may have formed the nucleus of this last; at least there are some books in it which were printed near the beginning of the present century.

This last library contained about 250 volumes. The number of books in the others cannot be learned, but probably it was not large.

In 1880 a library was organized known as the "Haverhill Library Association," and had its origin in the idea of furnishing useful and attractive reading for the young. Mrs. Augustus Whitney was the person who started the idea. Also, a reading-room was considered in the plan, but that was afterwards abandoned, and only the library was matured. The library opened with 90 volumes of new books, to which were added about 150 volumes from the defunct "Social Library" of 1845. Any person could become a member of the association and continue so, by the payment of one dollar as the initiation fee, and a yearly tax of fifty cents. The original officers were Mrs. Charles B. Griswold, president; Mrs. George F. Putnam, vice-president; Miss Kate McK. Johnston, librarian; Mrs. Griswold, Mrs. Stephen Cummings, Mrs. Whitney, Miss Johnston, committee on books.

The library has steadily grown from its foundation, about 50 volumes being added each year, and much interest has been taken in its care and progress, until now it contains with the 150 volumes from the Social Library, about 750 volumes of generally well and carefully selected books, many of them being standard works in different lines of knowledge. The library is an assured institution, and has a hopeful future of good and usefulness to the community that sustains it.

But its present great need is a library building, which at one time it was hoped might be supplied before now, but which has not yet been realized. But this idea is not relinquished, and the friends of the library do not despair of seeing a suitable home for this most praiseworthy institution.

NEWSPAPERS.

The newspaper made its appearance in Haverhill at the close of the last century. A small paper was published here for six months before 1800 by Daniel Coverly, and Mosely Dunham also printed a magazine for a short time. These incipient endeavors to found the popular educator of our times was followed by the Coos Courier in 1808, but it was short-lived. The next attempt was in 1819, when Sylvester T. Goss started the New Hampshire Intelligence, which was really the first permanent newspaper printed in Haverhill and had a life of about seven years. He also printed the Evangelist, a religious paper. The material and press of the Intelligence afterwards passed into the hands of

John Reding, who was the founder of the Democratic Republican in 1828, and which was published with success and edited with ability by him till he went to Congress in 1840, when it passed into the hands of his brothers, H. W. and Silvester Reding, who continued its publication till 1863. This was by far the most influential paper ever published at the western county-seat. Meantime, other attempts were made at printing newspapers at Haverhill. The Masonic Cabinet, "designed for the benefit of Free and Accepted Masons," was established in 1824, but it lived only about two years. In 1827 the New Hampshire Post and Grafton and Coos Advertiser was begun. This paper continued till 1848. It was first owned by Atwood & Woolson. Afterwards Atwood withdrew and John L. Bunce became part proprietor, and later George S. Towle bought the paper and published it with much spirit till it was moved to Lebanon in 1848, the name being changed to Granite State Whig. Other papers were the Whig and Argus, Haverhill Herald (Woodsville,) afterwards called Advertiser and Budget of Fun, the Woodsville Enterprise, and the Oliverian. All these were of short duration except the Enterprise which was established in 1883, and is now owned and published by Bittinger Bros., who also are the owners of the Cohos Steam Press from which the Grafton County Register is issued. This last paper made its first appearance Jan. 1, 1886, and is now the only paper published at the western county seat. The paper is clean, bright, and carefully edited and has a good field to work in.

The outfit of the Cohos Steam Press is of the best material and machinery, and the office has a large and yearly increasing patronage. The proprietors are college trained, understand the "art preservative," and are sending off work which speaks for itself. Previous to the establishment of the Register, W. Cone Mahurin bought the material of the Democratic Republican, and began the publication of the

Grafton County Signal; after two years he sold to Joseph W. Dunbar who continued the paper at Haverhill for about a year, then had it printed at Hanover, next at Littleton, when in a short time it was merged in the Littleton Journal. The history of newspapers in Haverhill is marked by variety and numbers at least.

TWO GREAT PLAGUES.

Two great disease-plagues fell upon the Town in its early history. The first as near as can be learned was in 1803. This was the small-pox plague, and was very general and of a severe character. Two hospitals, or pest-houses, as they were called, were built for the care of those who were attacked with the disease. One was located near the Oliverian on the north side at the foot of the high ground south of Mr. Flanders' house. The other was farther north, near where Mr. Jewett now lives. Both were remote from any dwelling, and were only visited by nurses and the doctor. Dr. Carleton was the physician at that time. Miss Cross related to me an amusing incident of her brother William who was an inmate. He became convalescent amongst the first, and was able to be around. On one occasion he got on the roof of the little hospital, and waved the red flag and began to crow, so as to make his fellow pestites feel jolly. His pranks were quite amusing to his sicker companions. In consequence of the severity of the disease many died. Small-pox has visited the Town since in general form on several occasions, when the whole population was vaccinated, but the disease of subsequent years was not as severe as that of 1803. This is due no doubt to the discovery of vaccination which took place in 1796.

The other plague was in 1815, and was known as the "spotted fever" or "black plague." It prevailed in other places, notably in Warren, where the death-rate was fearful, almost whole families and neighborhoods being swept away, and the disease seemed to baffle all medical skill and treatment. When the plague fell upon Warren, people called to mind many omens the year before of a sad coming, but this was due more likely to an alarmed imagination under which the people suffered in the presence of the dread enemy, than to any real signs or wonders of its advent. The disease in Haverhill was of a milder form, and little seems to be known of it, except the fact that it was somewhat prevalent. Persons taken with the disease were seized with chills and fever, and their bodies were covered with spots, so that the disease was called "spotted fever" from this fact. Death often followed soon after the disease came on. After death the bodies turned black, and this gave the name of "black fever." Burials took place immediately after death, as the disease was thought to be very contagious, and often in the night when no one was around but the undertaker and some one to assist him. The people were awe-stricken by the suddenness with which persons were seized, seemingly in the enjoyment of good health. It began in the early autumn and did not cease till the severe winter weather. Dr. Wellman, a very prominent physician of Piermont, went to Warren to aid the sufferers and fell a victim of its ravages.

BANKS.

The first bank in Haverhill was chartered in 1803, and was called the "Coos Bank." It had a capital of $100,000, and George Woodward, the lawyer, was the first cashier. The charter was renewed in 1821, but the name of the bank was changed to "Grafton Bank" from January 1st, 1822. The charter was renewed again in 1846, and extended in 1857, but the bank was not continued after the latter date. The "Grafton County Bank" was incorporated, with a capital of $100,000,) but the bank never went into operation. There was also a charter in 1879 for a savings bank, called the "Grafton County Savings Bank," but the bank was never organized. The Cohos Bank and its continuation under the name of Grafton Bank, was the only bank in the county for many years, and was a strong and influential monitary institution. The Lebanon Bank was not incorporated till 1828, and the Lancaster Bank till 1832.

HANGINGS.

Haverhill as the shire-town has been the scene of several executions for capital crimes. The first person hung in Haverhill was a mulatto, Thomas Palmer of Lebanon, convicted in May, 1796, on a charge of rape, and ordered to be hung on July 8th, but a reprieve was granted until July 28th, when the execution took place. David Webster was sheriff. Hangings then were in public.

The next execution was that of Josiah Burnham, who killed Russell Freeman, Esq., and Capt. Joseph Starkweather. Burnham and his victims were in prison for debt, and occupied the same room. The cause of Burnham's murderous assault is not known, as the prisoners had conducted themselves with general mildness and submission whilst confined together. Burnham in his speech from the gallows says, "I was carried away with my passions," from which it may be inferred that the prisoners had got into a dispute which led to the fatal act. The deed was done with a double-edged knife which Burnham, it seems, had concocealed on his person when he was put in jail, and the crime was committed in the evening of the 17th of December, 1805. Both victims died of their wounds on the 18th. Indictments were found in both instances at the May term, 1806, and Burnham was tried, convicted, and sentenced to be hung on the 15th of July between the hours of 12 M.

and two P. M. But application being made to the Governor for a postponement of execution, on the ground that the prisoner "may have a further time to prepare for death," the application was granted, and the 12th day of August next between the hours of 10 A. M. and 2 P. M. was set for carrying the sentence into effect. David Webster was sheriff.

The hanging of Burnham was a great occasion. It is estimated that fully 10,000 people gathered on the west side of Powder House hill, where the execution took place. They came from near and far, in carts and in wagons, on horse-back and on foot, old men and young men, beaux and lassies, mothers with babes in their arms, and even invalids. The event took place with much ceremony. A military guard escorted the prisoner from the jail to the scaffold, and a long sermon, preceded by singing and prayer, was preached by the Rev. David Southerland of Bath to the immense concourse of people who listened with deep emotion to the preacher. After these were ended Burnham was given an opportunity to address the multitude, which he did in a faltering and broken speech, the substance, however, of which was a confession of his crime and the justice of his punishment. One suggestive thing he mentions in his speech, which illustrates the peculiar theological bias of the times, viz., that he had been a believer in the doctrine of universal salvation, and but for this he would not have committed the crime for which he was about to suffer, and he admonished his hearers to beware of this doctrine. He was entirely unmoved during all the ordeal at the gallows, evincing not the slightest feeling at the eloquence and impressive words of the preacher, which melted the vast audience into tears and sobbing.

The next execution was that of Enos G. Dudley for the murder of his wife. Dudley was from Grafton, and was a Methodist minister. He committed the crime in March,

1848, was tried and convicted in January, 1849 at a special term, and sentenced to be hung in May, 1849. He was hung in the jail yard. Joseph Powers was sheriff.

The other capital punishment was that inflicted on Samuel Mills, an Englishman who was at work in the mines at Lisbon. He was indicted in March, 1867, for the murder of George Maxwell at Franconia in December, 1866, convicted in March, 1867, and sentenced to be hung on the first Wednesday in May, 1867. Grove S. Stevens was sheriff.

Mills is said to have been a desperate fellow, and at one time during his confinement in the county jail he broke loose, but was re-taken, and finally suffered the penalty of his crime. The execution was not in public.

CYCLONE.

During the history of the Town the usual number of more than ordinarily severe storms has visited its borders. One, however, surpassed all others in its fierceness. It struck the south-east part of the Town on Sunday, Sept. 9, 1821, beginning at a point a little eastward of the late Alonzo W. Putnam place, and moved in a north-east direction across the unbroken forest, reaching the high land just south of where the East Haverhill depot stands, and then passed to Owls Head beyond. The gale was so violent that a path was cut through the forest, prostrating every thing before it, as a scythe would cut grass through a field. The marks of this cyclone remained visible for many years in the immense hemlocks which strewed its pathway, even after the undergrowth had obscured its course. No lives were lost and no houses or barns were destroyed, as the path of the cyclone was through unknown forest.

POWDER HOUSE.

This land-mark stood on a high knoll on the left hand side of the road leading from the corner to the Brook, and gave name to the eminence on which it stood, Powder House hill. It was built in 1812, and was a magazine stone-house during the War of 1812. This section then, as during the Revolution, was a point of exposure, and troops were stationed on the frontier north. It was built of massive slabs of granite about twelve feet square, and was a landmark for three-quarters of a century, when it was taken down and the stones used in the construction of a receiving vault at the cemetery on Ladd street. It was an unfortunate thing that this ancient land-mark was not allowed to stand and to be restored to its primitive condition. This the more so, as there are very few monuments of any sort that link the present with the past. The first churches are gone, and only a few of the earlier houses that are at all historic are left, — the old Bliss (Leith) house, the Col. Johnston house, and a few others so changed in outward appearance as hardly to be recognized. Powder House, built of solid granite, the last to disappear, yielded to the behest of utilitarianism. I fear the Town is not as deeply imbued with a sentiment for the past, as ought to inspire her, in view of her historic character. We have truly been iconoclasts.

STEAMBOATS.

Haverhill at one time enjoyed the convenience if not the luxury of steam-navigation. In 1830 the first steamboat ascended the Connecticut river as far as Wells River. The name of the boat was "Ledyard." An attempt was made to go up further, but just above the "Narrows" the boat struck a sand-bar which could not be got over. The boat came from Hartford, Conn., and made only one trip. Two years later the "Connecticut River and Transportation Company" put on five boats to run between Hartford, Conn., and Wells River, Vt. These boats made trips during the summer of 1832, and were then taken off, and the project of navigating the upper waters of the Connecticut by steam was abandoned. The water was found to be too uncertain, even at that day, and the great bends in the river at various points made the channel unstable on account of the shifting sands.

MAKING CIDER.

Cider-making was not an institution peculiar to our forefathers, but it was much more of an occasion than it is now, especially with the young who looked forward to the day with liveliest anticipations. The girls had no part in this work, unless perhaps it was picking up the apples before they were carried to the mill, as it was called. But this fell mostly to the boys. Making cider was hard work with all the fun there was in it for the younger folks. The farm hands started out early on crisp October mornings. The apples were crushed by large cog-wheels driven by a crank, to which a horse was hitched, walking around in a circle, and the apples in passing through these wheels made a peculiar dull groan, as if protesting against being so unmercifully squeezed. One or two boys, with wooden paddles, sat on a board lying across the tank into which the apple-pulp fell, to scrape out the pulp between the large cogs. The grinding usually consumed the greater part of the morning, after which began the building of the cheese on a plankbed, near the edge of which was a canal to conduct the cider as it oozed from the cheese to the receiver at one side. The cheese was perhaps three or four feet square, and built in this way — a twisted rope of clean bright rye-straw, two or three inches thick, was laid down inside the canal and the pulp was filled into above the level of this, and then another rope of straw was laid on the top of the first, and so on, tier after tier of straw and pulp, till the cheese rose to the height of three or four feet. Later, a crib took the place of the straw-cheese. The earliest press was a powerful frame with an immense log twenty or more feet long, fastened between two large upright pieces. The cheese was at the fastened end of the log, while the other end was let down on the cheese, the latter acting as a fulcrum and the log as an immense lever. Long before the log was let down on the cheese the cider began to flow in rivulets by the pressure of the cheese as it grew in height, and as the boys were through at the cog-wheels, and there was little for them to do now, they had armed themselves with rye straws and like busy bees were hanging on the edge of the canal sucking the sweet cider as it flowed along. Oh, the jolly fun of sweet cider sucked at the press through a straw! It was a joy almost for ever, for a boy could manage to "put himself outside" of an immense quantity of apple juice, and for an indefinite time. His stomach took on an elasticity which would discourage the most yielding gutta percha, and suggested the thought of a bottomless reservoir. Then later in the afternoon, often in the twilight, the tired company drove home, hard to say which was fullest, the boys or the barrels. But a glorious time was cider-making on a dreamy October day.

TEAMING.

Early roads were rude and difficult to draw loads over, but as the years rolled on they were improved, so that teams went back and forth from the Cohos Country to Boston, Portsmouth, Salem, Newburyport, and wherever they could find a market for the products of the soil and the forests, and brought back on the return trip such articles as were needed in the new country. In summer great teams of six and eight horses with covered wagons passed over the roads, many of which came down from Vermont.

There were also numerous teams of pods and pungs, one and two horse sleighs in winter, with their bells that made the crisp air jingle with music mingled with the shouts of the drivers. The road from Haverhill to Warren was the great thoroughfare to "down below" from the Cohos Country, so that these caravans or trains of pungs and pods were often a half mile or more in length. Frozen hogs, butter, cheese and poultry, mink, fox, sable and bear skins, sheep-pelts, and all articles of country produce was carried in this way to market. Taverns were numerous along the way, and were filled in the night with teams and travelers, many of whom carried with them their own food of cold meat and fowl, pies, cake, and cheese, and only took lodgings and drink at the tavern. Many also carried their oats for the teams. They made the country lively along the route, and the trips with now and then an accident or dismal few days of thaw, were full of jollity and incident. The children at home would listen with wonder at the recitations of what was seen in the great towns "below."

TRAINING-DAY.

The annual muster was the great day of the year in former times, when the colonel who led his regiment in the march with flying colors and stirring strains of music, felt prouder than a French marshal under the First Emperor. The companies were not indeed the truest and steadiest that ever were, nor were they exactly Falstaff's miscellaneous crowd, but they presented a somewhat picturesque and striking appearance — all ages, all sizes, hump-back and bow-legged, thick and slender, tall and short, erect and bent, but all inspired with a true military spirit. Who of those still living of a former generation does not call to mind training-day with vivid recollections! None were prouder of their position on such occasions than the drummers and fifers, some of whom were remarkably skillful and adept, and could awaken music in the dullest breast. It was this music that so filled the hearts of the boys and quickened the blood in the veins of the old men.

And everbody went to the general muster. Bright and early the entire population was on the move, over hills and along valleys, on foot, on horse-back, in shays and wagons, young and old, women and children, peddlers, showmen, victuallers. All around the parade-ground were tents and booths, where could be bought ginger-bread, nuts, candy, cider, beer, and something more tonic. Here peddlers shouted themselves hoarse in their frantic efforts to sell their wares to the hundreds that thronged the parade-ground. The showman's tent was well patronized by the curious and eager, and country beaux led their sweethearts from place to place, to see the sights and to watch the manœuvers and marches and sham fight of the proud soldiers. At the close of the muster, after feasting on the attractions of the booths and tents, and drinking in to the fill the unabated excitements of the day, the multitude turned their foot-steps homeward, tired and with less elastic tread than it came in the morning, and with a feeling almost akin to disgust that so much was endured for the short fun and pleasure they got, but next year found them just as eager as ever, and the same great crowds thronged the muster-field. Many were the incidents of these times that were told over in the long autumn and winter evenings by those who "went to muster." When the muster came to Haverhill the parade-ground was at Horse meadow, or in the field east the of Ladd street cemetary. The soldiers wore white pantaloons and dark coats, and were furnished with arms. Officers were in full uniform. Marching and counter-marching, in companies, in battalions, in full regimental ranks was the drill of the day, the whole ending with a sham fight which was attended with the greatest excitement, and filled the crowds as well as the soldiers, with the utmost enthusiasm and military zeal. Every boy longed impatiently for the day when he could participate in these scenes and have his sweetheart watch his martial step with swelling heart. Oh, the muster-days that were and are not!

THE GREAT ACCIDENT.

In the year 1844, during the Polk and Clay campaign, there was a mass meeting at Haverhill on the 4th of July of the followers of "Gallant Harry of the West." Distinguished speakers were invited to address the crowds that came in from the surrounding country both in New Hampshire and Vermont. In the evening there was to be a great display of fire-works. In those times such things were more of a novelty than they are at the present day. Cannon boomed morning, noon and evening, and when the curtains of night had sufficiently shut out all signs of day, every thing was in readiness for the pyrotechnic display. Immense crowds gathered in the vicinity of the Columbian Hotel, where the fire-works were to be set off. This hotel stood on the site where Mr. Nathaniel M. Page now lives. The balconies of the hotel which reached to the third floor were packed with a mass of eager persons who had crowded there to see the fire-works. Just as the first rocket was to be set off, the crowd in the balconies lurched forward to see, when crash! down came the upper balcony with its living freight of men, women and children, and all were precipitated into one promiscuous mass of ruin. A death-silence reigned for a moment as the mass came down, and then a fearful cry of despair arose from the wounded and living. One person, a young girl, was instantly killed by a falling timber, and many others were borne away helpless and wounded. Several died from injuries which were then received, whilst others never recovered from the effects of the disaster, and the village was a hospital for some weeks. And so ended the great Clay rally of 1884.

THE GREAT FIRE.

Haverhill has had her great fire which in proportion to the size of the village, was as disastrous and extensive as the great fires of large cities whose losses mount into the millions. This was in 1848 when the stage lines were still in full tide of operation. The number of buildings burnt were seven, and these were amongst the largest and most valuable properties at the Corner. Two were private dwellings standing south of the Brick Block, and owned and occupied by John R. Reding and Col. John McClarey. One was the large and famous Towle tavern, and the others were business places which were situated on the ground which the Brick Block now occupies. The four houses were separated by narrow alleys. The fire caught in the Towle tavern by defective flue, and before the fire-engine could be got ready or water secured, was beyond control. The wind was from the northwest, and but for that circumstance the Smith hotel and all of north Main street would have been at the mercy of the devouring flames. As it was, Milo Bailey's house caught fire, but by the most super-human exertion the house was deluged with water and the flames were stayed from going further north. A double line of men being formed from the burning building to a large reservoir on the south park, and pails of water were rapidly passed to and fro and dashed upon the burning roof and sides. But in the other direction building after building fell a prey to the devouring element, with no hope of arresting it, till by the intervention of a wider space between the old Dea. Barstow place and the Grafton Bank building, which the flames did not leap, the fire was brought to a stand and further destruction was arrested. The Brick Block took the place of the four buildings which stood on the ground. These buildings were owned and occupied by William Cummings, general merchandise; W. S. Thompson, merchant; Henry Towle, jeweler; R. N. Brown, tin-smith; John R. Reding, printer. The post-office was in the Reding building. The loss was heavy and severely felt by the place, from which it only partially rallied with utmost difficulty. This great calamity taken in connection with the stopping of the stage lines in a few years, marked the point where Haverhill saw her proudest day ended, and the glory of former times departing forever, unless her citizens become imbued with a larger public spirit, and open her natural advantages to the flow of tides of enterprise which are coursing along these valleys and sweeping up to the foot-hills and mountains.

FIRST JERSEY STOCK.

Haverhill has the honor of being first in this region, if not in Grafton county, as regards the introduction of Jersey stock. The first animal of this famous breed brought to Haverhill was a full blooded bull calf from Belmont, Mass., and was owned by E. A. Filley of St. Louis. This was in January, 1860, and the animal was placed on the farm of the late Hon. Joseph Powers. Afterwards several full blooded Jersey heifers were added, and the stock was increased from time to time by purchase and production, until it became famous in Grafton county and in Vermont, and from which for a number of years full bloods were sent to different parts of the surrounding country. When the Jerseys were first brought to Haverhill, Mr. Filley was blamed for introducing such looking cattle, but their great value for the dairy were soon learned, and now Jersey cows either pure or mixed are the rule with farmers. The herd of Jersey cows now on the Powers farm owned by Mrs. Filley, is one of the choicest in all this section.

A ROMANCE.

Elsewhere is mentioned the fact of a famous willow, but in the biographical chapters, is in danger of being overlooked by the majority of readers, just as the average Bible reader skips the books of Kings and Chronicles because they seem little more than a catalogue of names. So I give the story a new lease of life amongst the miscellaneous, which are sure to be read by everybody.

This willow stands on Ladd street near James Woodward's. It measures over seventeen feet in girth, and gives every evidence of having been a mute witness to a century of Ladd street history. It has lost much of its top, and the trunk is now in a state of considerable decay. The year of its planting was 1790, and Samuel Ladd, Jr., was a bright and handsome inn-keeper of a hotel just back of where the willow stands.

This willow has a very romantic story connected with it. In this same year Dr. Jonathan Arnold of St. Johnsbury, who was a lonely bachelor, went to Charlestown to spy out a wife, in which mission after some entreaty he was successful in winning the heart of Cynthia Hastings, and arrangements were immediately made for their marriage and return to St. Johnsbury. The journey was made on horse-back, and on the morning of their start a roguish cousin of the young bride handed her a willow stick with the request that she might need it to urge on her horse when its spirits needed quickening, and after she got through with it for that purpose, she might plant it by the door of her second husband. The last words were a sly hit at the Doctor's age, which was considerably above that of his young bride. The willow stick, however, was accepted in good part, and the journey was begun. On the evening of the second day they arrived at Haverhill, and stopped at the inn of Samuel Ladd, Jr., for the night. The next morning as they were ready to proceed on their way the gallant landlord presented Mrs. Arnold with a new stick, and the old one was left behind. After Dr. Arnold and his bride had started out, the willow stick was planted in the door-yard, and came to be the large tree now standing on the site of the Samuel Ladd tavern. Dr. Arnold died within a few years, and his young widow on her way to Charlestown to visit her friends, had occasion to spend the night in Haverhill at the Ladd tavern. Being invited to make her home at the Ladd inn whenever she had occasion to pass that way, she accepted the courteous invitation, and afterwards became the wife of the friendly young landlord, and saw the willow stick which her cousin presented to her on the morning of her first marriage, grow to be a large tree, and his good natured mock-words turned into a prophecy.

THE CUCUMBER STORY.

The story of a mammouth cucumber which grew in Haverhill in the summer of 1826, I get from the late John L. Bunce of Hartford, Conn., through his daughter, Miss Alice, who often heard her father relate it. Mr. Bunce was at that time living in Haverhill, and was president of the Grafton bank. The cucumber grew in the garden back of the bank-house, and reached the extraordinary length of over ten feet. It was taken to Orford to a fair, and unfortunately when the cucumber perished, none of the seeds were saved. The original seed, it is said, came from Rutland, Vt. The box in which it was carried to the fair was afterwards used in a hotel stable in Orford to run oats from a bin in the barn to the stables below.

The story of the cucumber was also told me by the Hon.

John R. Reding, and the corroberation of the truthfulness of the story is so striking, that I give it in his own words as near as I recall them. Mr. Reding went to Congress from the fifth district in 1841, and was then living in Haverhill. When members got tired in the routine duty of the House, they were accustomed to gather in social groups in the smoking room or lobby below, and amuse each other with stories, some of which were very extravagant. One day Mr. Reding ventured to "put on the market" the Haverhill cucumber story, and after he got through, all his brother-members in the smoking-room gathered around him and good naturedly proffered him their hats in token of his being the "champion liar," and for some days after they asked him to repeat the story, as it seemed so apparently to be made of whole cloth, which was rather annoying to Mr. R.

Before long, however, Mr. Reding happened to be speaking with Mr. Herrick of Maine, who was in Congress with him, when the latter said, "I believe, Mr. Reding, your home is in Haverhill." "Yes, sir." "Well, a good many years ago I was engaged in surveying a canal route from Lake Champlain to the sea, and I passed the greater part of the summer in Haverhill, and have many pleasant recollections of the place." "Pray, what year was it?" "That was in 1826." Mr. Reding at once thought of the cucumber story, and this might be his chance. "Well, Mr. Herrick, while you were in Haverhill did you ever hear any thing about a monster cucumber that grew there about that time?" "Oh, yes; it was the summer I was in Haverhill. Every body went to see it. I went to see it myself one day, and as I passed the tailor's shop, I stepped in to get some paper-tape which tailors then used for measuring, to measure the cucumber with. It grew in a garden back of the bank-house. I forget who was president of the bank." "Mr. Bunce?" "Yes, that's the name. The cucumber measured ten feet and ten inches." "You're sure of that, Mr. Herrick?" "Yes, I'm perfectly sure, for a few days before I left for Washington I was looking over some papers, and among them I found the *identical paper-tape measure, and on it was written the length of the cucumber*, as I measured it."

Shortly after, Mr. Reding was again in the smoking-room, when his brother-members, calling him, said, "Reding, tell us that cucumber story." He said nothing, but beckoning to his side a page, he directed him to go up to the House, and tell Mr. Herrick from Maine, that a gentleman wished to see him in the smoking-room. In a few moments Mr. Herrick made his appearance, when Mr. Reding said, "Mr. Herrick, I want you to tell these gentlemen the story about the monster cucumber that grew in Haverhill, in my state." Mr. Herrick, entirely ignorant of what had been going on, told the story to his fellow congressmen exactly as he had told it to Mr. Reding a little while before. When he got through, the members by unanimous vote transferred the "champion liarship" from Mr. Reding to the gentleman from Maine. But one wag remarked, "Mr. Reding, you have got New Hampshire out of the scrape pretty well, but the story sticks to New England."

LOCAL NAMES.

Different sections and neighborhoods of the Town were designated by different names which were early given to them, and which had their origin in various circumstances. Beginning at the south end of the Town, there is the locality known as the "Corner." This name was given to it from the fact that in the settlement of the boundary question between Piermont and Haverhill, a jog was formed in the disputed territory which was known as the "Corner." The name which at first was applied to the territory, was afterwards given as a local name to the village of Haverhill, so that the village is often called "Haverhill Corner." The territory lying east of the village, and forming part of the jog in the Town, was early known as "Out-on-the-turnpike," and extended somewhat indefinitely from the village eastward, and got its name from the old "Cohos Turnpike" which passed through it. From the foot of the hill northward of Haverhill village, to beyond the Oliverian as far as cemetery road, was called "Oliverian Village." In later times this locality has been generally known as "The Brook." Beginning at the cemetery road and extending to the foot of the hill beyond James Woodward's, to this section was given the name of "Ladd street," so called from the fact that at one time a number of persons by the name of Ladd lived in this part of the Town. No one of that name is now living there; the families have either died out or moved away. "Dow Plain" is a locality where Gen. Moses Dow, a prominent lawyer and citizen of Haverhill, owned a large farm and is still often called by his name. This plain is situated south of Pool brook, where the River road going north turns sharp to the east after crossing a deep ravine. The road formerly ran along the bluffs overlooking the river, but has long since been changed, leaving the "Dow Farm" buildings a little north-west of the present road. At the foot of the hill descending from the Dow Plain, is a locality on the right hand of the road, which was known by the bibulous name of "Toddy Brook." A little stream of clear, fresh water runs close by the road, at which in former days horses used to be watered. The name "Toddy Brook," tradition says, was given to it from this circumstance. Many years ago some one was coming down the hill from Dow Plain with a barrel of rum in his wagon, when the barrel got loose and rolled from the wagon into the brook and was broken, mingling its contents with the water. "Slab City" was a name early used to designate North Haverhill and the plain on which the village is built, and is said to have originated in this way. It was the fashion years ago when Swasey's saw-mill was turning out large quantities of lumber, for the people in that section to use the slabs in building their fences and in battoning the roofs of their houses and barns. The slabs were furnished at very little cost, and this was an inducement for their general use, and so gave rise to the local name of the place. The locality on the River road north of North Haverhill village, is known as "Horse meadow," a section of territory about a mile long. This name was given to it as noted in the article headed "Horse meadow" in this chapter. Next north of this is the "Kimball neighborhood," so called on account of several families of that name that lived there. One of these was Col. John Kimball who was a prominent man in the Town and deacon of the church at the North End. "Woodsville," which has now passed the stage of a mere local name, got its name from John L. Woods, an extensive lumber dealer years ago, who lived in that neighborhood, and was the owner of the mills and lands near the north of the Ammonoosuc. Eastward of Woodsville some two miles is "Sanborn Hill," a locality which was so called because a man by that name owned a farm on that hill. He was known as "Uncle Argy,"—the *g* being pronounced hard,—and this name was given to him from the fact that in expressing his ideas or opinions about any matter, he was accustomed to say, "I argy," meaning I argue. "Briar Hill" is the local name of a section in the north-eastern part of the Town, a farming region of considerable extent, occupied early by several families by the name of Carr, whose descendants still continue there. This region was very prolific in blackberry and raspberry bushes which were called briars, from which circumstance the neighborhood was called "Briar Hill." To the south of Briar Hill is the "Wilson neighborhood," which took its name from two brothers that lived there. "The Centre" is a name given to the central part of the

Town, which is also blessed with another name, "Bangerstown," and which had its origin in the following incident. A company of shingle-makers were engaged in manufacturing shingles in the pine woods in this part of the Town. Near by lived a family by the name of Hildreth. One of the sons, Ephraim, had a notorious reputation for his extravagant stories, though he was not a malicious person, and was not known to tell these to the injury of any of his neighbors. Usually, he was the hero of his own wild tales. On one occasion the story-teller, whilst making a visit to the camp of the "shingle-weavers," as they were familiarly called, was entertaining them with his pretended travels in "York State," which was in those days the far West of the civilized part of the country. Taking it for granted that no one of his hearers had been as far west as he claimed to have been, he told them of a number of places which he said he had visited, and to which without the least hesitation he gave fictitious names. One of his amused auditors, knowing his propensity, asked him if in his journey he had gone to Bangerstown. "Oh, yes," was the prompt reply, and then he went on with a full description of the place. Meantime, the men had given to each other the knowing wink, and were enjoying the joke which had been played on him, when Ephraim seeing that he had been caught at his own game, owned up and declared that there was no such place. The story of course got round, and the region was thereafter known as "Bangerstown." North of "The Centre" is the "Swiftwater road and French pond neighborhood." The eastern part of the Town on the Oliverian was early known as "East Haverhill," but that name is no longer a local one. The "North Benton road" is a name which designates a neighborhood along that road. The "Bath road," as it was more generally called in former times, leading from Haverhill depot north-east to Swiftwater, was also used as a

local name for the region through which the road runs.
And so of " Brush-wood road."

Some of these names are more local and limited in their
use, whilst others pass current amongst the people all over
the Town, and are employed in common speech to designate
localities which are as well understood as the name of the
Town itself.

MASONRY.

A lodge of Free Masons was organized in June, 1799.
Gen. Moody Bedel and others had petitioned for a lodge in
January previous, and their request was granted by the
Grand Lodge. The time appointed for the inauguration of
the lodge was June, 1790, and Grand Master Nathaniel
Adams of Portsmouth was present to organize the same and
to install the officers. Who the officers were the records do
not show, but in all probability they were among those
named in the charter, and perhaps in the order named. The
names in the charter are Michael Barron [of Bradford, Vt.,
probably]; John Montgomery, Moody Bedel, William Wallace, [Bradford, Vt.]; Arad Stebbins, [Bradford, Vt.];
Andrew B. Peters, [Bradford, Vt.]; Joseph Bliss, William
Cross, Artemus Nixon, John Haley, William Lambert, and
Amasa Scott. The services were public and were held,
probably in the " meeting house," as Grand Master Adams
wrote the committee of arrangement to " request of Mr.
Smith permission to use his meeting house " for the services.
He also suggested that they invite some minister to preach a
discourse on the occasion. Mr. Forsith of Orford, who had
officiated at a similar service before, preached the sermon,
though it is not certain whether he was a member of the
order or not.

The name of this earliest lodge at Haverhill was " Union
Lodge, No. 10," and had in its list of membership many of

the leading men at that time. In 1809 the Lodge was removed to Orford, and was held there under its original name until about 1860, when it was changed to "Mount Cube Lodge." The members of Union Lodge, No. 10, who lived at Haverhill, did not find themselves sufficiently accommodated by the removal of the Lodge to Orford, and accordingly were organized into a new lodge called "Grafton Lodge, No. 46." This Lodge continued until 1844, when on account of a failure to make returns, its charter was declared forfeited by the Grand Lodge.

The present Lodge in Haverhill, called "Grafton Lodge," is the renewal of the Lodge of 1826-44, and was re-habitated in October, 1857, by having its charter restored.

The communications or meetings of the old "Union Lodge," were held at Newbury and Bradford, Vt., as well as at Haverhill, according to convenience. Amongst the earlier officers of Union Lodge was Micah Barron, master in 1802; Ross Coon, treasurer; and William Lambert was the first secretary. The latter was master in 1805. John Montgomery was master in 1804.

The present Lodge is in a flourishing condition, has a neat hall for its meetings, and includes many of our leading citizens in its membership. The present officers are, H. P. Watson, worshipful master; Tyler Westgate, senior warden; A. J. Randall, junior warden; John Farnham, treasurer; W. P. Smith, secretary; F. M. Tucker, senior deacon; C. J. Pike, junior deacon; C. J. Ayer, senior steward; C. N. Miner, junior steward; A. F. Thomas, tyler; E. W. Stoddard, chaplain and representative to Grand Lodge.

When the brick church was built, the corner stone, it would seem, was laid under Masonic ceremonies, at least the church whose corner stone was laid by D. D. G. M., Calvin Benton of Lebanon is described as a "new Methodist

Episcopel chapel." "Calvin Benton" sounds sufficiently orthodox to lay the corner stone of any church.

PINE GROVE FARM.

Both correspondence and a visit to the farm have failed in securing all the information which is desirable in regard to this well-known stock farm. The farm is historic, aside from its present history and fame, being owned in the early settlement of the Town by Gen. Moses Dow, a distinguished lawyer of Haverhill, and was known as the "Dow farm," and is sometimes still called by that name. It was bought many years ago by Hon. Henry Keyes, of Newbury, Vt., and has been in the Keyes family since that time. At present the farm is owned by Harry Keyes of Newbury, Vt., who continues it as a stock farm. Mr. Keyes is a graduate of Harvard University, and takes a deep interest in the farm and its stock, fully appreciating the importance of such farms in maintaining high-grade stock. Holstein and Jersey have been the chief lines of cattle which Pine Grove Farm breeds and of these it has some of the finest in the country. At present the number is one hundred twenty-five head, and these cattle are sold far and near. Also, the farm breeds Cotswold sheep and Norman horses. At state and other fairs Pine Grove Farm has taken the highest premiums on various occasions, and has a wide and well deserved fame. The buildings are large, airy, and thoroughly adapted to the purposes of a stock farm, and nothing is spared to secure the best results of breeding. Mr. Keyes is a gentleman of means, and is able to add to or improve his herds in whatever way will increase their value and perfection. The farm consists of 800 acres, part on the river, the rest lying back, and the tillage portion is in the highest state of cultivation.

ODD FELLOWS.

Mooschillock Lodge, No. 25, I. O. O. F., was instituted at Haverhill Corner in 1848 by Grand Master J. C. Lyford. The lodge grew in members, but never became very large, and contained in its membership some very prominent names. Ex-chief justice, J. E. Sargent, Hon. Ellery A. Hibbard, J. D. Sleeper, Esq., Chas. G. Smith, and others. After a useful mission of about ten years it ceased to exist. The cause of the decline of the lodge is said to have been due to the general decline of Haverhill after business was diverted by the advent of the railroad.

The lodge was resuscitated at Woodsville in 1874 through Quincy A. Scott and Joseph Kidder, with the following charter members: M. H. Parker, G. A. Davison, Q. A. Scott, K. Marshall and M. V. B. Perkins. Fifteen new members were admitted the first month, and the lodge has had a steady growth since its re-constitution, having received 190 members in all. Its present membership is 130. It held its meetings for a time in a hall in the Mt. Gardiner house, but in 1882, having outgrown its quarters, it purchased the Tabor property and erected a three story building, 60x40, with stores on first floor, tenements on the second, and the lodge hall on the third. The lodge holds property valued at about $5,000, and has been wonderfully successful under the wise, prudent and zealous care of those who have had the management of its affairs. Growth, thrift and progress have marked its history from the first, keeping full abreast of the enterprise and progress of the active and stirring village in which it is located. Its membership includes many of the best and most prominent citizens of Woodsville and vicinity, and its influence is exerted in the line of moral and honest and conservative life.

PATRIARCHS MILITANT.

Grand Canton Albin, No. 4, Patriarchs Militant, I. O. O. F., of Woodsville, was mustered in 1887 with seventy-five members, by Lt.-Gen. John C. Underwood commanding the army, P. M., and is composed of Patriarchal Odd Fellows who are members of the different lodges and encampments in this vicinity, and has components at Bradford, Vt., and Littleton.

This body is a military branch of Odd Fellowship and is organized and officered the same as the United States Army. Capt. John E. Bisson was its first commandant. The three components are organized as a Battalion under the command of Major Q. A. Scott. The Canton was named in honor of Hon. John H. Albin, a leading lawyer of Concord and a prominent Odd Fellow.

GOOD TEMPLARS.

Bluff Lodge No. 47 of Good Templars was chartered in 1866, and instituted the year following. The first officers were Rev. J. M. Bean, worthy chief; Mrs. N. H. Batchelder, vice chief; M. B. Carpenter, secretary; A. F. Thomas, marshal; Fannie Morrison, deputy marshal; Horace Morrison, past worthy chief; Frank Morrison, chaplain; Joseph Weed, outside guard; Alice Woodward, inside guard. The meetings were held in a hall on the second floor of the building now owned and occupied by the Cohos Steam Press. The lodge met on Thursday of each week, and was prosperous for some time, and its membership was composed of ladies and gentlemen. The object of the lodge was to promote the cause of temperance, and it achieved some success in that line. It is to be regretted that it did not have a longer lease of life.

CHAPTER XXII.

APPENDIX.

Principal Town Officers and Representatives from 1763 to 1888.

MODERATORS.

1763.	John Hazen, *	1780.	James Abbott, s
1764.	Jacob Bailey.		Timothy Bedel, s
1765.	Elisha Lock.		Timothy Bedel.
1766.	John Hazen.		Timothy Bedel, s
1767.	James Abbott.	1781.	Timothy Bedel.
1768.	Timothy Bedel.	1783.	Moses Dow.
1769.	John Hazen.	1782.	Timothy Bedel.
1770.	John Hazen, s †		Charles Johnston, s
	James Bailey.		Charles Johnston, s
1771.	Charles Johnston.	1784.	Timothy Bedel.
1772.	John Hazen.		Charles Johnston, s
1773.	Charles Johnston.		Daniel Stevens, s
1774.	Ephraim Wesson.	1785.	Charles Johnston.
	Capt. Wesson, s	1786.	Moses Dow.
1775.	Simeon Goodwin, s	1787.	Asa Porter, s
	James Bailey.		Moses Dow.
1776.	James Bailey, s	1788.	Moses Dow, s
	Thomas Simpson.		Charles Johnston.
1777.	Capt. Wesson, s		Charles Johnston, s
	Thomas Simpson.	1789.	Charles Johnston, s
1778.	Thomas Simpson, s		Charles Johnston.
	Thomas Simpson.		Charles Hutchins, s
1779.	Charles Johnston.	1790.	Charles Johnston.

* Town officers for this year, except moderator, were appointed by the Proprietors, as is learned from their records.

† Officers with s attached to their names held their positions at special meetings.

1790.	Moses Dow, s	1804.	S. P. Webster,
1791.	Moses Dow,		Capt. J. Pearson, s
	Charles Johnston, s	1805.	Sam'l A. Pearson, s
	Asa Porter, s		Stephen P. Webster
	Obadiah Eastman, s		Amos Chapman, s
1792.	Asa Porter, s		Isaac Pearson, s
	Charles Johnston,	1806.	S. P. Webster,
1793.	Charles Johnston, s		Jno. Montgomery, s
	Andrew S. Crocker,		Moses Dow, s
1794.	Charles Johnston,		John Osgood, s
	Moody Bedel, s		Asa Boynton, s
1795.	Charles Johnston,	1807.	Moody Bedel,
	Asa Porter, s		Simeon Towle, s
	A. S. Crocker, s	1808.	S. P. Webster,
1796.	Charles Johnston,		Richard Gookin, s
	John Montgomery, s		Moody Bedel, s
1797.	Charles Johnston,		J. Montgomery, s
	Michael Johnston, s	1809.	S. P. Webster,
1798.	Charles Johnston,		Alden Sprague, s
1799.	Charles Johnston,		Charles Johnston, s
1800.	John Montgomery,	1810.	S. P. Webster,
	Amasa Scott, s		Moody Bedel, s
	Daniel Stevens, s		Charles Johnston, s
	Charles Johnston, s	1811.	S. P. Webster,
1801.	Amasa Scott, s		John Kimball, s
	Moor Russell, s		Charles Johnston, s
	Moody Bedel, s		John Smith, s
	John Montgomery	1812.	E. Kingsbury,
	Daniel Stamford, s		Jacob Williams, s
1802.	Amasa Scott, s		Israel Swan, s
	Ross Coon,	1813.	S. P. Webster,
1803.	Asa Porter,		S. P. Webster, s
	Charles Johnston, s		Israel Swan, s
	Moses Dow, s	1814.	E. Kingsbury, s
	Joshua Swan, s		E. Kingsbury, s

1814.	Israel Swan, x	1828.	John Nelson, x
1815.	E. Kingsbury,	1829.	Joseph Bell,
	David Webster, x		Isaac Pearson, x
	Noah Davis, x	1830.	John Smith,
1816.	E. Kingsbury,		John Nelson, x
	Israel Swan, x		Joseph Bell, x
1817.	Moody Bedel,		Caleb Morse, x
	Isaac Pearson, x		Ezekiel Ladd, x
	E. Kingsbury, x	1831.	John Page,
1818.	S. P. Webster,		R. N. Powers, x
	E. Kingsbury, x		Moses Dow, x
1819.	S. P. Webster,		Bryan Morse, x
	Jona. Sinclair, x	1832.	John Angier,
1820.	S. P. Webster,		John L. Rix, x
	Benjamin Merrill, x		John Angier, x
	Tim. A. Edson, x	1833.	John Angier,
1821.	Joseph Bell,		Ezra Niles, x
	Thomas Morse, x		Moses Dow, x
1822.	Joseph Bell,		John L. Rix, x
	Ezekiel Ladd,	1834.	Joseph Bell,
	Ezra Bartlett, x		Sam'l Cartland, x
1823.	Joseph Bell,		John Nelson, x
	S. P. Webster, x	1835.	John Page,
1824.	Ezra Bartlett,		E. Kingsbury, x
	Ezekiel Ladd, x		Jonathan Bliss, x
1825.	Joseph Bell,	1836.	John Page,
	John Smith, x		Jonathan Sinclair, x
1826.	Joseph Bell,		Moses H. Sinclair, x
	Ezekiel Ladd, x	1837.	John Page,
	Jonathan Pool, x		J. B. Rowell, x
1827.	Joseph Bell,		Jona. Sinclair, s
	Ezekiel Ladd, x	1838.	John Page,
	John Smith, x		Caleb Morse, x
1828.	Joseph Bell,		Nehemiah Woods, x
	John Kimball, x	1839.	John Page,

1839.	Jacob Williams, s	1860.	James P. Webster,
	Moses H. Sinclair, s	1861.	James P. Webster,
1840.	John Page,		Samuel Carr, s
	David H. Collins, s	1862.	James P. Webster,
	Samuel Page, s	1863.	James P. Webster,
1841.	Samuel Swasey,		D. C. Kimball, s
	A. M. Brown, s		Nath'l M. Swasey, s
	Hosea S. Baker, s	1864.	James P. Webster,
1842.	John Page,		G. W. Chapman, s
	John Carr, Jr., s		A. J. Edgerly, s
	Samuel Swasey, s	1865.	J. P. Webster, s
	John S. Bryant, s		J. P. Webster, s
	Henry W. Reding, s		Samuel Carr, s
1843.	Chandler Cass,	1866.	Daniel Batchelder,
	Samuel Swasey, s	1867.	Daniel Batchelder,
1844.	Samuel Swasey,	1868.	Chas. G. Smith,
1845.	Samuel Swasey,	1869.	Chas. G. Smith,
1846.	Samuel Swasey,	1870.	Chas. G. Smith,
1847.	Daniel Morse,	1871.	Chas. M. Weeks,
	Nathaniel Rix, s	1872.	Chas. M. Weeks,
	D. C. Kimball, s	1873.	Chas. M. Weeks,
1848.	Daniel Morse, 2d	1874.	Henry P. Watson,
	Samuel Swasey, s	1875.	Chas. M. Weeks,
1849.	Daniel Morse, 2d	1876.	Chas. M. Weeks,
1850.	J. D. Sleeper,	1877.	Chas. M. Weeks,
1851.	J. D. Sleeper,	1878.	Chas. M. Weeks,
1852.	Joseph Powers,		Enoch G. Parker, s
1853.	J. D. Sleeper,	1879.	Enoch G. Parker,
	John R. Reding, s	1880.	Chas. M. Weeks,
1854.	James P. Webster,		Chas. M. Weeks, s
1855.	James P. Webster,	1881.	Chas. M. Weeks,
1856.	James P. Webster,	1882.	Chas. M. Weeks,
1857.	James P. Webster,		Chas. M. Weeks, s
1858.	James P. Webster,	1883.	Chas. M. Weeks,
1859.	James P. Webster,	1884.	Chas. M. Weeks,

1885. Chas. G. Smith,
1886. Chas. B. Smith,
        Chas. G. Smith, s
1887. Samuel B. Page,
1888. Samuel B. Page.

TOWN CLERKS.

1763.	Jesse Johnson,	1819-20.	Ezra Bartlett,
1764.	(No record,)	1821-9.	E. Kingsbury,
1765.	John Taplin,	1830.	J. Woodward,
	John Hazen,	1831-3.	Henry Barstow,
1766-7.	Elisha Lock,	1834.	John L. Chapin,
1768.	Timothy Bedel,	1835-6.	Henry Barstow,
1769-70.	James Abbott,	1837.	N. B. Felton,
1771.	Charles Johnston,	1838.	T. K. Blaisdell,
1772-3.	James Abbott,	1839-40.	John McClary,
1774-82.	C. Johnston,	1841-42.	John A. Page,
1783-4.	Moses Dow,	1843.	N. B. Felton,
1785.	Joshua Young,	1844-46.	N. M. Swasey,
1786.	A. S. Crocker,	1847.	A. E. Haywood,
1787.	Charles Johnston.	1848-9.	J. T. Barstow,
1788-90.	A. S. Crocker,	1850.	Chas. G. Smith,
1791-93.	Moody Bedel,	1851-2.	J. T. Barstow,
1794-5.	Samuel Brooks,	1853.	Chas. G. Smith,
1796.	Moody Bedel.		Geo. W. Aiken,
1797-8.	John Osgood,	1854-7.	Nath'l Bailey,
1799.	Joseph Ladd,	1857.	Jacob Bell,
1800-03.	Joseph Ladd,	1858-63.	A. K. Merrill,
1804.	John Osgood,	1863.	Michael Carleton,
1805-6.	Joseph Ladd,	1864.	A. K. Merrill,
1804-8.	David Mitchell,	1865.	Albert Bailey,
1808-11.	E. Kingsbury,		A. K. Merrill,
1812.	John Page, Jr.,	1866-73.	J. L. Ham,
1813-15.	H. H. Goodman,	1874-88.	Enoch R. Weeks.
1816-18.	John Osgood,		

SELECTMEN.

Year	Selectmen
1763.	John White, James Bailey, Edmond Morse.
1764.	(No record.)
1765.	John Hazen, Elisha Lock, Jonathan Elkins.
1766.	Timothy Bedel, Jonathan Elkins, Jonathan Sanders.
1767.	James Abbott, Ezekiel Ladd, Edward Bailey.
1768.	Timothy Bedel, Ezekiel Ladd, Nathaniel Wesson.
1769.	Joseph Hutchins, James Woodward, Simeon Goodwin.
1770.	James Bailey, Maxi Hazeltine, Charles Johnston.
1771.	A. S. Crocker, Charles Johnston, James Bailey.
1772.	Ephraim Wesson, Charles Johnston, Simeon Goodwin.
1773.	Charles Johnston, Ephraim Wesson, A. S. Crocker.
1774.	Ephraim Wesson, James Bailey.
1774.	Charles Johnston.
1775.	Charles Johnston, James Bailey, Ephraim Wesson.
1776.	Thomas Simpson, Capt. Ladd, Simeon Goodwin.
1777.	Capt. Ladd, James Woodward, Charles Johnston.
1778.	Maj. Hale, John Page, Maxi Hazeltine.
1779.	Joshua Hayward, Daniel Stevens, Charles Johnston.
1780.	Charles Johnston, Ephraim Wesson, Timothy Barron.
1781.	Charles Johnston, Timothy Bedel, James Woodward.
1782.	Chas. Johnston, Timothy Bedel, James Woodward.
1783.	James Woodward, Moses Dow, A. S. Crocker.
1784.	Charles Johnston, A. S. Crocker, Nathaniel Merrill.
1785.	Charles Johnston, A. S. Crocker.

1785. Nathaniel Merrill,
1786. Charles Johnston,
A. S. Crocker,
Nathaniel Merrill,
1787. Charles Johnston,
Joshua Howard,
Ezekiel Ladd,
1788. Charles Johnston,
A. S. Crocker,
Nathaniel Merrill,
1789. Charles Johnston,
A. S. Crocker,
Joseph Hutchins,
1790. Moses Dow,
Nathaniel Merrill,
Amos Kimball,
Charles Johnston, *
A. S. Crocker,
Amos Kimball,
1791. Joseph Hutchins,
Nathaniel Merrill,
Moody Bedel,
1792. Moody Bedel,
Amos Kimball,
Moses Porter,
1793. Ezekiel Ladd,
A. S. Crocker,
Moody Bedel,
1794. Samuel Brooks,
A. S. Crocker,
Nathaniel Merrill,
1795. Samuel Brooks,
A. S. Crocker,

1795. Daniel Stamford,
1796. Alden Sprague,
Nathaniel Merrill,
Moody Bedel,
1797. Charles Johnston,
Ezekiel Ladd,
Amos Kimball,
1798. Charles Johnston,
Ezekiel Ladd,
Amos Kimball,
1799. Charles Johnston,
Nathaniel Merrill,
William Porter,
1800. Nathaniel Merrill,
Moor Russell,
Michael Johnston,
1801. A. S. Crocker,
Amasa Scott,
Ross Coon,
1802. Nathaniel Merrill,
Moody Bedel,
Asa Boynton,
1803. Stephen Morse,
Asa Boynton,
Ezekiel Ladd,
1804. S. P. Webster,
John Kimball,
Ezekiel Ladd,
1805. S. P. Webster,
John Kimball,
Ezekiel Ladd,
1806. Asa Boynton,
John Kimball,

* This second list of Selectmen was chosen at a special meeting, for what reason is not stated.

APPENDIX.

1806.	Nathaniel Merrill,	1818.	John Kimball,
1807.	Moody Bedel,		Benj. Merrill,
	John Kimball,	1819.	John Page, Jr.
	Tim. A. Edson,		John Kimball,
1808.	Simeon Towle,		Edward Towle,
	Richard Gookin,	1820.	John Page, Jr.
	John Kimball,		Benj. Merrill,
1809.	John Kimball,		Tim. A. Edson,
	Richard Gookin,	1821.	John Page, Jr.
	Michael Johnston,		Obadiah Swasey,
1810.	John Kimball,		Benj. Merrill,
	Ezekiel Ladd, Jr.	1822.	John Page, Jr.
	Michael Johnston.		Benj. Merrill,
1811.	John Kimball,		Obadiah Swasey,
	Ezekiel Ladd, Jr.	1823.	E. Kingsbury,
	Jacob Williams,		Jacob Williams,
1812.	S. P. Webster,		Jonathan Wilson,
	John Kimball,	1824.	E. Kingsbury,
	Uriah Ward,		Jacob Williams,
1813.	John Kimball,		Jonathan Wilson,
	David Merrill,	1825.	E. Kingsbury,
	Israel Swan,		Jonathan Wilson,
1814.	David Webster, Jr.		Jacob Williams,
	Israel Swan,	1826.	John Page,
	John Kimball,		John Kimball,
1815.	Israel Swan,		Caleb Morse,
	John S. Sanborn,	1827.	John Page,
	E. Kingsbury,		John Kimball,
1816.	Israel Swan,		Caleb Morse,
	Chester Farman,	1828.	John Kimball,
	Enoch Chase,		Caleb Morse,
1817.	John Page, Jr.		John Nelson,
	John Kimball,	1829.	John Nelson,
	Benj. Merrill,		John Kimball,
1818.	John Page, Jr.		Caleb Morse,

1830. John Page,
John Kimball,
Joshua Woodward,
1831. John Page,
Simon Stafford,
Jonathan Wilson,
1832. John Page,
Simon Stafford,
Jona. B. Rowell,
1833. John Page,
Simon Stafford,
Jona. B. Rowell,
1834. John Page,
Jonathan Wilson,
Simon Stafford,
1835. Jonathan Sinclair,
Jona. B. Rowell,
John L. Corliss,
1836. Jona. B. Rowell,
Jona. Sinclair,
John L. Corliss,
1837. Jno. B. Rowell,
Samuel Page,
Jacob Morse,
1838. Joshua Woodward,
Caleb Morse,
Moses Southard,
1839. Samuel Page,
Jacob Morse,
Daniel Carr, Jr.
1840. Samuel Page,
Daniel Carr, Jr.
Joseph Stowe,
1841. Samuel Page,
Joseph Stowe,

1841. Daniel Carr, Jr.
1842. Samuel Swasey,
Nathaniel Rix,
John Page,
1843. Nathaniel Rix,
Newhall Pike,
Alvah E. Haywood,
1844. Alvah E. Haywood,
Samuel Swasey,
Isaac Morse,
1845. Dudley C. Kimball,
Isaac Morse,
Alvah E. Haywood,
1846. John McClary,
Isaac F. Allen,
Josiah Jeffers,
1847. Dudley C. Kimball,
Samuel Page,
Isaac Morse,
1848. Dudley C. Kimball,
Isaac Morse,
W. W. Simpson,
1849. Dudley C. Kimball,
Isaac Morse,
W. W. Simpson,
1850. John R. Reding,
Isaac F. Allen,
Itham Howe,
1851. Dudley C. Kimball,
Isaac Morse,
Nathaniel Kimball,
1852. Samuel Page,
Luther Colby,
Nathaniel Kimball,
1853. John R. Reding,

1853. N. M. Swasey,
N. S. Davis,
1854. Samuel Page,
Samuel Carr,
Nathaniel Kimball,
1855. James P. Webster,
Samuel Carr,
Hosea S. Baker,
1856. James P. Webster,
Hosea S. Baker,
Luther Butler,
1857. Samuel Page,
Luther Butler,
David Merrill,
1858. Luther Butler,
Russell Kimball,
Stephen Metcalf,
1859. Stephen Metcalf,
John L. Rix,
Solon S. Southard,
1860. Stephen Metcalf,
John L. Rix,
Solon S. Southard,
1861. Stephen Metcalf,
James A. Currier,
Joshua Carr,
1862. James A. Currier,
Joshua Carr,
Roswell Elliott,
1863. Dudley C. Kimball,
Daniel Merrill,
N. M. Swasey,
1864. Dudley C. Kimball,
Harry A. Albee,
Edward L. Page,

1865. Edward L. Page,
Hosea S. Baker,
Nathaniel Bailey,
1866. Chas. M. Weeks,
Langdon Bailey,
Isaac Morse,
1867. Charles M. Weeks,
Langdon Bailey,
Jacob Morse,
1868. Ezra S. Kimball,
Charles Fisher,
John W. Cutting,
1869. Ezra S. Kimball,
Charles Fisher,
John W. Cutting,
1870. Charles G. Smith,
James L. Bisbee,
Calvin Merrill,
1871. Charles G. Smith,
Calvin Merrill,
Samuel H. Crocker,
1872. Charles G. Smith,
Samuel H. Crocker,
Sylvester Jeffers,
1873. Charles G. Smith,
Sylvester Jeffers,
John E. Carr,
1874. Charles G. Smith,
Sylvester Jeffers,
Henry F. King,
1875. John E. Carr,
Wm. C. Marston,
Horace E. Noyes,
1876. John E. Carr,
Wm. C. Marston,

1876.	Horace E. Noyes,	1883.	Caleb Wells,
1877.	Horace E. Noyes.		Ira Whitcher,
	A. W. Thomas,		Charles W. Pike,
	Daniel W. Meader,	1884.	Caleb Wells,
1878.	Daniel W. Meader,		Ira Whitcher,
	S. H. Cummings,		Charles W. Pike,
	Ezra B. Mann,	1885.	Charles W. Pike,
1879.	N. P. Ridout,		Wm. C. Marston,
	George C. Jeffers,		Seth P. Stickney, *
	Enoch G. Parker,	1886.	Caleb Wells,
1880.	Ezra B. Mann,		Ira Whitcher,
	S. H. Cummings,		Levi B. Ham,
	Nathan P. Ridout,	1887.	Henry F. King,
1881.	Ezra B. Mann,		Levi B. Ham,
	S. H. Cummings,		W. W. Coburn,
	Horace Eaton,	1888.	D. L. Hawkins,
1882.	S. H. Cummings,		W. W. Coburn,
	Horace Eaton,		E. C. Kinney.
	Caleb Wells.		

TREASURERS.

1771.	James Bailey, †	1793-4.	Charles Johnston,
1772-3.	Simeon Goodwin,	1795.	Daniel Stamford,
1774-5.	James Bailey,	1796.	Moody Bedel,
1776-9.	Simeon Goodwin,	1797.	J. Woodward,
1780-2.	J. Woodward,	1798.	Ezekiel Ladd,
1783-4.	Simeon Goodwin,	1799.	Michael Johnston,
1785-6.	Moses Dow,	1800-06.	John Osgood,
1787.	J. Woodward,	1807.	David Mitchell,
1788.	Ezekiel Ladd,	1808.	Charles Johnston,
1789-92.	Moses Dow,	1809.	John Kimball,

* Resigned and Stephen H. Cummings was appointed.

† The treasurer was chosen this year for the first time. The duties of the office before this date were performed by the Selectmen.

APPENDIX.

1810-11.	Ezekiel Ladd, Jr.	1841-2.	John A. Page.
1812-13.	John L. Corliss.	1843.	(No record.)
1814-15.	H. H. Goodman.	1844-6.	N. M. Swasey.
1816-18.	John Osgood.	1847.	D. C. Kimball.
1819-20.	Ezra Bartlett.	1848-49.	J. T. Barstow.
1821-30.	E. Kingsley.	1850.	Chas. G. Smith.
1831-33.	Henry Barstow.	1851-2.	J. T. Barstow.
1834.	John L. Chapin.	1853.	Chas. G. Smith.
1835-6.	Henry Barstow.	1854-7.	Nathaniel Bailey.
1837.	N. B. Felton.	1858-65.	A. K. Merrill.
1838.	T. W. Blaisdell.	1866-73.	L. B. Ham.
1839-40.	John McClary.	1874-88.	Enoch R. Weeks.

REPRESENTATIVES.

1783.	J. Woodward, *	1806.	Nath'l Merrill.
1784.	T. Bedel.	1807.	Moody Bedel.
1785-7.	Classed with other towns. †	1808-12.	S. P. Webster.
		1813-14.	John Kimball.
1788-9.	J. Hutchins.	1815.	Ezekiel Ladd, Jr.
1790-1.	Moses Dow.	1816.	S. P. Webster.
1791.	J. Hutchins. (?)	1817-18.	Moody Bedel.
1792.	Samuel Brooks.	1819-20.	John Page, Jr.
1793.	Moses Dow.	1821.	Joseph Bell.
1794-6.	Nathaniel Merrill.	1822-4.	John L. Corliss.
1797-8.	Moody Bedel.	1825.	Samuel Cartland.
1799.	Moor Russell.	1826-7.	John L. Corliss.
1800.	Moor Russell.	1828.	Joseph Bell.
1801.	Moody Bedel.	1828-30.	Caleb Morse.
1802.	(None.)	1831.	Jona. Wilson.
1803-5.	J. Montgomery.	1831-2.	Samuel Page.

* First representative sent this year.
† This year and the two following years the representative was either from Piermont or Coventry, as the towns were classified with Haverhill, and formed our representative district.

1833.	John Angier, *	1854-5.	Isaac Morse,
1834.	Ezra Bartlett, *	1856.	John L. Rix,
1835.	John Page, *		Isaac Morse,
1836.	John McClary,	1857.	Nath'l. Bailey,
	John Angier,	1857-8.	Russell King,
1837.	John McClary,	1859.	J. P. Webster,
	Jona. Wilson,	1859-60.	Geo. S. Kelsea,
1838.	Hosea S. Baker,	1861.	Daniel Morse, 2d
	John S. Sinclair,		N. Westgate,
1839.	Jacob Williams,	1862.	Albert Bailey,
	Samuel Swasey,	1862-3.	M. W. Nelson,
1840.	Samuel Swasey,	1864.	P. W. Kimball,
1840-1.	Samuel Smith,		J. B. Cotton,
1842.	N. B. Felton,	1865.	P. W. Kimball,
1842-3.	Samuel Swasey,		John N. Morse,
1843-4.	Eber Eastman,	1866.	Chas. G. Smith,
1844-5.	Daniel Morse, 2d		H. B. Leonard,
1845.	D. Batchelder,	1867.	Chas. G. Smith,
1846.	Samuel Swasey,		H. B. Leonard,
	Nathaniel Rix,	1868.	G. F. Putnam,
1847.	Samuel Swasey,		Chas. M. Weeks,
	Isaac Morse,	1869.	Chas. M. Weeks,
1848.	Samuel Swasey,†		G. F. Putnam,
1849.	Daniel Morse, 2d	1870.	L. Bailey,
	Samuel Page,		J. W. Cutting,
1850.	Samuel Swasey,	1871.	Henry Holt,
	T. B. Jackson,		J. W. Cutting,
1851.	D. C. Kimball,	1872.	N. M. Swasey,
1851-2.	C. G. Thompsom,		Silvester Reding,
1853.	N. B. Felton,	1873.	N. M. Swasey,
	Jacob Morse,		Silvester Reding,
1854.	John L. Rix,	1874.	Levi B. Ham,

* Only one representative chosen.
† Only one sent.

1874.	A. J. Edgerly,	were chosen in November, bi-annually.)	
1875.	Levi. B. Ham,		
	Chas. A. Gale,	1880.	John E. Carr,
1876.	Ezra B. Mann,		W. C. Marston,
	Chas. A. Gale,	1882.	W. W. Coburn,
1877.	Ezra B. Mann,		W. F. Westgate,
	Samuel T. Page,	1884.	Geo. H. Mann,
1878.	John E. Carr,	1886.	Samuel B. Page,
	Samuel T. Page,		Samuel T. Page.

(After 1878 representatives

CORRECTIONS.

PAGE 29, Read *Charlestown*, for Charleston.

41, "Moses Hazen died in Albany, N. Y., in 1785." Another account gives 1803.

55, Read *Moses Swasey of Newbury, Vt.*, for Obadiah Swasey of North Haverhill.

59, Read *Mr. Ethan Brock* for Mrs. Ethan Brock.

68, *Moses Little as justice of the Court of Sessions, is credited to Campton.* Whether the Campton and the Haverhill Little were the same person is not clear.

70, John Hurd died in Boston in 1809, and was probably buried in the old Germany graveyard, where his wife and son are buried.

72, Joseph Hutchins also, it is said, led an independent company at the time of Burgoyne's Surrender.

108, To the synopsis of Chapter VII add Woodsville settlers.

131, *May Rix* was probably Timothy Rix.

151, Read *Jacob Bailey* for James.

157, Read *It was an earlier marriage*, for it was the first marriage.

191, Read *Gen. John McDuffee* for Gen. John Duffee.

193, Same as above.

193, Read *1834–5* for 1795.

324, Read *Moses Elkins* for Moses Elkin.

375, Read *Courts and Court Houses* for Court and Court Houses.

393, Read *Joseph H. Dunbar* for Joseph W. Dunbar.

INDEX.

Academy, 211
Adams Stephen and family, 120
Area of Town, 22
A Great Accident, 403
Appendix, 418
An Episode, 157
Aim of Author, 17
Ayer Perley and family, 121
Animals, danger of 152
" wild, 367
Angier, John 294
" Joel 295
" J. Dorsey 311
" Geo. W. 311
Abbott, James 68
" Chester 148
Arnold, Jonathan 66
" Cynthia Hastings 67
" Lemuel 67
A Noted Character, 371
A Romance, 406
Author, material of 17
Appendix, 434.

B

Bailey, Jacob 41, 42, 173
" James 58
" Albert 141
" Nathaniel 141
" Milo 141
" Azro 141
" Allen 141
" Langdon 148
Barron, Timothy 68
" William 91
Blaisdell, Daniel 269
" Timothy K. and family, 135
" Alfred 97
Barstow, Henry 112
" William 112
" James 113
" Thomas 113
" Ezekiel H. 113
" Mrs. 113
" Alfred 313
" Anson 314
" George 314
" Charles W. 314

Barstow, John 314
" Mary 315
Baker, Hosea S. and family, 123
" Peyton 124
" Oliver R. 124
" Solon H. 124
Bacon, Timothy R. 140
" Asa 140
" Sumner P. 312
" Elmer C. 312
Batchelder, Daniel 140
Banks, 394
Bartlett, Ezra 292
" Ezra, Jr. 293
Babcock, Mrs. Louisa P. 312
Bracket, Anson 295
Bedel, Timothy and family, 48
" Moody and family 49
" Hazen 315
" John 316
Bell, Jacob and family, 119
" James, 119
" LeRoy 119
" Joseph 262
" James 317
" John 317
Bean, John V. and family, 141
Brewer, James P. 317
Birth, first 56
Bridges, 193
Bliss, Jonathan 270
" Joseph 93
" Mrs. 93
Bittinger, Rev. J. Q. 227
Bryant, John S. 278
Boundaries, 20
Bounties to Soldiers, 159, 162
" to Families, 161
Brooks, North Branch 26
" Pool, 26
" Samuel and family, 90
" George W. 91
" Samuel 319
" Edwin 320
Boyington, Asa 102
Blood, J. G. 143
Brown, Edwin J. 305
Bunce, John L. 132
Burbeck, Wm. H. and family, 122
Burbeck, Edward C. 320

Burbeck George 321
Butler, Luther 146
" Geo. C. 148
" Thaddeus 289
Burial places, 154

C

Changes in Life and Habits, 19,361
Charter, Date of 35
Carr, Daniel 97
" John 97
" Samuel 97
Carleton, Michael and family 122
" Michael Jr. and family, 122
Carleton, Horace D. 123
" Edmund 268
Clark, James B. 309
" Wm. R. 136
" Henry H. 136
" Clarence H. 305
Care of imbecile, 154
Canal, 192
Cartland, Samuel 268
Carbee, Samuel P. 302
" Moses D. 304
Chapman, Geo. W. 280
Census, 154
Cohos Country, Reports of early discovery and exploration 29
Cohos Country, Measures to explore 29
Cohos Country, original plan to take possession of 29
Cohos Country, Marking road to 31
Cohos Country, Indians at 42
" , Rapid Settlement of 57
Cohos Turnpike, 190
Corrections, 433
Coon, Ross 103
Crocker, A. S. and family, 85
" Frederick 321
Collins, H. D. 276
Committee of safety and correspondence, 58
Cross, Wm. and family, 95
" Eliza 95
" Jeremiah 96
Courts and Court Houses, 375
Currier, James A. 142
" F. P. 142
Cutting, James 136

Cutting Abijah 136
" John W. 136
" James A. 321
Cummings, Wm. H. 139
" Stephen H. 140
" George S. 148
" George E. 149
Church, Congregational, 222
Church, Methodist Episcopal, North Haverhill 228
Church, Methodist Episcopal, Haverhill Corner 231
Church, Methodist Episcopal, East Haverhill 233
Church, Methodist Episcopal, Woodsville 236
Church, Baptist, North Haverhill 234
Church, Freewill, East Haverhill 235
Church, Union, Centre 235
" Advent, 235
" Episcopal, Woodsville 236
Cucumber story, 407
Church-going, 360
Cyclone, 397

D

Dartmouth College, 209
Davis, Noah 119
" Judge Noah, 323
" Darius K. 142
" John L. 147
Day, Charles H. 146
Davidson, Geo. A. 148
Death, First 56
Deer, Reave 153
Delano, Rev. Samuel 225
Dentists, 309
Disputed boundary, 383
Drinking habits, 382
Dow, Benjamin 148
" Moses, 254
" Moses, Jr. 258
" Joseph E. 259
Doctors, 287
Duncan, Wm. H. 271

E

East Haverhill, 25
Eastman, Wm. and family, 69
" Eber, 69

Eastman Oliver D. 307
Early Settlers, domestic habits of 354
Early Settlers, Houses of 355
" Furniture of 357
" Living of 359
Edgerly, Andrew J. 145
Emery, George 148
Emerson, John D. 226
Elliott, Roswell 135
Elkins, Jonathan 63
" Col. Jonathan 64
" Moses 324
" Henry 64
Egyptian Plague, 368
Edson, Timothy A. 118
" Mrs. Edson 118
Education, 206

F

Family, First 56
Families, Number of 22
Flanders, Chas. N. 324
Fairs and Markets, 366
Farm Products, 20
Farnam, Chester 121
" Jeremiah 121
" Samuel L. 121
Farnsworth, D. L. 324
Frary, Rev. Lucien H. 325
Fleming, Rev. Archibald 225
Felton, Nathan B. 271
Few early Clearing on Oliverian, 178
French, Richard 105
" David A. 148
Fish, Salmon 137
Fish, 367
First Jersey Stock, 405
First Vote for President and Governor, 155
First Representative, 156
First Saw mill at Hosmer Brook, 177
Fire proof Vault, 164
Founders, Character of 17

G

Grantees, Names of 38
Grantees common to Haverhill and Newbury, 40
Gale, Charles A. 142
Gray, Michael 326

Game, 367
Granite Quarries, 27
Great Flood, 369
Great Pines, 381
Great Fire, 104
Great Accident, 403
Greeley, Rev. Edward H. 226
George, Isaac K. 148
Gibbs, Rev. Joseph 225
Gibson, Chas. R. 307
Griswold, Chas. B. 144
Goodwin, Simeon 73
Gookin, Samuel 101
" Richard 102
" Warren D. 326
Good Templars, 417
Glover, Truman W. 148

H

Harriman, Jaaseel 47
Hawkins, D. L. 149
Hangings, 395
Hale, Jonathan 73
" Samuel 89
Hazeltine, Maxi 72
Hayward, 68
Hayward, Benjamin 135
" Nathaniel, 135
" Alvah 135
Ham, Levi B. 112
Hazen, John 40, 42, 43
" Moses 41
" William 45
Hayes, Henry 297
Haverhill, Corner 23
" Academy 84
" Prominence of 165
" Exposure of 165
" Troops at 168
" Scouts from 168
" Threatened in 1776 169
" Second threatening of 169
Haverhill, Military road from 170
" People of, wide awake 171
Haverhill, Beef for troops at 171, 174
Haverhill, Ammunition for troops at 171
Haverhill, Domestic enemies at 172
Haverhill, Alarm of 1781 at 171
" Effects of War on 175
" Stage Center 197

438   INDEX.

Haverhill in War, 237
" of Revolution, 237
" of 1812, 241
" of Rebellion, 242
Haverhill, Lawyers of 250
" Doctors of 287
Haverhill Abroad, 310
Heath, Simon B. 296
Historic Farms, 379
Howard, Joshua, and family 46
Howland, Moses N. 309
Horn, Amos 113
Houses, The first 355
" Furniture of 357
Houses of Refuge, 370
Horse Meadow, 373
Hog Reeves, 374
Huskings, 360
Hurd, John 70
Hutchins, Joseph 72
Hunt, Caleb 140
" Caleb Jr. 326
" Horace 327
" Prescott 327
" Hellen 327

I

Island, Howard's 27
" Johnston's
Intervals, 25
" Clear 22, 43
Indians, 31, 364
" Surprised by 31
" Carried away by 31
Indian Trail, 31
" Names, 363

J

Jackson, Samuel 140
" Thomas B. 140
" John W. 140
Jeffers, James 122
" Josiah 122
" John 122
" Sylvester 122
Johnston, Michael 42
" Chas. and family, 74
" Michael 1st and family 82
Johnston, Michael 2nd and family, 82
Johnston, Hale A. 269
" Hannah 328

Johnson, Thomas 47, 173
" Jesse 57

K

Kent, Jacob 41
" Col. Henry 41
Kimball, Amos and family, 94
" Jno. and family, 95
" C. C. 129
" Russell 128
" Peabody W. 128
" Chas. C. 129
" Joseph P. 148
" Ezra S. 148
" John 328
Kingsbury, Ephraim 115
King, Henry F. 148

L

Land, Division of 35
" Clearing of 60
Ladd, Ezekiel and family, 65
" Ezekiel Jr. 65
" Samuel 66
" John 66
" David 66
" James 66
" Samuel Jr. 66
Law-suit, 154
Leighton, Albert H. 149
Leith, Wm. H. 329
Leonard, Henry B. 302
Little, Moses 68
Liberal offer for Blacksmith, 177
Libraries, 390
Limestone, 27
Lovewell's exploring party, 31
Lovewell, Aim of 34
Lot, Meadow 39
" Privileged 40
" Gov. Wentworth's 40
" Numbering of 40
" Laying out of 151
" Drawing of 151
Lock, Elisha 58
Local Names, 409
Lombard poplars, 83

M

Marriage, First 52
Mails, 194

Making Cider, 399
Manson, Alexander and family, 130
McClary, John 130
Marston, Wm. C. 135
Mann, Ezra B. 147
" Edward F. 147
" Melvin J. 149
" Geo. H. 149
Mattocks, Edward 298
Masonry, 413
Meadows, Names of 40
Meader, Daniel W. 144
Memorable contest, 163
Merrill, Nath'l and family, 86
" David 116
" Schuyler 116
" Benjamin 116
" Abel K. 116
" Henry 117
" Arthur 117
" John 117
" Daniel F. 118
" John L. 329
" Benjamin 329
" Charles H. 329
" William 329
Mill at North Haverhill, 180
" at Brook, 178
" First Saw and Grist 44, 176
Mill Privilege first granted, 177
Mountains, 25
Morse, Caleb 92
" Lafayette 120
" Isaac 120
" Isaac S. 334
" Jacob 120
" Daniel 120
" Stephen and family, 91
" Dea. Morse 93
" Geo. W. 332
" Peabody 331
" John N. 92
" John 121
" Joshua 92
" Robert 336
" Joseph B. 323
" Edmund 93
" Luther C. 284
" Bryan and family, 92
Muster day, 360

N

Name, Origin of, 20
Newspapers, 391

Newcomb, Charles 308
Nelson, William H. 143
" John 260
" Thomas L. 337
Niles, Joseph B. 130
" Alonzo F. 337
" Horace L. 338
Nichols, Jonathan S. 134
" Geo. B. 338
" Nellie P. 339
" Clara I. 339
North Haverhill, 24
Noyes, Timothy and family, 110
" Person 110, 339
" Benjamin 110
" Horace E. 110
" Royal H. 110

O

Ores and Minerals, 27
Odd Fellows, 416
Osgood, John 96
Old Debt, 158
Olcott Edward, R. 269

P

Pattie, John 42
Page, John and family, 51
" Hannah Green 52
" David 279
" Samuel 55
" Samuel T. 284
" Samuel B. 284
" William H. 55
" Moses S. 340
" John A. 339
Palmer, Haven 304
Parker, Enoch G. 147
Paper Currency, 155
Paring bee, 359
Patriarchs Militant, 417
Pearson, Joseph and family, 89
" Isaac and family, 89
" James H. 341
Phelps, Martin 289
Pike Station, 25
Pike Isaac and family, 125
" Alonzo F. 126
" A. F. Mf'g Co. 180
" Isaac Jr., 127
" Edwin B. 127
" Chas. W. 128
" Burns H. 128

Pike, Chas. J. 128
" Oscar B. 128
" Samuel P. 342
Pigeons, 369
Piermont Boundary dispute, 383
Pine Grove Farm, 415
Pond, French 27
" Long, 27
" Woods 27
Porter, Asa 82
" William 84
" John 258
Polls, Number of 22
Powers' Exploring Party, 32
Powers, Aim of 34
" Joseph, 144
" Rev. Peter 173, 220
" Grant 223
" Elizabeth A. 342
" Mary W. 342
" Henrielle M. 342
" Geo. C. 342
Population, 22
" Influx of 35
" In 1767, 57
Poor, The 374
" Care of 178
Poor Farm, 160
Powder House, 398
Putnam, A. W. 139
" Geo. F. 282

Q

Question of Conscience, 157

R

Reding, Jno. R. 133
" Silvester 134
" Warren 134
" John 343
Religion and Churches, 217
" in Colonial Times, 218
" Protest against, 219
Record Book, 152
River, Connecticut 25
" Ammonusuc 26
" Oliverian 26
Rixes, "Major" 131
" John L. 131
" Nathaniel 131
Roads and Bridges, 28, 185, 194
" First, only bridle-paths, 185
" From Plymouth, 186

Roads, Portsmouth, 187
" First mention of in Proprietors' Records, 187
" First into Town, 187
" River, 188
" Change of, 188
" Imperfect, 190
" Character of, 191
" Grades of, 191
" Rail, 192
Rodgers, Levi 343
" Carleton 343
Rowell, Jno. 13, 135
" Jonathan H. 344
" Chester 345
Russell, Moor and family, 100
" David Moor 100
" Wm. W. and family, 101
" Alfred 101
" William W. 101
" Frank W. 101
" Walter W. 101
" Charles J. 101

S

Stark, John, 31
Sprague, Alden 256
Sanders, Jonathan 58
Swasey, Obadiah and family, 98
" Samuel 99
" Charles J. 99
" Nathaniel 100
" John H. 100
Swan, Joshua 97
" William 97
" Charles 98
" Israel 98
" Charles J. 98
" Phineas 98
" Henry 98
Spalding, Phineas 292
Sabbath, Observance of 62
" Traveling on 157
Stages, 195
Stage Drivers, 197
" Drinking habits of 198
Settlements, River 109
" Back 109
Settlers, First White 42
" Living of 358
" Drinking habits of 382
Scenery, 20
" Longfellow's view of 21
Stevens, Simeon 17

INDEX.

Stevens, Parker 105
" Caleb 105
" Grove S. 143
" George W. 143
" Lyman D. 345
Special Choice of Selectmen, 157
Searle, Moses C. 226
Sleeper, Jonas D. 277
Steamboats, 398
Simpson, Thomas 73
Smith, Eleazer 137
" Charles G. 137
" Chas. B. 147
" Rev. Ethan 222
" Rev. John 223
" Lyndon A. 347
" Stephen S. 347
" Carlos 347
" Frank A. 347
Stickney, Seth P. 148
Southards, Moses 129
" Aaron 129
" Lyman M. 129
" Samuel F. 130
Stowe, Amos 132
" Joseph, 132
" William P. 348
Stoddard, Eugene W. 228
Soil, 27
Sloan, David 262
Stone, Uriah 61
Scott, Amasa 290
" Quincy A. 149
Soap Stone, 27
Soper, Horace O. 345
Store at Corner, 182
" at Brook, 183
" at No. Haverhill, 183
" at Pike Station, 183
" at East Haverhill, 183
" at Woodsville, 183
School Troubles, 160
" Houses, 207
" Centres, 209
Schools, Early 206
" First Money for 206
" First districting of 206
" Re-districting of 206
" Graded, 207
" At Corner, 208
" at Woodsville, 208
" Liberality for 208
" Dartmouth College, 209
" Academy, 211
Soldiers Monument, 162
" in War of Revolution, 238

Soldiers in War of 1812, 241
" in Mexican War, 241
" in War of Rebellion, 242
" in 2nd Reg., 242
" in 4th Reg., 243
" in 5th Reg., 244
" in 9th Reg., 245
" in 11th Reg., 246
" in 15th Reg., 248
" in 18th Reg., 249
" in First Heavy Artillery, 250
" In First Cavalry, 251
Sugar Making, 359

T

Taplin, John 65
Tarleton, William 105
" Josiah B. 348
" George W. 349
" James M. 349
" Horace 349
" Thos. G. 349
" Albert 349
" Amos 349
Taverns, 198
" of olden times, 202
" Famous 203
" News Center of 203
" First Families Kept 204
Taxes first abated, 153
Treasurer, First 153
Teams, 201
Tenney, Homer H. 302
Teaming, 400
Time,—Changes, 354
Tything-man, 374
Towle, Simeon and family, 114
" Henry 114
" Edward 114
" Susan E. 114
" Emily H. 115
" Frederick 350
" James H. 350
Town and Proprietors Meeting, First 150
Town Officers, First 150
" First full list of 151
Town Officers, Character of 163
Town Meeting, First Annual 151
" Places of 155
Town, Area of 22
" Expenses, 152
" Work, Wages for 152

Town on State of Country, 159
" House, 160
" Duty of 162
" General progress of 177
Troublesome Persons, 156
Two Classes, 354
Two Great Plagues, 393
Thompson, Charles E. 279
Trotter, William 91
Tucker, R. D. 146

V

Vermont Union, 387
Villages, 23

W

Water-power, 28
" Storage, 28
" On Oliverian 179
Warren, Luther 135
" George 135
Waif, 155
War of 1812, 159
" Rebellion, 161
Watson, Henry P. 306
Wesson, Ephraim 73
Wells, Caleb 145
Wheeler, Glazier 104
Weeks, Enoch R. 143
" Moses M. 143
" C. M. 147
Webster, David 110
" Stephen P. 111

Webster, Mrs. 111
" James P. 111
" John V. 112
" Caleb 112
" Samuel C. 274
Westgate, Nathaniel W. 281
" William F. 286
Wetherbee, Myron S. 309
White, John 68
" Samuel 287
Wilson, Nathaniel 114
" Geo. L. 114
" Nathaniel 350
" Edward B. 352
Wilmot, Timothy and family, 122
" Harvey B. 352
Whitney, Augustus, 142
Whitcher, Ira, 147
" David, 147
" Daniel, 147
" William F. 352
Wild Animals etc. 367
Wood, Rev. Henry, 224
Woods, John L. 146
" John L., Jr. 352
" Frank P. 353
Woodsville, 24, 180
Woodward, James and family, 59
" Chas. B. M. 123
" George 259

Y

Young, Joshua and family, 94
" John 94
" Tryphena 94

MEMORANDA.

These sheets are added for the convenience of those who may be interested in noting important events of the Town as they occur.

www.ingramcontent.com/pod-product-compliance
Lightning Source LLC
Chambersburg PA
CBHW032000300426
44117CB00008B/845